Your Journey to Peace

*Bridging the Gap
between
Religion,
Spirituality,
Psychology,
and Science*

Rosemary McCarthy

YOUR JOURNEY TO PEACE
BRIDGING THE GAP BETWEEN RELIGION,
SPIRITUALITY, PSYCHOLOGY, AND SCIENCE

iUniverse books may be ordered through booksellers or by contacting:

iUniverse
1663 Liberty Drive
Bloomington, IN 47403
www.iuniverse.com
1-800-Authors (1-800-288-4677)

ISBN: 978-1-4917-5162-6 (sc)
ISBN: 978-1-4917-5161-9 (hc)
ISBN: 978-1-4917-5160-2 (e)

Library of Congress Control Number: 2015902065

Print information available on the last page.

iUniverse rev. date: 10/21/2016

www.yourjourneytopeace.com

Attitude is everything about everything.

We cannot always choose our circumstances,
but we can always choose our attitudes.

To my three sons, Shawn, Scott, and Brad, who showed up
on this Planet much more evolved than I did.
I love you all so much and thank you for showing me
where my misalignments still lie just by being who you are.
To Lindsey, Finn, and Sonja, we are all so glad you are part of our family
and for the love you have brought into our lives.

To my sister-in-law Francine,
my nephew Mitchell, his partner Emma, and my niece Mayora.
May we always share the bond that Brian brought us, and
know that he will always be watching over you and guiding us all.

This book is also dedicated to:
All people who wish to find peace in their lives;
to anyone who wants to understand why we are the way
we are—individually or collectively;
to those curious about how our past and present formed us;
to others confused about all the inconsistencies in
and conflicts because of our religions;
and finally to those who want to know how we
can create a safe and abundant future
for ourselves, our families, our communities, and the world.

Chapter Titles

Contents

(All the illustrations with their page numbers
are listed at the end of the Contents)

Part I
Our Journeys

Part II
Other Subjects Related to Who We Are, Our Journeys, and the Oneness We Are a Part Of

Illustrations

(Credit goes to Jeremy Shantz for his original designs for illustration #'s 1, 4, 5, 6, 11, 15, 16, and 17; and to Bianca Basso for her original designs of illustration #'s 2, 3, 7, 8, 9, 10, 12, 13, 14, 18, 19, 20, 21, and 22. Bianca also modified illustration #'s 1, 4, 5, 6, 11, 15, and 16 so that they now exemplify the current meaning of the associated concept, and prepared them all for production).

Preface

My Journey to Peace

Almost twenty years ago I embarked on a journey to find peace in my life. I never went looking to find God, per se. In fact, I was actually ambivalent about the concept of God. Nor did I ever feel the need to ask, "Why am I here?" One day I realized I simply didn't like myself. This realization started my journey.

Along the way, I started to understand that my unhappiness and frustrations had less to do with my circumstances and more to do with the perceptions I held of myself, others, and the world around me. I often let the attitudes or actions of others affect me. I projected my needs upon those around me, and if they did not answer my call to satisfy them, I felt hurt and disappointed. I was finally able to understand that there was something wrong with the way I was looking at life. In the words of *A Course in Miracles* I started on a quest to "find a better way."[1]

In my pursuit for self-understanding, I was guided to basic readings about how we can improve our lives and how we can create and choose our realities. I started to connect the dots between my past and present perceptions and their projections, realizing that they affected how I had and was still experiencing life. I was further directed to more advanced philosophies and useful practices within different self-help, spiritual, religious, and psychological disciplines.

I noticed many similarities within the practices and disciplines I was directed to. This struck me as important. I sensed that there was a puzzle with a million little pieces that all fit together to become one big masterpiece. I was and still am intrigued when I hear something from two completely different belief or thought systems that ultimately say the same thing, but with different slants and focuses, using different vernaculars, and aimed at different audiences. This commonality suggests there is a universal truth that underlies and thereby connects us all. It is one of the major themes throughout the book.

My awe and curiosity for the similarities between different religious ideologies and spiritual thought systems has allowed me to delve into them without negative preconceptions or biases. I have no particular attachment to any of them even though I encourage the positive aspects of and practice and embrace certain elements of many. In fact, throughout this writing process I have felt so neutral I often said I feel just like Switzerland! Because of my detachment, I believe that I have been able to unravel the mysteries of the truths that underlie all these different areas of study and connect the threads that bind the different representations together.

Like so many of us, I lived most of my life unaware of the false illusions I had internalized about myself. This impacted my peace and happiness because I approached life and reacted from within those false illusions which colored my perceptions of others, the world around me, and how life should be. I was often frustrated when others did not bend to the notions and ideas I suggested or to my demands. This created further frustration within me, created conflict with others, and generally added turmoil to my life.

Although not a tell-all book, as I aim to bring understanding to our unconscious influences and clarity to seemingly vague philosophies and concepts, I interweave some of my personal stories to show how these influences show themselves and how their false perceptions play out in our lives. I also share my personal experiences because my own journey is what gives me the credentials to bring forth this work: I have walked the road.

My Qualifications

While I do not have any formal education in theology or psychology, I am educated and have two semi-completed degrees, in business from years ago and more recently in English. However, for many years now I have had an insatiable curiosity to investigate, study, and understand the concepts you will find in this book and their relationship to our peace and happiness and ultimately, to our spiritual growth.

My years of self-inquiry into the many deep-set inner beliefs I held that created the misperceptions I operated under allowed me to connect the dots between my false beliefs about myself, others, and the world around me and see how these led me to experience life as difficult. Completing the lessons of *A Course in Miracles* was the final step to me overcoming my negative tendencies, and I felt the urge to study and practice all its concepts intensely in order to really understand them and unlock more layers of my false illusions, the misperceptions they created, and the negative reactive responses they lured me into. I now take responsibility for my own life experiences, no longer blaming others for my frustrations or unhappiness.

I offer the insights and the wisdom garnered on my journey from anger and frustration to inner peace and harmonious relations with others in the hope that some of you may recognize how you may be working from unconscious patterns that may not be serving you well, or, so that you can better understand others who are caught up in a web of reacting to life negatively. We succumb to reacting badly and blaming others simply because we have not been taught how to do otherwise. These unconscious automatic responses create our Default Position, and unknown to us, they actually perpetuate further frustrations, unhappiness, and conflicts with others, keeping us in limitation and distanced from our sense of empowerment and Best Selves.

I have thought in the last few years that all my curiosity, study, practices, and self-evaluation are the equivalent of a master's degree in spirituality. I now understand it served as the groundwork preparing me to present the ideas in these pages in a nonjudgmental way. In that sense, this book is my thesis!

I believe I have surmounted the challenge to unearth and release the underlying influences that were running my life, and in doing so, came out the other side calmer, happier, more confident, and in control of my life. I now feel empowered and so can anybody! From a place of humble confidence, I believe I *found the words* to express and share these understandings, and am optimistic that if you are searching for answers you can find some encouragement and direction within these pages.

Acknowledgments

I would like to acknowledge all those in the various disciplines who preceded me in their quest to understand themselves, the world around us, and the whys and wherefores of our existence. You guided me, inspired me, and helped me find peace in my life! A further thank you to all whose work I have drawn upon in this book.

A universal thank you to all the mentors who entered my life: whether you guided me for a short or longer period of time, you have all been valuable to my journey.

I also wish to extend a heartfelt thank you to my family and all my friends (new and old) who stood by me the past few years, showing interest in my project, encouraging my efforts, and offering help in a myriad of different ways—from practical household assistance that freed me of some of the everyday burdens, to including me in social activities that kept me grounded in the real world, which helped me avoid becoming too lost in the esoteric concepts that permeated my days.

To my many editors who stood alongside me and helped me turn over a thousand pages, dozens of copybooks, and a myriad of notes of uncoordinated material into something viable, I thank you all for your valuable input. To Linda Chechik, who helped me reduce and refine masses of unorganized material into something more manageable, I thank you for your invaluable help. To Shannon Lee Figsby, who further helped me fine-tune the material, meticulously guiding me in the technical aspects of writing, I am extremely grateful. To Ania Johnstone, Anita Ashtakala, Bev Brownrigg, and Rima Hammoudi, I thank you all for your valuable input for helping me in various editing capacities along the way. For the last phases, I also want to thank Vivienne Schami for helping me to further reduce and fine-tune certain chapters, and to June Weiss for polishing the manuscript and giving it the final edit. And a *very special thank you* to Rachel Greeve, who has been with me from almost the beginning right through to the end, for your attention to detail and judicious eye which helped me fine-tune, tweak, and substantially reduce the material again and again in its various stages as well as for the final proofread.

Another big thank you must go to Catherine Gabriel-Ferland for the invaluable research she did for me, often finding material and authors when I had given her very little information to go on. I also want to acknowledge, thank, and give credit to Jeremy Shantz and Bianca Basso for the 22 illustrations they provided for the interior of the book. The detailed credits are located on the Illustrations page, located after the Contents.

A heartfelt thank you to Erik Riley from GPro Computers, who over the years has endlessly helped me with all my computer-related needs. I also thank and acknowledge Tony Snippe and Lindsay Presley, my web-designing team at Creative Unity, for their patience and expertise in building and helping me maintain my website which supports this book.

And finally, my deepest appreciation to Carol Fitzpatrick, a visionary, channel, mentor, and teacher who has guided me since February 2012, helping me clarify the direction this book was to take and elucidate certain concepts within its pages.

Introduction

Why This Book, Why Now?

A few years ago, shortly after writing the first draft of this book's introduction, tentatively entitled "Why This Book, Why Now?," I received an e-mail message suggesting I might be interested in a book by well-respected professors H. Ronald Hulnick, PhD, and Mary R. Hulnick, PhD: *Loyalty to Your Soul: The Heart of Spiritual Psychology*. That book's introduction was also entitled "Why This Book, Why Now?" This reminded me that we are all on this journey *together,* unraveling higher truths, helping and supporting each other in a myriad of ways. The synchronicity of my link with the Hulnicks astounded me, and I was proud to find myself on the same wavelength as them. I felt the cosmic connection of our purposes.

I believe that the *why-now* theme is so prevalent today because we have finally reached a point in our history where we are ready to embrace all that we are, and all we are meant to be. We are ready to find peace in our lives: for ourselves, our families, our communities, and the world around us. We are ready to step into our empowerment and support others to step into theirs. We are ready to acknowledge the Oneness we all share. We are ready to tap into joy.

Whether we can articulate it perfectly or not, more and more of us are reeling from the effects of lives lived amassing material possessions, climbing social, academic and career ladders, blaming others for our circumstances, and pitting ourselves against one another for personal gain and power—endeavours *we believed* we needed to undertake to be safe, happy and feel empowered. Being ensnared in these activities we have often ignored our spiritual needs and now find ourselves unfulfilled and exhausted.

My purpose in writing this book is twofold: to share my journey to peace with you and to reveal the many commonalities I noticed on my journey between religion, spirituality, psychology and science in the hopes of illustrating the truth of who we are, **Our Truth, and the** common *truth we all share,* **A Binding Universal Truth**. Although these truths and their understandings are esoteric in nature, the search for a *higher meaning* in life and/or the inner peace we all yearn for is a common thread that runs through us all—even if it is deeply buried within our consciousness. The path to that inner peace is embedded in the intended meaning of the teachings of all these disciplines.

Our Truth: Our True Reality. We are love; we came from love; we are all *unconditionally* loved by our Creator; and we hold all the power of that creator energy. Even though we have forgotten this, we are still connected to that reality.

A Binding Universal Truth: We *all* came forth as loving expressions of the creative force of the Universe. Thus there is a pervasive Oneness that binds us together.

Because Humanity has been caught in a paradigm whereby we do not access the love inherent in us or the universal truth of the Oneness that unites us, we have upheld illusionary ideas that separate us from each other. This book aims to help us access Our Truth—the *truth of who we are*, while reconciling *the truth of who we are being*.

We Are Awakening: to Ourselves and Our Connection to All Others

It is time for us to *wake up* to Our Truth, as well as from the illusion that there is no way out of the unhappiness, struggles, limitations, and the conflicts that Humanity has unknowingly fallen prey to. We are finally ready to acknowledge that we have chosen poor substitutes in attempting to answer the deep longings we have within us, which only a connection to Our Truth can fulfill.

However, what comes with the knowledge that we can be in tune with Our Truth is the need to take responsibility for our part by pointing our attitudes in the right direction. Our egoic mind (whose negative influence is somewhat analogous to what some call Satan) has a strong hold on us and wants authority over our lives. We inherited this tendency to allow our ego to shape our attitudes and thereby run our lives from Humanity's past, however we now have the knowledge to address and change them. Our personal and collective attitudes have shaped our past, affect our present, and create a blueprint for our future. They affect us individually and on a collective level. To release ourselves from the negativity that has plagued us, individually and collectively, we must understand that the relationship between the judgments, blame, angers, hatreds and fears in our personal lives manifests and is displayed in the world around us. This is because we are all connected.

We are all interconnected in a weaving link of energetic, organic patterns. When we make peace with ourselves, we are in touch with this shared energetic link and from that place of inner connection, can more easily make peace with those around us, and then extend it to all those on the Planet, even if they seem different. We are able to do this because we are in touch with the

Oneness—the shared energy that pervades us all. This is its natural effect. When we strive to live in harmony and cooperation with all people on earth, we work together for the benefit of our Planet so future generations can live in a peaceful environment and enjoy the abundance it has to offer. And we have the cosmic support to bring this all about—this is what we have been feeling and witnessing as Gaia embarks on a shift in consciousness.

What Is this Shift, and Why Now?

Individually, this Shift is the process of leaving behind dense, lower third-dimension[1] attitudes, which distance us from our True Selves and separate us from each other, in order to embrace lighter, higher fifth-dimension[2] attitudes that unite us. On a cosmic level, this Shift is the process of our Planet, or Mother Earth or Gaia, taking its place in these higher realms. We do this in tandem. This is the cosmic time for our Planet and its inhabitants to ascend to the higher dimensions where peace, love, acceptance, fairness, equality, and abundance reign. We are invited to make the Shift with Mother Earth and take part in ushering in the thousand years of peace the Bible describes in Revelations 20. It is a time of global Ascension! Ascension is further explained in chapter 10, "Ascension."

The much-discussed December 21, 2012, Mayan calendar date was not about the end of the world but about the beginning—a new era in which the proverbial lion will lie down with the lamb. We are awakening from the darkness that Humanity has embodied for eons. In the cosmic scheme, it was our Planet's time to take its place in the realm of a higher consciousness, and we, as its occupants, were invited along with it.

This date was a fixed cosmic happening, but anchoring in its concepts is a process. The degree to which we collectively raised our vibrations out of our third-dimensional density influenced how successful our Planet would be in raising itself up. In her *Fire the Grid* talk of a few years ago, Shelley Yates explained that "2012 is a birth date for our planet and whatever energy is the greatest will prevail."[3] Clearly, enough of us changed our attitudes and raised our consciousness to an adequate level for our collective energy to allow for our survival.

Even though you will be reading this book in 2016 or later, it was sometime around December 2012 that Gaia chose to ascend to embrace the realms of a higher consciousness. At levels beyond our conscious awareness, all of us living on earth now chose to be here and accompany her at this time. We have actually been moving toward a higher consciousness for eons; however a global cry went out to the Universe some seventy years ago, and the Universe responded.

Eradicating ourselves was never part of our cosmic plan, so after the atrocious events of WWI and WWII the next generation came forth leaning more toward peace, however, those in power were too entrenched in their old ways to support its flourishing. The cosmic convergence in 1987 (further explained in chapter 7, "Science and Other Related Topics") brought powerful celestial energy to encourage us to embrace compassion, equality, fairness, and peace. This twenty-five year convergence came to a head around December 2012. However, the fulfillment of this Shift is a process. Fully anchoring in all what this entails will take years, individually and collectively.

It was the energy in the final years of the convergence that helped to raise our consciousness to collectively demand honesty and transparency in our governments, and fairness, equality and respect for everyone in the world, thereby paving the way for us all to live happy, safe, and peaceful existences with all our needs met and in control of our destinies. Individually, this final push has affected us in many ways. At a soul level we chose to be here at this time of the Shift, which means having to release all that is not in alignment with Our Truth. This energy has brought a huge impetus toward change!

Effects of the Shift's Influx of Energy

Within the last few years, some of us may have had the impulse to work toward seeing more fairness expressed in the world, to become less selfish and more concerned about others, or reacted with peace instead of anger, with acceptance instead of judgment, and with graciousness instead of bitterness. Some may have finally been able to release fearful, limiting, or victim attitudes as they found their empowerment, while others may have had the impulse to let go of what depletes them, choosing instead to embrace what energizes and brings them joy.

These shifts in our attitudes empower us and encourage unity rather than separateness with others. This is part of the energy the Shift has ushered in, as it has brought the impetus to release any manifestations not aligned with the fifth-dimensional characteristics of love, joy, peace, harmony, and unity. It is no longer time to allow for negative attitudes to diminish us, push *against* what we do not want, or judge, control, or undermine others in any way—no matter how different they are from us.

It is time to fully embrace uplifting precepts and bring forth the manifestations of these impulses. However, the decision to live in harmony and joy, the desire to let go of past negative and limiting attitudes, or the impulse to do good in the world do not necessarily mean that we will be able to heed this inner call at all times. A period of shifting and anchoring in the concepts of self-love, compassion, acceptance, fairness, and harmony will be necessary both individually and as a collective. To fully move into the higher consciousness we yearn for that embraces these precepts often involves a journey of self-understanding.

In recent years, buried issues not faced or fully dealt with before may have come to the surface for acknowledgment and release. However, we may not have been able to pinpoint the past issue and simply felt disappointed or disillusioned. Something within us knows that *all should be well*, but because of the influences Humanity has been stuck under, our personal and human history has not complied. Families have not offered unconditional love. Society has not encouraged fairness and equality. Schools offered rigid rules. Many religions' dogma-based teachings could not address our spiritual needs, and even as they evolved some still held to us-vs-them concepts that encouraged a me-better-than-you attitude and bred divisive outlooks. As we went through life we attempted to appease our discontent by *doing things differently*, but our efforts also eventually led to disappointments because of unconscious influences.

New Understandings Help us Embrace Our Sense of Empowerment and God-given Power

Within the disciplines of religion, spirituality, psychology, and science we have now cracked the codes that allow us access to our individual powers. This new understanding can help us to dispel our illusionary beliefs of being separated from the universal force that created us—what many call God. Our connection to that powerful energy force was in fact never broken! We just forgot how to access it. As we begin to connect to Our Truth we can also see that truth in others. We see the Oneness that connects us instead of the illusions that separate us. Our ultimate goal is to release *all* the faulty foundations we have unknowingly upheld, thereby enabling us to align with the loving, joyful, powerful universal beings we truly are.

This God-given power offers us the capacity to create what we want. Thereby we *can* bring about a different or better life experience for ourselves. All we have to do is adjust our frequency to align with the laws and principles that govern the Universe, and thereby us, to bring what we want into our sphere. (See chapter 2, "Universal Laws / Kingdom Principles"). These new understandings also allow us to realize that we do not have to be in competition with others, because there is enough love, success, and material goods to go around—for us and everyone, as the Universe operates under the principles of abundance and limitlessness.

The faulty unconscious beliefs about our powerlessness have kept us separate from one another because we believed we had to hold to conflicting agendas for survival. These ways of being do not emanate from a place of love, compassion, sharing, and unity and have pitted us against one another further perpetuating our separateness. Now is the time to reconnect to our God-selves and the inner power held within it, so we can once again align with the limitlessness inherent in our nature and reclaim our sense of empowerment. Embracing these realities is all part of this Shift.

Philosophical Explanations, Practical Tools, and Scientific Connections

From a philosophical perspective, I seek to help the reader understand why we are the way we are and how we got here. I will outline the importance of our connection to the intelligent, creative force in the Universe—Spirit, God, Source, Holy Spirit, whatever we may call it.

Even if one is not interested in lofty spiritual concepts or does not believe in God, most of us can acknowledge the existence of an energy or universal force that created and holds the Universe and everything in its place. With the understanding of the recent scientific discoveries that this energy force is organic, and since we are part of the Universe, we *can* allow for the possibility that just like every organism within it, we are constantly acting and reacting with this universal energy force.

We actually tap into this universal energy force as easily as we breathe—every second of every minute of every day and in doing so are always sending it messages and requests—whether we are aware of it or not. So developing an awareness of the messages we send to that energy force and recognizing what it returns to us is vital, as this is what gives us control over our lives. The various religions and spiritualities, diverse areas of psychology, and countless self-help groups are now at our disposal to help us find our empowerment and reconnect with our God-selves.

The scientific elements expressed in this book help us to link the spiritual mysteries of our existence to cosmic truths. Our third-dimensional living has kept us ignorant of these connections. In ancient times, scientists, cosmologists, holy people, philosophers, and truth-seekers respected each other, worked together, and understood that connection. However, as science moved away from including philosophical and cosmic understandings and as religion became more dogmatic, a gap was created and continued to grow—until recently. We now understand that the universal principles we must follow in order to embrace our God-selves and create the lives we want contain a scientific component.

The creative force of the Universe is benevolent and offers only unconditional love within which is complete forgiveness for everybody—for all that we have, or have not done. However, when we are not connected to this love we cannot *feel* it, and in our yearning to feel love and loved we accept crumbs. We may also have unresolved guilt that undermines our ability to feel we deserve love. We may have an unconscious belief that we are not good enough, strong enough, smart enough, or are limited in our abilities, etc. So we vie for externals to feel loved and empowered. We must understand that we were created from this all-encompassing loving energy, we are still connected to it, and that the time has come to fully realize this.

We Chose to be Present at This Time of Gaia's Shift

Say what? I don't remember choosing *to be here.*

If you are new to any of these concepts, you must by now be thinking all this is absolutely ridiculous or that I am delusional. And from your point of reference, you are right. For most of us it takes years and lots of backup—having mentors, reading and rereading material, listening to talks, and going to workshops—to understand what this is all about. We are so entrenched in our third-dimensional way of thinking and out of tune with Our Truth that we cannot imagine anything beyond what we can see or feel with our physical senses. In an attempt to overcome the emptiness this disconnect creates along with any unconscious influences we have amassed along the way, we act and react in ways that ultimately create stress, add conflict to our lives, and keep us distanced from others. Many refer to this as acting from our egoic mind.

The Egoic Mind

In *10% Happier*, Dan Harris humorously tells of his personal journey from a skeptic of all spiritual and woo-woo concepts to someone who now meditates a half hour a day. He still works as a successful international journalist, still has ambitions, and still considers himself somewhat of a workaholic. However, he devotes less chaotic energy to his pursuits. His practice and new way of looking at himself and life has simply bought him a more peaceful existence. After a live broadcast mishap, Harris knew he needed to do something to relieve stress. At some point his wife gave him Eckhart Tolle's *A New Earth* to read, and when he first started to read it was "often rolling his eyes," finding it full of "irredeemable poppycock" and "jargon like 'conditioned mind structures'" that drove him crazy.[4] However, sufficient snippets rang true to keep him engrossed.

While Harris felt compelled to read on, he was annoyed with the terminology and esoteric concepts. One minute he would be thinking, "This guy gets me," then the next that what Tolle was saying came straight from "crazy town."[5] Nonetheless, through the maze of what he considered nonsense and way too out there, Harris started to connect the dots between his own inability to relax, how his mind functioned, and what Tolle was trying to convey about the hold our egoic mind has on us. As the words within the pages brought Harris understanding, he felt as if Tolle "must have somehow spent an enormous amount of time inside my skull." In a momentary flash Harris realized that all the behaviors he felt embarrassed and guilty about, like doing drugs, his preoccupation with his hair, judging others for their beliefs, ignoring his wife while being glued to his Blackberry, and being lured into dangerous assignments just for the thrill of it were all ego-driven. He finally began to understand the scope of his obsessive behaviors saying they had kept him "sleepwalking through much of my life—swept along on a tide of automatic, habitual behavior."[6]

Harris realized there must be *some* legitimacy to what Tolle was saying. Slowly but surely, as he investigated the egoic mind and attended workshops with all kinds of people within the spiritual community, he found a meditation practice that suited him which relieved enough stress that he could cope much better with daily life. Most of us are not guided to esoteric journeys walking around in robes chanting "om." However, the majority of us would be happy to learn that a small daily practice can help us become calmer, relieve stress, lessen the conflicts in our lives, and quiet the bantering of the egoic mind which often lures us into situations that ultimately do not serve us.

We Said "Yes" For Many Reasons

By virtue of you reading this book at some point, be that yesterday or years ago, somewhere within your being you said *yes* to this invitation (whether you are aware of it or not) to find peace within yourself, live a conflict-free life, and/or join with Gaia in the journey to a higher consciousness. Or you may have been born with peace in your heart, and a conscious choice may not have even been necessary. If you are within the latter group reading this book, your alignment with peaceful concepts has acted as a beacon of light for those of us who have had to struggle to find that peace. I remember noticing people enduring far more difficult circumstances than mine, yet were less frustrated and more happy and peaceful, and would ask myself, "How do they do that? This sparked something in me to go searching for what they had. So know how important you are to the process of the Shift!

However, this book does not claim to offer all the answers. It is simply an attempt to thread together what we now know from the various disciplines discussed so we can unravel a few more of the mysteries of our existence. This enables us to start to find our way out of the dualistic and separating systems we unintentionally created so we can live peaceful, happy and fulfilled lives, in harmony with others, and create a more loving and fairer world.

It Is My Hope

Many of you have lost faith and lost touch with your original belief systems and do not know where to turn for guidance. I believe I can point you in the right direction, either within your original belief system, toward a different one, or to other practices that can bring you peace, happiness, and a sense of empowerment.

It is my hope that the words, insights, philosophies, and practices I offer will inspire some of you to start your own journey of self-discovery and self-fulfillment—without fear; or, that they help you better understand the people around you, others who have different perspectives, and even those creating heinous crimes to Humanity. I also aim to help explain why the world is the way it is, how we got stuck in this fear-hate-blame-judgment paradigm, and what we can do to get out of it.

Some of the concepts within these pages may instead help you reach the next level on your journey to peace. Perhaps you have hit a plateau and are stuck at a certain level of understanding, or are confused about your beliefs.

For those of you who feel despondent or depressed about your life, I believe that the energetic vibration held within these pages can uplift, energize, encourage, and give you hope regarding your future.

As well as discussing our personal journeys, I also seek to help alleviate much of the confusion and information amassed throughout the ages about how and why we came about, as well as endeavor to reconcile some of this with how our religions evolved to what they are today and the whys and wherefores of much of the misunderstandings within them. I also aim to unravel some of the mysteries regarding the physical laws with the laws of the Universe that so directly affect us and our spiritual growth, as well as attempt to put to rest some of the confusion regarding the extraterrestrial connection we can no longer deny.

Many within the traditional religious belief systems are uncovering these truths themselves. In placing these new awarenesses alongside how we now understand philosophy and our new appreciation for what spirituality means today, and intertwining all this with our current knowledge of psychology and recent scientific findings, I believe we can all benefit from what is being unearthed. This will help us all glean a greater understanding of the mysteries of life, while at the same time offer us considerations that will unite rather than separate us.

Laying Thought Systems alongside One Another

While my original intention was to offer equal space to all the major world religions, most of the conceptualizations here seek to reconcile the

Judeo-Christian thought systems of the Bible with various current spiritual understandings. This is simply how this work flowed out of me. I will often refer to *The Course*, my abbreviation for *A Course in Miracles*, a highly comprehensive spiritual practice I embraced a few years ago that had a profound effect in helping me to undo my unconscious influences. Its metaphysics is the thread that ties this patchwork quilt of different forms of similar concepts together. Notwithstanding its title, *A Course in Miracles* is not a religious work. The miracles it guides us toward are the everyday little attitude shifts one can make to relinquish our reactive defaults of judgment, blame, and the myriad of approaches that focus on our differences and separateness which our egos so love to lure us into. Once we learn to shift these responses to more loving, accepting, and inclusive ones we discover a sense of peacefulness flowing through us as the new vibrations we are creating connect us to our True Self, helping us discover our Best Self.

In contrast to the highly evolved *The Course*, I also draw on insights, stories, and journeys of many people who work in various fields. Their stories are strewn with sensitivity, humor, and intelligence. Their insights demonstrate that our journeys are not about becoming new, strange, and different people, but about becoming better versions of ourselves.

Finding What Works for You

Many different belief systems and practices are presented in this book. Some are of a spiritual or religious nature, some are not. I in no way suggest that you must investigate, study, or embrace *The Course* or any other philosophy, religion, teacher, or tool mentioned in this book. For those who are interested in more information, a List of Recommendations is located at the back of the book including practices, tools, teachers, websites, CDs, DVDs, YouTube videos, and so on, that have inspired me and that may be of interest. This includes resources that adhere to no particular belief system as well as those within the spiritual and religious arenas.

Along with this list, at the back of the book I have also included the worksheets offered, a Definition page of the key terms used throughout the text (those that are defined and capitalized) and a section of some of the tools (meditations, visualizations, affirmations, etc.) noted that might be useful to you, the Reader.

Most concerns are best addressed with human tools and with the appropriate approaches. Lofty spiritual concepts can serve as sound background information to understanding why we are the way we are (and why the world is the way it is), but we must aim to heal ourselves at the level appropriate to the issue at hand. Telling ourselves "God loves us" over and over again (or any other affirmative phrase) is a good adjunct to any tool we are using, but is not intended as a stand-alone exercise when attempting to overcome negative influences—especially with serious issues like addictions. Nor do I suggest we ignore collective concerns.

We can no longer ignore, be insensitive to, or accept that any human suffering or unfairness is ok. The explanations I give as to why we and the rest of Humanity have behaved badly do not suggest we should focus on, or deny what was done—they simply help us understand *why*. This helps us avoid further negative responses, facilitates us forgiving others, eases any guilt if we have acted in unloving ways, and gives us insight as to why our ancestors acted as they did.

At their base, all religions, spiritualities, and thought systems speak many truths and aim to help aspirants return to wholeness, offering great wisdom in how to go about this. They are all perfect in this way; however we have often misconstrued the intended meanings. As they spoke to us from past eras and through various cultural norms, we have often had difficulty differentiating between their inherent wisdom and the specific details they offered to the people then. They also spoke to us at different levels. Our scriptures guided us on how to behave in every-day life so that we could align with spiritual or Godly concepts. They also attempted to explain our beginnings and our connection to and the workings of the Universe. As much of this information was way beyond our comprehension, many "it is like" similes, metaphors, and parables were used, and over time, given the varying interpretations, many of the core messages or meanings had been misunderstood or lost. We have now uncovered their intended meanings, discovered that we are powerful beings able to direct our minds and create and bring forth change, and have the spiritual maturity to use that power wisely to manifest positive changes for ourselves and the world.

~

You may find what appear to be inconsistencies in this book. This is because explanations need to be expressed on different levels. For example, I might say that everything, including us and the Universe is an illusion. Shortly thereafter, I might talk about some aspect of our physical reality and how to deal with it that is within the illusion. My approach to one subject may make another thing I said appear to be false. Context is very important and I have tried to frame my explanations so that the reader knows from what level I am speaking.

It was humanly impossible to touch on every concept and belief system that exists, although I am certain that there are valuable elements in all of them. Some simply did not enter my sphere of awareness during my personal journey or the writing of this book. So if those that I have presented here do not resonate with you, by all means explore others.

You can visit the book's website— www.yourjourneytopeace.com —to leave me comments, ask questions, seek clarification, join my mailing list, subscribe to my weekly articles, or find out about upcoming events.

Part I

Our Journeys

I have been a door opener to myself,
I can be a door opener to you,
and you can be a door opener to others.

CHAPTER 1

Why We Are the Way We Are

There are things known and there are things unknown,
and in between are the doors of perception.
—Aldous Huxley[1]

Have you ever wondered why you feel, think, act, and react a certain way? At some point in our lives we may ask ourselves what has made us what we are. Why am I different from my siblings? We came from the same genetic pool and were nurtured by the same parents. Why am I different from my friend? Our backgrounds are similar. How did I become the person I am now? Why is it others with more difficult circumstances than me seem more happy, peaceful, and have more harmony in their lives? Have you ever wondered why the world is the way it is? Have you ever wondered: Why did this happen to me?

We also often ask, Why did God let this happen? Why is this happening in the world?

We are the way we are individually because of our perceptions and beliefs about ourselves, others, and the world around us. These perceptions stem from our inherent personalities, filtered through past influences: familial, generational, and cultural. Our tendency to allow false perceptions to be created has its roots in our very beginnings.

Humanity is the way it is because we got stuck in a dualistic *me-against-you* paradigm, birthed out of decisions we made at our beginnings billions of years ago and before form—at levels beyond our current awareness.

What happens to us and in the world is not brought about by a trick of nature or a vengeful God but is a response to our playing out and attempting to rebalance within the dualistic system we are now trapped in. I will first look at why we are the way we are individually, and later in the chapter why Humanity is the way it is and how we all got here: our beginnings.

Our Perceptions

Our perceptions of ourselves and the world around us stem from the impressions and interpretations we have incorporated into our Emotional Bodies, a term I borrow from Inelia Benz's Ascension 101 program,[2] although I do not use it in exactly the same way. As we internalized these from our

3

environments while growing up they became part of our makeup, and we created expectations that formed inner beliefs and attitudes which upheld the perceptions we originally created.

> **Emotional Body**: The storage house of all the impressions and interpretations that we have gathered from our life experiences. Our innate characters influence to what degree these affect us.

From these inner beliefs and attitudes about ourselves and the world around us we developed responses to deal with the emotions and feelings held within our conscious and unconscious memories from our past. How we interpret and process these memories affects all aspects of our being: physical, mental, emotional, and spiritual. As such, our Emotional Bodies can hold positive or negative aspects that influence our happiness, attitudes, behaviors, and responses in different ways.

Our Emotional Worlds

The presence of any unacknowledged emotional factors retained in the memory bank of our unconscious minds can cause us to react negatively rather than respond calmly. Whether we *react* aggressively or passively, buried emotions from past events keep us from *responding* consciously to the present reality of the situations in which we find ourselves as well as keep us anxious about the future. In her article, "5D Spring Nesting Instincts," Angela Peregoff asks us: "Why are you so fueled from emotional memories that you react rather than respond to a present situation? Why are the voices over future concerns so loud that you are pulled from the quiet simplicity of the life that is before you?"[3] This Shift is nudging us to become more aware of our reactions and modify them if necessary, so that we can be fully present to what is happening now.

To overcome our inclination to react rather than respond to others and situations we need to adopt some sort of daily or regular practice to center us like prayer, yoga, meditation, taking quiet time for reflection, or to spend time in nature. This aligns us to our True Selves. We also need to employ a self-examination tool to help weed out unwanted past influences that are brought into the present, or affect our thoughts about the future. This will enable us to live life as we really want, rather than be undermined by past shadows. Journaling is a common tool used to help us understand ourselves—the fears, buried issues, inner beliefs, etc. that unduly influence us. In chapter 3, "What We Can Do about It," I further explain these concepts and explain the tools in more detail.

Thoughts and emotions buried within our Emotional Bodies create layer upon layer of unconscious fear that form *reactive* mechanisms and act as protective devices. So instead of responding to situations as they are, we bring these reactive and protective mechanisms to them in inappropriate ways.

Aggressive or Passive Reactions Stem from Past Fears

When we live on the surface level of our emotions, reactionary mechanisms and defensive and protective strategies play out in aggressive or passive approaches inappropriate to the situation.

Depending on our innate character, personality, and early life experiences, we may react aggressively and lash out in situations that appear to threaten our closely held inner beliefs. If for example, you harbor an inner belief that being successful will wreak havoc on your personal life (perhaps your parents broke up as a result of being too career-oriented), you may react in an aggressive or defensive way to anyone who suggests you focus on having a good career. Our inner beliefs are also dictated by protective strategies. If a situation is reminiscent of past experiences that frightened us, we may react passively and turn the present feelings inward, fearful of repercussions. Our inner beliefs might dictate that not speaking up in order to keep the peace is better than expressing our minds.

These inner beliefs and the emotions they engender not only affect our reactions to present situations but also bring about fears regarding our futures. Although these fears are based on outdated interpretations, their influences have us believe that our current perceptions are showing us a true picture—the present reality.

Our Perceptions of Reality

The Course suggests that much of our thinking is actually upside-down and that our reality is not what we perceive but what we *project* onto others and situations. We believe that what we see is a reality, but it is actually only a perception, based on a projection.

Take for example, a chair made of oak with a blue, striped cushion. From a scientific perspective, it is a group of molecules in the form of a chair. Now, let's say you simply do not like this chair. Your dislike is based on individual preferences: you might prefer modern furniture to country style. So long as this preference does not come with any strong sentiments that bring up anger or defensiveness, this is a healthy, normal response. However, sometimes our perceptions are colored by biases and emotional reference points. If the chair was dug up from Grandpa's garage and was dusty and dirty, would it conjure up feelings of love or feelings of conflict? This would depend on your internalized emotional impressions of your grandfather's demeanor and your relationship with him.

Misperceptions and Illusionary Constructs

> **Illusionary Constructs:** Thoughts, attitudes, beliefs, and ideas based on past emotional impressions that we unconsciously constructed or appropriated from others, or from past situations. These are held within our Emotional Bodies and create misperceptions about current situations.

We project our Illusionary Constructs onto others or different situations in many ways. If our early life was characterized by an impoverished background and powerlessness, we may have constructed attitudes and belief systems to avoid being disempowered in life. These may manifest as a powerful need to be successful in life no matter what or a desire to marry for money. If a sense of victimization typified our early life experience as a result of having an abusive parent, we may have become controlling or overly aggressive ourselves to avoid being hurt or becoming a victim in life, or, if we have a quiet character we may have became passive.

For example, my mother was a 1950s housewife who was unhappy, distant, and morose. She alienated herself from life and didn't find joy in anything. Because my father was an aggressive, loud bully, she fell into a poor-me, passive, victim mentality. So when I married at nineteen and had my first child at twenty-three, I decided there was no way I was going to be a housewife; I associated this with being weak and a victim of one's circumstances. While that was a common viewpoint for my generation, I was also wary of any implication that would leave me seemingly vulnerable.

I had a kind and hardworking husband. While we suffered the usual frustrations of a young married couple, every area of our lives was colored by my projections of my background. I went back to work shortly after my first son was born and subsequently resumed part-time studies as well. In doing so, I lost opportunities to enjoy being a young mother, all to avoid following in my mother's footsteps.

Not only were the times different, but my husband had a quiet temperament, while I had an innate, natural confidence. Looking back, I now realize that I took innocent comments and observations about life and motherhood such as "You could stay home for a few years and enjoy the baby" as suggestions that would result in my being *stuck* in life like my mother. Instead of simply enjoying the benefits of marrying a decent man who wanted to work hard to get ahead for himself and his family, I took every innuendo to mean that he was going to get ahead, move forward, and then stomp on me as my father had on my mother. The truth was that I did not know how to tap into joy, live in the moment, feel empowered, or be appreciative of what I had or what was in front of me. I did not perceive my situation as it really was.

Past emotional responses create the Illusionary Constructs we live under. These bring misperceptions to our interactions with others and to situations. Coming from this place of distorted reality, we generate biases and judgments to uphold our illusionary beliefs. These affect our actions and reactions as the false realities we created that are there to protect us. We then become distanced from our True Self and the power it holds, thwarting our ability to become our Best Self. This creates further frustration and we thus become caught in a cycle of wanting and reaching, while our illusionary beliefs and their limitations keep what we want just beyond our grasp.

Becoming self-aware and having clarity of vision and insight enables us to see others and situations for what they really are, with our reactions to life based on the realities of what is now in front of us. We can greatly affect the quality of our lives by understanding the relationship between our perceptions and projections! Worksheet 1 helps us investigate any misperceptions we may hold.

Worksheet 1: Illusionary Constructs, Misperceptions, and Projections

Conscious Awareness vs. Unconscious Awareness

We act out of desire,
which itself is the result of some prior action
recorded in the unconscious mind.
That desire manifests itself as a resolves for action.
—The Upanishads[4]

We are affected by both our Conscious and Unconscious Awarenesses. However, our levels of Conscious Awareness are what will set the stage for peaceful and contented lives. If we are under the influence of Unconscious Awareness, our lives may be fraught with frustration, dissatisfaction, and conflict. Understanding that our perceptions may be projections from past issues helps us avoid living under resultant negative unconscious influences.

Conscious Awareness

Conscious Awareness: When living consciously we are aware of, have made peace with, or are simply not under any negative influence from our personal, cultural, or generational conditioning.

When we live consciously, we can embrace any positive past influences and are aware that negative past influences have nothing to do with who we are now and should not affect current situations. We can move toward happiness and our full potential, as we act in ways that do not thwart our happiness or infringe on others, which would cause disharmony or create more guilt or emotional hurts. Living with Conscious Awareness, we are conscientious of the effects of our attitudes, words, and actions.

Unconscious Awareness

> **Unconscious Awareness**: The effect of our created perceptions that were birthed from the attitudes and inner beliefs we amassed within our Emotional Bodies and that we appropriate to the world. If our Unconscious Awarenesses hold biases, negativity, or misappropriated perceptions, we will develop *needs* to try to uphold them and *strategies* to keep them buried.

We keep these perceptions buried and unconscious because we are afraid to look at them. In *Mindfulness*, Dr. Ellen J. Langer reminds us that Freud considered our unconscious thoughts or awareness to be "motivated-not-knowing" because it is undesirable for us to consider them.[5] We are afraid of the emotions they might incite, like loss of control, as well as any associated shame or guilt that may be lurking. We do not know how to deal with them, so we avoid them.

Our Unconscious Awarenesses can take on many forms. If they hold negative associations, they are always characterized by a sense of need to safeguard ourselves from further pain or disempowerment; they are teeming with agendas and defensive mechanisms. For example, a woman might feel a strong need to have a large family because she witnessed the burden her grandparents were on her mother, who was an only child. She also might develop a need to always be first at everything because of witnessing her mother being marginalized. These needs may be somewhat conscious, but we are largely unaware of the power they hold over us.

Personally, I developed *survival needs* as a result of witnessing the oppression and victimization of my mother. I judged that being quiet and unassuming was disempowering and led to being victimized. I believed that being loud, aggressive, and bully-like was empowering, as this seemed to create a sense of control.

Our Unconscious Awarenesses are based on our personal, cultural, and generational conditioning. These can be positive or negative in nature, although it is the influence of the negative aspects that distance us from our

True Selves, thereby detracting us from becoming our Best Selves. Depending on our innate natures and personalities, these play out differently in all of us.

True Self: The truth or memory of who you really are—free of any Illusionary Constructs.

Best Self: We are our Best Self when we are aligned with our True Self. This manifests as happiness, acceptance of life and our circumstances, and connection to that part of our self that feels empowered, confident, assured, loving, giving, and emotionally healthy.

The negative influences that keep us from being our Best Selves display themselves in the unintentional motivations behind our thoughts and actions, created from our unconscious minds.

Unblocking the Unconscious Mind: The Shadow
Self and Our Spiritual Evolution

When I first embarked on this journey to *find peace in my life*, I was not aware that this was a spiritual endeavor. Many within the religious community still believe that psychology has nothing to do with spirituality. I have learned that it does, because by unblocking that which is held deep within the recesses of our minds, we make way for Spirit, God, Source, or whatever we consider the creative force of the Universe to be, to work with and through us. If we don't, barriers remain erected, making it impossible for our connection to Source to flourish.

This concept of the unconscious mind and its hold on us has also been described as the *shadow self*, a theory introduced by Carl Jung. Jung studied the relationship between unlocking that which is held in our unconscious minds, or our shadow selves, and the ability to reach higher levels of consciousness and awareness in our human and spiritual evolution. When we unlock what is held in our unconscious, we clear the path to access these higher levels. In *Encountering the Shadow in Rites of Passage: A Study in Activations*, Amy Casement explains how Jung used the term *shadow* as an expression of our own dark side, which he said holds "inferior and primitive" impulses that we experience as our ego. She explains that Jung also believed that our shadows contain all our "greatness, but that it is usually latent."[6] It is when we unlock all that is in our unconscious minds that our greatness can be accessed and our Best Self shines through.

In order for us to access our greatness, or our Best Selves, we have to be aware of and control any negative influences that block it. We cannot always choose our circumstances, but we *can* choose our attitudes. If we are under the influence of negative unconscious influences, we have to *consciously* choose to override them.

When we adopt more positive attitudes, not only do we experience more peace in the moment, we also invite more positive circumstances into our lives. Our newfound attitudes also pave the way for us to feel more joy.

Our Perceived Needs and Negative Attitudes Are Intertwined

While there are many qualities that run through our unconscious fabric, it is the impulse to satisfy our Perceived Needs that wreaks the most havoc in our lives.

> **Perceived Needs**: What we think we need to do and who we think we need to be, to appease any disempowering, negative inner beliefs we have amassed in our Emotional Bodies.

Aggressive attitudes such as control, anger, impatience, and overcompetitiveness, as well as passive attitudes like timidity, passive-aggressiveness, and victimization, are birthed from the original hurt, fears and misperceptions we have accumulated into our Emotional Bodies. These developed into inner beliefs that have to be acted upon, as we deem them necessary for our emotional stability.

Hosts for Others' Needs

We are always trying to meet our needs, whether they are real desires based on preferences, from what Spirit has put in our heart (our soul contracts), or from emotional neediness or Perceived Needs. While we are trying to fulfill them, our emotional antennae go out searching for others to be hosts. This concept works whether we hold positive or negative influences in our makeup. If we hold positive influences, we will simply attract those who will complement our desires or add to our lives. However, if we hold negative influences our antennae will invite others with negative influences that clash with ours into our sphere and conflicts ensue.

For example, someone who has developed a need for control through his or her unconscious influences will tend to attract someone with a propensity towards victimization. Someone with a need to be a doer or creator may unconsciously seek a less active, more passive partner who is a nurturer. All these types of relationships can play out in positive or negative ways, depending on whether the needs being satisfied were created from true soul urgings or from unconscious Perceived Needs.

We are all born with different personalities, and the fulfillment of our souls' contracts (lessons we came here to learn) play out through our relationships and show up as differences to maneuver through. For example, we may have manifested on earth choosing that our soul's lesson in this lifetime would be to learn patience, or overcome neediness. The associated relationship would then offer us opportunities to do so. However, when one or both parties are beset with negative unconscious influences, the paring is fraught with conflict and/or emotional pain. Soul lessons and their contracts are more fully explained in chapter 6, "Words, Symbols, Rituals, Concepts, and Prayers." We can examine the quality of our needs with worksheet 2a.

Worksheet 2a: Desires/Needs: Real or Perceived

Unconscious Influences and Neediness

Desires arising from our unconscious influences seeking to fill a void will often drip with neediness. Mine were. However, as we attempt to fulfill the neediness, instead of feeling satisfied, we expose ourselves to further hurt or disappointment because these types of longings cannot be satisfied by others or by outside sources. Our neediness, often played out as an insatiable drive for intimacy, is our way of trying to heal the disconnect between our created selves and our True Selves. As our neediness draws us to those who either ignore our needs completely or who use our neediness to manipulate and control us, we invite more disconnect, disempowerment, and conflict into our lives. We thereby create a vicious cycle.

When we are needy, we are not loving ourselves or existing from our power bases. We are giving in to our unhealed emotions. All memories, conscious or unconscious, hold an emotional component. In fact, the proverbial emotional roller coaster is an aspect of unhealed negative emotions playing themselves out.

If we want to feel empowered in our lives, we have to overcome our disconnect from the power base held within our True Selves, so that we no longer attempt to draw on the power of others through our neediness. Instead of attracting true intimacy and love into our lives, our neediness is always vying to be satisfied, and we eventually alienate the other because truly satisfying relationships require healthy emotional boundaries. Our neediness hinders us from really loving close friends and family members, as fully loving another is an unselfish act: there is no neediness or agenda behind it to fulfill. Our neediness draws others in, but there are strings attached, because by the Law of Attraction those we attract to us will counteract our neediness in other ways that will bring more hurt into our lives.

Neediness does not come into play when we love unselfishly, as the true gift of love requires no reciprocity. This does not mean that we do not turn to others in hard times, but our ultimate aim should be to eventually find our own inner strength. The more we are in touch with our True Selves, the greater our level of self-confidence.

Unleashing our neediness creates frustration, conflict, and unhappiness in our lives. Our neediness is always lurking around vying to be satisfied, and as we try to find peace and love in our lives, we look to whatever appears to fulfill it. However, the externals that we look to will never fully satisfy us or they will eventually disappear, and we will feel lost again. They are only mirages that lure us with false promises of fulfillment, while actually drawing us further away from our True Self, as each disappointment is recorded in our Emotional Bodies. The cycle continues.

Conflict is neediness' best friend. As with any form of wavering insecurity, when we are needy, we bait others to enter a lose-lose playground of emotional warfare with us. Under the influence of our Illusionary Constructs, our fears play out through neediness, revealing themselves by our reactionary states as either aggressive or passive behaviors. If we become aggressive and vie for control over situations, we become the victimizer. If we become passive and succumb to the victimizer's ways by either being defensive or not standing up for ourselves, we have accepted their invitation to play. Control can be wielded in many ways: a parent who still wants to control his or her children's lives, an ex-partner struggling to hold on to a terminated relationship, or a child vying for attention. With a tear, a few directed words, a yell, a pout, or even a sigh, we lure others into this murky arena. We play the victim, the offender, or both and unleash our emotional warfare upon others with aggression, defensiveness, or weakness, and conflict entails. We can examine how our neediness plays out in our lives with worksheet 2b.

Worksheet 2b: Neediness: How It Plays Out in My Life

When we are needy, we often have unhealthy boundaries, as we will pull others toward us to fulfill our Perceived Needs or keep people at a distance to protect ourselves.

Boundaries

Healthy boundaries allow us to maintain our individualism while sharing our lives with others. Maintaining healthy boundaries is crucial to our ability to experience the world fully in a healthy, empowering way. This means being confident enough to be all that we can be without overstepping others' boundaries and being open enough to others and new experiences without fear of victimization. Unhealthy boundaries can create conflict in our lives and keep us frustrated or alienated.

Even though our boundaries are created in childhood, learning to trust or distrust is influenced by our innate characters, as well as our souls' journeys. This is why within families, children can all respond differently to the atmosphere that surrounded them—whether it was filled with love and warmth or conflict and detachment. If children do not learn how to get their needs met in healthy ways, their boundaries become confused.

In *Boundaries: Where You End and I Begin*, Anne Katherine explains that children come into this world with many needs that demand to be met. If the parent's needs have never been met, then meeting the child's needs becomes an overwhelming burden. Katherine explains that the parent becomes either distant or cold, emotionally checking out, or verbally or physically abusive. The child consequently suffers as emotional and/or physical needs go unanswered.[7] When our emotional needs were not met as children, as adults our need for love, affection, and intimacy compels us to enter into situations or relationships where our boundaries are wide open or closed shut.

When our boundaries are wide open, we either give too much of ourselves or fall into situations where we are not appreciated. We have not developed the ability to turn away from people or situations that tax us emotionally or physically. We often feel hurt and that life is not fair and may blame others or the situations for our frustrations. We may also develop boundaries that are too closed off. Instead of allowing people into our lives and embracing situations that provide us with emotional connections, we are afraid to open ourselves up to what life has to offer because we fear being hurt or rejected again.

I once heard that we should let others into our sphere like windows that we can open and shut—not have wide-open doorways that let everyone in or walls that shut everyone out. Worksheet 3 investigates our boundaries.

Worksheet 3: My Boundaries

Confusing emotions about love that surrounded us growing up not only spawn unhealthy boundaries, they also create conflicts within our Emotional Bodies. These conflicts produce imbalances and like a pendulum cause our emotions to shift from one pole to the other. Unhealthy boundaries can also encourage codependency, whereby our happiness is wrapped up in others'. These responses all create pull-and-push scenarios, which cause more inner conflicts to develop that keep the vicious cycle going, making it difficult to break out of until the underlying causes are dealt with.

When we embark on this journey to find more peace in our lives, we have to unearth, understand, and be on guard for the aspects of our thought systems that do not serve us in ways that will ultimately bring us inner peace and harmony with others. Most humans are deeply conflicted because we are born into a society that extols the virtues of love, caring, and honesty but is biased in carrying out the representations of these virtues. This compounds the pulls-and-pushes within us.

Conditional Love and Conflicting Messages

The history of Humanity has been based on conditional love. This has manifested within our families, community support systems, and even our religions. Conditional love has created conflicting messages within us because while we often extol the virtues of love, we may not uphold them. We tell our children we love them or want what is best for them; however, this is often influenced by our limited perspectives based on perceptions, or we unconsciously inflict our neediness or Perceived Needs on them. We have been told that God loves us but also that he is vengeful. Our psyches have thereby become riddled with conflicts about love.

Similarly, mixed messages about success and money are quite common. We may have the desire to excel and/or succeed at something, but deep within us may fear success which hinders our aspirations. I came from what was perceived by most in my school as an affluent background. But we were not. My father was a well-respected school principal of the only English Catholic school in town, and we lived in a nice house on a hill. However, this was not because we were wealthy but because my parents were *very* frugal. My mother watered down the ketchup, diluted the milk, and scraped food off the plates. We ate beef almost every night, but as it became more expensive, my mother bought the cheaper cuts. We had the appearance of a nice middle-class family, but conflicts surrounding our station in life abounded. For example, my father drove a nice car and had pride in our house but also bemoaned attachment to money. I remember many loud protestations about the evils of money and success. So I grew up conflicted about my value and worth, as well as about money and success. We can examine conflicting messages within us with worksheet 4.

Worksheet 4: Conflicting Messages and Their Pulls-and-Pushes

If we have Perceived Needs vying to be satisfied, we have likely developed Hidden Agendas to play these out.

Hidden Agendas

Hidden Agendas: Ulterior motives or unconscious driving forces created by our Perceived Needs that we constructed for our emotional survival.

Hidden Agendas develop as we aim to nourish the Perceived Needs that our misperceptions uphold within our Emotional Bodies. We erect them to either avoid being hurt or to pursue a course of action that we believe will help us avoid hurtful situations. These agendas are self-serving, aggressively pursued, and strongly defended.

The degree of the *need* to uphold the inner beliefs within our Illusionary Constructs and their perceived solutions keeps us from being aware of our Hidden Agendas, or at least understanding the complete hold they have on us. Below are some concrete examples.

Susan developed a Hidden Agenda as a *need* to control all aspects of her life. She grew up in a chaotic situation with an alcoholic parent and therefore never knew what atmosphere she was coming home to. However, the control patterns she created in an attempt to generate stability in her life produced conflict with those around her, and a peaceful existence still eluded her. George lived in an emotionally distant environment where feelings were kept under the surface and never validated. This caused him to develop a *need* to create connections with others, but his attempts usually just invited in highly emotional situations which created drama in his life. They never fulfilled him and always left him feeling lost and further alienated. Peter's early life experience was one of impoverishment, and his family members were snubbed because they lacked social status. He developed a *need* for success, which he relentlessly pursued, ignoring intimate family connections, as all his relationships were built on business associations. His family life suffered because he alienated them.

In my own life, I developed a Hidden Agenda to be in control of situations and to create a perfect household, having always felt a lack of love in my life due to an emotionally distant mother and a critical, bullying father. I tried to fill this void by creating a nice house rather than a loving home. I also created emotional barriers so as not to become vulnerable and therefore lose control of my life. While I was somewhat aware of this, I was not aware of the depth of my *need* for control nor of how blind I was to some of its repercussions. We can explore any Hidden Agendas we may hold with worksheet 5.

Worksheet 5: Hidden Agendas

The self-serving attitudes within our Hidden Agendas can undermine our happiness and efforts to reach our full potential. As these blindly feed our neediness or appease our Perceived Needs, we may be unaware of their destructive nature, but our unconscious mind is aware of everything. As with all masked influences, Hidden Agendas infuse our being with unconscious guilt, an ally of negative attitudes.

Unconscious Guilt

As we wield these Hidden Agendas (or exert any other negative attitude or behavior), our unconscious minds are aware of the dishonesty. They record every little nuance within our Emotional Bodies associated with all that we think, say, and do. We then amass associated unconscious guilt, which further entrenches negativity into our beings and distances us from our True Selves. Any thought, word, or action that is not in alignment with our True Self builds up traces of emotional guilt within our psyches. This guilt lurks about seeking opportunities for release by projecting onto others through our negative attitudes and behaviors. Our unconscious minds then believe the guilt has been released.

Pendulum Swings of Our Emotional Bodies

When we live under the influence of Unconscious Awareness, we can aggressively push our neediness, defenses, and agendas onto others and situations, or we can become overly passive burying more emotions. As we aim to appease our unconscious influences, our emotional pendulum usually swings through center way to the other side. For example, we might swing from neediness to aloofness back to neediness. As we become dependent on others through our neediness, we pull them into our spheres. We then become dissatisfied as our neediness cannot be satisfied by others, and end up undermining the relationship and push it away. Then as distance naturally develops, we feel alienated and try to pull others into our lives. Illustration 1 shows what happens when what is held in our Emotional Bodies looks for an outlet and attempts to correct.

#1: Pendulum Swings of our Emotional Body

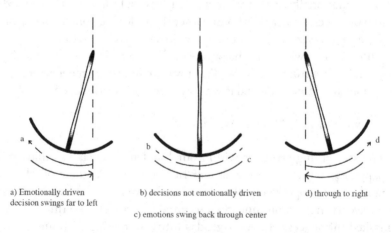

a) Emotionally driven
decision swings far to left

b) decisions not emotionally driven

c) emotions swing back through center

d) through to right

These swings will continue until we release the original emotions they stem from.

These outlets manifest as aggressive or passive behaviors or pull-and-push scenarios, which cause the pendulum to swing back and forth, keeping us unbalanced. As I explain in chapter 2, "Universal Laws / Kingdom Principles," the Law of Balance aims to guide us back to center, so we will continue this *pull-and-push* scenario until we overcome or deal with what is creating the swings. We usually find these attempts to attain balance unsatisfying and even painful, as they are feeble attempts to feel loved or empowered. All illustrations are listed with their page numbers at end of Contents pages.

An example of this would be to confidently and even boldly pursue a relationship or job situation that is not really right for us to appease a need to feel loved or successful. However, because we have extended our self out of a Perceived Need, any feelings of love or success will be short-lived, and our ego will be hurt. We may then pull back all the way through center to self-pity, where we may stay and lick our wounds for awhile, until our next attempt to appease a Perceived Need.

Once we trade in Unconscious Awareness for Conscious Awareness and become aware of what is driving us, we can begin to understand the pulls-and-pushes in our lives that have been, or still are, keeping us from being our Best Selves. Being consciously aware empowers us: we can honestly show up in life and be at the *cause* of our experiences. Conversely, when we live unconsciously, we are always at the beck and call of influences we are not aware of: we are disempowered because we are at the *effect* of what these undue influences bring into our lives.

Being the Cause of Our Life Experiences vs. at the Effect of Our Unconscious Influences

The main advantage of conscious living is that we can become the *cause* of our life experiences, instead of being at the *effect* of our thoughts, attitudes, and actions, which usually create negative life experiences, or short-lived positive ones. This is one of the main tenets of *The Course*, as its lessons guide us to uncover and acknowledge what is held in our unconscious minds or egos, so that we can move away from their influence. Shifting away from living as an *effect* of the unconscious mind to being at the *cause* of our experiences is also the basis of many other spiritual and religious practices.

By being aware of our thoughts and attitudes we can modify our thinking so we can move away from the negative—what is not creating the harmony or life experiences we want—to the positive and our Best Selves, which will bring us more positive experiences. No matter how meager our efforts to become more conscious and shift to the more positive, this process is supported by Spirit, God, Source, or whatever we call the conscious, intelligent force of the Universe that wants us to live happy, empowered, and fulfilled lives. Even small shifts in our attitudes give us results. All our efforts are recognized.

The Masks of Fear

All angers, hurts, and frustrations stem from fear. Although we are usually not aware of these deep-set fears, if we trace any of our negative or disempowering attitudes back to their origins, we will find some aspect of fear at the base.

To appease these deep-set fears, we lash out in many ways. Fearing that we are undeserving of love, we push it away by undermining ourselves. Fearing we are not good enough, we try to prove ourselves, often with unsatisfying results. Fearful of being hurt again, we are timid and overly cautious. We are afraid of not having our Perceived Needs met, believing if our perceived superficial selves and its needs are not satisfied, we will be void and empty vessels. When we operate superficially aiming to feed our neediness and Perceived Needs, we are not connected to our True Selves and are afraid of looking within for our fulfillment. Aggressive and passive behaviors are manifestations of our fears, played out by the unconscious influences within our Illusionary Constructs.

Being under the influence of our Illusionary Constructs and their limiting beliefs and insecurities, we develop mechanisms to survive and uphold our inner beliefs. We vie for changes and maneuver things to suit what we think will appease our needs, but often they do not. If we connect the dots between how we think, feel, and act, we can pinpoint the fear beneath any anger, frustration, insecurity, attitude, or behavior that is undermining our peace and happiness. Once we face the underlying fear, we can start to unblock it and in so doing release the hold it has on us.

An Example of Being at the Effect of Negative Unconscious Influences

In an attempt to appease the conflict and pain that is held in our Emotional Bodies, our misperceptions and unconscious fears can influence us to make choices that we think will circumvent our perceived problems, but they will not ultimately make us happy. We think our problems will just go away, but they will follow us despite whatever we change in our lives.

In 1991, my young family and I moved from Saint-Bruno to Beaconsfield. I had been *dying* to get out of Saint-Bruno because of the many constant reminders of some family tragedies. Using the guise of needing to move westward because of my husband's job, I set my heart on Beaconsfield in the West Island. It seemed like a cool place, and I decided that this was the town where I would find security and happiness. I was terribly wrong! Unfortunately, we couldn't find a house within our price range in the areas we liked near the lake. My spouse had suggested other towns along the Lakeshore, and I now know I would have ended up liking that area, but I wouldn't hear of it. So we found a house in Beaconsfield but it was stuck between two highways and far from the lake and its peaceful environment. It was a nice house, but I hated living there! It was very different from our quiet Saint-Bruno home tucked away at the bottom of a mountain. This part of Beaconsfield was busier than what I was used to, and we had to navigate traffic lights to even go out for an ice cream on a hot summer's day. I made my family and ultimately myself, unhappy for nine years all because my life had become an *effect* of my unconscious influences.

We *can* create the realities that we want and be the *cause* of our experiences, rather than at the *effect* of unconscious choices, but to do so we must free ourselves of the fears our unconscious influences create in us. This is a wonderful power we hold, but many of us have not been aware of it. We can examine where we might be at the effect or the cause of our experiences with worksheet 6.

Worksheet 6: Being at the Effect or the Cause of My Life Experiences.

To go from being at the **effect** of our unconscious influences to becoming the **cause** and creator of our experiences, we have to understand the difference between being responsive and reactive.

Being Responsive or Reactive

Being in a responsive state means that we respond to others or situations at face value, unemotionally and with neutrality. Being in a reactive state, we respond with heightened emotions, imposing past perceptions and their projections into the now and/or future picture.

Reasons for Being Reactive

As explained by Arten in an excerpt from Gary Renard's book *The Disappearance of the Universe*, most of our reactions and actions come from a need to release because we live in a world of "tension and release."[8] This concept is rooted in motivations that come from a lack of connection to our True Selves and the fear this brings up in us. Arten further explains that all our tensions exist because we live in a world characterized by duality. All negativities or tensions we have amassed in our Emotional Bodies are rooted in fear and fueled by a belief in lack, which is a characteristic of this duality playing out in our lives. This belief in lack convinces us that there is not enough love, money, or success etc. to go around. As we are stuck within these false, limiting illusions, we are disconnected to the love and abundance inherent in the Oneness we emanated from and thereby further perpetuate the false belief as we aim to look for it.

This sense of fear and lack results in our competing with others to have our Perceived Needs met, our Hidden Agendas answered, or our neediness satisfied. Any inkling that these perceived requirements will not be answered arouses strong reactions. This stems from the authority our unconscious influences have over us, as well as the void they create within as they disconnect us from our True Self. Our unconscious influences need to be understood and released if we want to live choosing our life experiences rather than being at the effect of our unconscious influences.

We often try to get something to relieve something else. Hunger for something is really a yearning to fill a void. If we expect something from someone else, we are actually trying to meet a need, as all expectations stem from a lack of connection to our True Selves. Then when the person does not provide what we expect or something we had hoped for does not happen, we become disappointed, hurt, depressed, or angry and react involuntarily.

Even when our Perceived Needs *are* met, we will often yearn for something else or something better or bigger. We continue to be disappointed, and the void grows. The *need* to fill a void within ourselves manifests itself in the unconscious demands we put on others, in our relationships, or in our incessant striving for material possessions and status. The answer is to stop looking for satisfaction from outside ourselves and to look within. When we are in touch with our True Selves, we find the satisfaction within. The yearning of love and appreciation that we hunger for exists within us all, and we will always attempt to go looking for it if we cannot find it in ourselves.

I was very outwardly reactionary for most of my life. I blamed everybody and everything for all my frustrations, which I now understand were caused by my neediness, Perceived Needs, and Hidden Agendas. I was often angry at those around me for not getting down in the muck and joining me in my misery.

It took a lot of studying, journaling, and reflection for me to begin to understand where my reactions and frustrations came from and to unravel it all. And it took a lot of courage to "go there." Listening to and attending uplifting talks and workshops energized me, kept me focused on the positive aspects of the process, and helped me anchor in the fact that no matter how I felt now or acted in the past I was unconditionally loved and forgiven. All my efforts led me to believe that I could come back from it all, thrive in all ways, and become my Best Self. Once I understood that we can and need to choose our attitudes, I then had to *consciously* practice to shift from blaming others to taking responsibility for my own happiness. Until we become adept at all this, the need to react helps us release internal tensions from the conflicts within us. I call our automatic reactionary or nonreactionary state our *Default Positions*.

Our Default Positions

Default Position: The reactionary, nonreactionary, or responsive way of dealing with others or situations. We respond with aggression, passivity, or neutrality.

Our Default Positions can show up in many ways when we are affronted or criticized: aggressively with judgment, anger, or blame; passively with timidity, denial, or withdrawal; or neutrally with calm, self-assuredness, without needing to defend ourselves or our positions.

A Positive Default Position

Positive Default Positions do not create conflict, as we respond neutrally to others or situations. Our responses promote harmony because we are confident and do not feel the need for retorts. We may express our opinions, but do so without blame, aggression, or judgment. And we are not invested in others agreeing with us, because we are self-assured. Under the influence of the positive we tend to be easygoing. We may still work hard and move forward confidently, but without greatly overtaxing ourselves.

This approach is usually the product of having experienced and witnessed loving, accepting, and hopeful attitudes toward ourselves and others. Being somewhat easygoing, we would be more responsive than reactive. We would not have developed unconscious agendas that need to be satisfied, so we would be less invested in outcomes.

People with positive Default Positions would not uphold limiting beliefs for themselves, others, or the world. Although innate personalities come into play, there can still be a range of underlying characterizations. With positive

Default Positions, we might have gentle, quiet natures not prone to taking stands on issues. However, we would have enough inner strength to avoid becoming victimized. We could also have strong, outgoing characters, defend others, and still pursue what we want in life but do so in a fair and balanced way aiming to maintain harmony around us.

A Negative Default Position

On the other hand, negative Default Positions create conflict. They stem from early experiences or witnessing of aggressive and/or passive behaviors or strong biases, leading to the formation of limiting beliefs. For example, if a woman experiences or witnesses controlling, manipulative, or other aggressive behaviors toward women within a family situation, she might form the inner belief that women are *weak* and *vulnerable* and cannot achieve what men can. Those perceptions could also potentially sway her to the opposite end of the spectrum, and she could become an aggressive or bullying high achiever, often to the detriment of her relationships.

If we have a negative Default Position, we have limiting beliefs about ourselves, our potentials, and the world around us. Not having the self-confidence of inner strength, we react either aggressively by defensively judging or blaming others or passively by falling into victimization roles and not defending ourselves or others. These reactions tend to generate conflict; acting aggressively brings immediate consequences, while the effects of passivity usually find an outlet at some other time.

We can hold overlapping Default Positions, whereby both negative and positive aspects are at play. We can also shift away from a Default Position (e.g., a person who normally reacts positively can have a negative reaction), though we usually return to our defaults quickly. Permanently changing from a negative to a positive Default Position is possible, but requires conscious effort, as underlying negative influences are at play and pull us back. But it can be done. I did it!

The more we uphold and reinforce our Default Positions, the more they become our primary natures. Understanding how our internalized past experiences and personalities created and sustain our Default Positions will allow us to gradually shift away from negative reactions that do not serve us to embrace more positive ones. We can examine these reactive mechanisms with worksheet 7a.

Worksheet 7a: My Default Position

Our Default Positions act as masks for our limiting inner beliefs and the insecurities they create. We falsely believe these inner beliefs and all other unconscious influences to be the truth and that the reactions that stem from them are necessary, because they feel vital to our emotional survival. We thereby feel the need to protect and defend them.

Protective Mechanisms

> **Protective Mechanisms:** The methods we use to uphold, protect, and defend false, limiting inner beliefs, biases, and insecurities.

Our Protective Mechanisms seek to hide and mask our fears and deep-set neediness, Perceived Needs, and Hidden Agendas. This keeps us mentally and emotionally on guard. Our Protective Mechanisms create menus of *how-it-should-be* rules, which we use as barometers of how we think things should be compared to how we *perceive* things actually are. I say perceive because our unconscious influences cause us to indentify situations falsely. For example, a person may feel their spouse is not attentive enough, but it is *their need* for attention that cannot be satisfied. Judgments then ensue to support these viewpoints.

Holding these mechanisms in place keeps our minds active with worry and our emotions taxed, even affecting our health. This stress creates anxiety, depression, phobias, and dependencies, as well as physical symptoms, such as high blood pressure and insomnia. In *Your Body Speaks Your Mind: Decoding the Emotional, Psychological, and Spiritual Messages that Underlie Illness,* Debbie Shapiro says that "the role of the mind with relation to health is inseparable from emotions ... there is an undeniable and close interconnection between what is going on in our life, with our thoughts and feelings, and the physical reactions that manifest in our body."[9] I further explore the effects of our mind-sets on our health in chapter 8, "Health and Healing; Death and Dying." We can investigate our fears and their protective devices with worksheet 7b.

Worksheet 7b: Protective Mechanisms: My Masks of Fear

Neediness, Perceived Needs, Hidden Agendas, negative Default Positions, and Protective Mechanisms are all unconscious influences that result from living under Illusionary Constructs. Why are we prone to getting stuck in illusion? Was it always like this? If not, how and when did this happen? Are we relegated to staying stuck in limitation? No! We *can* choose whether or not we wish to live under the influence of the illusions we have fabricated. We can embrace every moment connected to our True Selves. Which reality do you want to live under? How do we shift realities? We must look at Humanity's past and our very beginnings to unravel how we became entrenched in such a deep illusionary nature.

Why We Are Like This

As individuals we have become stuck in a paradigm of lack and fear and live under the ruse that conditional love is normal. The illusions we created around this idea are now part of our operating systems, and we further anchor them in by playing them out through our attitudes, actions, and reactions. As a collective, Humanity has similarly become trapped and entrenched in its illusions of fear and lack.

We cannot see that we exist within a false, illusionary state of *me-and-you* and *us-and-them* that ultimately keeps us divided. It is incomprehensible to us that we can consciously choose anything other than our reactions. But we can! Within this false paradigm that we have unintentionally embraced, we hold separate, conflicting agendas, born of our illusions. Where has all this come from?

Loss of Connection

Many philosophers, as well as spiritual and religious teachings, suggest that all our internal and external conflicts are the result of the original loss of connectedness to God, Spirit, or our Source: to the Oneness we emerged from. A separation is alleged to have occurred, but did it? Before that original loss of connectedness, all we knew was the blissful, fearless love within the Oneness.

Our origins, our connection, and this loss of our connection to God have been outlined in all the ancient religions and thought systems, and their stories, parables, and myths have given us various interpretations which attempted to explain the unexplainable. From within our level of awareness, we cannot understand the full scope of it all.

The Judeo-Christian story of the Garden of Eden is one depiction of this loss, commonly known as the *fall of man*. However, some believe that the fall occurred on levels well beyond our awareness—before physical form. This does not mean that a Garden of Eden did not exist on earth at some point, where we lived in peace and harmony with each other, all animals, and in tune with the Planet. But using a metaphoric point of view gives us a frame of reference that goes back to why the fall, or the perception of a fall, occurred.

We all originally emanated from Oneness, an all-encompassing energy: the creative force of the Universe. This is what we call God, Source, Creator, or

24

the many other names given to who/what created us. This Oneness is pervasive and completely nondualistic, meaning it holds no concept of anything, even itself, and it completely embodies unconditional love, abundance, and fearless sharing. **It just is!**

> **Oneness**: The pervasive universal creative force that everything and everybody emanated from, are still connected to, and will eventually return to: we still hold a memory of that Oneness within us.

In *Awaken from the Dream*, Gloria Wapnick tells us that this beautiful but distant memory of our origins is what creates longing within us:

> In the Beginning, before there was even a concept of beginning, there is God, our Source and the Source of all creation: a perfection and resplendence whose magnificence is beyond comprehension; love and gentleness of such an infinite nature that consciousness could not even begin its apprehension; a pristine stillness of uninterrupted joy; a motionless flow without friction to impede it; a vast, limitless, and all-encompassing Totality, beyond space, beyond time, in which there is no beginning, no ending, for there was never a time or place when God was not ... Creation, like spirit, is abstract, formless, and unchanging.[10]

First there was only the Oneness, an energy characterized by blissful love. That love energy created abundantly and fearlessly and had no awareness of itself or its creations. These creations are our beginnings: we *are* the extensions of the Oneness, albeit further along the line. Created by the Oneness and fully meshed with it, at this point we had no fear, ideas of limitation, or any concept of separation or "other." Wapnick further tells us that there was "no perception, simply the total knowledge of who we were: a glory of such unified resplendence that concepts of within-without have no meaning."[11] There was total unity. This Oneness, this all-encompassing creative force of the Universe may be the "one unifying principle" physicists have been looking for. Inspired by an illustration by John English, a writer, teacher, and shamanic healer, illustration 2 is my rendition of the Oneness extending itself:[12]

#2: Creative Universal Force Extending Itself

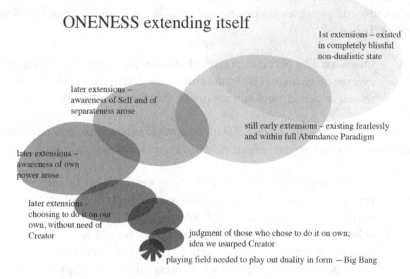

ONENESS extending itself

1st extensions – existed in completely blissful non-dualistic state

later extensions – awareness of Self and of separateness arose

still early extensions – existing fearlessly and within full Abundance Paradigm

later extensions – awareness of own power arose

later extensions - choosing to do it on our own, without need of Creator

judgment of those who chose to do it on own; idea we usurped Creator

playing field needed to play out duality in form — Big Bang

World of multiplicity created; we are fragments of these original fragments.

These early extensions occurred without any awareness of themselves or the other extensions, as within the Oneness there is no perception. They expressed themselves fearlessly without limitations because they were in tune with the Abundance Paradigm.

> **Abundance Paradigm**: An awareness of enough—without any awareness of limitation or lack.

Before any perception or separateness arose, these extensions were our original beginnings. Speaking metaphorically, within the creation model of the Bible, this would be considered as the Garden of Eden, as these original creations experienced abundance and limitlessness and were still aligned with the Oneness paradigm whereby fear, lack, and limitation did not exist. We were co-creators with the God-energy/Oneness we emanated from and created as we wanted. We effortlessly brought forth glorious realities merging the powerful Father energy and the creative Mother energy in perfect balance, while still maintaining the concept of a unity of consciousness and purpose, all within the auspices of free will. I explain the Father and Mother energies in chapter 6, Words, Symbols, Rituals, Concepts, and Prayers.

Somewhere along the way, however, an awareness of Self arose, and then the thought *The Course* explains as, "a tiny mad idea" arose that "I can do it on my own," apart from the original creative force. As free will was in place, this could occur. In time, both unity of purpose and all the concepts inherent to the Oneness were ignored, leading to duality and polarity. The concepts of yin and yang within some forms of the Eastern Taoist and Confucianism belief systems are considered explanations of this duality and polarity, understood as aspects that need to be played out within the Law of Balance, as explained in chapter 2, "Universal Laws / Kingdom Principles."

Within these extensions, while some ignored the original tenets of the Oneness paradigm, others judged them for doing so. This *judgment* swung the pendulum off balance. At some point from within this doing-it-on-our-own concept, a spark was ignited to create the Universe—the Big Bang—as a playground was needed for this new game of duality and polarity. We have been caught up in the pull-and-push of this dualistic nature of judgment, guilt, shame, and blame ever since that time.

The thought of doing-it-on-our-own, thereby usurping our Creator, is akin to the original sin mentioned in the first chapter of Genesis in the Bible. The temptation to judge others for doing so is akin to the temptation of Adam and Eve to not eat from the tree of the *knowledge* of good and evil. Knowledge of good and evil = judgment.

Longing for Unity and Connectedness

The fearlessness within the Abundance Paradigm as well as the Oneness and its sense of unity and interconnectedness is what we long to reconnect to. The common thread that runs through the world's religions has been to help us understand these principles of Oneness so that we can reconnect to it.

The Judeo-Christian belief systems aimed to reconcile the Oneness paradigm and our ideas of separation by moving away from the ancient practices of worshipping many different gods. The Eastern religions hold to a belief of the One expressing itself as many in our world of multiplicity. In *Ten Theories of Human Nature*, L. Stevenson and D. L. Haberman explain that one of the main tenets of Hindu philosophies (Buddhism, an offshoot of Hinduism also holds to this belief) is "that there is a single, unifying principal underlying the entire universe. At the level of ultimate realization, the world of multiplicity is revealed to be one of interconnected unity."[13]

Eastern philosophies and *The Course* (A Course in Miracles) suggest that only the Oneness exists and that everything else is an illusion: we are an illusion, the masters are illusions, the Universe is an illusion, and even Spirit or Holy Spirit (our connection to the Oneness) is an illusion. The separation we thought we had brought about by doing-it-on-our-own never occurred:

this is the first illusion we bought into. As our basic premise was erroneous we existed under a false operating system, which lead us to create illusion upon illusion. We further perpetrated the illusions by believing those we created until they all became our perceived realities. In fact, the basic premise of *The Course* is that even the Universe—*all* form—all of us in bodies or on the ethereal levels, and even *all thought is not only an illusion, but a projection of the original thought of separation* from the Oneness.

It compares the illusion we live under to a dream—and we are the dreamer—projecting it all with our mind. However, because we have no awareness of any of this, we have to work within the illusion and our current awareness. All words, teachings, and ancient texts have spoken to us from within the illusion, in form, to help us remember our true reality: our connection to the Oneness. I explore these concepts more thoroughly in chapter 7, "Science and Other Related Topics."

A main philosophy of *The Course* suggests that it is the mind that is the decision maker and we can and need to consciously direct it away from egoic thinking. Others see it is a bequest given to us to help us become aware of who we really are. In *The Messenger of the Soul*, G.W. Hesketh tells us "The human mind has the capacity to question everything—that is the gift of consciousness." He continues to explain that we have mostly used our mind at a superficial level without using it as a tool to investigate the "deeper parts of our consciousness" and to question our existence—as it was intended. Not using our mind for inquiry about the whys and wherefores of our existence has kept us within our illusions because we never questioned the status quo.[14]

Within the illusion, there are different levels of awareness or realms. Like the other lower realms, our third-dimensional reality is characterized by form, is physically dense, and has a weak sense of interconnected unity. The higher levels of awareness occupied by those who have passed on, as well as the light-beings, archangels, and ascended masters like Lau-Tzu, Buddha, Muhammad, and Jesus, etc. are characterized as more ethereal, and their sense of Oneness is strong. Illustration 3 offers us a visual of what the different non-linear levels might look like in linear form. This illustration is an amalgamation of many interpretations I have come across over the years but inspired mostly from a depiction by JRobert in one of his workshops.

#3: Levels of Consciousness Within the Different Realms

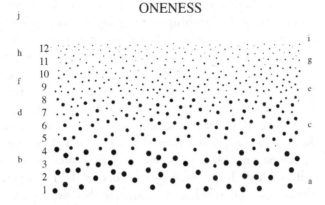

ONENESS

a) 1st 4 dimensions, world of form, separation is manifest
b) all life form, including humans and lower level ET's
c) 5th – 7th dimension, more ethereal, less awareness of separation
d) evolved live forms, higher level ET's, lower level Light-beings. Can take form
e) 8 -10th dimension, completely ethereal, concept of separation foreign. Rarely take form
f) highly evolved light-beings who run the Universe.
g) 11-12th dimension, completely ethereal, no awareness of separation. Very rarely take form
h) highly evolved light-beings that supervise the running of the Universe. Domain of Archangels and Seraphim. Almosy never have taken form.
i) No conscious awareness of Self, separation, its creations or us.
j) 13th - Original creative force we emanated from: God

The Garden of Eden and Choosing to Try It on Our Own

Within the Judeo-Christian belief system, the concept of temptation and original sin in the Garden of Eden can be seen as a metaphor for partaking in the "*knowledge* of good and evil," mentioned in Genesis 2:17—or *judgment*. The *perception* of the dualistic concepts of right and wrong, good and bad, lie in the temptation to evaluate another's actions: in judgment. The value of *The Course's* practice of forgiveness[15] recognizes and deals with our thoughts, decisions, and judgments of today, with an understanding that they represent not only our present issues but also everything since that original separation.

Looking at the creation story in the Bible as a metaphor, *The Course* suggests that we were never forced out of the Garden of Eden. Rather, inner guilt arose from what it calls the ego (comparable to Satan) and lured us into a false belief that we had committed a sin in acting independently, not wanting or needing the support of the original Oneness. We believed we had severed that connection, but we never really did, because we could not have. Just like the child who runs away from home, the DNA of the parents is never lost, no matter how much guilt the child may feel or how hard the child may try to ignore the fact of his or her blood connection. Unfortunately, that belief in the severed connection became and is still the basis of our operating system.

Ego: On an *individual* level, ego is the manifestation of the separated Self. It is engrossed in itself, in the "I" of it all. It gives a running commentary of everything that is going on, could go on, or has gone on with us, with others, and in all situations. It upholds all ideas of separation, luring us away from being present in the moment, thereby separating us from the truth of who we are. It constantly compares, judges, and blames, thereby further separating us from others. It can be relentless, needs to protect itself, and is thereby defensive of upholding all its ideas of separateness. On a *cosmic* level, the ego, or Satan, is the negative energy that arose from the original judgment of the *false* notion that we separated from our Source, and thereby relinquished all the qualities it embodies. Ego was perpetuated by shame and guilt of what we thought we had done, as well as the fear of retribution. All our issues and everything that is *not of love and unity* is a manifestation of ego (or Satan).

We were not sent away by a vengeful God. We bought into the ego's deception that we had *broken* our connection to our Source, and so were filled with remorse, guilt, and fear of retribution. Even though the connection was never actually broken, we projected our shame and guilt onto others through *judgment* believing that we could rid ourselves of it. Shame, guilt, and fear, judgment and projection, as well as our belief in lack took us out of the Abundance Paradigm and this has been the basis of the human predicament. As Humanity progressed, the memory of joyfully creating and the sharing of purposes was completely lost, to be replaced by the principles of detachment, independence, and competition—we became ensnared in survival mode leading us to create separate agendas to protect our continued existence.

Me-against-You Approach

This survival attitude and its inevitability of separate agendas created a *me-against-you* approach to life, pitting one against the other. As this reality became our normal way of existing, a never-ending cycle of fear, greed, conflict, and hate ensued. As the Law of Attraction's "like attracts like" further entrenched us in the paradigms we had chosen, we forgot our origins. The Law of Attraction is further explained in chapter 2, "Universal Laws / Kingdom Principles."

Somewhere deep within the crevices of our minds lies the cellular memories of the original feelings of living within a harmony-ruled paradigm—and it remains a longing deep within us. The original purpose of all mysticism, spirituality, and religion was to reawaken those memories within us and help us return to the state that is inherent in us, but remains buried. Their intentions were to help us let go of the fear-based consciousness that controls and separates and instead turn us back to the love-based consciousness and the unifying principles that accept rather than divide.

Upholding a metaphoric concept of the Garden of Eden, believing that God did not create the world, and embracing the concept that God is not a vengeful being and did not throw us out of the Garden of Eden helps us to make peace with some of the conflicts within our religious dogmas. We superimposed our misperceptions onto the texts which were intended to help us find our way back. However, we are now unearthing the truths held within all these texts, and I am sharing some of them with you.

Missing the Mark

Whether we take the stories and mythologies depicting the separation of man from God as metaphoric or as physical, we can all concur that at some point we lost our way. However, a memory or spark as well as a roadmap of who we are still reside within all of us. After eons of trying it our way, we have forgotten our way home; we have actually forgotten that we have a home. The map tucked away deep within the recesses of our souls is soiled, crumpled, and ripped—by our own hands. We often asked for help, but even misunderstood those who showed up pointing us home, and then further entrenched ourselves in the darkness as we tried to reconcile the misperceptions we created with their messages and misinterpreted many of the *it is likes*.

Although we are now stuck with our unconscious influences because of Humanity's journey and its perpetuation of them, we also have uncovered the way out. All the truths that we are unearthing within religion, spirituality, psychology, and science tie together to help us find our way back to who and what we really are. Having believed ourselves separated from the Oneness and its paradigms of unconditional love and limitlessness, we are now ready to reconnect to it and rediscover our True Selves. As we remove the illusions of our separateness from God or our Source, we are also removing what prevents us from embracing the unifying principles we share with all others. All we have to do is dismantle the barriers that block us accessing Our Truth.

Our Unconscious Influences and Inner Beliefs

Whether positive or negative, our unconscious beliefs influence us without our consent or real knowledge of why. In his series broadcast "Miraculous Probabilities: The Science of Faith," based on his book *The Anatomy of a Miracle*, Dr. Jim Richards explains that even if we decide to do something or want to make changes in our life, if our "heart beliefs" (our unconscious inner beliefs) do not match our mind beliefs (what we consciously decide to do), we will undermine ourselves, as these inner beliefs are "written on our heart" and will override our mind beliefs.[16] This is because they unconsciously influence how we really feel about ourselves and how we think we must navigate the world, as they are deeply embedded within our latent, emotional memories. Our unconscious influences float about in our psyches like sparks of love or daggers of fear. They will influence how we feel, act, react, live, and love.

Even If the Heart Is Programmed, We Can Direct the Mind

Dr. Richards also tells us that to change the programming of our hearts we have to use the mind, because we *can* control where the mind goes. It is the mind that directs the emotions. The mind will *decide* if something is fearful. It then bases its direction on the intentions we give it, like "I have to *protect* myself." If we can shift our intentions with the mind—instead saying to ourselves, "I will be fine"—and act on the impulses to support that new belief, we can influence our emotional responses.[17] When our emotional responses shift, our heart beliefs also shift. However, those new impulses will wane quickly, so we *must* act upon them asap.

Most of us have not been trained to consciously choose with the mind. In fact we likely didn't even know this was an option. I didn't. We are accustomed to simply responding to how we feel. However, sometimes our feelings are based on misappropriations of past emotions. Except for the teachings within some of the Eastern religions, which value training the mind and self-examination, Humanity's history has been to allow our emotions and inner beliefs to run our lives. Power hungry leaders even fostered a sense of fear and lack, so our natural response has been to succumb to fearful and limiting thoughts. However, we can overcome these deeply entrenched inner beliefs.

While it may appear to be an overwhelming undertaking to shift from the negative or limiting unconscious influences we have held all our lives, we do get help, as our higher Selves are on board. We just need to make a conscious choice and then remember to use our mind and its decision making power to get the recalibration process going. We *can* take control of our mind and shift away from any negative thoughts, attitudes, or habits it wants us to act upon. I explain the many things we can do to help get this process going in chapter 3, "What We Can Do about It."

Unconscious Beliefs and Our Preferences vs Those That Undermine Good Intentions

Most of our life choices develop from preferences. Whether we come from a large or small family, a comfortable or impoverished background, a busy city or the quiet country will affect our likes and dislikes. However, our inner beliefs can also influence us.

For example, if you grew up in the city and your family enjoyed city life, you would not have amassed any emotional scars concerning living in the city. But if your personality or your soul's journey drew you to country living, you would automatically be vibrationally aligned toward work that would accommodate country living, and you would naturally draw partners and friends who want a quiet living environment.

Although no matter how good or pure our intentions and motivations may be they sometimes get thwarted because they automatically intertwine with an inner belief system that is contrary to what we want. For example, perhaps you want to be successful because in your family life you witnessed others who were disempowered and victimized. However, some of the negative attitudes from those around you became embedded in your psyche, and your inner beliefs may not match your desire to succeed. Inwardly you are conflicted about success, and you may thereby undermine yourself by failing exams because of a lack of discipline, being late for interviews or meetings, or not getting papers or reports in on time. You may also not be cooperative in work situations, as you have created shoulds about how you think things need to be run. You have put limitations on your success because you are unconsciously driven to undermine yourself.

Compulsions, Dysfunctions, and Addictions

Our unconscious beliefs can show up as annoying compulsions, harmful dysfunctions, and life-altering addictions. Sometimes we are aware of the negative effects on our lives from habits such as overeating, overdrinking, or doing drugs, but we are often unaware of the connection to the original need that fed these dysfunctions, and as such they may be difficult to override unless we address their cause.

Addictions and serious dysfunctions must eventually be dealt with if we are to be fully functional. We do this by following the appropriate treatment recommendations, but it is also important to address and unravel the unconscious influences they stem from. Even non life-threatening dysfunctions thwart us from becoming our Best Selves, as our focus on satisfying them draws us away from more productive activities, and keeps us at arms-length from other people as they usually require a degree of secrecy which prevents true intimacy. Guilt and shame are also factors in dysfunction and addiction and undermine our sense of inner peace. Professional help is often necessary to fully unlock any serious addictive behavior, as there may be layers of buried and unaddressed emotions, as well as a familial propensity to addiction that may need to be addressed.

In *Survivors of Addiction: Narratives of Recovery*, Mary Addenbrooke tells us that much shame and guilt accompany addictions, making treatment difficult. Drawing on Carl Jung's findings that we limit and stifle ourselves by trying to fit in and maintain a facade based on society's norms, Addenbrooke says she encourages her patients to understand that it is their *own* inner voice and the acknowledgment of their innate special strengths that helps bring about their healing, rather than succumbing to the pressures of societal dictates.[18] Unaddressed addictions and dysfunctions not only affect our life, they often affect that of those around us further adding to our guilt. I discuss addictions in more depth in chapter 8, "Health and Healing; Death and Dying."

Compulsions, on the other hand, can be much more subtle but they still create limitations in our lives and distance us from others. Compulsions show up as us fixating on something superficial instead of facing or dealing with what lies in our unconscious mind. As it vies for attention, our unconscious mind may encourage us to place emphasis on the external, less-important aspects of life. For instance, my focus on providing a physically stable household superseded my ability to recognize the greater importance of providing an emotionally secure home. Although compulsions may not be as destructive as outright addictions, compulsive subtleties affect our being present to those around us. We can examine any of these distractions with worksheet 8.

Worksheet 8: Compulsions, Dysfunctions, or Addictions

Conflict from Adherence to Strict Principles and Ideals

Our unconscious influences can spawn ideals and principles, which create attitudes and actions that align with their precepts. While some principles may be good to uphold, such as "I will be an involved parent," others only hinder our potential and spiritual growth. The workforce is now far more of an organic entity than it was say fifty years ago, so the ideal of working at the same company for thirty-five years then retiring is now an outdated principle. Many of our ideals birthed from our belief systems, such as our attitudes regarding gays and same sex-marriage are also now outdated principles, as they are judgments and do not endorse the concept of unconditional love. If we adhere too strongly to what was normal in the past, we will create unnecessary conflict as we push against the new ways of thinking and possibly thwart our or the evolutionary growth of our children.

In *Radical Honesty: How to Transform Your Life by Telling the Truth*, Brad Blanton, PhD, explains that adhering to the strict ideals and principles that society deems correct decreases our ability to think for ourselves and thereby thwarts our instinctive input. Principles often come about because we have created a framework to exist in, either by default, from the past, others' influences, or through fear. Reminding us that Fritz Perls said "principles are substitutes for an independent outlook," Dr. Blanton further explains that many students brought up under strict codes, such as within the traditional Catholic schools and old law schools, learned to live by their strict codes and not think independently. This, he believes, squelched their ability to solve their own problems without rules to follow, even to the point that many of his patients from strict upbringings want him to tell them how to fix their lives rather than allowing for the normal process of him guiding them to figure it out for themselves.[19]

It is often difficult to give up the ideals and principles of our family or those held within our belief systems, no matter how outdated they may now be. In *Change Your Conversations ... Change Your Life*, John D. Knight explains that in general the human tendency is to stick to our limiting beliefs even when they are outdated, because "they feel like trusted friends" and are the framework we have lived under.[20] We can examine any limiting beliefs and strict principles and ideals we hold with worksheet 9.

Worksheet 9: Unconscious Limiting Beliefs and Outdated Principles and Ideals

Are We Going toward or Running Away from Something?

What we pursue in life can create burning desires within us, which can be directed either toward achieving, as in going toward something, or in circumventing, as in running away from something. The results of these diametrically opposed motivations will differ greatly; however, they each come with strong impulses. Going toward something holds endless possibilities, while running away from something holds the negative emotional components we accord to what we are attempting to leave behind.

To better ourselves we must continue to move forward and grow, as this path forward is the channel to becoming all that we are and can be. And we must embrace the changes this encompasses, because they create confidence within ourselves paving the way for more fulfilling futures. However, major changes in our lives must be steeped in self-honesty and built from true heart desires, rather than excuses to run away from awkward or uncomfortable situations, outdated ideals, or to please others. If our desires for change are birthed from an attitude of moving toward something, such as having a successful career in order to have a comfortable life for our family, then we will probably have positive experiences, unless of course we end up focusing exclusively on success.

I realized many years later that when I wanted to move away from Saint-Bruno, I was running from painful reminders of my past. This desire to run from something directed me to look to outward solutions for an internal issue, so I was never happy where I ended up. Of course, moving away from harmful or abusive situations is to our benefit. We can examine whether we have or have not been honest with ourselves regarding our desires to make changes in our lives with worksheet 10.

Worksheet 10: Moving Toward or Away from Something

All our conscious and unconscious influences work in an interweaving pattern of threads that hold together the patchwork quilt of our makeups, like matrixes that overlay our lives. I call these our Life Matrixes.

Our Life Matrix

Life Matrix: Is the lens through which we see and navigate the world. It holds *all* our underlying perceptions or misperceptions and our unconscious influences. It supports what we think we need to be, as well as what we think we need to do to uphold our perceptions, whether real or false.

Our Life Matrixes can bring about positive or negative experiences for us. We usually develop dominant Life Matrixes, but since living is an organic ebb and flow of thoughts and emotions, we may vacillate between the positive and negative influences of both forces. If something throws us off-center and we react out of character, our heart beliefs cause us to quickly revert to our normal attitudes. Our Life Matrixes may predispose us to dealing with today head-on, procrastinating, staying in denial, or reacting to life with passivity or aggressiveness.

A Positive Life Matrix

Living under the influence of positive Life Matrixes, we may embody optimism, confidence, and hopefulness. We may feel lucky, be fearless, as well as accepting of others since our own self-confidence shields us from being judgmental. We may sometimes succumb to arrogance, impatience, or single-mindedness as our personalities dictate, but emotional reactions will generally be composed. Most of our dealings with others will likely be propelled by responses rather than reactions. As our general outlooks are positive, we will quickly return to these attitudes should we fall into negative ones.

A positive Life Matrix may temporarily shift to a negative one, but we are usually pulled back as our underlying inner belief systems hold a positive approach to life. The same holds true for a negative Life Matrix as we may have times of positivity, but we generally default to the negative. A negative Life Matrix *can* be shifted more permanently to the positive, albeit with a sincere and conscious effort.

A Negative Life Matrix

If we are living under the influence of negative Life Matrixes, we may tend to be pessimistic, hesitant, doubtful, and feel disadvantaged. Often frustrated and blaming others for our failures, we may act with aggression, timidity, or passive-aggressiveness, or vacillate between these. Positive feelings are usually undermined, as our negative heart beliefs will eventually pull us back under their influence. With a volatile emotional component we will be overtly reactive rather than responsive. Some of us may respond to life with seeming passivity, but are internalizing our angers or frustrations keeping our inner world in turmoil.

Our emotional state is very important because it defines who we are now being which influences what our future may hold. It has only been in the last century or so that psychologists have been able to connect the dots between unconscious influences and how we experience life.

We often feel that we do not experience enough love in our lives; however, our capacity to truly feel love and to love others is in direct proportion to how much we love ourselves, and this is in direct relationship to what is held in our Life Matrixes. Whether from our conscious or unconscious minds, every thought, belief, attitude, and action emits a vibration. To become the cause of our experiences and the creator of our realities, instead of at the effect of our unconscious influences, we must be cognizant of the vibrations we are emitting.

~

The conscious and unconscious beliefs and life philosophies within your Life Matrix govern everything you think, say, and do and thereby what you invite into your life. The lens through which we view others and the world around us is how the world will show up for us. You become what you think you are, and you create based on how you view the world.

We Attract from Our Energetic Vibrations

Every thought, emotion, attitude, belief, response, action, and word spoken emits a vibration. To become the creators of our realities, rather than at the effect of our unconscious influences, we have to recognize that the energetic vibrations we emit into the Universe are our requests for life experiences. Our vibrations are held within every cell of our being, and make up the fabric of our Life Matrixes. To shift anything held within our Life Matrix, we must change the vibrations we give off. To shift our vibrations, we need to shift our inner beliefs and corresponding attitudes and thoughts.

The reason we attract people, things, and situations into our lives is that we have requested them through the vibrations our thoughts, emotions, words, and attitudes emit. When we emerged from the Oneness God-energy the gift of conscious co-creation came with us, and it was through the vibrations of our thoughts, desires, and ideas that our creations could come about. Having lost the awareness that this is how we create, we have also forgotten that this is how the Universe responds to us. It perceives our underlying Life Matrix and then gives us back the same. The vibrations we emit are felt and recorded.

The stronger the emotional attachment to something, be that an intense like or dislike, the stronger the pull to attract the same back to us. It is like a resonating energetic vibration and acts like a boomerang. The Law of Attraction is always at play. The more loving and accepting we are toward others, the more we will draw love and acceptance into our spheres, as that is what we have requested with our energy. The more we are critical and judgmental toward others, the more we will draw others toward us who are critical and judgmental. And because we are all energetic beings, we may infringe on each others' energetic vibrations.

Sometimes when we feel drained, stressed, or conflicted it is because we have picked up another's energetic output. So we must be attentive to what we are absorbing from others. Once we realize we have picked up something from another, we just have to remove ourselves from their presence as soon as politely possible. We must also be conscious of what energy we are emitting. We usually do not recognize when we are sending out vibrations that are affecting others, however, in our neediness and desire to express ourselves, we may inflict others with our hyper, pushy, or negative tendencies.

Drawbacks of an Unbalanced Life

An unbalanced life will derail what will ultimately make us happy unless we have our eyes wide open to any unconscious influences that may be undermining us. The classic example are workaholics, who spend all their time focusing on success, money, and/or power and leave no time for relaxation or family life. They may be unaware or in denial of the consequence of their single-mindedness on themselves and the effects of their selfish pursuits on others, or, they may have their eyes wide open and not care about anything else at this point in their lives, which is their own choice and okay.

For those of us in denial or unaware of the consequences it is usually a distorted picture of reality caused by our Illusionary Constructs that creates imbalances in our lives. And something always suffers. This is usually related to health, family life, career, or our ability to connect to the subtleties in life. We need to ask ourselves whether or not our decisions will bring us peace of mind and *ultimately* make us happy.

On his website talking about his healing sessions, Gerry Clow reminds us that as a society we have tipped the scales way off center as we have replaced the more subtle aspects of life with the harsher ones: "Most of our lives we are reactive, rather than reflective. We spend our time searching, not sourcing; looking, not listening; finding, but not feeling. We involve ourselves in life, forgetting often how to evolve ourselves in life, not realizing it's essential—and healthy—to be on both pathways at the same time."[21]

The more we ignore the reflective and feeling parts of ourselves, the deeper we become entrenched in the false realities we have created and the further we disconnect from our True Selves. This disconnect produces many fears that live within us, and as these play out they perpetuate the disconnect. In reality there is only love! Everything else stems from fear.

Everything Stems from Love or Fear

All thoughts, attitudes, and actions stem from either love or fear. Our positive feelings and attitudes come from the love we feel within ourselves and from our being connected to our True Selves and aligned with the Abundance Paradigm. Our negative thoughts, feelings, attitudes, and actions are based in fears amassed from the impressions and interpretations we have gathered from our life experiences now buried **in our Emotional Body**. These fears need a voice and are often released in dysfunctional ways as we project them out into the world. Illustration 4 shows some of the aspects of love, and illustration 5 shows some aspects of fear.

39

#4: Aspects of Love

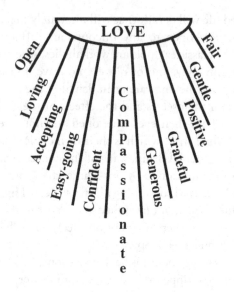

#5: Aspects of Fear

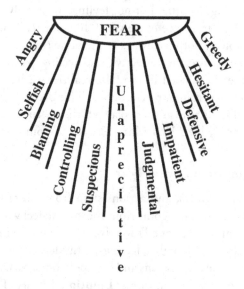

Love

All the joy and passion that we feel, any harmony that manifests in our lives, and all the other positive attitudes (many shown in illustration 4) stem from love. We are able to bring these about because we are connected to the spark that we emanated from. There is a memory of that spark within all of us, and it is easily accessible if no roadblocks were erected in life to squelch the connection. In positive, loving people, that connection can show up in either overt or covert ways, depending on their personalities. Even when the connection is stifled, as in my case, it can still be accessed with external reminders. A baby's smile, a spectacular sunset, the abandonment that arises in us from the exhilaration of an extreme sport, or the passion that is reawakened within us from music, dance, art, or anything else that moves us can rekindle the spark of love, joy, and fearlessness we originally held. What we are feeling or how we are being stems either from love, or from fear.

Fear

Fear is at the heart of *all* of our issues. We do not recognize it as such, as it masks itself in many different manifestations that aim to protect us, but they ultimately keep us from being able to access joy, find our empowerment, and become our Best Selves. They also create conflict in our lives thereby distancing us from others. We may get hurt feelings because someone ignored us, withheld a compliment, or didn't include us. This stems from a fear that we are not loved, appreciated, or good enough. Not having inner confidence, we may fear failure and in turn get defensive at an innocent comment about where we are in life.

When we are not in touch with our True Self and its power-base, we may fear pursuing what we want and become judgmental of the successes' of others. We may fear poverty because of long-held perceptions of the poor, and thereby strive tirelessly, ignoring the urgings of Spirit. We may feel a lack of love or connection in our lives and be fearful of being alone and thereby fall into relationships that are unfulfilling or abusive in some way. Experts suggest that children of parents with addictions often tirelessly aim to control their environment as their home life was never predictable. However, this often backfires as the controlling attitudes usually create disharmony in their current home life, as succumbing to the underlying fear of instability creates another bad situation.

As well as the results of our attitudes or behaviors that arise because of not addressing our issues, all these manifestations of underlying fears create more of a misalignment with our True Self, and this distancing creates more neediness that aches to be satisfied. A vicious cycle ensues. We do not recognize these manifestations as fear, because the original hurts we seek to protect and/or the origins of any limiting attitudes or biases we hold are buried deep in the recesses of our Emotional Bodies. Our fears can manifest as neediness, or may be played out through our Perceived Needs, Hidden

Agendas, or Protective Mechanisms—all aiming to avoid further hurt or feelings of disempowerment.

As we attempt to protect ourselves from further onslaughts against our fragile psyches, we project the manifestations of these unconscious influences onto others, acting in aggressive ways, or if our reactionary states are passive, turn them inward and bury further hurts and angers. This may manifest as us being judgmental, aggressive, controlling, manipulative, defensive, or passive-aggressive. However, when we honestly look at the issues in our lives and use tools that can uncover the original buried emotions, we can connect the dots between these outer demonstrations and the associated inner-fears they were derived from that manifested in unhelpful, inappropriate, or harmful ways. And even though this may seem a scary endeavor, there is a *net* that will catch us and guide us throughout the process: our connection to Spirit. Worksheet 7b can help us to connect the dots between our issues and their original fears.

Worksheet 7b: Protective Mechanisms: My Masks of Fear

Fear's Allies: Neediness, Guilt, Shame, and Judgment

Neediness, False Needs, and Inner Beliefs

The neediness within us is held in place by fears that our Perceived Needs will not be met. Any guilt or shame that we buried is projected outward with our judgments. Illustration 6 shows some of the ways our neediness shows itself.

#6: Our Neediness and its Manifestations

The more we plan, manipulate, and plot to satisfy our neediness, and all other unconscious influences, the more we disconnect from our True Selves. The more convoluted our efforts become, the more we wreak havoc in our lives and the lives of others, while a peaceful life is passing us by. God, Spirit, or the creative force of the Universe is benevolent, wants us to connect to our True Selves, and offers us a net that will catch us. However, we have to allow ourselves to believe in it. Spirit wants us to experience inner peace and joy, feel empowered, and become our Best Selves, but we have to let go of the shackles that are keeping us from these experiences. When we continuously fuel our neediness by pushing through our perceived wants and desires, we are not allowing ourselves the gift of the net that will catch us. We ultimately become frustrated when our neediness is not satiated, and thereby the cycle of frustration continues.

Sometimes our desires stem from our souls' purposes and show up as honest yearnings, like when I felt a strong desire to go back to school a few years ago. I had a burning urge to return and take some English courses. I didn't know why exactly, except I felt I had something to say, but I knew it wasn't based in any ego desires. At other times they are based on our unconscious influences as we attempt to fulfill our neediness or Perceived Needs, like when I wanted to move away from Saint-Bruno.

Giving Up on the Dictates of Our False Needs

It was very scary for me to think of not being able to get away from Saint-Bruno. I *felt a strong need* to get away but was too afraid to acknowledge what was really pushing me. Putting our trust in something other than what we *feel* an urge to do is a frightening concept for most of us, especially if we don't know about the connection to our True Selves that supports and guides us and the net that will catch us. When our desires and dreams are born from any of our Illusionary Constructs and their protective devices, there is a deep-set fear of doing anything other than yielding to their urges. We sense that if we do not answer their calls, we will be opening ourselves up to more pain and/or to becoming vulnerable. Our Protective Mechanisms were created to avoid pain and protect us from becoming vulnerable. However, putting our trust in the creative force of the Universe is very different than putting our trust in ideas that our minds conjure up or that society has deemed correct.

God's Better Plan for Us

There is a better plan for our lives than what our limited perspectives conjure up. Abraham-Hicks (a group of light-beings that call themselves Abraham and who speak through Esther Hicks) often remind us that what Source has in escrow for us is well beyond what we could ever imagine. I now realize that, like in the writing of this book, my life was full of so many more possibilities than to just be able to feed the scraps of my perceived wants, desires, and neediness. I never in a million years thought that I would be able to make peace with and overcome all my anxieties and frustrations in life and then be able to write about, and pave the way for others to overcome their issues or frustrations.

At this point in Humanity's evolution, we are being guided to understand our neediness and give up the false inner beliefs that have kept us disempowered, limited, or detached from our feeling natures. But to do so, we must be aware of the subtle workings of the ego.

Guilt and Shame

Guilt and shame are the insidious repercussions of any negative attitudes and behaviors we hold or carry out and are the ego's best allies. We can also infuse our beings with guilt and shame because of what others have put upon us, as we are sometimes told by people or society that we brought it about ourselves. Although some guilt may be at the surface of our awareness, most is unconscious. Either way we attempt to get rid of it by projecting it onto others in negative ways. Shame is more covert as it often masks as shyness but can be evident in our body language. Both guilt and shame can lead to illness or dysfunction.

Acting as our conscience, Spirit makes us aware of things we have done that are not in alignment with our True Self. However, the purpose of bringing these to our attention is for us to see where we are out of alignment and adjust—not for us to amass more guilt, which is what we are inclined to do. Sometimes there is a benefit to feeling guilty, as we can feel so awful when ridden with guilt (shame too) that it may help us turn to more positive attitudes and actions. The danger is that we get *stuck* in the guilt or bury it.

Buried guilt or wallowing in shame are the principal thieves of emotional happiness and undermine our sense of self-worth. They are tricks of the mind and have no substance. The underlying causes of guilt and shame are in the past and should therefore be relinquished. We have to forgive ourselves and move on from the heavy burden of the guilt associated with our misalignments and the shame we may feel because of them: we have to embrace the prodigal-son philosophy. Once guilt and shame are relinquished, the mind and heart are liberated from the heaviness of the burden, and we can regain our sense of self-love.

Judgment: The Root of All Evil

An important element to keeping the ego alive is our propensity to judge. Judgment is what fuels divisive attitudes, so while people often say that money is the root of all evil; I say that *judgment* is the root of all evil. Although at the highest levels there is no right or wrong in the Universe, for our purposes we will focus on the importance of understanding how judgment affects our everyday lives. And I am not talking about our day-to-day decisions and preferences, but the judgments we make of individuals, groups of people, or situations that we take issue with. Being critical, upholding concepts of blame, being overly invested in outcomes, needing to prove ourselves right and others wrong—especially when we aim to condemn the other are judgments bathed in *right-and-wrong* and *me-and-you,* mentalities which uphold and create divisiveness.

All beliefs and ideals that uphold ideas of right and wrong or good and bad are judgment calls because they are man-made constructs. One never knows what is right for another person, what their soul's life plan is, or what they have to experience to find their path in life. Maintaining dissatisfaction with our or another's situation is also a judgment that where we or they are now in life is wrong,

When we judge with strong emotions, resort to blame, aggressively defend beliefs and ideals, or focus on our differences, we are feeding the ego's ideas of separation. We are all different, with different backgrounds, purposes, and soul journeys. We also must understand that others are just doing their best to make their way in the world doing what they think they need to do to be happy or a good person. Judgment manifests itself through our attitudes in aggressive, passive, or other alienating behaviors. When we hold judgment in our Life Matrixes, we are defensive of our feelings and points of view. We often believe we are acting on our feelings when we react in negative ways towards another, but we are really just projecting our fears, shame, or guilt with our judgmental attitudes onto them. When we judge others, we ultimately judge ourselves.

Your unconscious mind doesn't recognize whether your emotions and judgments are aimed at yourself, others, or situations. This is because the unconscious mind internalizes all emotions and their vibrations. So, by the Law of Attraction, our judgments invite judgment upon us, as well as attract new situations into our spheres that will tempt us into judgment. Until we address the particular misalignment that is causing us to judge, judgment will continue to be an issue for us.

Even when discussing or dealing with what is going on in the world today, while not turning a blind eye to unfairness, inequality, or cruelty, we have to ensure that we *focus on solutions* rather than allow blame or revenge scenarios to be at the forefront of our thoughts.

No Need to Judge

If we saw everybody as they really are, love incarnate, and their misalignments simply manifestations of being disconnected from their True Selves, condemnation would not ensue. If we saw negative situations as the playing out of the duality we are all trapped in, we could put our energies into helping alleviate the issues, instead of judging which further disconnects us from our True Self. This is what Jesus meant when he said, "As you see him, so you shall you see yourself." Judging others ultimately means judging ourselves! Judging others or situations is actually a form of self-hatred, and we are in effect sending daggers into our psyches, as well as into that of others. Many of us have unhealthy boundaries and an injured self-worth and judging them just adds to their burden.

Being gentle with those who seem sensitive or defensive is the loving and compassionate way to deal with people. We don't often do this, as much of our society is built on judging, pointing out the weaknesses in others, and proving people wrong. However, there have always been light holders in the world, some within our families, some famous like Mother Teresa, and even groups of people here and there who could love unconditionally, void of blame or judgment.

On one of his PBS telecasts, the late Wayne Dyer tells of an indigenous tribe in Africa who did not believe in judgment and punishment. If one of them were to do something wrong, the villagers would surround that person or child in ceremony and tell them how smart, wonderful and great he or she was and how much he or she was loved. They did this until the person no longer felt badly about him or her self. The irony is that the ceremony was rarely needed *because* the tribe upheld the concepts of unconditional love and acceptance and everybody felt validated. The people thrived in that atmosphere and were not inclined to act in any way other than a loving manner.

Those who exhibit negative attitudes are simply acting from errors in perception. They are misperceiving who they are, and their connections to their True Selves are very weak. When we judge others—even judging those who judge—we are also acting from errors in perception. Even if we have a somewhat more positive life attitude than another, when we judge others or feel acutely aware of our differences, we are not completely connected to our True Selves. When we are completely connected, we do not see the differences: we see only others' *truth* and *light. The masters, and those rare beings who could unconditionally love everyone, were fully connected to their truth and light.*

Other Manifestations of Our Misalignments

There are benefits to evaluating our inner worlds. When we examine our attitudes and behaviors, we can often avoid bringing chaos into our lives. Self-examination even existed in the ancient world. Socrates responded to peoples' questions who came to him for advice with questions they could ponder, so they could figure out their own issues, and the ancient Egyptians practiced introspection to ensure their souls were light as feathers when they passed into the judgment hall.

> Ambition, Success, Power, Pride, and Greed—are all attitudes that we can fall prey to, but that can easily derail our lives if not kept in check.*

> Aggressive Behaviors and Attitudes such as Control, Manipulation, Criticism, Bullying, and Impatience—are protective devices whose intent is to make us feel powerful, but as they come from a position of weakness they further lower our sense of self-esteem.*

> Passive Attitudes and Behaviors such as Helplessness, Victim Mentalities, and Passive-Aggressiveness—come about because of low self-esteem and fear of failure, but as I once heard Dennis DeYoung from the band Styx say at one of his concerts, "people like me do well and are successful mostly because we failed and got back up and tried again and again, many, many times."[22] *

> Behaviors that Can be Aggressive or Passive such as Self-Indulgence, Envy/Jealousy, and Defensiveness—are attempts to placate our neediness, and as such do nothing to increase our self-esteem and thereby keep us in a negative mind-set.*

We can examine our aggressive or passive tendencies with worksheet 11.

Worksheet 11: Aggressive and Passive Behaviors

> Limiting Attitudes such as Minimalistic Tendencies and Small-Mindedness—develop because we feel we are not deserving enough, or believe there is not enough love or goods to go around.* We can examine limiting attitudes with worksheet 12.

Worksheet 12: Other Limiting Attitudes or Behaviors

We all have differing personalities, strengths, and weaknesses that are expressed in how we navigate the different aspects of our lives. This is normal. However, our unconscious influences need to find outlets. We often believe our ways of reacting to events are attempts to gain authority over our lives, when they are just feeble efforts to counteract feelings of disempowerment.

*I further explain** how these aggressive, passive, and limiting tendencies play out in article, "Aggressive, Passive, and Limiting Attitudes and Behaviors," located on the book's website.

Some type of self-examination is necessary to unearth the causes of aggressive, passive, and limiting attitudes and behaviors that keep us from being the best we can be and in conflict with those around us. However, when looking at our past or current errors in perception, we must always be on guard against self-condemnation. The purpose of self-examination is not to make ourselves feel wrong but to uncover and release what is blocking our connection to our True Selves. It also helps us to become conscious.

Becoming Conscious: Mindlessness vs. Mindfulness

Because we have been unaware of being under the influence of unconscious authority and that the separation we feel toward each other is an illusion, we have gone about life mindless to the effects of these illusionary influences.

Mindlessness

When we operate from a mindless state we act impulsively, foolishly, or single-mindedly, often blind to other possibilities and the effects our decisions will have on ourselves and others. We are not concerned with others or maintaining harmony in situations, as we are acting from unconscious impulses aiming to either protect us or get us what we think we *need* to be happy or feel empowered. An example of this might be a spouse who, without consulting his or her partner, takes a job that makes more money but means less time for family. The partner making this decision may have been influenced by a disadvantaged background and be blind to the effects this decision would have on the rest of the family. By making this decision on their own they are being mindless to the reasons they want the job as well as to the effect on those around them.

Mindfulness

Conversely, if we are mindful when making decisions or taking action, we are not in denial of the reasons for our desires or choices, and we are aware of their effects on others. We instinctively maintain harmony in all situations. While all this self-examination may sound tedious, it isn't. If we exist within positive Life Matrixes, we don't have to continuously examine all our thoughts and attitudes through a microscopic lens, as we will naturally be mindful. It is when we are trying to shift our Life Matrix away from the negative that a conscious effort is required.

As expressed in *Mindfulness*, Dr. Ellen Langer explains that although the practice of true mindfulness within Eastern teachings is quite complex, focusing mainly on meditation to bring about a "mindful state" that influences our actions, Westerners have adopted a simplified version to help guide us to live more consciously. We aim to become more mindful by examining our focus, thoughts, and motives, and by making choices considering their impact on our and others' well-being. We understand our past and present experiences through a clear lens, so there is no need to blame or project our frustrations or miseries onto others.[23]

When we are mindful, we are empowered and do not expect others to fix our problems. Nor do we wait for any higher being to take them away, as we are doing our part. We can examine whether we are mindful with worksheet 13.

Worksheet 13: Mindfulness and Mindlessness

The Power to Choose

There is an old Cherokee tale where a grandfather explains to his grandson about the conflict that goes on within us. "He said, 'My son, the battle is between two 'wolves' inside us all. One is Evil. It is anger, envy, jealousy, sorrow, regret, greed, arrogance, self-pity, guilt, resentment, inferiority, lies, false pride, superiority, and ego. The other is good. It is joy, peace, love, hope, serenity, humility, kindness, benevolence, empathy, generosity, truth, compassion and faith." When the grandson asked "Which wolf wins?" his grandfather replied, "The one you feed."[24]

When I blamed others for my unhappiness, I didn't realize that I could choose my attitudes in circumstances that disappointed or upset me. Nor did I understand that I was feeding my negativity by maintaining attitudes of frustration, blame, and discontent. At the time, my unconscious influences kept me disempowered because of my constant state of blame and frustration, and I was unknowingly perpetuating the problem, which further affected my opportunities for peace and happiness.

Aided by reflection, self-examination, journaling, and light meditation I was able to start to become more mindful, make conscious choices, and take responsibility for my moods and discontentment. My circumstances and overall well-being began to improve. Once my unconscious influences were no longer buried, it was easier to see clearly where my choices were coming from, and I could avoid inviting more negative experiences into my life by making bad choices. I now feel and act completely differently.

From Mindlessness to Conscious Mindfulness

Our minds can decide whether our emotions are showing us true pictures or are based on false created Selves that do not guide us to ultimate satisfaction. Unless we are mindful, we *will* fall prey to emotions influenced by our unconscious. For example, it is our neediness, which speaks through emotions, and wants us to overeat or indulge in something that is not good for us. We have to use our conscious minds to override those emotions. And even though being mindful may conjure up visions of a Zen or a holy person in perfect meditation pose, being mindful is about being aware of where our minds are going so that we can live better, normal lives.

We do not *need* to meditate, do yoga, take up Tai Chi, etc. to become mindful, but these types of practices do quiet the mind, keep us centered and connected to our True Self, and help to reduce the incessant chatter of the ego. Embracing something like journaling, taking quiet time for reflection or prayer, or spending time in nature works too. Nonetheless, many do find that some type of formal daily practice *is* helpful. My day just goes better when I do yoga, tai chi, or a simple meditation—even if my mind wanders all the way through. People who read or meditate on the Gita, the Bible, or any other holy book daily say the same thing. Dan Harris tells us in *10% Happier* that he is not sure what impact the half-hour daily meditation practice he recently took up will have on him in the future, but it has calmed him down and so long as it can help him cultivate "mindfulness, happiness and not being a jerk," he will continue to embrace it.[25]

When we are mindful we can avoid acquiescing to our ego and its emotional whims. It is louder than the whispers of our soul, and is always competing to be heard above peaceful or enlightened thoughts. We need to be aware of this and utilize a tool to quiet it. Our ego is always vying for our attention and lures us to be constantly concerned with our body's needs, our emotional world, our wants and desires, and our social requirements.

The Human Collective

As explained earlier, as the history of Humankind unfolded and we played out the game of duality and separation, the misperceptions that we unknowingly engaged in perpetuated themselves throughout time. This further entrenched us all within a web of self-deceit, and eventually we forgot everything about our origins. We asked for help but ignored the master's messages, as the spark of that desire was not the predominant factor in our consciousness.

Instead of taking responsibility for our own misperceptions of the light and dark forces within us, we shunned the teachings of the masters who came. We were so entrenched in our own ideas of how things should be and so unaware that we were under the influence of false illusions that we superimposed much of it on their teachings. With the egoic, fear-based thought system still deeply entrenched within our beings, we were not able to overcome the dark forces within us that further distanced us from our True Selves. Divisive attitudes were the norm instead of those that encouraged unity.

As the *me-against-you* paradigm became ingrained in us, greed, control, power, and unfairness became the mainstays. Church and state were not immune. Those who were most supposed to guide, help, and protect us often became the worst perpetrators, and along with the powerful and the wealthy, held us prey to their whims. A collective Default Position emerged.

Humanity's Default Position: Reprogrammed for Failure

In order to play by society's rules, we had to adopt survival-mode attitudes and thereby reprogrammed ourselves for failure. The title of Dr. Jim Richard's book *Wired for Success, Programmed for Failure* puts forward that we all have the wiring to be safe, happy, and to thrive, but are working under the wrong program. We have been reprogrammed for eons as Humanity anchored in its negative Default Position. Our original wiring has been all but snuffed out, but we can reignite it! We must not only overcome our propensity to undermine ourselves individually with our false illusions, but must also stand up for ourselves against the elite and most powerful in society who aim to keep us under their control. This is why this struggle has taken so long.

Time to Shift Humanity's Default Position

The time has come. Today, we are witnessing the crumbling of the power structures that have plagued our world and manipulated its people. We are no longer silently accepting the suppression of individual rights, the greed of corporations, corrupt governments, and the prejudice, intolerance, and untrustworthiness within religious organizations or anywhere. We are beginning to realize that the realities of Humanity and our Planet have not been based on the good of the many, but on the good of the few. Those in power have perpetuated false beliefs long enough, and this is no longer acceptable to us. This is all part of the Shift we are ushering in.

What we see unfolding within the collective is indicative of what we have held within us individually. Until as individuals we shift to giving up *all* our egoic, fear-based prejudices and judgments based in divisiveness rather than unity, until fairness with each other is the mainstay, and until we abandon ideas of separate agendas with those around us, we will still see injustices playing out in the world arena. Each individual can ultimately affect the world with his or her attitudes. As we uphold concepts of fairness, this beams out toward others and inspires them to make shifts within themselves. They then affect others and so on.

Even if some of the concepts and theories in this chapter seemed lofty, spiritual, and impossible to attain or even grasp, a variety of simple and comprehensive tools exist to help us shift from any false realities we are now working under that are keeping us from being our Best Selves. And many of the tools hold no religious or spiritual overtones. We *can* shift a negative Default Position to the positive and move away from the influence of any Hidden Agendas or Protective Mechanisms that undermine our happiness. We *can* change any negativity within our Life Matrix and get past the underlying forces that run our lives and the confines of any attitudes that limit us. **We can *all* become our Best Self!**

> *God is like a musician who creates the harmonies of the Cosmos*
> *and gives each individual his own particular theme to play.*
> *If the music of life seems discordant to us,*
> *we should not blame the Master Musician, but ourselves.*
> *We are the out-of-tune instrument*
> *which mars the beauty of his composition.*
> —The Hermetica[26]

Now that we understand why we are the way we are, we can examine the Universal Laws / Kingdom Principles within the cosmos that affect the more subtle aspects of the Universe and thereby us, just like gravity affects the Universe's more-solid facets.

CHAPTER 2

Universal Laws / Kingdom Principles

*Just as there are proven laws, such as gravity,
that govern our physical world,
there are also Universal Laws, or Kingdom Principles,
that govern our Universe.*

This chapter's focus is the intrinsic nature of the creative force of the Universe that pertains to us. Laws and principles were set out at the creation of our cosmos, and because we emanated from and are still linked to that original creative force, some of these laws and principles influence us and govern our relationship with it.

The Standard

The Standard: What we must align ourselves to so we are working at our highest potentials: happy, peaceful, and in harmony with everything in the Universe, embracing the qualities of its creative force, or God.

The principles that govern the Universe apply, and have always applied, to everybody and everything in creation. Throughout the rest of the book, when I refer to the Standard, I mean the qualities of that creative force.

The Standard is the term that came to me when I was searching for a generic word or phrase to describe the qualities, characteristics, principles, and laws we need to abide by in order to align to our highest potentials and become our Best Selves in form here on earth, as well as assist our soul's journey into it's next phase. Because of the nature of this book and its audience, I was looking for a nonspecific term to denote the qualities of the creative force that formed the Universe and holds it in place. Although I use Spirit, God, Source, and Universe interchangeably throughout the book, I also wanted to use a term that would represent the qualities these uphold without any preconceived interpretations.

However, these laws and principles do not hold commands; they hold vibrations. If our vibrations are aligned with the Standard, they are in harmony with those of the creative universal force and we can tap into its power. All aspects of love and anything that upholds harmony and aims to unite, aligns with the Standard. When we live under the influence of attitudes akin to hate that provoke conflict and aim to separate, we are not aligned with the Standard.

These laws and principles are simply explanations of how to uphold the required vibrations to align to the Standard. When we do not adhere to these laws and principles that govern us and everything, then by default, our own internal thoughts, ideas, and judgments prevail.

Forces That Kept Us in Illusions, Fear, and Negativity

Much of the reason the Universal Laws and Kingdom Principles eluded us throughout the ages was because those who sought to maintain control over us for their own power and gain kept the attributes of these laws and principles hidden from us. Both church and state kept us dependent on them for our spiritual and physical well-being.

The belief in a judgmental and vengeful God was further anchored into our belief systems because the energy of our negativity drew some dangerous beings from other planets to us. We became hosts for their control and greed. Although these beings were technologically more advanced than us, they were still within the illusion and under the auspices of duality with some of them exhibiting its qualities of greed and control. However, because they appeared to come from a higher place, we treated them as gods and confused them with the true creative force we emanated from. I further explain this in chapter 6, "Words, Symbols, Rituals, Concepts, and Prayers," and chapter 7, "Science and Other Related Topics."

~

I have grouped the Universal Laws / Kingdom Principles that make up the Standard into six different categories. These are just general guidelines. There are others, and some people divide them up into more details, or use different names, but most of what we need for our purposes here is contained within these. First, the *Law of Openness* denotes that we have to be in a state of receptivity. Second, the *Law of Authenticity* indicates that we need to come from an honest place within ourselves. Third, the well-known *Law of Attraction* maintains the principle that like attracts like. Fourth, the *Law of Cause and Effect* clarifies that we are the cause of our experiences, not at the effect of the world around us. The *Law of Balance* suggests that we have to make peace with all parts of ourselves as well as the world around us. And finally, the *Law of Expansion* comes into play in our lives once the other laws are well integrated into our beings, whereby the exponential function allows us to take a sharp upward turn and expand into all that we can be.

The Role of the Spirit

Although aligning our vibrations to the Standard and these Kingdom Principles is essential, there is another part to the equation: Spirit, who acts as our partner, guide, and helper. Spirit has always been there helping and guiding us. Once we have made the decision to embark on this journey, we ignite a spark to that original link we emanated from, and our connection to Spirit becomes stronger. Aligning our vibrations toward the lighter and higher aspects of the Universe is what *we* can do. Spirit, who has a consciousness, can then reach down (metaphorically speaking) and lift us up, bestowing gifts upon us. However, this only kicks in once we take the first step. *The Course* tells us that "A little willingness is all that is required," but we do have to take that first step.

Law of Openness

Jesus said, "Come to me like children." Paralleling the expression "the heart is the seat of the soul," the Law of Openness means that our hearts have to be open—*childlike*—so that we are open to receive the universal love and its gifts that are rightfully ours. Being open means coming from a heart-centered place, whereby we can accept and freely give love and its qualities, like kindness, understanding, compassion, fairness, and acceptance. The limitations and protective barriers we put up block this openness. With an open outlook we can be confident but still remain humble. If we are open and living spherically, we can gain a wide variety of opportunities that would not be available to us if we were closed off.

Being open allows us to have faith that our needs will be met and that what is supposed to happen will happen. Worry does not cloud our awareness or block our connection. Existing from within this paradigm, we are flexible and can accept whatever is going on at the moment regarding ourselves, others, and situations.

As mentioned previously, all dysfunctional thoughts, attitudes, and behaviors are rooted in fear. When we live with open hearts, we are living in our highest, purest forms. The channel to the Universe and its gifts and knowledge are completely open: love, guidance, and information flow freely back and forth. Conversely, when we live with closed hearts, from a mind-centered place, we are living within the lowest densities available to us: the communication lines are either infused with static or blocked completely. When the benchmarks we live by are worry, fear, control, prejudice, judgment, or any other limiting or divisive factors, we are unable to take full advantage of the creative force of the Universe. Illustrations 7, 8, and 9 give us visuals of these concepts.

#7: Open to the Universal Powers

#8: Closed off from the Universal Power

#9: Static in Connection to the Universal Powers

Law of Authenticity

The Law of Authenticity suggests that we must come from an honest place within ourselves, in touch with all aspects of our being. A good gauge is whether we are able to be honest with ourselves and others, regarding where we have been in life and what we now want. Being authentic means we are able to do the following:

We are able to honestly express what we want out of life and why and act upon it. (Not necessarily the details but the emotional component);

- We are able to communicate to some degree what is running our lives, even if the words are not eloquently formed or the connections completely clear;
- We are able to connect to the fact that we may not have been acting consciously regarding past attitudes, behaviors, or actions;
- We express our hurts and needs honestly but eloquently;
- We are able to see ourselves clearly—who we are being and what we are doing—and are happy with what we see;
- We can spend a day, a week, or even longer alone because we are comfortable with and accepting of who we are;
- We are not overly discouraged by failure as we know something else will come about.

To come from an honest place within ourselves and be honest with others, we have to be able to connect to and express the subtler parts of ourselves. We cannot do this if denials or barriers surround our innermost thoughts and feelings.

Law of Attraction

This law implies that like attracts like. The term *Law of Attraction* was popularized by Abraham-Hicks and has lately become prevalent in spiritual circles. Though considered a New Age term, it is not a new concept at all. It is a universal law that was stifled by most Western religions. All religions that I refer to in this book, whether working under a Christian umbrella or any of the spiritualities, teach principles that parallel the Law of Attraction. They just use different terminology.

Joyce Meyer often encourages her listeners and readers to let go of anger and worry and to "stop grumbling." When we adhere to these suggestions, our vibrational makeups shift from negative to positive. We then attract more positive experiences into our spheres. Meyer also regularly encourages us to be grateful for what we have.[1] Gratitude moves us into a high vibration that allows more good stuff to come our way.

The Law of Attraction is simply the reality that within the Universal Matrix, we will attract back to us the same that we send out energetically. The thoughts and attitudes held within our Life Matrixes emit vibrations that the Universe reads as requests. This suggests that whatever vibrations we emit with our thoughts, actions, or underlying attitudes will be returned to us, although not necessarily under the same exact circumstances. This returning of what we emit is not a judgment from God, nor a trick of nature. It is just a natural phenomenon, a Universal Law, just like gravity.

Law of Cause and Effect

The Law of Cause and Effect builds on the premise of the Law of Attraction. We now understand that we bring into our lives that which we ask for with our vibrations. So it only follows that if we want a different experience than what we are getting, we need to change our vibrations to positively reflect what we want. It also follows that if we act and react unconsciously, unaware of the vibrations we are emitting, so then to change them we must first become aware of what is driving us. Once we are aware of what any negative attitudes, habitual responses, or long-held underlying misperceptions we hold are having in our lives, we are in a better position to change them.

Once we change our thoughts and attitudes, our vibrations shift automatically, bringing us better experiences. Because Spirit is on board with us, even the most meager of efforts benefit us. We do not even have to be aware of this vibrational shift. The understanding of this vibrational aspect has not been at the forefront of Western religious teaching, but any who have made personal shifts in attitudes have experienced the benefits.

With these shifts in thoughts and attitudes, our actions also change for the better because they are a follow-through of the thoughts and attitudes we uphold. We then have less conflict in our lives.

Law of Balance

The inner resources cannot be accessed when
you are more familiar with the outer than the inner realities.
Eternal renewal comes when the inner and outer realities are one.
—Almine (Tri-Ech-Ma)[2]

The Law of Balance infers that to hold all the other laws in place, we should strive to live in a way that promotes a sense of equilibrium in our lives and harmony in our beings. If we are unbalanced in any areas of our lives, such as overworking, overeating, or oversocializing, the Law of Balance will aim to bring us back to center—at one point or another. This is also true of overspiritualizing our lives, and many fall into that trap. You can refer again to illustration 1, from chapter 1.

JRobert and Oasis[3] always promoted the 50/50 rule, meaning that we need to find a balance between concerning ourselves with material matters and spiritual matters. If we become overly concerned with material matters, such as success or the focus on our bodies, we will be thrown off kilter and not be in full access of the universal powers. If we become overly concerned with spiritual matters, we will also become unbalanced and find life difficult. In the movie *Eat, Pray, Love*, based on Elizabeth Gilbert's book of the same title, Ketut, the medicine man she visits in Bali, also explains this concept of 50/50. He tells her that to be happy and to get along in the world we need to live a balanced life with "not too much God, not too much selfish," (with God meaning our spirituality and selfish meaning worldly concerns).[4]

Some people's life purpose is to serve God and the world in a particular way, like the clergy, rabbi's, yogis, or monks, and their lives are dedicated to service, prayer and/or meditation, but most of us are simply meant to express our spirituality and serve God through every day dealings with people and the world while keeping to that 50/50 balance between the physical and spiritual, otherwise we would find life difficult. However, there may be times in our lives that will call for us to tip the scale of balance to one side, like caring for a newborn baby, being an intern training to be a doctor, or doing an extended spiritual retreat. I experienced an unbalance during the final couple of years of putting this book together, but was aware of what I was doing and why.

I am sure I will take extra quiet and relaxing time once the book is out, to rebalance my being.

Law of Expansion

Our Universe is that of an expansive energy, and its form (our bodies, earth, and the cosmos), with the duality it offers, is still a necessity for us to complete our lessons on our way back to reemerging with the Oneness. When we continuously tap into the Universe's power and yield to its laws and principles, we become one with the expansion process, until eventually we take an exponentially sharp upward turn. We can see a visual of how this works with illustration 10.

#10: Our Exponential Function

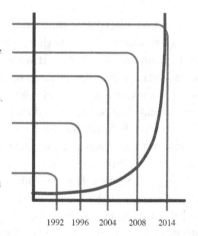

Have arrived: feel happy, peaceful and confident, and are empowered in life, embody life purpose

New doors open up: people and situations fall into place in many areas of our life

Confident: in Self and the process. Allow for possibility of us happy and peaceful.
Inspired: to make positive and empowering life changes. Get glimpses of life purpose

Sometimes able to: connect the dots between our perceptions and our life experiences
Feel: less anger, frustration and blame; are more accepting, peaceful and empowered

Decision: Start sincere search to find peace in life; or Major life upset: Forces us to look at life differently and process beings

1992   1996   2004   2008   2014

As we continuously apply ourselves to aligning all the different parts of ourselves with these laws and principles, we anchor in the confidence from all the little gains we make. All this plays together in concert, and we are then primed to step into our full potential and expand into all we can be. And our efforts do not necessarily have to be hard work. They simply can be the letting go of what is in the way of our becoming or attaining what we came here to express. However, our successes could also come with a combination of things falling easily into place, spurts of hard work, and times of inertia or what feels like hitting brick walls. Getting this book out was like that for me. As well, cosmic forces are always at work, and sometimes it is simply cosmic timing, such as the energy of the Shift of December 2012, that brings about the final push.

Constance of the Universal Laws and Principles

Whether we are conscious of them or not, the Kingdom Principles are at work in our lives all the time—for better or worse. How they affect us depends on the quality and strength of our vibrations. With our thoughts, mind-sets, attention, and vibrational outputs, we invoke these cosmic laws. They are underlying principles that govern our experiences, just as gravity governs form and structure.

Everything we will ever need to know is at our disposal just waiting for us to download, so long as we are tuned into the right station. Every thought, idea, action, reaction, or inaction from the beginning of time, through to the present, and into the future until the Universe actually does disappear is held in a universal bank known in Eastern and spiritual circles as the Akashic records (explained in chapter 7, "Science and Other Related Topics"). The masters, the great scientists, and inventors, as well as the most profound philosophers of our world have all tapped into this data-bank of knowledge. We *all* have access to it; we just have to tune in to the right frequency.

> *We have a magical relationship with the Universe,*
> *but we have forgotten it.*
> —Louis Pauwels, Jacques Bergier[5]

In the next chapter we will explore what we can do about the unconscious effects that Humanity has fallen prey to and perpetuated throughout our history that are keeping us from aligning with the Standard, Our Truth, and becoming our Best Selves.

CHAPTER 3

What We Can Do about It

When we create peace and harmony and balance in our minds,
we will find it in our lives.
—Louise L. Hay[1]

Are you content? Have you ever experienced pure joy? Are you able to consciously control your life and experiences? Can you connect the dots between what you are thinking, who you are being, and who you want to be? Are you aware that your inner beliefs and attitudes are connected to how you experience life and how it unfolds? If you answered no to any of these questions, are you willing to look deep within to align your mind-set with who you want to be, how you want to experience life, and what you want to achieve?

When we begin the journey toward finding inner peace, we must stop blaming others for our frustrations or problems, or looking to outside sources for their solutions. While anger or blaming may provide temporary relief by releasing tensions in the moment, this band-aid solution only serves to keep discord in our Life Matrixes. We will never find peace and harmony in our lives until we offer it in our attitudes. And so the journey begins to make the shifts.

The Journey

It takes courage to look within to examine if the way we think about ourselves and behave toward others and the world around us impacts how we experience life. Will we have to acknowledge that we have been wrong? Possibly for most of our lives! Perhaps! However, as shown in the first couple chapters of this book, most of us have unknowingly been working from a limited knowledge base: we were missing information. By acknowledging and removing any mental barriers that prevent us from engaging our True Selves, or our God-selves, we can open the door to our Best Selves and work toward feeling peaceful, content, confident, and whole.

The path to a peaceful existence requires that we be open to seeing life through a different lens: one that allows Our Truth to come through, and allows us to see that *truth* in others. To clear this lens, we must unearth any obstacles that stand in the way of us perceiving ourselves and others as we truly are—not what our illusions interpret. This may seem a daunting task, but it is the only way to gain control of our mind and its unconscious influences, and the thoughts, attitudes, and associated reactions and stresses they engender that keep us distanced from our True Selves unable to become our Best Selves. In *10% Happier*, Dan Harris highlights Dr. Mark Epstein's remark that the way our minds are always running amuck with their "insatiable wanting, the inability to be present, the repetitive, relentless, self-referential thinking" is really a 2,500-year-old analysis by the Buddha himself of how we are plagued by the mind. Harris quotes Epstein's description of the ego as "constantly murmuring, muttering, scheming or wondering to ourselves under our breath ... I like this, I don't like that. She hurt me. How can I get that? [and that] much of our inner dialogue is this constant reaction or experience by a selfish, childish protagonist."[2]

Most of us will recognize at least *some,* if not many, of these characterizations in ourselves. However, with a little self-honesty, patience, and some helpful tools, we can shift from the underlying influences that create these thought processes and hold us in stress-inducing patterns that keep us from becoming our Best Selves.

<u>We Must Incorporate Two Elements to Making this Shift:</u>
A) Connect To and Anchor in *Our Truth*
B) Dismantle What Is in the Way of Accessing *Our Truth*

A) Connecting to and Anchoring in Our Truth

Understanding Our Perceptions; Accessing Our Truth

As previously explained, to reach our Best Selves we have to align our attitudes and their expressions to the qualities held within the Standard by adhering to the precepts of the Universal Laws. We do so by rediscovering and connecting to who we really are: Our Truth, while at the same time dislodging any misperceptions and false inner heart-beliefs that we innocently cemented into our being and that now run our lives without our conscious consent. Our true reality lies buried deep beneath the recesses of these false Illusionary Constructs.

Our ability to connect to Our Truth and the negative unconscious influences underlying much of our attitudes and behaviors are interconnected: one influences the other. When we shift our thinking processes, our attitudes change; as we change our attitudes, new mind-sets develop, and our inner heart-beliefs shift. As our inner heart-beliefs shift, our energetic matrixes will become characterized by lighter vibrations. We are then more in tune with our true reality, which will enable us to access our latent inner power. However, to make these shifts, we have to understand any misconceived attitudes and how they define us, and then we have to remove them.

The Truth of Who We Are: The Truth of Who We Are Being

The famous biblical phrase "the truth will set you free" (John 8:32) can have a dual meaning: (1) recognizing the *truth of who we are at our core*, will set us free, and (2) *recognizing* the *truth of who we are being*, will also set us free. Powerful shifts will occur in us when we acknowledge the *truth of who we are* while at the same time reconciling *the truth of who we are being*.

Anchoring the love within us is the first and most important step in our journey to peace. Feeling peace and being happy and empowered requires that we believe in our hearts that we deserve to feel peaceful, happy, and empowered. That peaceful place is within us. However, we must open the door to our True Selves and allow its love to permeate us. Then we will be able to connect to it whenever we wish. It is only when we open ourselves up that we can apply any philosophical, spiritual, or biblical teachings: our hearts must be open to receive and properly perceive the teachings. We have to keep to the Law of Openness. Being open to the love within us we are then better able to extend that love and the acceptance it engenders to all others.

Our current society and Humanity's past have operated under the premise of *conditional* love. Like an addict, we have unknowingly become hooked on conditional love. We do not remember what it was like to not live under its influence. Until *unconditional* love is fully anchored in our beings, we will have to continuously override our propensity to not believe it.

In order to infuse and anchor this love into every cell of our beings, we must adopt practices to help us believe that this love is real and accessible to us and adhere to attitudes and behaviors that uphold the belief. And we will have to consciously and continuously remind ourselves—especially at first. It takes time to override old programming. The following seven steps can help us do this. (These seven steps are listed in the "Recaps" section in "Meditations, Visualizations, and Other Practices" at the end of the book. They can also be downloaded from the book's website through the "Download" link by keying in the associated code located on the last page of the book).

Seven Steps to Help Us Connect to, Anchor in, and Align with Our Truth

1) Aligning to Material that Supports Ideas of Unconditional Love and Joy, Opens Us Up to that Love, and Reawakens Our Being.

Reading, listening to, and watching material that underlines the inherent nature of unconditional love is essential to make shifts in our unconscious influences, as it reawakens it in us. We have to reprogram our hearts and minds, as Humanity's Default Position has been based on conditional love. Unconditional love has not been a tenet of living. Prayer groups, workshops, self-help groups, and listening to beautiful or high-vibrational music can help us to become centered in this love, and guide us to whatever will open us up in a comfortable way.

I was first guided to the *Conversations with God* books by Neale Donald Walsch, and even though I don't remember much of what was written, they answered a growing longing in my soul for answers and confirmed a knowing that had been rising in me that Mother Nature's intention was goodness, and that all would be well. (At the time the term Mother Nature represented for me the who or what that created and looked after the Universe and all that was in it including us, that it was benevolent, and that it intended harmony for everything and everybody). I also read, studied, and meditated upon the words found in Marianne Williamson's books *A Woman's Worth* and *Illuminata: A Return to Prayer*, which spoke to the woman in me who needed to access the love within and find her empowerment. I also spent much time journaling and listening to uplifting music.

I was fifty years old before I finally began to understand that joy is not only an option in life but is part of our inheritance. We emanated from love and love is still retained deep in our hearts, as is the joy it engenders—we just have to rediscover it all. I had to work hard at accessing my connection to joy and anchor it within me, but I succeeded.

In one of her broadcasts, Joyce Meyer said that when she was primed to write her first book and had already formulated her ideas, Jesus guided her to write something else. He wanted her to teach people how important it is to first anchor his love for them within their beings. This first book is called *Tell Them I Love Them; Receiving a Revelation of God's Love for You*. In Christianity, Jesus is the symbol of unconditional love, whereby God's love can come through to us through our abandonment of our love for him. Abandonment breaks down our barriers and opens us up.

In Hinduism, practitioners are encouraged to love and worship their guru with abandonment, as it is understood that the abandonment of the heart opens one up to connect to the love within. Abandoning ourselves to the beauty or power of music, art, or even the splendor of a flower can open our hearts and uplift us. These all help pave the way to connect to the love within and all the good things that come along with it.

2) Reaffirming through Repetition

To get this process going, we have to *consistently* align with what will energetically shift our vibrations, as well as help us to override any inner beliefs or negative attitudes or thought processes we hold. Reading and listening over and over again to different types of uplifting material that reaffirms the love residing within will help us connect to it. We should regularly immerse ourselves in whatever uplifts and reconnects us to the more-subtle heart aspects of our being, be that music, poetry, painting, or being in nature until we can easily access a peaceful feeling. Overriding years of aligning with the dense, fear-based, limiting, and negative attitudes may take perseverance, but does slowly start to happen. I now just have to sit in the chair I use for meditation, reflection, and journaling for my being to align with peaceful feelings, as it automatically reconnects to the vibrations I often evoked there. Even when I am out and about, I can call that peaceful feeling up whenever I feel disconnected from it.

An acquaintance once mentioned how she had to read Gary Renard's book *The Disappearance of the Universe* seven or eight times before she fully understood the concepts enough to apply them in her life and for the shifts to start to happen. James Frey, author of *A Million Little Pieces*, told Oprah on one of her last shows that he read, reread, and meditated on the *Tao Te Ching* when he was in rehab to help him overcome his propensity for addictive behaviors. In *10% Happier*, Dan Harris also revealed that it was only by the time he read Tolle's *A New Earth* a third time that he really started to get it. When we reread or relisten to inspirational material, not only do the concepts sink in, but we are also infused with the energy of their intentions.

3) Directing Our Thoughts and Words with Concepts of Empowerment and Self-Love

Our thoughts and words must align with the new identities we are aiming to embrace. If they do not, we have to replace our negative "stinking thinking"—Joyce Meyer's phrase—with loving thoughts about ourselves. This requires *consciously* training our minds to shift to the positive.

If for example, we tend to berate ourselves over making errors or being slow to learn something, we have to consciously replace those negative thoughts with positive ones. We can substitute a thought such as "I always screw up" with "I made a mistake; maybe next time I should recheck my work." We can shift our thinking from "This is too hard. I'm stupid and will never get it" to

"It is taking a long time for me to get this, so I'm sure it will be worth it when I finally do." Always, always, always encourage yourself positively! Doing so is crucial to staying or becoming happy, strong, and empowered.

We can also tell ourselves, "I am love," "I am loved," "God loves me," "I can _____." JRobert, the channel for Oasis, used to tell us to look in the mirror and tell our self, "Je t'aime" ("I love you" in French) and to say it with *vigor*. He also told us to "smile at ourselves," enthusiastically and with love, in the mirror every morning. These are beneficial practices to keep up throughout our lifetime. I once heard Louise L. Hay, the prolific American self-help author and publisher, say in one of her talks that even after years of working on reprogramming herself, every morning she still looks at herself in the mirror, smiles at herself and says "I love you" to her image.

Replacing negative self-talk with a more-positive spin helps us to develop compassion for ourselves, and setting up our day with positive reinforcements helps to get us aligned. This effort is understood by Spirit as our attempt to take steps toward our healing, and the partnership gets stronger.

4) Lightening Up and Infusing Our Lives with Joy

Desires born from our connection to our True Selves rather than from neediness or any other unconscious influence will bring us true joy. Whether working with our hands, bodies, or minds, if we embrace activities that bring us joy, we will be happy and fulfilled and will bring pleasure to or provide a function for others. Whether we enjoy carpentry, painting, sculpting, gardening, dancing, yoga, any sport, racing cars, working with numbers, the law, or medicine, if we follow what we love to do, we will be happy and find joy. The more we embrace these with lightness, joy, and abandonment, the more this will strengthen the connection to our True Selves.

Embracing joy is a powerful thing. In her promotion for a recent workshop, "Open Your Heart, and Allow Joy to Be Your Guide," Carol Fitzpatrick said, "The feeling (of love, joy, peace) has all the structure of the universe. It's the rocket fuel that gets us to where we want to be."[3] To help us embrace our wholeness, we have to embrace joy. When we cannot easily connect to joy, we can look for what will ignite it again. Sometimes we just stumble upon it, because even when our joy or need for expression has been suppressed, Spirit often finds a way to help us overcome the repression.

I discovered dancing at the age of thirty-five by going to exercise classes at a dance studio—and it became a passion. Growing up, I was not encouraged to do anything that was not family or church oriented, and my mother always wanted me to stay home with her. She was displeased with and discouraged any activities I joined or friends I made. However, once I discovered dancing, I came alive by being able to express myself. It took me years to fully let go in dance class or on stage, but once I did, I never lost the freedom of expression dancing afforded me.

To allow joy to express itself in us, we also need to lighten up and embrace laughter. Taking life too seriously, not appreciating humor, or overlooking opportunities for laughter keeps us distanced from joy. All the spiritual teachers I have come across encourage us to not only find joy in life but also to lighten up and not take everything so seriously. Part of the Default Position that Humanity has fallen into upholds tendencies toward worry and seriousness. The creation story of the Bible says that God created and it was good. It does not say that He created, then worried about it or second-guessed himself. Humor and laughter break down our barriers and allow us to connect to our God-selves.

5) Calming Our Minds; Centering Our Beings

To connect to the joy buried deep within, it is helpful to adopt practices and habits that quiet the mind, center our beings, and help us live from a heart-centered place. This keeps the chatter of the mind and its maladapted efforts to protect us at bay. Getting lost in activities we love also helps connect us to that peaceful place within. As I explain in chapter 6, "Words, Symbols, Rituals, Concepts, and Prayers," one of the purposes of singing and worship in spiritual or religious settings is to quiet our minds and open us up. During my workshops with JRobert and Oasis, music was always a key component. It helped us to withdraw from our minds and go into our heart spaces. In addition to music or other activities that uplift us, practicing conscious breathing, doing yoga or meditation, and being in nature all help us to calm our minds and become centered.

Slowing down our breathing allows our consciousness to drop into our heart centers or chakras, allowing for a closer connection to our True Selves. In his book *Conscious Breathing: Breathwork for Health, Stress Release, and Personal Mastery*, Gay Hendricks explains that some type of "conscious breathing" is essential to overcoming our propensity for tension, stress, and mind chatter, as it slows down our mind and creates a general sense of well-being.[4] Conscious breath work, meditation, or yoga, all slow down our breathing. A few meditation practices are located on the book's website. You can access them from the "Download" link by keying in the associated code found on the last page of the book.

Being in nature helps us to reconnect to our origins. In Hermann Hesse's *Siddhartha*, Siddhartha explains to Govinda that we are all made of the same thing and that nature in its purest form can speak to us. He tells Govinda the tale of a ferryman who said "the river's voice spoke to him" and that "every wind, every cloud, every bird, every beetle is equally divine and can teach just as well as the esteemed river."[5] Nature can communicate truths to us because it is the cleanest and purest channel within our realm.

6) Aligning with the Oneness Paradigm

We all emanated from Oneness and retain a memory of our connection to it. We can connect to the Oneness in ourselves by embracing the tenets of its paradigm: love and all its qualities, the Standard, and its Universal Laws. We also reconnect by acknowledging that this same Oneness exists in others, because we all emanated from the same energy, share this connection, and are all interconnected. This is one of the explanations of the well-known biblical phrase "give and you shall receive." By offering the tenets of Oneness to others, like fairness, compassion, understanding, etc. they are returned to us. By being judgmental instead of accepting of others, people will be judgmental of us.

The strong connection we have to nature mentioned above extends to all of Gaia and everything and everybody on it. (I explain this connection more fully in chapter 9, "The Planet and Abundance"). We separate ourselves through our perceived differences because we have forgotten the part of us that embodies the Oneness that pervades everything and all of us. The discord within our cultural and religious backgrounds reflects the separation from the Oneness playing out on the world stage, as does the abuse we put upon Gaia. We are beginning to realize that we have to bridge the gap between our differences, but we still identify so strongly with them that it is hard to let go enough to focus on our similarities instead of our differences. This is true of us as individuals as it is within our societal structures.

To fully embrace the God-part of ourselves that all of Humanity shares is to understand that no matter what religion we were born into, we are all the same—equal in God's eyes. Regardless of our sex, orientation, race, culture, or social standing, we are all equally loved by the Creator, and deserve the same freedom to express ourselves. We have to focus on working toward peace and equality for all, not on finger-pointing or revenge. We also have to offer love and forgiveness to all, even those who victimize us.

Many people throughout history have embraced these concepts. These light holders have encouraged us to love unconditionally, to work toward peace with each other, and to support equality for all. Their energies are embodied today by brave young souls, like Malala Yousafzai, the young Pakistani girl shot in 2012 by the Taliban for advocating education for girls in Pakistan. In Malala Yousafzai's case, you need only look at how she wished for a good education and good lives for her perpetrators' children to see unconditional love at play.

7) Taking Control of Our Lives; Aiming to Live Consciously

If negative unconscious influences have been running our lives, they will be firmly anchored into our attitudes and habits. Even though we decide to take the above steps to reconnect back to our True Selves, we have to follow our inner promptings to make the changes required to fully align with it. We are aiming toward living consciously rather than under unconscious influences.

To align with our True Selves and become our Best Selves, we may be guided to join workshops to attune to higher vibrations and/or to address unconscious influences. We may have an impulse to get physically fit, and then be invited by a friend to join a gym or yoga or dance class. Our physical body is the vehicle to express our spiritual being and all aspects are affected by our emotional world. The healthier and more vibrant our body, the higher its vibration and the easier it is to align with the higher vibrational attitude changes we wish to make. It is our negative unconscious influences (coupled with familial tendencies) that have enticed us into dysfunctional and addictive behaviors. On our journey to becoming our Best Selves we will be guided to address our dysfunctions and even our addictions.

We may feel the need to make new friends and partake in activities more in alignment with who we want to become and then be invited to social gatherings that uphold these notions. Some friends may still lure us into activities that are not in alignment with our growth toward wholeness; therefore, we may have to drop them.

In his book *Conversations with God for Teens*, Neale Donald Walsch answers a young man's question about being "on the outs with the group" he was hanging out with. He was feeling pressured to do something he did not really want to do anymore. Walsch answered, "Remember, this is for the rest of your life … The group will go away. One day it will simply not be there. Yet *you* will *never* go away. You will be with your Self until the end of time."[6] Even though Walsch was addressing teens, the idea that we will always be with ourselves, living our lives, and being at the effect of the experiences we engage in, speaks to us all. Giving up friendships or activities that no longer align with our new goals may seem hard at first, as we are social beings, but new friends whose attitudes, habits, and passions align with our objective to reach our Best Selves will come along, however we must be open to these changes and make room for them in our lives.

We *must pay attention to and act upon* the impulses that fall across our path, as they are the practical ways that support our inner shifts. We will be guided toward what now aligns with our personal journey, however, when uncertain whether a prompting we receive is for our growth, or based on neediness or any other unconscious influence, we simply need ask ourselves if this will ultimately help us to become our Best Self. Journaling helps us pinpoint and untangle any fears or emotions that may come up during this process of change, and writing lists helps us clarify what we want our future to look like.

Writing lists of where we want to be in one, two, five, and ten years from now is highly recommended, as is making lists of what we have to do or give up to get there. Many self-help and spiritual aids, such as those of Tony Robbins, Earl Nightingale, and Dr. Richard's in his Heart Physics program guide us to make life lists. You can also use worksheet 14.

Worksheet 14: Life Lists and Goals

I have included a list of the Seven Steps to Anchor in Unconditional Love at the back of the book in the "Recaps" section of "Meditations, Visualizations, and Other Practices" and have provided instructions for downloading it from the book web site. Printing this out and keeping it handy along with worksheet 14, "Life Lists and Goals," will help focus your mind on moving forward. I keep mine in a plastic see-through folder at my bedside and read it before I sleep and upon first waking.

The purpose of all these practices and tools is to dispel and override the illusions that we are not of love, helping us reconnect us to our True Self. These illusions have undermined us into believing we are less than we actually are. We must replace the outdated heart beliefs keeping us in emotional bondage with new ones that will set us free. We must aim to live consciously. Until we do so, we see life though a clouded lens that blocks our True Self from shining through and our Best Self from blossoming. Once this love is anchored enough within our beings that we can sense ourselves shifting to a more-positive outlook and embracing joy more easily, we can proceed to removing obstructions to our accessing that love.

B) Dismantling What Is in the Way of Accessing Our Truth The Lens through Which We See Life

Our True Self sees life through a clear lens. It sees sameness and light and love within everybody and everything, because we are connected to Our Truth and the light and love it holds within us. Our created Self sees life though the murky distorted lens of illusions, focusing on our differences and imperfections. It sees ugliness in others and in things because it is disconnected from our true reality and from this place of disconnect it cannot the beauty.

A Clouded Lens: Focusing on the Ugliness not the Beauty

Noticing and focusing merely on negativity and ugliness is an ingrained habit that comes from our not being connected to our True Self. Do we see the beauty in the world or the ugliness? If we notice the ragged clothes of a child instead of his or her keen spirit or the weeds in a garden instead of the beautiful flowers, we are looking through a clouded lens. Our outlook on life, or what is held in our Life Matrix, mirrors how we view ourselves, others, and the world around us. Before I started finding a better way to perceive life, I viewed the world through a murky lens.

I remember once seeing a child waving a paper excitedly, running up the hill from school to meet his mother. What I saw was a scrawny, disheveled little boy with mismatched clothes, hair askew, shirt out, skinny legs sticking out of shorts, and one brown sock halfway up his calf and the other one invisible, likely squished inside his shoe. I did not see the happy little spirit of the child excited to show his mother his accomplishment. What I perceived was only an outward appearance of my mind's inner workings.

Another time, I recall being with my mother-in-law in her garden as she was showing me a beautiful flower that had just bloomed, some exotic flower she had grown from seed. She may have still been working on the garden or perhaps this plant had flowered early, but all I saw were the weeds and neglected overgrowth surrounding it. I really did not notice the beauty of the flower. We both had a love of gardening and flowers, and she was just sharing the beauty of this first bloom, which sadly, I missed.

Inability to Find Joy by Our Focus on Seriousness

When we are consumed by the seriousness or the harsh aspects of living we often cannot, or do not, allow for joy in our life. So entrenched in seeing life through the veil of negativity, we become focused on the dramas and overly concerned with the details of life or what a struggle life has been, is, or will be. This focus does not allow for an appreciation of humor and robs us of our connection to joy. Many medical and psychological specialists now include laughter, comedy, and lighthearted or uplifting shows in their prescriptions. All spiritual teachers and mentors I have known interject humor and jokes into their messages. I once read somewhere that there is no proof that there is anything serious in the Universe. However, the ego loves to make us think there is, and even uses our spiritual journeys to impose its ideas of drama and seriousness onto them.

As we aim to understand spiritual concepts, many of us can get very serious about it all and get bogged down in the mental aspect. I know I did, and still can if I don't watch myself! Our egos love to make this esoteric stuff very important and serious and want us to get it mentally, which distracts us from the purpose of our journeys: to relieve us of unhappiness, stress, and any serious attitudes we may hold so we can experience joy and love's bounty. Trying to figure it all out is even counterproductive. The more we allow our mind to get caught up in the mental aspect of it all, the more we distance ourselves from our True Selves—the antithesis of what we are attempting to do. Our ego will attempt to lure us to go down the rabbit-hole of the darkness we and the world has been caught up in. And it aims to lure us into taking our spiritual journeys seriously as a last-ditch strategy to keep itself alive, as it thrives on mind-games, and their drama, negativity, and divisiveness. This is one of the reasons there is so much conflict and strife within the different religions and spiritualities.

So, even though we are encouraged to investigate the effects our past has on our current life, we *must* do so with full forgiveness for ourselves and anyone else involved—without shame, guilt, or blame. We *can* do this because we now understand where the negativity came from and how it perpetuated throughout history. But we *must* keep it light. This is why the practices are kept to fifteen to twenty minutes. Having a lighthearted attitude is actually a spiritual tenet and a sign of really getting what life is about.

To discover whether our lens has been or still is clouded, we have to acknowledge how we have or continue to see the world around us. This new-found awareness is not to make ourselves wrong, but to help us shift our focus from the ugly to the beauty, and from seriousness to light-heartedness. As we do so, our inner being will start to acknowledge the lightness and beauty within. To help uncover how you view the world, use worksheet 15.

Worksheet 15: Lens through Which I View the World

Understanding Our True Reality and Natures—Not a New Idea

Around the time of Buddha about 2,500 years ago, other ancient philosophers were also aiming to help us expand our limited views of ourselves, our true nature, and the true nature of the Universe. In his poem *On Nature*, the Greek philosopher Parmenides encourages us to understand that there is only the present moment by telling us, "How, then, can what is be going to be in the future? Or how could it come into being? If it came into being, it is not; nor is it if it is going to be in the future."[7] Buddhist concepts like self-examination and contemplation aim to move us away from the business of the mind so we can experience the present moment. Other philosophers of the time also encouraged practicing self-examination.

Socrates, who is thought to have had a huge influence on Plato and is a key figure in Plato's dialogues, was known as the "talking prophet" because as he traveled about people gathered around him to hear his philosophies. However, when people asked him questions about situations in their lives, he encouraged them to come to their own conclusions. He answered their questions with questions. These back and forth questions and answers encouraged the person to probe his or her perspective on the situation, and to examine if their perceptions were correct or unfounded.

Although the Eastern thought systems have always maintained some form of self-examination in their philosophies, this past century self-examination has again come to the forefront in our quest to attain peace within ourselves and harmony with others. Byron Katie's practice, The Work, invites us to ask ourselves questions to help us deal with our current issues.

Noticing our thought patterns and shifting them is the key to releasing the hold the negative ones have on us. In *Women's Bodies, Women's Wisdom: Creating Physical and Emotional Health and Healing,* Dr. Christiane Northrup guides us to do this:

> notice during the day how often your thoughts about what you want turn to the negative. Gently bring them back. Make it a habit to concentrate on what is working in your life. Cultivate the habit of noticing what is good and appreciating it.[8]

I was unaware of these connections, and thus my twenties and thirties were fraught with much anger, frustration, judgment, and projection. By the time I was in my forties, I was starting to study and understand that which really helped me to see the connection between my projections about life and my experiences in life. Years later, with a much deeper understanding of these concepts and using *The Course's* practice of forgiveness, my Life Matrix is much, much clearer.

We can ask ourselves a few questions to see if our lens is clear and if we are aligning with the affirming qualities within the Standard to become our Best Self. Do our thought processes allow us to see others or the world as positive or negative? Do they encourage self-love? Support what we are trying to create in our life? Promote harmony and unity with others? You can further examine these with worksheet 16.

Worksheet 16: My Thought Processes: What They Invite into My Life

Required Shifts in Perception

The first leg of this path usually requires some shifts in perception with regard to our self, others, situations, and the world around us. Our perceptions set the stage for either a life of peace and contentment or one fraught with frustration and dissatisfaction. If there is anxiety or conflict in our lives, we can change this. As we change our ways of looking at things, our internal mind-sets start to shift, as do our Default Positions, Protective Mechanisms, and eventually our complete Life Matrixes.

We may hold false perceptions regarding what love is and what our real needs are. If we have unconsciously erected blocks to the love within us, we will have difficulty receiving and giving love to others. Our capacity to love others is in direct relationship to how much we love ourselves. Are we supportive of our loved ones, or do we undermine their hopes, dreams, and passions? If we truly love ourselves, we can easily offer love, gifts, support, or help to those around us— without wanting reciprocation of any kind. We also may hold false perceptions about what we or others need to be or do to be happy and contented, and may try to impose those beliefs onto others in the guise of helping them, fuelled by our how-it-should-bes. We all feel strong impulses to connect to the truth, but our past efforts to do so may have been met with disappointment and created conflicts with others.

We have looked for love in all the wrong places and not filled the hunger. Looking to another, wealth, or to success to fulfill us is based on the false belief that we cannot find contentment within ourselves. Now is the time to recognize any disempowering inner beliefs so we can free ourselves of their influence. With a greater understanding of how our perceptions and inner beliefs affect our life experiences, we can also now recognize how they may affect and undermine the happiness of those around us. We can examine these with worksheet 17.

Worksheet 17: False Perceptions, Their Beliefs, and How-It-Should-Bes

Once we understand the influence of our false perceptions and the inner beliefs they created, we are better positioned to make the necessary shifts to release their holds on us. As we unravel all that binds these together, we move through six steps. (These six steps are also listed in the "Recaps" section in "Meditations, Visualizations, and Other Practices" at the end of the book. They can also be downloaded from the book's website using the "Download" link by keying in the associated code located on the last page of the book).

Six Steps to Unravel What Is in the Way of Accessing Our Truth

- Recognizing
- Acknowledging
- Understanding
- Forgiving
- Letting go: Releasing Emotions / Shifting Attitudes
- Uncluttering the Inner and the Outer

We often move through many of these steps simultaneously and effortlessly, as it all works like an intertwined matrix. However, other steps may take amazing faith and will. But I did it, and so can you.

1) Recognizing

The first step to healing is to recognize that something is not working for us or is in need of change. At any point in life we may look at ourselves and think, *I'm not happy, I don't like myself,* or *I don't like the direction my life is taking.* The recognition that *something is off* may come about slowly, as small awareness creeps into consciousness, or in the wake of a pivotal or life-changing event.

For me it was a combination of both. I gradually became aware of others in more difficult situations than mine who seemed better able to navigate life, all the while with a positive attitude. Additionally, the death of my mother brought a surge of conflicting emotions to the surface that I could no longer deny or ignore. It was time for me to address them and start to unravel all that I had buried. My journey to wholeness began.

Recognition is akin to quitting smoking. Some quit cold turkey, never looking back, while others may take ten years, stopping and starting again and again until eventually they succeed. Once the decision is made that something has to change in our lives, we just have to follow the path that will unfold for us, as our higher Selves guide us in our journey toward wholeness.

2) Acknowledging

Once we recognize that something is off in our life, we are ready to acknowledge that we may have been living in denial and perceiving life through false understandings and beliefs, and can see that decisions made from within that false paradigm may not have served us well.

If we can acknowledge that at least some of our life situations and frustrations may have a lot to do with our perceptions and that we can affect the directions our lives take by making some attitude or life changes, we have stepped onto the path toward healing and wholeness. We will then be guided to information, tools, practices, guides, and anything or anybody else that will help us on our path.

Slowly, as we are given insight and start to connect the dots between our misperceptions and false beliefs and how we experience life, an internal shift begins to take place and with it an understanding of what is not working for us and why, and how to move in the direction of peace and happiness.

3) Understanding

As we get in touch with our feelings and connect the dots, we begin to understand how our false perceptions and past hurts influenced our attitudes and that many of the frustrations we blamed on others or on life actually came from our feelings and their reactions. While this realization may come with mixed emotions, such as anger or embarrassment, this understanding will enable us to make peace with our past and how it influenced us, so that we can eventually move past its affect on us. This will have a *huge* impact on how we now feel.

As we allow the realities and emotions of past hurts, upsetting events, or bad choices we made to surface for release, we need to continue the previously mentioned practices to ensure we are keeping unconditional love anchored within us. This keeps confusing or mixed emotions from further affecting us negatively and helps us from falling into self-condemnation. This is a good time to start journaling.

Journaling

Journaling, expressing ourselves on paper, helps us to understand our feelings, pinpoint those we cannot easily access, and make connections to long-buried emotions. We can look for an answer to a specific question, ask for clarity on a complex issue, or simply try to uncover why we are angry, frustrated, or not able to become our Best Self. Be prepared to devote a few minutes in a quiet setting.

- Allow your mind to go to the concern or question;
- Write down all thoughts and emotions—even if you cannot articulate them very well;
- Old remembrances may come back to you. Invite them in. Without judging, allow and accept whatever emotions surface, be that anger, rage, shame, or embarrassment. But do not force it;
- Insights or answers may come; you may make some connections of current feelings to past events; or they may come to you later;

- Continue until you feel satisfied or complete, empty or emotionally spent. But go no longer than twenty to thirty minutes.
- When finished, let it all go. Do not deeply analyze anything.

Like most people, when I first started journaling it felt contrived, and what came out seemed silly and superficial. This may be because we are not accustomed to accessing our deep feelings and usually only scratch the surface of our inner worlds. After a few sessions, you will find that you can pinpoint your current feelings and delve further into them. Whether during the session, or later, insights will eventually come that enable you to connect past events or emotions to more-recent feelings or events. When this happens just treat it as an aha moment, and let it go. Do not scrutinize it.

Talking things out with other people is also helpful, be that a close friend, minister, professional, or a healing and sharing workshop that deals with our inner workings. So long as the other is a good listener and offers us a safe haven to express ourselves without judgment, making us feel shame or guilt, or giving unsolicited advice, this can have many advantages. A good listener can allow us to express freely, which can sometimes help us to find words for thoughts and feelings that have been difficult to pinpoint.

Any tool we use to understand and work through our misperceptions, negative attitudes, or habitual reactions will release the grip of the original unprocessed emotions of the associated past event.

4) Forgiveness.

Forgiveness entails making peace with our self, others, situations, and/or the world. And we start with self-forgiveness.

Self-Forgiveness

No matter what "bad things" we have thought, believed, supported, done, or not done, we can turn our lives around and rise above what has held us in negative attitudes, hurting our self or others, and kept us from being our Best Selves. A vital step is forgiving our self.

Self-forgiveness requires giving up and releasing guilt and shame. Guilt is the principal thief of emotional happiness, but it is only a trick of the mind and has no substance. The underlying causes of guilt are in the past and should therefore be relinquished. Once we understand that we only say or do hurtful things because we are not connected to our True Selves and thereby misjudge who we and others are, it is easier for our unconscious to exonerate itself. We can thereby connect more fully to the concept of unconditional love and forgiveness for ourselves.

Room is then made in the deepest part of our self to connect to the peace and general feeling of well-being that occurs when the emotions of what we have done are acknowledged and understood, and the associated guilt of projecting our unconscious influences onto others is lifted and the shame we feel dissolved.

Our higher Self wants us to embrace the concept of unconditional love as expressed in the parable of the prodigal son I mentioned in chapter 1. Depending on both our innate personality and what we need to forgive our self for, this can be immediate or take years of work. Even those who have committed crimes and are in jail can experience God's unconditional love and forgiveness. In *Letter to a Prisoner: From a Career Criminal to a Seeker of Truth*, Joe Wolfe, an ex-prisoner with a criminal past, describes his long journey to accept God's love and forgiveness within himself through the forgiveness practices outlined in *The Course*.

We practice self-forgiveness when we recognize thoughts we had, words we uttered, deeds we did, or things we didn't do that are causing us angst, guilt, shame, or discomfort and then release the associated negative emotions surrounding the issue. Whether we are aware of it or not, it is the denial and burying of these shadow parts of ourselves that keep us in emotional bondage, take away our current peace of mind, and cause us to act in ways that continue to hurt ourselves and others. We have to make peace with these negative parts of ourselves so that we can finally release them and their hold on us. Releasing techniques are discussed below in item 5, "Letting Go; Releasing Emotions / Shifting Attitudes." We can examine areas that might need self-forgiveness with worksheet 18a

Worksheet 18a: Self-Forgiveness

Forgiving Others

To fully move away from self-condemnation, requires that we shift our mental image to see *all* others as innocent. This is a trick of the mind, but one we can use to our advantage. When we offer love, peace, or forgiveness to everyone who crosses our path, our unconscious recognizes these as qualities that we want to adhere to, even if we fake it at first. Spirit understands what we are trying to do and will support our efforts, no matter how meager they are. For example, if someone cuts us off in traffic and we get angry and really want to give them a rude sign, we can diffuse this inclination by telling ourselves that although we feel upset, we want to move away from allowing ourselves to be bothered when someone does something that pushes our buttons. We do this with an understanding that we are *all* just playing out our misperceptions in different forms of negativity and that the first step to move away from their influences is to acknowledge them; the second step is to override them. This we can and must do consciously—even if we have not yet made any connection to why we act or react in certain ways.

Forgiving those around us for their minor transgressions may be hard enough to wrap our heads around, so forgiving anyone for major wrongdoings against us or those who perpetrate heinous crimes may seem almost impossible. But we must reconcile our feelings. Otherwise, we internalize the emotions further hurting ourselves, or we end up feeling hatred, turning to blame, or exacting revenge, considering these justifiable responses. This further anchors negative responses within our being, as well as perpetrates them as acceptable responses to life in general and around the world. In his book, *How Can We Forgive Murderers*, Greg Mackie maintains that we have to "recognize the Christ" in everyone, even people like rapists and child molesters. This perspective allows us to recognize that no matter how 'bad' their behavior it is only a manifestation of their error in perception, *not* a sin."[9] Christ is used here as the symbol for forgiveness and unconditional love.

Mackie explains that when we choose to forgive, it is a "decision to look past what we *think* people are, and invite the Holy Spirit's version of what they *really* are in our minds."[10] In doing so we actually anchor our own forgiveness into our being through a combination of Spirit's recognition of our attempt (no matter how futile) to forgive all, as well as through the vibrations we emit that shift our Life Matrixes. Like many of *The Course* students and teachers, Mackie uses the symbol of the Holy Spirit as our conscious, active guide.

Seeking to forgive murderers or those who commit other heinous crimes may not make any sense for most of us. It requires the understanding of ultimate forgiveness, and also delineates the higher consciousness we need to aspire to so that *we* can find peace in our lives, and encourage peace in the world. Light holders throughout time have shown us the way, like Malala Yousafzai, who not only forgave those who tried to kill her for standing up for Pakistani girls' education but also wished them and their families well and their children a good education. The more of us that aim to take the high road, the more possibilities will open up for us individually and for humankind as a whole. We can examine where we can make peace with others' attitudes and behaviors with worksheet 18b.

Worksheet 18b: Forgiving Others

Forgiving Situations

In addition to forgiving ourselves and others for acting on errors in perception, forgiving situations is paramount to our inner peace. If you were partly responsible for a situation, for example, if a gambling compulsion led to your life partner leaving, then you have to forgive the situation as well as yourself. If alternately, another brought about a situation, you have to forgive him or her for being the instigator, but must also forgive yourself for any part you think you *may* have played in allowing it to happen. For example, if your life partner had an affair you need to forgive him or her for having betrayed your partnership, forgive the other person involved in the affair for invading your relationship, and yourself for any part you may or may not have played, perhaps neglecting your loved one. Even when we have done nothing wrong our unconscious mind can infuse guilt into our being.

We practice forgiveness regarding situations by recognizing and acknowledging that these come about because Humanity exists within the paradigm of duality. While under this influence, we are all being offered life lessons whereby situations allow us to choose to respond with attitudes derived from love, or from fear. We may be born with physical ailments or into impoverished situations; situations may befall us which cause us or our loved ones physical or emotional pain and suffering; or we can fall prey to financial insecurity. All these situations are unfair and can create unhappiness, depression, or conflict in our lives.

Until we have made peace with any past or current situation that causes us anguish or feelings of blame or shame, the related emotions are like dark blemishes in our Emotional Bodies, which can contaminate or even fully block our connection to our True Self and the powers in the Universe, which affects our ability to become our Best Self. These effects are portrayed in illustrations 7, 8, and 9 from chapter 2. We can examine situations that might require forgiveness with worksheet 18c.

Worksheet 18c: Forgiving Situations

Forgiving the World: Humanity and Its History

It is easy to focus on and point out all that is wrong in the world today. However, with the understanding that we have all been living under the shadow of duality throughout our history and of the misperceptions that created within us individually and collectively, we still have to forgive the world for all that has happened. This does not mean condoning the wrongdoings that have and still occur in the world, but to fully anchor in the connection to Our Truth, we have to make peace with all aspects of ourselves and others regarding all current and past situations. It is still appropriate to act in ways to make the world a better place, but we have to leave judgment, blame, vengeance, and any divisive attitudes aside. Otherwise we will simply attract these back into our spheres to be played out again and again: within ourselves, our communities, and on the world stage.

Any divisive attitude we hold onto like, *we-are-better-than-them*, will add to keeping the world, and its people, divided with separate, conflicting agendas. As previously mentioned, *The Course* teaches that there is no hierarchy of illusions. And although it is hard to accept, thoughts of revenge do as much damage as what was perpetrated—just on another level. We are either aligned or misaligned with the concepts of love and thereby send out into the world the vibrations that focus on love that unite, or those that focus on fear and its hate that divide. We can examine areas that upset us regarding the goings on in the world with worksheet 18d.

Worksheet 18d: Forgiving the World

One way or another, our peace and return to wholeness depends on forgiving ourselves, others, all situations, and the world. When we forgive ourselves, we can more easily forgive others and any difficult situations. And as more of us do so, the accumulative, collective effect is immeasurable.

5). Letting Go

Letting go entails releasing buried emotions. It creates a lightness in our being because it lifts emotional burdens allowing for more peace and joy to come through. Releasing negativities we unknowingly allowed in our Emotional Bodies rids us of their holds on us, which in turn shifts our attitudes and improves our reactions. It is a necessary step in overall healing on the path to wholeness. Until we face and make peace with past issues we did not deal with properly at the time, they will have a tendency to be dragged into the present through our attitudes and behaviors. They also affect our thoughts of the future. The worksheets in this book strive to bring awareness to the misperceptions, inner beliefs and attitudes we unknowingly created that do not serve us. When we allow unhealed emotions to rise, the hold they have in our lives is released. When we acknowledge the attitudes we hold and our habitual reactions that stemmed from these, we can become more conscious of our predisposition to react negatively, which keeps us distanced from our Best Selves. We can then consciously work on shifting them to more positive ones. I have worked with the concept of letting go or releasing for over ten years now.

A Simple Technique I Have Used:

- Invite your higher Self, Sprit, God, your Best Self, or any deity to join you;
- Sit in a comfortable quiet place. Take a few deep breaths;

- Focus on either a specific concern, a general feeling of dissatisfaction, or ask a question;
- Ask for clarity;
- Allow whatever impressions come to surface;
- As thoughts, memories, or visions appear, allow the associated emotions flow through you until they abate.
- We may get clarity on a confusing situation, experience anger, or have aha moments. Practical answers may come, or we may become aware of attitudes that are creating our frustration.
- Journal your thoughts or feelings, as finding words for what we think and feel helps to crystallize them.
- Allow for twenty minutes to half an hour at the most for each session.

Once the session is over we are to forget about it, go about our daily lives, and let the process work, as rehashing the details in our mind is counterproductive. Spirit, or our higher Self, knows what we are attempting to do and works with our unconscious. In its supreme wisdom it knows what and how much we can handle and will give us insights during the session to help us make some connections. Shortly thereafter we also may have associated thoughts, become aware of new connections, or have more aha moments. This happens without really interfering with our routines, except to maybe take a little time here and there for quiet contemplation or journaling. (Other examples of releasing techniques are located on the book's website. You can access them using the "Download" link and keying in the associated code found on the last page of the book).

Once we have worked through and released the effects of past, hurtful, buried events, acknowledged any negative attitudes we may have held, and made the connections to how these affected our past feelings and how our life has played out, we are ready to accept how any current negative and disempowering attitudes we still hold can affect our present and future life, and can act to change them. These processes of self-inquiry guide us to understand and assess current feelings, attitudes that may be creating our situations, or misperceptions we have of others or situations. With this understanding, we discover that no matter what is happening in our lives, we can leave anger, blame, and judgment behind. We can then create harmonious attitudes toward others. We can also overcome any propensity for self-doubt or passive tendencies that keep us disempowered.

To prevent any guilt from seeping into my unconscious from what was uncovered during my releasing sessions, and also to help anchor in the sense of empowerment I was attempting to attain, I read, re-read, and meditated on Marianne Williamson's books I mentioned above (*A Woman's Worth;*

Illuminata, A Return to Prayer; A Return to Love). And once I really understood how *I* had created much of my frustrations with my negative attitudes and slowly shifted them, I realized I felt more peaceful and empowered when being positive. I started to develop a real inner confidence that was no longer influenced by what I *didn't* want to be (like my mother) but based on all that I *could* be: happy, fulfilled, empowered, in harmony with others, and successful in all areas of life. As I came to understand what I had unconsciously created to protect myself, my neediness abated and other Illusionary Constructs began to fade.

Fully letting go of what is held within our Emotional Bodies is usually a slow, gentle process, combining releasing techniques, forgiveness opportunities, and often some humbling realizations about our attitudes or misperceptions. And while doing all this, we *must* continue to anchor love within ourselves. But we mus*t not* rehash it all, try to figure out the whys and wherefores, or allow our *minds* to go deeply into our issues.

The purpose of any good spiritual practice is done at levels beyond the mind with Spirit guiding the process. Involving the mind not only diminishes its effects, it overrides Spirit's involvement—as well as its protection, and entices our egoic mind (the Devil) to go into the darkness of it all. This can make us feel bad, depressed, or even be dangerous. Delving into the recesses of the mind without proper mentoring is a dangerous undertaking. It is akin to conjuring up dark forces. I discuss this more thoroughly in the section Dark Forces / Powerful Energies in chapter 6, "Words, Symbols, Rituals, concepts, and Prayers."

During any period of consistent releasing or deep spiritual practice it is advisable to take breaks from the work regularly—especially if you start to feel bad, depressed, or guilt or remorse has seeped in. Even *A Course in Miracles* with its profound philosophies and 365 lessons that bring about *major* shifts in our awareness suggests we go about it at a pace that is comfortable for us, and if we start to become depressed we are to put it down for a while. The daily lessons are on a small page and it is recommended that we read and meditate on them for only fifteen to twenty minutes a day, and that we do no more than one a day. Only very advanced spiritual practitioners complete them within the year, and most who do the lessons take *much* longer, with some never finishing but still getting many benefits.

Even though the arc of our return to wholeness is a slow, gentle release from our unconscious issues, throughout the process there may be instances of great release, like a huge moment of clarity, or a few days of heightened emotions. I go into these more thoroughly in the next chapter, "Along the Way." Even so, as some of the associated emotions are understood and released and their invisible chains on us start to dissipate, we begin to feel lighter, calmer, and more content as the burden of buried emotions is lifted. Others may even notice and comment on these changes in us.

6. Uncluttering

Along with doing internal clearing out, engaging in external cleaning uncomplicates our lives and helps us to further align with our True Selves. When we get rid of unnecessary physical baggage, we also get rid of the emotional attachments to the objects. Hanging on to old stuff clogs our energetic field with the past and can keep us from fully moving forward in life. The lighter our past emotional attachments, the more room there is for the new us to come forth. The less complicated our lives, the less we have to navigate through to the peace within ourselves, and the less complicated our internal world. Joyce Meyer often says that complicating our lives goes against what God has planned for us and takes away our joy.

For further information on how these six steps play out, an article entitled "How the Six Steps Guide Us Toward our Best Self" can be found on the book's website.

Other Concepts That Help Us Shift

Start with the Little Things

Because we have to start somewhere, and since the unconscious doesn't distinguish between small and large issues, we can start by noticing the little things in life that annoy or anger us, steer us into losing our peace, or reinforce our passivity. The first principle in *The Course* is that there is no hierarchy of illusions. We are either aligned with the love and compassion held within the Standard and feeling empowered or we are not.

So while it may appear that making peace with small issues like the guy cutting us off in traffic can't do much to change the misperceptions we exist under, they do. Consistently making these shifts has a *huge* impact on our psyches. As he expressed in his speech to the Liberal Arts graduates of the Kenyon College class of 2005, the late David Foster Wallace suggested that we should not ignore any small and inconsequential progress we make.[11] Small shifts in attitudes start the ball rolling! When we make the effort to shift our propensity to react negatively to even minor upsets and reap the benefits of feeling more peaceful, we are encouraged to continue with more peaceful responses. Our trajectory starts to change.

For those of us who tend to be passive, taking small steps like speaking up with regard to minor matters builds confidence. In continuing to speak up, we may come to feel more empowered around bullying, controlling, or manipulative people. This is an immeasurable self-esteem booster! We then become ready to tackle larger issues. Worksheet 19 can help you to investigate small attitude shifts you can make.

Worksheet 19: Small Attitude Shifts I Can Start With

We can consciously choose *better* attitudes and actions—even if it doesn't feel natural!

- We can aim to replace judgment with acceptance!
- We can aim to replace blame with understanding!
- We can aim to replace anger with self-control!
- We can aim to replace indifference with empathy!
- We can aim to replace that which causes discord with that which embraces harmony!
- All we need is a little awareness and willingness!

When we understand where *our* misperceptions come from, it is easier to understand another who has not yet made that connection and is still under the influence of his or her unconscious beliefs. Furthermore, as we begin addressing the small areas where *we* are not aligned with loving thoughts, words, or actions, it is easier to forgive others who are still misaligned.

Once we are comfortable with forgiving the little things, we are then better equipped to deal with any larger or more sensitive issues that may be holding us from our Best Selves. And even though we have been told we are unconditionally forgiven for *all* our errs in perception and that there is no hierarchy of illusions regarding forgiveness from God, Spirit, Source, etc. for what we have or have not done, our unconscious does not believe this. So we *must* forgive the larger issues as well. However, this all takes time and practice, so until it comes *naturally* to feel positive and loving and to forgive even small affronts against us we can help ourselves along by pretending: *we can fake it.* We can use worksheet #19 for any large issues as well.

Faking It

If negative attitudes have been our mainstay, we may not be comfortable with these new approaches. It helps to fake positive responses initially, until the new habits are solidified.

Faking our way to where we want to ultimately end up is a psychological technique often used in couples therapy. By the time couples finally seek counseling, they usually don't feel very loving. One of the first things they are often asked to do is fake being in love again by being nice, touching each other lovingly, doing special things for each other, and abstaining from blame—even when they do not feel like it. The idea is to create an atmosphere in which healing can begin. Even when we fake more positive responses, our intention to change alters our vibration, somewhat neutralizing the effect of our desire to respond negatively. And Spirit recognizes our attempt, so we get points for our willingness to shift. When negative thoughts or attitudes trickle into our consciousness, we can also use trigger words or phrases to interrupt the flow of any negative consequences these would have on our Emotional Bodies.

Choose a Trigger Word or Phrase

To help get this process under way, you might choose a trigger word to remind you to become aware when you lapse into your habitual negative thoughts or behaviors, be that anger, blame, judgments toward others, or even self-deprecating thoughts. As I was becoming aware of my propensity to judge others, I borrowed the phrase "Oops, I did it again" from Britney Spears's song to use as a reminder that I was judging others again. Using this phrase was my way of recognizing my error, but at the same time, the lighthearted tone of the song encouraged a spirit of self-forgiveness. To avoid beating myself up for thoughts or words that were self-deprecating or behaviors that were not congruent with where I was or wanted to be in life, I also adopted Gilda Radner's phrase "*Neeever* mind." Although this might seem embarrassing, we do not have to speak them aloud; no one needs to know.

It is courageous to recognize our misperceptions, but important to avoid falling into a trap of *seriousness and guilt* associated with these admissions. *We have to practice self-examination, not self-condemnation.* We may be inclined to shy away from consciously examining where our minds go or from using tools or tricks to direct them to go where we want, but doing so will empower us and moves us in the right direction.

Further Understanding Our Misalignments

Our Propensity to Judge Everything

I was led to *The Course* early in 2009. At the time I was more consciously aware of the underlying negative influences that I had lived by, and my Default Position and Protective Mechanisms had shifted drastically. However, I recognized that I was still prone to judge—not big judgments like hating people or certain groups of people, just little thoughts like "This person is like this; I am not" or "That person has a bad attitude; mine is better." I had come a long way, but was still not as deeply in touch with the concept of acceptance as I knew I could be. Another layer had to be peeled off. I was still projecting my own misalignments with Self onto others or their situations. Judgments operate through the lens of separation. They are infused with concepts of *me-and-you* and *us-and-them*, as well as *me-better-than-you* and *us-better-than-them*. As such, judgment is the perfect vehicle to play out our Self separated from the Oneness paradigm.

When we judge others, whether based on our differences or their seeming imperfections or inefficiencies, we are making judgment calls with incomplete information. We have not understand how duality is played out, how our return to wholeness works, or how we are all working from some sort of misalignment and on different legs of our paths. In *Mindfulness*, Ellen Langer reminds us that while we all come from our own perspectives, when we become "mindfully aware of views other than our own, we start to realize that there are as many different views as there are different observers."[12]

Another's viewpoint or attitude may not resonate with us, but for that person, in his or her current awareness, it does. For example, it may appear that someone is projecting hurts outward, but that may be exactly what that person needs to do at that time. Maybe he or she has lived disempowered most of their life and is attempting to find their voice but is still not adept at it. (Abraham Hick's guidance scale in the next chapter explains how we move slowly from burying to expressing our emotions, which may manifest as showing anger until we learn to deal with the emotions in the best way). Since we have not lived the other person's life, we cannot know his or her circumstances nor how his or her journey needs to progress.

Importance of Nonjudgment

Judgment is so pervasive, and we wield our shoulds and should nots at every unsuspecting bystander. Even though people can be rude, unruly, or inconsiderate to others and the environment, sometimes we just catch them at a difficult time, whereby a behavior we witness is an anomaly and doesn't necessarily have anything to do with the person's character.

I once read an article about a man who was on the subway late at night with his three young kids. The kids were running amok, loud and out of control, as the father sat there seemingly oblivious to their actions. Someone approached him, annoyed and judgmental, and asked why he didn't control them. Looking up distraught, he slowly and quietly answered that they were returning from the hospital, where his wife had just died. The judgment was silenced. These misinformed judgments often happen.

When my youngest son was ten days old, he developed a rash and was put in the hospital. I also had a two-year-old and thirteen-year-old at home.

I was torn between being with my baby, who had tubes coming out of his head because the needles wouldn't fit into any other veins, and being with my two-year-old who was already dealing with being usurped as the baby of the family. For almost a week I spent one night at home and one night at the hospital, which was not close by, sleeping in a cot in my baby's room. I was completely exhausted and stressed.

During that time, I took my two-year-old son to McDonald's for a treat one afternoon, as he loved the park there. After we ate, we shared some fun mommy-and-son time as he played, and I got to relax. It was a nice break for both of us. After he finished playing in the park, I took him to the bathroom, and on the way back I noticed our tray still on the table askew with leftovers. With a sigh and the heaviness of one more thing to do, I consciously made the decision to leave without putting anything away. As a rule, I never did that, but that day I succumbed to the fatigue of the past few weeks, and I left it without guilt. The restaurant was almost empty as it was the middle of the afternoon, but as we passed a mother and her young daughter, I heard the woman loudly and haughtily proclaim, "See, that lady is leaving the mess for others to clean up. We should never do that." Too tired to even respond, I continued walking. I knew that I cleaned up after myself 99% of the time, and the criticism was her issue.

This is what we often do. In this woman's mind, she was teaching her daughter to be responsible, and she was, but instead of showing compassion as well, she judged. A compassionate way of dealing with that situation might have been for the woman to wait until I had left and then go over and take the tray to the bin, explaining to her daughter that it is good to clean up after ourselves and maybe that mother had forgotten or was having a bad day. She would have taught her daughter compassion as well as responsibility. I invite you to complete worksheet 20 if you feel judgments are keeping you from being your Best Self.

Worksheet 20: Judgments of Self, Others, Groups, or Situations

Judgment keeps us in anger and creates conflict—if not with others within ourselves. Not engaging in conflict helps us live lighter. In *Loyalty to Your Soul*, Drs. Ronald and Mary Hulnick use the metaphor that when we choose to forgo conflict or practice forgiveness, it is like we are "taking rocks out of our backpack" of life.[13]

Further Understanding Conscious and Unconscious Guilt

Every time we think, say, or do anything that is not aligned with love and acceptance, we amass unconscious guilt—whether we are aware of it or not. Although we may sometimes allow guilty thoughts and feelings to surface, most of guilt's tendrils are held in our unconscious minds, which are aware of and record every hint of negative emotion we have. This is why it is so important to release any negativities held within our unconscious minds to prevent them from accumulating in our psyches. Otherwise they lie in wait for opportunities to release using a plethora of negative attitudes and behaviors that we project outward towards others.

When we release emotions associated with unconscious guilt from this lifetime, we are also releasing past remorse that we had not dealt with from other lifetimes. Because of the holographic nature of the Universe, our souls' spiritual journeys do not adhere to linear time, and so how we deal with events in this life can influence our souls' whole journeys. Our souls hold the cellular memory of every emotion they have ever experienced, attitude held, and behavior exacted.

Through the infinite wisdom of the Universe, the circumstances of our current lifetime also give us opportunities to release unconscious guilt or other issues that we did not make peace with and let go of in past-lifetimes. This is why we may have recently or are still facing issues in our lives that we cannot make sense of. However, we do not have to know what happened in a past life, we just have to deal positively with our current issues. And while this may seem unfair, we all chose to be here at this time of the Shift to release any current or leftover negativity still in our beings. We just may not have recognized, fully understood, or refused to listen to the clues we were getting to solve our angst. We may have been afraid.

If we have not been told or do not believe that we are unconditionally loved and fully forgiven for all that we have or have not done, or that there is a net that will catch us if we address our issues, it is very hard to allow for the possibility to rise in us that they stem from us and how we approach life. The solutions may also point to changes we do not want to make, so we remain stuck. Past lives are explained more fully in chapter 6, "Words, Symbols, Rituals, Concepts, and Prayers," and the holographic nature of the Universe in chapter 7, "Science and Other Related Topics."

The Lure of Drama and Conflict

Many of us are addicted to the dramas in our lives and even the conflicts arising from them. As we talk about, rehash, and discuss all the ins and outs of life situations around us, we feel important, think we can figure things out, and thereby feel in control of outcomes. We get a sense of personal validation from it all. We also feel significant when we are knowledgeable and discuss world events with great vigor. However, focusing on drama is just our egos vying for attention. We sometimes also create drama or conflict in our lives as way to ignore or deny issues that need to be dealt with or because they offer us a sense of excitement.

In *The Lemurian Science of Immortality*, Almine tells us that we unknowingly generate our life dramas because of the dullness of our "self-made cages [which] hem us in like prison bars." They attempt to override the limitations we have created.[14] We ineffectively thrash through life trying to break these bars down, but as our connection to our True Self strengthens the need to engage in or create drama subsides.

One of Byron Katie's philosophies is that *there is my business, there is your business, and there is God's business.* She teaches that to live a worry-free, peaceful life, it serves us best if we look after only our own business, let others look after their business, and leave God's business (earthquakes, floods, etc., which we have no direct control over) to God. Her premise is that if we focus on others' business, who is looking after ours?

Not Getting Stuck in the Old Story

As we delve into the past and what is held in our unconscious, it is important to avoid getting entangled in our old stories. We investigate our past and buried emotions to disengage from the web of insidious thought patterns we unknowing allowed to form. We do not do this to rehash the past. Whether we were the ones with negative attitudes who behaved badly or the victims, it is important to acknowledge and release *all* associated ties to these old stories, so we can forget about them and move on.

As we work on healing the emotions of our past that affect us, they will slowly dissipate, until one day they are gone. However, it takes a conscious effort to stop the loop that keeps replaying our pasts over and over again. The ego thrives on drama and will try to lure us into holding on to the past. If we do find ourselves falling into this trap, we must remember that the conscious awareness of an unconscious influence is a big step. If we do get caught up in our old stories, we can have a catchword or phrase ready to remind us of what we are doing; and if we still wallow in them we simply need to forgive ourselves and move on.

Our Upbringing Influences Us; So Do Many Other Factors

Even though we may disdain the attitudes that surrounded us when growing up, we often inadvertently uphold them. I often felt bad and complained about my father's yelling and my mother's bad attitude, yet I internalized and retained some of those very qualities in my own attitudes and behaviors.

Sometimes only one child in a family will fall prey to serious life struggles, while the others do not. With regard to our soul journeys, we may have chosen to come here to make peace with these issues, for our healing and/or for forgiveness lessons for those who love us.

In my own personal journey, I learned to understand how the attitudes I grew up with affected me. I eventually forgave my parents and my strict and limiting Catholic upbringing, as I had realized they were unaware of how their attitudes and behaviors affected their children, just as I unknowingly allowed some of those attitudes to become mine. Like all of us, my parents were products of their familial, generational, and cultural backgrounds, and many negative and limiting influences were deeply entrenched in them. Making peace with how I had been affected by my parents was a huge soul growth opportunity, but while it was all going on I just felt unloved, unappreciated, and that I was never listened to.

This forgiveness of ourselves, others, and situations, past and present, is key. None of us knew what was underlying our attitudes and behaviors; what the impact was of our upbringing, generational or cultural; how our inherent personalities were affected; or that we should/could change our attitudes. We have all just been stuck and reeling from what Humanity's history created. Nonetheless, our exposure to serious negative generational influences in our past, like abuse or addictions, does not mean we have to succumb to them.

Overcoming the Sins of Our Fathers

Although the concept of the "sins of our fathers" is not a universal rule, we often make it so. We may allow it within ourselves, or put it upon others. If we see life and respond to it through the lens of our backgrounds, we may succumb to this false notion and fall prey to negative attitudes, habits, or dysfunctional behaviors by allowing unconscious influences to rule our lives, unaware we are falling into patterns that can be overcome but which require conscious effort to do so. Our backgrounds may also have kept us so emotionally deflated that we feel we cannot fight our family's propensity to dysfunctional behaviors and give up trying.

We can triumph over what was ingrained in us generationally, as well as our own natural inclinations. With conscious effort, courage, faith, and a strong will, any negative tendencies can be overcome. An abused child may have a tendency to become an abuser, just as children of alcoholic parents may have a tendency, emotionally and/or physiologically, toward alcoholism. Being brought up in or witnessing these or any other dire circumstances, however, does not necessarily mean that life has to be lived in the same way.

In the last few decades, we have acknowledged and unearthed the psychosocial and the physiological issues that keep negative forces alive through generations. Around the same time, Oprah and Joyce Meyer both spoke of the sexual abuses they suffered at the hands of relatives. I have heard both of them say that they had not intended to talk about the abuses that day but that the words just spilled out.

I believe that their search for truth and their desire to help others was sincere and that Spirit, God, or Holy Spirit spoke through them, as it was deemed time for society to unearth these types of hidden abuses. The implications of sexual and all other types of abuses can only be healed and released once they are acknowledged. As these two women both had a platform to speak from, they got the conversations going.

Oprah opened the door for mainstream society to feel comfortable enough to unearth and deal with deeply held, buried, dark secrets that were affecting the quality of their lives. Meyer opened the door within the Christian community for people to acknowledge, deal with, and overcome sexual, as well as other emotional or physical abuses. I have heard her say many times that although we may not have had unconditional love in our lives growing up, God loves us unconditionally. Acknowledging and addressing these types of issues is all part of Humanity raising its consciousness to embrace the requirements of the Shift. We also put the sins of the fathers on others by blaming them for what their race or past generations did.

Throughout history our hate, fear, or distain for another race, nation, culture, or religion has often been based on past events. We carried it forward, instructed our children about what the "others" did to us or promoted we-are-better-than-them scenarios, thereby perpetuating the negative perceptions of the "others." We also do this today, imposing stereotypes on whole groups of people who have nothing to do with what has recently happened or events of the past. The perfect example of this is the blame or hate aimed at some of the innocent refugees emigrating to get away from violence, heinous crimes, and awful living conditions. They are suffering prejudices because of the sins of a few within their culture.

Attempting to Correct Our Imbalances

Our imbalances play out in many ways. They are based on emotions that have not been addressed, but still hold an energetic component that comes out, one way or another. When our neediness or Perceived Needs are not answered, we may get angry, controlling, or manipulative. This unaddressed energy may have us focus on the physical aspects of life as they are so much easier to deal with than the emotional ones. For example, we often ensure that our families are sheltered, clothed, fed, and given the material things they require for school and work, whereas intangibles, such as really listening, offering understanding, and acting with openness and tenderness often are more challenging to provide. I was a very organized mother capable of managing all the physical needs of my home and family. Sometimes their emotional needs were met too, but most of the time I was too busy answering the call of my unconscious influences in attempts to keep myself sane to be able to offer much emotional support to anyone else.

At some point, we may feel an inner impulse to correct our imbalances. This may be accompanied by an extreme swing the other way as we try to compensate for what was missing or how we behaved. For example, if we have been inattentive to someone around us, we may end up going overboard with attention and suffocate them. The same may happen when overcompensating for anger, control, or any other misalignment that we attempt to make right. With time, our pendulum swings will lessen and we will be able to respond appropriately to situations. Illustration 11 below, similar to illustration 1 from chapter 1, shows us how this plays out.

#11: Attempting to Rebalance a Misalignment of Inattentiveness

are inattentive to partner

recognition for need to change (eg. threat of divorce, had an affair, etc.)

big push for correction

smothering the other with attention
- expect complete together-ness now
- allow the other to get away with being overly angry, grumpy or abusive
- giving into excessive demands

Worry: A Major Culprit to Our Happiness and a Block to the Abundance Paradigm

Worrying is one of the main causes of unhappiness and fatigue on our Planet. It sucks the life out of joy, and in fact, where worry treads, joy cannot follow. It is an epidemic in our modern society. Worry has always been present. Individuals have worried about not having enough food for their families or a roof over their heads. There have always been wars, famines, floods, and diseases to worry about. Over the last few decades, especially in most Western countries, we have gone from worrying about real life-threatening situations beyond our control to worrying about situations that we could actually control if we simply uncomplicated our lives. We take on big mortgages, buy expensive cars, acquire the newest electronic devices, modern day household gadgets and appliances, and we think we need it all but it really just complicates our lives further, especially when we take it all so seriously. We forget that there is a whole Universe out there just waiting to help us with everything.

Scripture supports the idea that we are not to concern ourselves with our circumstances. In Philippians 4:6, Paul tells us "do not be anxious about anything." He is suggesting that even in the direst of circumstances, we are not to worry, because God *will* look after us and our needs. Psalm 37 also suggests that we are not to worry or fret about our situations, nor compare them to others, or become jealous or vengeful. We are told to be patient and trust in the Lord, and if we keep a pure heart, what is meant for us will eventually come our way. A pure heart here means there is no negativity in it, such as worry or jealousy, which would undermine our requests. Worrying emits a vibration that all will not be well in our lives and this interferes with what God has planned for us.

If we revisit illustration 9, "Static in Connection to the Universal Powers," it shows that when we worry, we are not able to take full advantage of what could be available to us. We can examine how open and closed we are with worry or other specific attitudes with worksheet 21.

Worksheet 21: Opened or Closed to Universal Powers regarding Different Attitudes

Compartmentalization as a Limiting Protective Mechanism

The mind perceives order as the compartmentalizing of life,
the separating of oneness
for the purpose of controlling through definition.
—Almine[15]

Our beings seek to be aligned to their True Selves. When we are not, our unconscious uses internal mind games to attempt to control our misalignments. Compartmentalization can be a useful tool to help us make decisions and simplify life, but within the ego's framework, it is a technique to keep track of the different rules of our Illusionary Constructs.

When the ego compartmentalizes, it labels and classifies people or groups as being this or that way, others as upholding our beliefs and ideals or not, situations as being good or bad, and things as helpful or harmful. We believe there is safety in these classifications, but they encourage biased, limiting beliefs that need to be sustained and defended. We may also compartmentalize our emotional worlds which keeps intimacy at bay.

As mentioned in chapter 1, if our boundaries are too closed, we erect restrictions around our emotional lives to keep others out. We believe this keeps us safe, but it actually distances us from ourselves. To fully experience the love within us, we have to extend love outward to others. As we make the shifts within us to break down our barriers, this compartmentalizing starts to disappear, and the boundaries that we constructed start to deteriorate.

Joy, Inner Peace, and Authenticity

The quest for peace and harmony may seem overwhelming to those who are new to many of the ideas being presented here, but this journey need not involve years of melancholic struggle.

While I did have low periods in my life, I am an innately cheerful and fun-loving person. However, because of my frustration at not being able to create the loving family I so badly desired, I became very reactionary and angry at home and blamed everybody around me for not being and doing what I had decided they all should be and do and not fitting into the idealized fantasy I had created in my mind. Apart from that, I lived a good life.

Nonetheless, I have had seasons in the past twenty years when I felt the need to retreat from an active social life to dedicate more quiet time for reflection, being in nature, or attend uplifting workshops. As we move through life, we do have to be mindful of keeping our connection to Spirit strong. When it wanes, we may need to step back from life a bit. For most of us, this does not mean quitting life, but simply taking time to reenergize or refocus. Once we do, we feel lighter, more peaceful, and encouraged because getting reacquainted with our True Self gives us a clearer vision of our future. Taking this time also helps us reconnect to and discover, or rediscover, joy.

Inner Joy

I was once incapable of feeling real joy, of receiving, easily expressing, and freely giving love, but no longer. These all come easily now, as does genuinely celebrating the happiness and accomplishments of others. This internal shift can often occur without our being aware of it. At a small spiritual gathering a few years ago, a new acquaintance told me that my hug was full of love and joy—welcome words after a lifetime of not even knowing that joy was an option in life.

Joy and our healing are found in the *experience* of our connection to who we are. Every spiritual teaching I have come across guides its followers to an experience, not to words or a philosophy. Most religious teachers today also guide us to discover our personal relationship with God. It is the key to discovering joy and having peace and harmony in our lives. As we start to peel away the layers between our created Selves and our God-selves, we begin to access our ability to experience joy. *When we are able to connect to the joy held within us, our authentic selves can come forth.*

Authenticity

Being authentic is to live and speak from the heart. Having acknowledged and dealt with our inner fears and unconscious influences, our heart spaces are open and we are better able to express honestly and confidently to others. Gone is the need to protect what lies hidden in the recesses of our unconscious minds. We are authentic when connected to our True Selves, and as such we do not need to puff ourselves up, yield to popular attitudes or beliefs, or succumb to pressure from others. We are sure of ourselves and confident in our value and strengths, and we view others and the world from a clear, unbiased framework without the need to blame or judge. From this newfound clarity we can bring forth all that we were meant to be.

In *Self Matters*, Dr. Phil explains that your authentic Self is the "*you* that can be found at your absolute core." When we are connected to our essence, we are not defined by our jobs or the roles we play in life. Nor are we inclined to be who or what others think or say we need to be or do. Dr. Phil says that the authentic Self is the "composite of all of your unique gifts ... talents ... strengths and values."[16]

What Is Held in Our Minds Is Reflected onto the World Stage

What is held in our minds and our individual attitudes is reflected in society. The blame, judgment, fear, and hate individuals hold toward one another play out in society. The conflict and divisive attitudes these promote affect the world as a whole because whatever we send out into the world is perceived as how we want it to be, therefore more of the same will be created.

When we promote ideals or beliefs, or how we think people should be in the world by pointing out how others are wrong—even if we are sincere—doing so only endorses divisiveness: it does not promote unity or God's love. Our ideals and beliefs may offer *us* very valuable life frameworks to live under and support systems to help us and by promoting them we are doing what we think is helpful or right, but we can be erroneous in our interpretation of them or misguided in our approach.

This Shift's energy is flushing out all divisive attitudes or actions, and they will be exposed for what they are. If in our approach we judge others and focus on peoples' differences, we create conflict. If we do not change our methods there will be fallout individually, as when we create conflict it always reverberates back to us, sooner or later. We are also inviting more conflict and divisive attitudes into the world.

When we push too hard to make our point, or push *against* anything, at this point in our evolution the Universe will push back—there will be repercussions for us individually, and for the world. If we adopt Mother Teresa's attitude of *marching for peace, not against war,* we give energy to what we want, instead of pushing against what we do not want. Groups of people who act from principles or policies that are based in judgment, promote divisiveness, or hold any echo of me-better-than-you will also feel the repercussions of these attitudes.

We may not be able to connect the dots between what we put out there and what is happening in our lives, communities, or in the world, but if we are experiencing conflict in our lives or are upset by what is happening around us or in the world, we need first examine *our* attitudes. The issues may not appear the same on the surface, but the mechanisms and motivations are the same. Until individuals drop their propensity to blame, judge, and hate, the world will not change. As individuals choose to adhere to the qualities within the Standard, the world will start to reap the benefits.

Embracing Unity Consciousness

Not only is it time to reconnect with ourselves, it is also time to connect with others through the Oneness that we all share. This begins by focusing on the things we have in common with our family members, neighbors, and those in our communities—instead of focusing on our differences. We can then extend this to all others around the world. Unity consciousness is developed by better understanding those around us, but we can only do so when we understand ourselves. Change and growth starts with us—with our conscious choices void of any protective devices, limiting attitudes, and free of their resulting biases and judgments. Ultimately, everyone's journey is the composite of each individual soul's journey back to Oneness.

We also need to extend the Oneness of love and compassion to Gaia, Mother Earth, the living, breathing organism who is our home and who has suffered from the abuses we have placed on her physically. She also reels from the effects of the abuses we have put on one another, as the vibrations of the mistreatment of our fellow man upon her has affected her Emotional Body. We have to support those who promote being kind to our Planet.

On a global scale, we need to encourage our governments, and religious and spiritual communities to reach out to Humanity as a whole in an effort to end the maze of unfairness, abuse, conflict, and confusion. This is the time to recognize the interconnection between the different religions and embrace our cultural differences while at the same time respecting our geographical borders.

~

The most important message of this chapter is that acknowledging the *truth of who we are* while reconciling this with the *truth of who we are being* triggers powerful shifts within us. Once we recognize who we are within ourselves and offer the attributes of unconditional love to others, the *truth of who we are* and *the truth of who we are being* meet. We will then start to fully experience our personal healing.

True happiness is always available to us,
but first we have to create the environment for it to flourish.
—Sakyong Mipham[17]

We now understand how to begin to fully forgive our past errors, find empowerment, and bring harmony into our lives, while at the same time influence the world in a positive way. In the next chapter, "Along the Way," I will further explain how our journeys play out.

CHAPTER 4

Along the Way

For the soul walks upon all paths.
The soul walks not upon a line, neither does it grow like a reed.
The soul unfolds itself, like a lotus of countless petals.
—Khalil Gibran[1]

Rewriting Our Lives

Once we begin this journey, it is as if we are rewriting our life and starting at page one. All stories start differently. Some delve right into the most gripping details, while others slowly trace the characters and situations through time. There are an infinite number of ways to write a story, and an infinite number of ways to write and rewrite our lives. And so it is with our journeys to wholeness.

Regardless of how our journeys unfold, we can all succeed. Much like a novel, there is always a conclusion. When we reach that juncture, we take with us all the insight and inspiration we have gleaned on this journey to wholeness. However, our paths will not likely follow a straight and narrow line. They will be windy and sometimes bumpy. But all will unfold as it should! It may even seem at times that we are caught in a paradox. The purpose of self-examination is to expose misperceptions, false inner beliefs, and/or buried feelings, but as we undo these and our unconscious influences fade away, rather than find clarity, we may feel confused. We have cleared out past perceptions that are no longer relevant to our lives but have not yet fully replaced them. This confuses our being and may even cause us to become dysfunctional in other ways. However, this is only temporary until we anchor in new ways of being.

As we aim to find our center, we may replace passivity with aggression. As we start to acknowledge our feelings anger may surface. These different ways of reacting may bewilder us, leaving us feeling lost, or even depressed. That which was buried was affecting us anyway, or we would have been happy, peaceful, and living in harmony with little need to look for another way to navigate life. Some confusion during the journey is normal. It is actually necessary and even good.

Disengaging with Who We Are Being

Acknowledging and Confronting Our Feelings

As explained in chapter 1, paying attention to how we feel is vital to our understanding what is going on in our inner worlds, as this directly affects how we experience the outer world. When we acknowledge how we feel, we can honestly express ourselves and then make empowered decisions. However, we must learn to distinguish between feelings that are based on true desires from our higher Selves and those that are steeped in neediness or from unconscious influences, and which cannot ultimately be satisfied.

Even though our wants and desires may be based on false illusions they are not easy to abandon, as they have often manifested as the dreams of our lives. They are often so deeply anchored within us, that we often cannot distinguish between true desires from our higher Selves that create dreams which will ultimately satisfy us, or those we created to attempt to heal wounds. Nonetheless, this *is* how we feel at the moment, and it must be worked through, expressed, and never denied.

It is important to understand the impact of our past and how it projects itself into our present neediness and Perceived Needs, for only then can we overcome its hold on us. By confronting my true feelings, anxieties, fears, and traumas I had suppressed because I didn't have the tools to deal with them at the time, I was able to move from unconscious to conscious living. As a result I no longer allow misperceptions or illusions to cloud my judgment. I have more clarity of vision. For instance, I recently moved again, but this time not to run away from emotional entanglements but because of what better suites my life now. Therefore, I did not accumulate any repercussions of acting from unconscious influences.

Once we delve into an underlying fear, look it in the face, and recognize it for exactly what it is—an illusionary state brought on by unresolved past issues or influences—we no longer fear the fear.

Heightened Emotions / Uncharacteristic Outbursts

In reality, nothing can be truly hidden, so any buried pain, anger, shame, guilt, or inner conflicts do, in fact, affect our lives through our thought processes, attitudes, and behaviors, often showing up as misguided decisions. The residual effects of buried fears, thoughts, and emotions can be overcome, however as we acknowledge and allow any associated emotions to surface, such as anger, or address any shame, guilt, or inner conflicts, we may find ourselves on an emotional roller coaster.

Although this journey is ultimately about freeing ourselves from strong emotions and their outbursts, as we allow what was buried to surface, we may start to react strongly to situations, whereas before we may have remained calm or silent. We may now speak up for ourselves and even become aggressive if others try to deny us this right. We may find ourselves crying or becoming upset for no apparent reason. Those around us may be baffled by our sudden assertiveness or release of emotions. We need simply explain that these uncharacteristic reactions are caused by blocked emotions surfacing and that releasing them is an important part of our emotional healing, finding our empowerment, and becoming our Best Self. And although this may all seem counterproductive, it is a necessary step to ultimately creating harmony in our lives. So we need not worry that we may be attracting more negative experiences by the emotions we are now allowing, or the acknowledgment of our thoughts or what is in our mind as we navigate through it all.

In *Ask and It Is Given*, Abraham-Hicks tell us that our thoughts are "not like a loaded gun that may wreak powerful and instantaneous destruction. For although the *Law of Attraction* is powerful, the basis of your experience is that of Well-Being."[2] What was unexpressed was affecting us negatively, so allowing pent-up thoughts and feelings to surface removes their influence on us and makes room for the intended experiences of well-being to come our way. The emotional hiccups we may now experience are the result of us navigating through our created illusions on the road to rediscovering our true nature.

Moving from Disempowering to Empowering Feelings

Even though our ultimate objective is to free ourselves from highly emotional or reactionary states, or to allow for overt reactions if we have been too passive, whatever we feel at any moment in time is real for us. Highly charged emotions are attempts to deal with inner hurts, buried feelings, or unresolved conflicts. It is important to address the emotions, however they show up. We do not have to act on them, but we do have to acknowledge them and allow them to rise up in us.

For example, if we find ourselves responding in anger at someone or frustration at a situation, we should acknowledge how we feel, giving ourselves permission to feel it until it dissipates and we feel peaceful again. When we acknowledge and give our current feelings a non-judgmental space to arise, the unconscious influence that created them loses power. We can use self-talk to help us acknowledge the emotional trap we have fallen into, like the lighthearted "Oops, I did it again" I mentioned in chapter 3. This helps avoid any uneasiness that may come about as we allow for the acknowledgement, as well as prevent any inclination to infuse our beings with any guilt or shame. Later, insights may come to us that will help us to connect the dots between these reactions or emotions and their origins.

By acknowledging the thoughts or attitudes our Default Position or Protective Mechanism dictate, we create room for powerful aha moments, inner shifts, and within the understanding of the duality we have all been caught up in forgiveness of self and others. Below are a few examples of self-talk we can use to acknowledge attitudes or situations that arise to help diffuse any tendency toward guilt.

General Self-Talks*

> Self-Talk for Anger: I feel angry at xx person at the moment. I understand that this anger is coming from within me and has nothing to do with them. Rather than direct this buried anger at xx, I want to release it and its hold on me. I want to feel peaceful, not angry.

> Self-Talk for Frustration: I feel frustrated at xx situation. Scenario 1) I want to find peace in this situation I feel frustrated about, but realize I must do all I can to help it. I want to feel satisfied, not frustrated! Scenario 2) I understand that this frustration is of my own making and originates from expectations I created within myself. I want to release the power these hold over me. I want to feel satisfied, not frustrated.

> Self-Talk for Falling into Victimization: I am falling into victimization mode rather than expressing my feelings or confronting xx person or dealing with xx situation. I understand that this tendency is coming from within me, and I want to acknowledge and release it. I want to feel empowered, not victimized.

> Self-Talk for Jealousy: I feel jealous of xx. I now recognize that this feeling is not really about wanting what xx has or being who he or she is but an attempt to appease my inability to create what I want in life or be who I want to be. I want to connect to my own inner power, not desire that of another.

> Self-Talk after the Fact: I succumbed to anger, jealousy, victimization, or xx, and I forgive myself for doing so and release any associated guilt. Although I am glad I now recognize this, I want to catch these tendencies and deal with them as they occur. I want to move beyond unconscious reacting.

*These "General Self-Talks" can be downloaded from the book's website using the "Download" link and keying in the associated code found on the last page of the book.

Unmet anger and feelings of frustration keep us in reactionary states. Falling into victimization or jealousy is disempowering. By acknowledging any anger and giving our emotions a voice, we make room for feelings of peacefulness. When we understand our frustrations, they lose their hold on us.

In *Ask and It Is Given*, Abraham-Hicks offer an Emotional Guidance Scale that explains how we move up the ladder of our emotions, from the disempowerment associated with negative emotions to empowerment by choosing more positive thoughts and attitudes. They explain that the words used in this scale may not exactly explain how we feel but are a general guideline.

Emotional Guidance Scale[3]
(Highest to Lowest):
1. Joy/appreciation/empowered/freedom/love
2. Passion
3. Enthusiasm/eagerness/happiness
4. Positive expectation/belief
5. Optimism
6. Hopefulness
7. Contentment
8. Boredom
9. Pessimism
10. Frustration/irritation/impatience
11. "Overwhelment"
12. Disappointment
13. Doubt
14. Worry
15. Blame
16. Discouragement
17. Anger
18. Revenge
19. Hatred/rage
20. Jealousy
21. Insecurity/guilt/unworthiness
22. Fear/grief/depression/despair/powerlessness

The higher we find ourselves on the scale, the closer we are vibrating to Source and the happier we will be. If we start off on the lower rungs of emotional states, such as hatred/rage or revenge, we probably won't move up to doubt or boredom immediately. However, Abraham-Hicks assure us that if we endeavor to find the "better-feeling"[4] thoughts like reaching for thoughts of anger when we feel depressed, our set point will improve. We do not move from despondency to joy immediately: the goal is to find a thought that brings some sense of relief, and that we will feel better with even the smallest shift up the scale of our emotions. They also tell us that the moment we take control of our thoughts, decide to look for a resolution to a problem, or take action, we start to move up the scale and will feel encouraged, as being on the middle rungs of the scale feels better than being on the lowest. The premise of seeking a better-feeling thought is applicable to all situations in life.

Recognizing that getting from the bottom of the scale to the top is a slow climb, Abraham-Hicks recommend that when directing our emotions, we should try to achieve the emotion just above the one we are currently feeling. If we feel rage, then we should find a relieving thought that brings about feelings of revenge. If we feel anger, to find a relieving thought that brings about blame. If we feel hopelessness, to reach for a relieving thought that brings about optimism, and so on. Joyce Meyers often says that our progress may feel slow, but we can encourage ourselves by recognizing that while we may not yet be where we want to be in life, we also are not where we were.

So even though we are ultimately aiming for the highest vibration feelings and attitudes, on the way there we may experience new outward signs of emotions that make us, and those around us, feel awkward. We may even feel as if we are going backwards—but we are not. However, we are overriding buried emotions, so we may feel unbalanced for a while. It is helpful to look back at past journals and see how we have progressed. When I peruse journals I wrote three years ago, I realize I have progressed since even then. When I come across those that go back ten years or more, I can barely recognize that person.

Clearing Away the Cobwebs of the Past

As we start to clear away the cobwebs of illusion and their related expectations, we make way for astonishing changes. Most of us have lived half lives, existing at the surface level, as what was below the surface seemed too frightening to look at. Although we may have encountered moments of peace and even pure bliss, we returned to our comfortable superficial living. However, once we acknowledge, look at, and clear away the cobwebs of the past, we open the door to living in Peaceful Honesty.

Peaceful Honesty

As we delve into and gradually release buried hurts, emotions, and conflicts we develop an honest connection to Our Truth. We start to feel lighter, emotionally and physically. One morning a few years ago, I woke up with an intensely peaceful feeling. It was as though every breath I took that morning went deep down into the core of my being. I had recently acknowledged, accessed, and released much of my old, buried hurts and feelings, and my True Self and the inner peace it held was now able to envelop me.

> **Peaceful Honesty:** The feeling that is created within the depths of our being when we no longer have buried hurts or pain, inner conflicts, or their attached emotions. As we have acknowledged the illusions that we created, there is no longer a barrier between our consciousness and our True Self.

By the time this Peaceful Honesty came upon me that morning, I had unraveled many layers that lay between me and my True Self, and the peace that was lying beneath them started to reveal itself. Having practiced the lessons of *The Course* for a little over a month, I had fully embraced them, as I understood and had opened myself up to the purpose of the process: to look at and remove barriers to the truth within me. I felt the shifts within my being and the benefits quite quickly, and this allowed me to further acknowledge the misperceptions I had long-held about myself, others, and my life experiences. The fears these had created within me started to dissipate.

Most of you will not follow the same path and adopt the same practices I did, and I am not suggesting that you do. Nor will you have the same experiences. We all unfold in our own ways. However, when you release buried emotions and honestly look at what you have created, you *can* look forward to developing an inner peace that will stay with you.

What Letting Go / Releasing Can Look Like

The process of letting go of past influences and their manifestations can take many forms. It can simply be an aha moment of sudden clarity, an epiphany that completely shifts our perceptions or way of looking at life, a realization that connects the dots between an attitude we held and a life experience, or many small realizations that meld together to slowly shift our perspectives.

Letting go can be experienced painlessly as we easily step onto our new paths. Or we can find the transition difficult if we have trouble acknowledging and releasing our deeply-anchored attitudes, beliefs, and habits. Any of these letting-go processes can be marked with new understandings that can blend easily into our life patterns, or can be characterized by frustration, moodiness, and crying as we fight our urge to hold onto the security of the familiar.

A Gentle, Slow Letting Go

Letting go is most often a slow, gentle process. Once we open the door to allow buried emotions to surface, the hurts we may have experienced in life may come back to us in memories, giving us the opportunity to acknowledge and then release the attached emotions. This usually manifests as moments in which we become aware of events that affected us emotionally, one way or another. We have our aha moments of clarity, and allow the emotions attached to the events to surface. Acknowledged and now experienced, rather than denied, their effects are released. A deeper awareness may soon set in, with a new understanding of how the associated buried emotions affected our general perceptions and how we experienced life. Emotions associated with very deep hurts may need to be released more than once, and those associated with horrific events need a professional to help fully release their affects on us and in a safe and timely way. Regarding the surface issues, these happen as we go about our day. A simple "Ah, I now understand" is sufficient to recognize and release them.

For the more serious or deepest issues we have buried, we may have periods (an afternoon, a day, or even a few days) when we find ourselves consumed with emotions. Again, once we work through any arising anger, confusion, conflict, or guilt, the issue is released from our being.

This unearthing of the real cause of our neediness or reactionary states allows us to understand our frustrations and helps to free us from further engaging others as a consequence of our illusions.

A Quick Letting Go

Within this letting-go process, we may experience a moment of clarity regarding a specific situation. We may simply accept this and move on. Sometimes major realizations come in a rush, and our whole misperceived illusionary thought system rises into our awareness. This can completely throw us off kilter and we may feel off for a few days, a week, or even longer. While somewhat unsettling, this is a very important aspect of releasing. Our inner world is adjusting itself and this has major benefits. This is where the real healing begins.

Like all other unloving thoughts, words, or actions, judgment is simply a misalignment with who we are, thus we cannot perceive others as who they really are. Much of my personal misalignments showed up this way. Beforehand, and while doing *The Course* lessons, I became aware of many internal scenarios concerning my judgments and was guided to acknowledge and release them. For others it could be the tendency toward, anger, blame, control, victimization, or any of the other ways our unconscious influences play out.

There was a short period of time during this process, maybe a month or two, when my judgments seemed to be constant and more blatant than usual. This often occurs, as we have given permission for the manifestations of our misalignments to show themselves. During that time, I often felt like a horrible person, but by then I understood the process enough to realize that a big part of inner healing is forgiving our self for what lays hidden in the recesses of our mind. I usually used one of my catchphrases, like "Oops, I did it again," as I also understood the necessity of avoiding internalizing any further guilt, knowing my ego would jump on my misalignment and attempt to instill fault into my unconscious.

We usually have very little awareness of the subtle workings of the ego, so unless we do something to deal with our tendency to self-blame, we bury more guilt. That is why it is so important to *fully recognize, understand, and address* any propensity for judgment, anger, control, defensiveness, victimization, or other ways our misalignments manifest themselves. They always hold some associated unconscious guilt. On the surface some of this may seem contradictory to how Abraham-Hicks suggest we *allow* or *invite* anger, for example, to rise in us to overcome feelings of despondency. In those cases, inviting the anger in is a conscious decision aimed at feeling empowered and thus is part of our healing process. Spirit knows when we are ready to fully acknowledge a misalignment and will provide the necessary conditions for it to happen.

One Christmas season a few years ago just prior to the family gathering at my home I fell quite ill with the flu. Once the festivities were over and my houseguests were gone, I was finally able to tend to my illness, which led me to lie vulnerable in a state of physical weakness and yes, self-pity. As I sat there one evening, I realized in a moment of clarity the extent to which I had judged *everybody* and *everything* throughout my entire life. I was already acknowledging my tendency to judge as it came up and had learned to forgive myself when it surfaced. However, this realization hit me like a ton of bricks and left me emotionally drained for days. I understood the process of letting go, but also recognized that this was a *huge* breakthrough clearing away years and possibly lifetimes of misalignment. So I took advantage of this quiet time after the holidays to indulge myself and simply relax, take baths, watch old movies, eat leftover goodies, and take long walks. I was given the time and emotional space to allow for its full impact, and for the guilt and shame to surface, so it could all be released.

Within three or four days, as this cloud of shame began to lift, I started to feel better. Within a couple of weeks, my flu was completely gone, and I felt physically and emotionally stable again. Since that time, my propensity to judge has been substantially reduced, and as a result of acknowledging, releasing, and forgiving my past judgments, and any that came up during the process, fewer opportunities to judge present themselves to me now. Judgment is substantially reduced in my Life Matrix.

Acknowledgment of what lies buried in our unconscious mind is a powerful tool, and if we do it honestly, we can release what is keeping us distanced from Peaceful Honesty and becoming our Best Self. Humanity has inadvertently held on to these negative attitudes and behaviors because our history has perpetuated guilt, shame, fear, hate, blame, and projection, as well as promoted a vengeful, wrathful God rather than a loving and forgiving Creator. Therefore we have been afraid to face the *ugliest* parts of ourselves. This is changing, but guilt, shame, fear, hate, blame, and projection are still deeply entrenched within our cellular memories as ways of dealing with our fears and emotions, so it is of vital importance to address our fears and flush out the associated emotions that cause our negative attitudes or behaviors so we can allow them to dissipate.

While exploring your past, know that if you have experienced any horrific events, you do not need to deal with these on your own. Much help is available today through psychology or guided spiritual or religious practices. I highly recommend using a support network to deal with horrific past events. I have often turned to help in its various forms. Sometimes we need professional guidance to unlock secrets so deep we are not even aware of them. Releasing our emotions manifests in many different ways.

Crying

Crying is a wonderful emotional release. A friend of mine once related to me how she cried for days after a memory came back to her of when she was sick as a child and called for her mother, who did not answer or come to her. During this period of release, other related memories began to flood her awareness. She remembered many instances when her mother never listened to her, causing her to continually vie for attention. As these memories continued to surface, she cried off and on for days, while releasing the buried emotions attached to these hurts.

At some point in those few days, she came to realize that the frustration and emotions she had buried regarding her mother had affected her throughout her whole life. Consequently, when she was not listened to or heard, hurt and anger would arise in her, and she would strongly react to the perceived affronts. Until she released the emotions of the past, regardless of why a person did not listen to her, my friend suffered a considerable degree of hurt and her reactions created undue conflict with others.

Although volatile situations with others are never solely the responsibility of one party, she was able to understand and forgive her part. She not only made peace with these past conflicts, but is now healed of creating further issues for herself because of her mother not responding to her.

Yelling

During early formal releasing sessions in the early 2000's I would sometimes resort to yelling in my personal sessions. I yelled at my parents for being who they were, for my upbringing, and for the seeming unfairness of it all. I complained about how in my mother's family of eight, I got stuck with the crazy one. I allowed her mean face twisted in unacknowledged anger to surface and had it out with her. I confronted her for her passiveness. I met my father head-on and told him what I thought of his bullying attitudes. I punched pillows during this time to release my frustrations—especially over my inability to get my life together.

Around the end of January 2012, another year loomed ahead, and this book, which I had put my life on hold to write, was not coming together. I spent days yelling at the Universe, Spirit, God, or whoever was listening. I had a real hissy fit! I voiced my frustrations at how I had done so much work on myself and had diligently completed *The Course*'s 365 lessons—when most don't. I felt stuck in nowhere land. I laid it all on the table. I brought up everything I had made peace with in my life: my parents and upbringing, my divorce and loss of an intact family, other people in my life who had been controlling and bullying, as well as the loss of some of the finer things in life. I reminded them (the guides and helpers who are with me—we all have many) of how fearlessly I had looked at every hurt I had experienced, as well as every judgment I had unleashed in my life.

Yelling at God, Spirit, or the Universe may seem over the top, but sometimes we get *so* frustrated with life or know there is something just below the surface ready to manifest, but feel stuck and just seem to be flailing around without getting any traction. Releasing that frustration energy can serve to get the ball rolling. And it is not that uncommon. I once heard Jennifer Hudson say that in her frustration of not knowing where she was going in life, she threw herself on church steps crying out to God to help her find her way. Shortly after that she went on *American Idol*, and from then on her life blossomed.

We often are so stuck in this third-dimensional density that we cannot find our own way out—even when we do the inner-work, understand it all, and pray or make our desires known to the Universe. Sometimes there is so much static in our connection to Spirit or the Universe that our requests go out as whispers. But as we energetically express our frustrations and/or desires they get through, and help often comes along shortly thereafter. Within a few weeks after my hissy fit, I was guided to meditations that got me un-stuck and catapulted me into a shift that finally allowed me to start to get this book together, thereby moving me toward feeling empowered. So always stay mindful of where the Universe guides you and follow the cues.

Emotional and Physical Changes of Letting Go

All parts of our being are accustomed to heavy, low-vibrational densities because of the weight of our thought systems and the burdens we have accumulated individually, generationally, and historically. As we exchange heavier attitudes for lighter versions, we may experience emotional and physical symptoms, as all aspects of our beings start to recalibrate themselves. We can help the process along by respecting what our body, mind, and soul tells us, no matter what others may say. Our heightened sentiments are just a manifestation of us now being in touch with our emotions, while the physical symptoms are our body and mind's attempts to hold on to that which they have been accustomed to.

As we let go of any buried hurts, disappointments, guilt, angers, or judgments we have accumulated, disconnect from the fears and survival modes we developed, and start to extend the qualities of love to others, we are automatically embracing a higher level of spiritual awareness: we are awakening. Our bodies and emotional systems must acclimatize to our new vibrational realities. This process will become easier, and as more of us let go of our issues and our vibrations shift, we will also be helping Humanity with its collective shift toward a fairer and more egalitarian world.

Impact on Every Aspect of Our Beings

The effects of allowing the contents of our unconscious surface into our awareness can be transferred to our emotional and physical beings in many ways. To help us maintain our sense of balance during this process, it is important to avoid undue stress or emotional teeter-tottering. Practicing some kind of aligning process can help too. This doesn't necessarily have to be esoteric; it could simply be doing what makes us happy and feel peaceful, like enjoying the company of friends and lighthearted conversation, being in nature, or walking our dog.

Our unconscious minds are at work 24/7 helping us to clear the debris. Along with the insights that may come to us during the day, they are working at night to release what is held there. Alongside Spirit, our unconscious mind works diligently through the layers of buried emotions. Since our Protective Mechanisms are off duty when we sleep, a great deal of progress can be made during this time. Far more goes on beneath our conscious awareness than most can imagine, so heeding any internal nudges we may get to support our efforts is highly recommended—even if we cannot yet see a clear path to an outcome. We may experience this clearing in our dreams.

Deep or Even Horrific Dreams

During this time we may experience deep dreams, and some people may even experience horrific events in their dreams. This is simply the unconscious letting go of emotions associated with past events—real, feared, or imagined. The details of these dreams are often metaphors representing recent events in our lives, something we saw on the news, or an incident held in our cellular memory, so analyzing them is often fruitless. It is not recommend reviewing any horrific dreams.

At this time of the Shift we are releasing not only what has affected us directly in this lifetime, we are may also be releasing events of our past lives and of Humanity's history as it is all held in all of our cellular memories. For dreams we are curious about, we can, if we wish, ask Spirit to enlighten us. Perhaps there is a hidden message that may be helpful to us. We can also do some dream analysis. However, it is important to try to forget any highly disturbing, traumatic dreams. Should they occur regularly, ask Spirit to stop communicating with you in this way, back off from the self-examination practices for a while, and engage in activities that bring you joy.

If we wake up feeling tired, empty, or even melancholy in the wake of a bad dream or from inner work being done on us by the unconscious, we can alleviate these effects by mending any weakness created in our energetic centers during this process by reattuning our energetic field.

Energetic Attunement 1: Healing Torn Energy Fields That Deplete You

- First thing in the morning as soon as you awake (or anytime something depletes you), take a few deep breaths, and put your awareness into your heart center.
- Then gently make the request that any torn energetic fields be healed.
- Take a few more gentle breaths, until you feel a bit lighter or in a better mood.

We can do the above exercise in the morning or whenever we feel depleted energetically in any way. (For quick reference this attunement is located with the "Meditations, Visualizations, and Other Practices" at the back of the book under "Energetic Attunements." Visualization 1 below, (+ 2 others) are also located there under "Visualizations." They can all also be downloaded from the book's website via the "Download" link using the associated codes given on the last page of the book).

Physical Symptoms

By dismantling any negativity held within our unconscious minds, we ignite a flame that will burn away these adverse attributes. This flame will produce smoke, which can materialize as anxiety in our bodies and manifest as fatigue, headaches, digestive problems, aches and pains, disturbances in sleeping or eating patterns, or many other minor but annoying symptoms. They signify the releasing of emotional toxins within our beings and this affects our bodies. It can be helpful to visualize these bodily upsets leaving us.

Visualization 1: Bodily Upsets Leaving: This visualization helps with any mild physical manifestations during the dismantling process.

- Take a few deep breaths.
- Connect with the anxiety, ache, pain, fatigue, or state of discomfort.
- Create an image in your mind of the upset leaving: a hand signal to offer them up to the Universe, a visualization of them floating away in a balloon, or any other symbol that works for you.
- Then visualize a cord being cut from the events.

Since many of these physical symptoms can also be indicative of underlying illnesses, if they are serious or persist longer than what seems appropriate for the matter at hand, consult a physician. A few years ago I attended a three-week spiritual retreat where I was in altered states for much of the time. I later ignored fatigue and lethargy that persisted for months, thinking I was still reeling from the effects of being in those altered states. Although that may have been the case at first, at some point my thyroid acted up. Looking back, I should have listened more carefully to what my body was telling me as I would have avoided months of feeling bad.

Releasing unconscious influences can affect how we feel physically, but it should not throw us completely off. For instance, we might see changes in our eating and sleeping patterns, or sometimes feel dizzy or experience a lightness of being. We may have headaches or muscle pain, feel tired or listless, or experience anxiety. I had to be reminded more than once that it is often in times of outer *inertia* when the real inner work is being done. This is very hard to accept for any of us who are doers, as we sometimes feel as if we are taking two steps forward and one step backward, or even one step forward and two steps backward. This can be very unsettling and make us anxious. For a while it may seem as if we are straddling two worlds. Although we may appear to be lost, we are now on the path to finding a better way. There are just boulders and rivers to circumvent before we get there.

Our Steps to Transformation

A book that really helped me navigate through this process is Michael Mirdad's *You're Not Going Crazy ... You're Just Waking Up!* In the book, Mirdad charts our journeys as a five-stage transformation process:

- **Dismantling**: Everything about and around us changes: life can seem to be falling apart. This could come about because we have been stuck or stagnant for too long and our souls are trying to shake us out of it, or we may have bottomed out. It could also be an inner call to let go of our attachments to earthly treasures that are not congruent with soul growth.
- **Emptiness**: Feelings of loneliness, depression, and emptiness are common in this stage of our journey. It may now become apparent that the energy we invested in others, life, and the world around us was all based on satisfying ego-based illusions. All of this often makes us feel despondent.
- **Disorientation**: Facing a sense of confusion and self-doubt, we become disoriented. When the way we navigate life changes, it seems our life falls apart, and we often do not know what to do or which way to turn. Experiencing this disorientation teaches us to let go of our need to control everything. Mirdad explains that this level of surrender "is an essential characteristic of a healthy soul."
- **Rebuilding**: Willing to now trust and surrender to the ebbs and flows of this process of personal transformation, we are open to the new ideas and inspirations that are based on Spirit love rather than ego fear.
- **A new life**: As we "reap the obvious fruits of the soul's transformation process," we are able to embrace our greatness and *true* divinity. We now have overcome the limitations that characterized our pasts.[5]

As the Process Unfolds / Living in the Meantime

The journey to wholeness is a process. It is ultimately an upward spiral, but one with its ups and downs. As such, this period of transformation often brings with it a sense of uneasiness. We are letting go of what we know, but have not yet anchored in what replaces it. One day we will realize that we are transforming into new beings. However, in the meantime, we have to live life as happily as possible until we make the complete transformation.

Most of us live at least some of life "in the meantime." Even though these periods of waiting or of major change often make us feel unsettled, we can and must find some inner peace in our *meantimes*. Whether we decide to quit school or a job because it did not feel like our calling or leave a relationship because it was unsatisfying or even abusive, the in-between time before our next step is revealed to us is often scary. In her book *In the Meantime: Finding Yourself and the Love you Want*, Iyanla Vanzant explains that this "meantime" is often experienced as a "time of vagueness."[6] We may not know what to do with ourselves, as it will feel as if we are living in a gray area. We have left one world behind but have not yet fully embraced the next. We may not know what to do or have trouble making decisions. Despite our successes in coming to terms with our unconscious influences, we can often become confused as their hold on us is strong. I discuss our meantimes more fully further along in this chapter.

Spirit's Voice: Our Internal Guidance System

As we clear the channel to the Universe, our senses are heightened, and we can distinguish Spirit's messages more easily. They can come through in many ways: strong impulses, inner whispering, and through dreams. Spirit also sends us messages through other people, either in person, in a book, or even on TV, the radio, and through all forms of media.

How do we know whether we are hearing Spirit or God, our own mind conjuring up ideas based on unconscious influences, or our egos blabbering away and vying for attention? It takes time to distinguish what is coming from our egos and what is from Spirit. This is why it is so important to be able to distinguish the voice when deciding to act on our impulses or when passing on messages to others.

Spirit's Messages / Urgings

Being able to hear and understand Spirit's or God's messages has been a challenge since the beginning of time. These messages do not always come through in a loud voice, with precise instructions, or with exact time frames. However, there are ways to help us differentiate and understand whether what we hear, or think we hear, comes from a higher plane or is simply ego clamoring away at us.

Distinguishing the Voice of Spirit from the Ego's

The best way to distinguish whether it is Spirit or the ego communicating with us is to ask ourselves whether following through on the message would be helpful or hurtful to us, or others. Will it bring harmony or discord to all involved? Is there an urgency implied? The prompts we receive are often quiet and subtle, and at the beginning most of us may think it is our imagination playing tricks on us. If the prompt is insignificant but helpful to us or others, it is likely a communication from Spirit. However, if we can sense negative repercussions, or it comes with a sense of urgency, it is likely not Spirit, unless of course it is a warning concerning our safety, or if we have been ignoring prompts that may now be coming through louder.

My nudging and insights do not usually come as words, but as a sense of knowingness in my being. Solutions to small daily issues, as well as larger ones, just seem to pop into my mind or cross my awareness as a thought, idea, or insight. This usually happens at no particular or significant time. And because they usually come through subtly, it took a while for me to recognize them as messages from Spirit. They may answer a question I asked, be a solution to a concern I had, a reminder of something that needs doing, or guidance regarding my next step to take in life. But they *are* difficult to distinguish until we get accustomed to them, because they do not come as lightening bolts. From time to time, I have also had words, loud and clear, that were written on my heart. I don't hear them, but it is as if they are said on my heart, usually as a quiet inner voice, but a few times as a loud voice. It is important to understand and recognize how Spirit speaks to us and to act upon it if appropriate to the situation. We can ask for a sign, symbol, word, or feeling so that when messages come though to us we will recognize them.

A Three-Second Pause to Let Our Higher Self Come Through

We engage our higher Self when we let Spirit's voice come through. If we pause for a few seconds before giving advice, voicing our opinions, or responding, we will find that what comes through is usually a more loving and less judgmental or defensive response. This pause gives time for the quiet, accepting nature of Spirit to come into play, rather than the aggressive or defensive nature of the ego. The ego loves to interrupt because it enjoys and needs to express itself. It feeds on drama, urges us to be judgmental and defensive, and will jump at any opportunity to reveal itself. The unhealed ego Self is aware that it is weaker than Spirit and is therefore constantly trying to prove itself. Spirit, on the other hand, is patient and does not need to feel validated.

By adopting a three-second pause, we quiet our own chatty, defensive, egoist mind, while offering a selfless space for others to fully express their feelings and thoughts. When we are unsure of what to do or say, we can always ask for the gifts of wisdom and discernment, and the courage and empowerment to uphold these. Taking the pause before responding—a few quiet breaths is sufficient, will allow for Spirit's voice to come through, as well as create an environment where it is possible to pick up on cues and the real intention of the speaker. We are not all adept at expressing what we really want to communicate.

Spirit's Messages and Timing

A message from Spirit can cause us to want to act immediately. However, despite our enthusiasm, it is important to be sensitive to the timing of our actions. A few years ago when some of the concepts for this book were coming together, I wondered how I would relay these messages to young adults, who I assumed would never buy a book like this but might benefit from some of the concepts. Suddenly, an idea popped into my head: a movie! That made sense to me, as many young people enjoy movies and the visual impact of the stories. So I took it upon myself to start writing a script. It started out well, but shortly thereafter didn't flow well and I became stressed about it. After a while I realized that I had asked a question and gotten my answer, but I was never told to *do it now*. I just started doing it even though I knew in my heart that this book was what I was supposed to be focusing on at the time. Quickly jumping on the idea and attempting to create a script not only caused me undue stress, I also lost some precious time by shifting my focus away from this book.

Our Best Ally: the Little Voice Within

Whatever we call our internal guidance system—intuition, Spirit, Holy Sprit, God, or our higher Self, that *little voice* that speaks to us in our hearts will become more perceptible as we progress on our journeys to wholeness. When deciding what to do or not do, the little voice will guide us to find the answers that will serve us best. And although others may have our best interests at heart, they are not us and are not on our path; therefore, we should trust that *our* inner guidance is our best barometer, so long as we have discerned it is not our overactive ego-mind speaking to us, or are not acting from unconscious influences. That little voice is always with us, whether we are making a life-changing decision about family or our careers or deciding on less consequential matters. The important thing is to take heed of the inner voice when we hear it.

Listening to Persistent Inner Urgings

True guidance will compel us to follow it—even if we do not know where it will lead. It will often feel as if we *can't not* follow the promptings! Advice from loved ones or those around us is always helpful as it provides perspective and support, but our inner voice is the ultimate guide, and it is important that we learn to recognize and trust it. If we are guided to make life changes on our journeys, the promptings will be strong. I felt a strong push to go back to school in my midfifties to get some writing credentials. I knew that through all my inner work I had something to say, but I had no vision yet of how this would manifest itself, however the urge was very strong. Some people around me questioned the wisdom of my decision, and I had to defend it firmly, even though I could not yet articulate why I was pursuing further education in something I had never been interested in before. Every once in a while I checked with myself to ensure this desire and push was coming from a pure place and not one based on arrogance, self-importance, or pride. It felt like it was coming from a pure place, so I continued.

The Little Voice and Physical Sensations

A few years ago, I was faced with a difficult decision, but my entire being told me loud and clear that the timing of my decision was off. I actually felt it in my body. One of my sons was living at home and was neither in school nor working. His father, brothers, and many of our friends felt that I should push him out of the nest and force him to experience the responsibilities of the real world. From a dispassionate perspective, this seemed justified—tough love and all.

One day, after many futile conversations urging him to at the very least, find a part-time job, I acquiesced to the advice, as well as my own desire not to further enable him, and informed him that he would have to move out within a month. Although I knew he had no work prospects, would have nowhere to live, and transportation would be an issue, I had given him many warnings over the last year, and so I was firm in feeling he had to figure out his life. As I was lying in bed that night, something in my being felt distinctly off. I felt very uneasy. I hardly slept that night and actually felt sick. The little voice inside was sending me a message through my body. I am not even sure whether I asked for help with this situation as I lay there, but help did come the next morning.

The phone rang early, and it was a friend of my son's, offering him a job, and a ride to it every day. It wasn't a fancy job, but it bought us more time. The more we unblock what is keeping us from our True Selves, the clearer our channel and connection to Spirit, and important issues will be looked after for us. This job offer was clearly a gift from Spirit—it was too coincidental not to be. A year later when it was the right time for him to leave home, it felt right. He had been the only one still at home when my husband and I divorced, so was most affected by the upheaval in the family. I saw this, but others did not. When our insights are validated, we not only help ourselves and those involved, but also sometimes help others.

A short time later, I bumped into an acquaintance struggling with similar pressure from her friends and family regarding her son. Although the circumstances were different, everyone was attempting to convince her she should tell him to move out, but she was uncomfortable with the idea. By sharing my experience, I believe I gave her a motherly and fresh perspective they did not have, but that may have helped her.

Asking for Spirit's Help in Our Lives and in Navigating This Journey

Spirit is always by our side helping, guiding and encouraging us, as was the case with my son's timely job offer. As we reinforce our connection to Spirit by asking for help and listening to and acting upon the promptings, we strengthen our ability to recognize and receive guidance. We can ask for favors to make life easier for ourselves and for others, and we may get them. We can ask for help to untangle our issues, and what will be most helpful will come along: a friend who loves and supports us, a book, workshop, prayer group, CD or DVD series that will help us on our next step. There is more on our requests and prayers in chapter 6 "Words, Symbols, Rituals, Concepts, and Prayers" in the "Prayers" section.

Asking for the qualities that will help us in life and on our journeys—like wisdom, discernment, courage, and empowerment—is helpful in making our way clearer and less bumpy. These won't appear like lightning bolts but as little insights, nudges, or understandings.

Shifting Perspectives and Positive Life Changes

When we embark upon this journey we have the whole Universe on our side, whether we are aware of it or not. As our attitudes shift, we may start to experience moments of complete peace and well-being, and are able to feel more love for those around us. Things will also fall more easily into place for us, and little gifts can appear out of nowhere to encourage us.

Subtle, Positive, and Palpable Shifts. Having disposed of the heavy burdens of anger, blame, jealousy, and judgment, we are no longer bothered by little things, and we feel calmer and physically lighter. We will be guided to align with activities that energize rather than deplete us. These changes are palpable, and others will notice them in us.

Seeing, Hearing, and Sensing More Beauty. As we clear away emotional debris from around our energetic fields, the veil previously clouding our senses thins, and not only do we come to perceive others more clearly for who they really are, we will also see, hear, and sense more beauty in the physical world.

Shifting Interests. As our vibrations shift from denser to lighter frequencies, our interests also shift. Not all that seemed so important to us just a short while ago will hold the same value to us, and we will be attracted to new interests. We may turn from being very sociable to needing more quiet time or vice versa. We may replace activities that promote competitiveness for pastimes that promote harmony.

Loss of Interest in Gossip, Dramas, and People Bashing. As we become more consciously aware, we are less inclined to participate in situations that focus on gossip, or fuelling or participating in dramas. Our inner shifts will instead nudge us in the direction of understanding and empathy.

We Attract Less Conflict and Things Falling into Place More Easily. As we align more closely to our higher Self, through the Law of Attraction we will find a decreasing incidence of conflict in our life. We may have a thought that we need xxx, and shortly thereafter it is in front of us. If we feel slightly deflated from doing all this inner work, someone may show up and say or do something to boost our spirits. This happened to me often.

Grace, light, energy, and unconditional love are continuously being beamed to us from the higher realms and to the Planet as a whole. (I explain this further in the various chapters in Part II). We have the power to receive and anchor these gifts within our beings, as well as to manifest them in our lives. Spirit is always pulling strings in our favor, or as Joyce Meyer says, "God's angels get to work for us."[7] If we live wholeheartedly, completely in faith, and without fear, we open ourselves up to the energies and opportunities available and can take full advantage of them. To exist from a place where the floodgates of the Universe are open to us, we simply have to keep the airwaves open. We must honor the Universal Laws of Openness and Attraction.

Living in the Meantime

It's a time of waiting, the meantime is.
You are waiting for further instructions, more guidance,
additional support, mental or emotional clearance.
—Iyanla Vanzant[8]

How we choose to live life "in the meantime" will likely be the deciding factor to our happiness, because most of our lives are spent in the meantime while we climb the ladder of life, with all our and others' emotional factors keeping us feeling unsettled.

Joyce Meyer frequently suggests that we should not allow ourselves to become discouraged because we are not where we want to be but should instead be glad we are not where we used to be. This encouraging advice perfectly sums up an attitude that will serve us best regarding the issues we are working on. It takes time for frustration, impatience, jealousy, anger, blame, and judgment to abate; for depression or despondency to lift; for feelings of powerlessness to fade; and to overcome succumbing to victimization. It takes time for the manifestations of our new attitudes to fully come into being.

Being able to forgive ourselves when we falter and still find joy in living *in the meantime* is the key to living as God wants us to. Even though we came from unconditional love, in which joy is inherent, we are not attuned to it. So we have to be good to ourselves.

In *A Thousand Names for Joy*, Byron Katie tells us we need to mother ourselves—be the mother we need.[9] We were not meant to be unhappy, worried, stressed, and burdened with life's difficulties. We were meant to live in love and joy. Vanzant also tells us that as well as embracing what brings us joy, we need to have faith in ourselves as the "dreamer[s]," the creators of our lives, and faith that the things we dream for will eventually come to pass.[10] Until that time, to keep an even keel, we need to stay open and positive, and both Katie and Vanzant suggest that to do this we have to stay in the moment and go with the flow of life, not push against it.

So, as we are living in our *meantimes,* possibly going through major life changes, it may take special effort to embrace what makes us feel good and treat ourselves as a loving mother would a healing child. It is time to look after our bodies, our minds, and seek out what will make us feel good in our "meantimes."

Looking for Happiness

Whether we are exactly where we want to be in life or still living in the meantime, we can find our own happiness. Someone I know who became very successful once said to me, "I am lucky, you know," to which I quickly replied, "Luck comes to them who go looking for it." This person had worked very hard for his successes. Though I do believe that we are often lucky, I also believe that luck finds us when we have gone looking for it.

Robin McGraw concurs and is a true believer of the power of going after what we want and thinks we need to go looking in life for what makes us happy. In her book *Inside My Heart: Choosing to Live with Passion and Purpose*, she explains that this was the driving thought behind her wanting to lead a Brownie troop when she was newly married.

Robin wanted to have children, but timing and finances were an issue. Following her instincts, she picked up the phone to call the Girl Scouts of America and told them she would love to lead a group of girls. Robin became a troop leader to eight little girls. She loved being a Brownie troop leader because she was doing what she loved to do: being with children and making them happy. She said, "To me there's a huge difference between expecting happiness to come to you because you deserve it, and going out and getting the happiness you believe you deserve."[11]

Finding Balance and Being Open

As we start to shift and change, we still must maintain balance in our lives and remain open. Although at times we may become off-balance, as certain aspects of living require different degrees of output at various periods of our lives, but we must always return to a state of equilibrium to remain healthy: emotionally, spiritually, and physically.

The optimal point of balance will be different for everyone. Some people will always work hard as it energizes them; others need regular relaxation time to stay energized. While opening ourselves up to others and being accepting of them and their attitudes is our ultimate aim, we must take care to ensure that our own energetic bodies are not adversely affected by others' negative attitudes or differing energy levels. This process sensitizes us to our emotions, so until we have worked through most of the layers of our negativity, the manifestations of others' misalignments may actually bother us more, just like a smoker who has quit is more sensitive to being around smokers. It also sensitizes us energetically, so being around those with different energy levels than us can drain or stress us and we may begin to feel fatigued, agitated, or energetically flattened.

Finding Balance between Being, Doing, and Helping

To feel whole we must love and respect all parts of ourselves, and part of this is finding the balance between *doing* and *being*. When we are *doing*, we are usually using our intellect, or the left part of our brain. Even when we have no awareness that our *doing* is coming from our brain, like when we get trapped in business always rushing around, getting *so* involved in *doing* what needs to be done often leaves us no time for *being in the moment* or allowing for joy. We can be *doing* while *being*, but the doing must be done with reverence. Otherwise, business develops from a myriad of little mind decisions aiming to satisfy unconscious influences. When we are *being*, we are attuning to our higher Selves and engage the right part of our brain. This is where inspiration comes from. I discuss reverence in chapter 6, "Words, Symbols, Rituals, Concepts, and Prayers."

Intellect is supposed to be a tool that follows through on what our inner guidance inspires us to do in life. However, intellect is usually running the show, with the right brain and its creative impulses at the beck and call of the mind. As we gain control over our emotional landscape, our mind chatter automatically lessens allowing creativity and the life we were meant to bring about flow through us.

When we experience a temporary imbalance in our lifestyles, find ourselves worn out and scattered, or lose our ability to feel joy, we should examine what is driving us. Are we fueled by Illusionary Constructs and so involved in everyday life or focused on being successful that we are always *doing with no time for* just *being or enjoying the fruit of our successes*? In our desire to help others, do we lose ourselves in their dramas, or allow their negative energy to affect us? Are we temporality imbalanced by a push to fulfill our souls' purposes and ignoring the 50/50 rule I spoke about in chapter 2. Taking the time to investigate the real reason for imbalances in our lifestyles can help us to avert continuing in a direction that will completely deflate us and ultimately not serve our best interests, or those of the people around us.

As with many things, there is a paradox in this journey. The aim is to unify and align our created Self with our True Self. However, as we go through the dismantling of our created Self we may feel we are fragmenting ourselves, even though the end result is reunification. Along the way, we will have moments when we get a glimpse of our wholeness, but may then subsequently lapse into familiar negative patterns, until something arouses that vision again. To keep moving forward, we have to keep faith in the process, continue to practice self-forgiveness, remember to take time to just *be,* engage in activities that bring us joy, keep up the practices we chose to help us along this journey, and be mindful of keeping our energetic balance as the openness we are now allowing often invite others into our sphere.

Being Open While Keeping Healthy Boundaries

As we open spiritually and move toward a more heart-centered existence and before we have found our stability within the new Self we are creating, we may have trouble striking a balance between being open and having healthy boundaries.

In an effort to be open and compassionate to others we may inadvertently allow them to walk all over us, get pulled into their dramas, or become victims of their neediness or agendas. Conversely, if in the past we were so open that we allowed everyone into our sphere, we may now find that we put up walls and close off to others in an effort to find our balance. And because we are more open, exercising good judgment in all areas of our lives is even more important. As Ronald L. Holt explains in an interview with Julia Griffin, "openheartedness [requires] conscious mindfulness ... If individuals do not commit themselves to impeccability in their behavior (which leads to a natural integrity), they fall prey to the ego agendas of themselves or others."[12]

Keeping our boundaries healthy while remaining open is a fine line to walk, but a necessary skill to hone. When around those who may tax us, we can envision ourselves surrounded by a cheesecloth type fabric. This will filter out negative energies while allowing the good ones in. We do not want to be closed off to what is available to us from the Universe.

Tapping into the Universe and Its Gifts

Once our inner self-awareness increases, our etheric body/energy becomes more pliable, and an expansion of consciousness occurs. Through this expansion, we become more attuned with those around us and all that is held within the Universal Matrix: we become more cosmically aware. Auditory, visual, synchronistic, and mystical experiences may be heightened. Our intuition increases because we can now more easily tap into the universal bank of knowledge, often referred to as the Akashic records which hold every past, present, or future thought, idea, or insight. The Akashic records are further explained in chapter 7 "Science and Other Related Topics."

The more closely we are aligned to our True Self, the more easily we can see through the filters of our illusions, or those of others, and make decisions based on facts, not what false illusions offer us. Spirit starts working through and for us: for our small, inconsequential requests, to the everyday issues and struggles, all the way up to the larger life issues. However, we must remain open to Universe flow.

Ensuring the Floodgates to the Universe and Its Gifts Remain Open

Below are three illustrations, #'s 12, 13, and 14, (similar to illustrations 7, 8, and 9 in chapter 2), that show the differences between keeping ourselves closed, open, or somewhat open to the universal energies available to us. I have used the example of wanting a new job.

#12: Closed Off to the Possibility of a New and Better Job

Illustration 12: The solid mass here shows us how our thoughts and attitudes close us off to the possibility of getting a job we want. If we think we will never get it, lie about our qualifications, or are critical of others who are successful, we create this solid block to the universal powers that can put things in place for us to get this job or at least another one that would suit us.

#13: Opened to the Possibility of a New and Better Job

Illustration 13: The openness shows how positive thoughts and attitudes keep the pathways open to getting this job. If we are sure it is a good time to change jobs, know we are qualified, are confident we will get it or another suitable position soon, and are genuinely happy for others' successes, we allow for the flow of universal powers to make things happen for us.

#14: Static in the Possibility of a New and Better Job

Illustration 14: The dotted effect represents how our thoughts and attitudes create static in getting the job we are applying for. If we are anxious about leaving the job we have, doubtful we will get the new one, and jealous of others who have made career jumps, we may not be creating a solid block to the universal powers, but we are creating roadblocks to their ease of flow.

These three illustrations show us the difference between being aligned, not aligned, or only somewhat aligned with the precepts of the Laws of Openness and Attraction, and between inviting in the Law of Expansion by stimulating our energy field with optimism, hopefulness, and confidence or diminishing it with negativity, jealousy, pessimism, or uncertainty.

In illustration 12, the energetic flow is blocked because of the person's lack of receptiveness. The individual is operating from a place of trepidation and will likely have no or only limited success. I say *likely* because divine intervention is always a possibility if one's heart is in the right place or if it is the cosmic time for this to unfold for them, no matter how little connection there is.

In illustration 13, the person is operating from a place of complete confidence. The opening is expansive, and the Universe's available insight, vision, guidance, and support is ever-expanding. Again, timing is always a factor for our manifestations to come about, as there are usually others involved who have to align to their part or be prompted by those working on the other side for us.

Illustration 14 portrays how, while we may not be completely blocked to universal help, some worry, jealousy, or lack of confidence creates vibrations inconsistent with the outcome we desire. This undermines our request, as it confuses Spirit as to what we want and may throw the timing off. It all becomes a bit of a crapshoot.

Unfolding of Our Life's Purpose

Once we embrace the higher-vibration aspects of living, our existence takes on more meaning and our life purpose starts to unfold. It is important to keep our minds open, as being attuned to our True Self will open up life possibilities that we never would have expected. Finding our life's purposes is invigorating and makes us feel alive. I spent most of my life having jobs to either make money or to keep myself sane from the perceived drudgery of being a housewife. Never in my wildest dreams did I imagine myself writing such a book. However, as my journey progressed, much of what I was learning yearned to be expressed and shared and is now coming to fruition with this book. I have had periods of great excitement as I realize I will now be able to share what I have learned on my journey to peace, and possibly help others on theirs.

New Possibilities / Clues to Our Lives' Purposes Appear

My background gave no indication that writing a book, especially one explaining my journey to peace, was in my future, although there were a few subtle hints along the way that I didn't clue into at the time. Not long after I went looking for another way of being, someone who knew me quite well and noticed changes in my attitude said, "You should write a book." A few years later, as I was starting to make greater strides in self-understanding, I heard a woman on a PBS show giving a talk on self-development and improvement, and a voice from deep within me said, "I want to do that." Although I had no conscious awareness or desire that I was ever going to do something like that, somewhere deep inside me was a growing awareness that I would one day be able to communicate my newfound understandings to others.

I also had *no* conscious awareness that I would be reconciling spiritual concepts with those from Christianity, especially about Jesus and his message. I was not a churchgoer, except perhaps at Christmas, had no relationship with him per se, and did not use Jesus as a symbol of Spirit or God's love for us, like active Christians do. However, about twelve years ago another clue appeared. While browsing though a bookstore as I waited for a long flight to Vancouver, I noticed *Mary, Called Magdalene*, by historical fiction writer Margaret George. I had thoroughly enjoyed her *Autobiography of Henry VIII*, so even though I never would have gone looking for a book about Mary Magdalene, I bought it. It was as engrossing as the book on Henry VIII and pulled me right into the story: while I was reading, it was as if I was back in Jesus' time, and every ounce of my being ached to follow him. Later I realized that one of the reasons I was guided to the book was because I was beginning to feel that I needed to make peace with Jesus and his teachings, and reconcile them with the other masters' teachings.

At this time of the Shift we all have to make peace with the conflicts within us that were created by the misperceptions or misrepresentations within the religions we were born into. I now realize that my recent life-purpose has been to investigate and attempt to put some of the pieces of the puzzle together and to share my findings with others.

Energy and Peace from Finding Our Life's Purpose

Most of my life was characterized by stress, frustration, and deep fatigue. I used to notice other women who had less luxuries or time on their hands and with more difficult circumstances than me and wondered where they got their energy from, and how they stayed calm, positive, and even seemed happy. It baffled me! I have come to realize that it was my unconscious influences that kept me frustrated, stressed, and angry—it was exhausting.

In the final phase of putting this book together, I worked harder than I ever have, as I had *so* much material to go through, collate, edit, reedit, double-check, and refine. Even though I have been plagued by some fatigue from working many hours a day, many days in a row, or even through the night from time to time, generally speaking I have felt more energized and peaceful throughout the whole process than I ever did when working regular jobs. I am also very excited to have discovered something valuable I can do with the rest of my life. We do not have to do something society judges as *valuable* to have a happy, peaceful, and fulfilling life, but I personally had an inner knowing that I had something to do. This is just how it all played out for me. I now feel energized, satisfied, and confident in different ways than before, and I know a lot of this is due to finding my life's purpose, which developed naturally along my journey to personal healing.

In *The Purpose Driven Life Journal*, Rick Warren suggests that as our life's purpose unfolds, we can experience "incredible joy from knowing God's purpose for [our lives]" and such a sense of peace as we "learn the big picture— how all the pieces of the puzzle fit together."[13] I have felt that sense of peace while putting this book together and am excited to follow this through. I have also realized how all the pieces of the puzzle of my life, with all its ups and downs, fit together to bring me to this point of finding my life's purpose and the resulting positive feelings. Warren further explains that understanding what we are supposed to do in life not only makes us feel more contented but also reduces our anxiety levels and makes choices easier because we are more confident in ourselves. I have found that to be true with me.

Even though we are guided to our life's purpose, we still have to do the work required. Conscientious diligence is a must to reach or bring forth our desires and reach our full potential. No matter what the purpose is, whether working toward a diploma or degree, making a team, or earning a promotion, dedication and consistent effort are absolutely necessary. Spirit inspires us, guides us, and helps us along the way, but we still have to do the leg work.

The Process's Pitfalls

Avoiding the Tendency to Become Holier Than Thou

As we continue on this journey, we must be careful not to identify too strongly with the *idea* of our newfound selves. This is a pitfall of many seekers: rather than identifying with our Best Selves, we fall into the trap of identifying with the trappings of a *good*, or *spiritual* or *religious* person. We must be wary of identifying as a *better-than-them* person.

We may become *super*sensitive to others' negative attitudes and become annoyed at those around us who are not making the same shifts. We all have our own time lines. Our judgment of those not on the spiritual path or not coming from a place of love is actually a trick of the ego (Satan, or whatever term you use) to promote separation. A *we-are-now-better-than-them* mentality can inadvertently insinuate itself just beneath our conscious awareness—the complete antithesis of what we are trying to achieve. Any judgments of the attitudes and actions of those not yet on this road indicate that we may not have traveled as far as we thought.

In Gary Renard's *Your Immortal Reality*, his teacher Arten offers the simple affirmation, "You are Spirit. Whole and innocent. All is forgiven and released."[14*] We can say this to ourselves when we fall prey to judging another for acting in a way that is not of love, as it reinforces within ourselves the premise that we are *all* pure love but have simply forgotten, and that we are both forgiven for simply misperceiving who we are. The judging is as much a misperception as is the acting out. Remember, there is no hierarchy of illusions. We are either aligned with the concepts of love, or we are not.

I have found this saying useful and have used it to help waylay my judgments of others and of myself. As we use this or any other saying or tool that offers understanding, we heal our minds of their cries of judgment and separation, and through the power of Spirit we also heal the minds of those we are judging, blaming, or criticizing. Everyone's ultimate goal is to heal his or her mind of it's propensity to focus on ideas of separation, but we are all on different legs of that journey. Every contact with another person is an opportunity to support a notion of unity and Oneness, or one of polarity and separation.

Overzealousness

Zealousness occurs when we have an inspiration from within us that may or may not come from a pure place. This energy is looking to find expression. Whether it is birthed from a new idea, an alignment with someone else's idea, or any realization that has created a powerful aha moment, an intense enthusiasm often comes with it. As this energy passionately pushes through our beings it may gain momentum and become relentless in its need to be expressed. This can sometimes blind us to realities, others' feelings, or simple common sense.

Being overzealous can lead to conflict if we try to force our ideas upon others. We may also develop tunnel vision and perhaps be blinded to new opportunities. Zealousness is a wonderful attribute, as expressed passion can evoke sleeping passion in another, but only if it is expressed clearly, concisely, with maturity, and in a manner that the recipient will understand

and appreciate. Overzealousness can be embarrassing at best and dangerous at worst. When first embracing a spiritual journey, we are often prone to overzealousness.

Nicky Gumbel, narrator of the Alpha Course DVD series which is basically a Christianity 101, explains that when he first became a Christian in his early twenties and was experiencing all the wondrous gifts of the Holy Spirit, he could not contain himself and went around handing out pamphlets, exalting this wonderful new discovery. Nobody listened to him. He realized later that his unabashed excitement, void of mature, clear, and relevant dialogue, just confused and turned people off.[15] When we have gained enough maturity within the discipline and are passionate but composed when presenting it, we will communicate far more effectively than when we are overzealous and aflame.

Ego's Influence Still Alive and Kicking Even Though We Have Made Great Strides

We have reached Rivendell, but the Ring is not yet at rest.
—Gandalf, to Frodo[16]

Even though we may have made great strides in understanding and releasing our unconscious influences, the ego is not yet completely at rest. Not that long ago and after many years of working on myself I presumed that I was now a very self-aware and spiritual person, but had a big wake-up call that my ego was still lurking around in my unconscious just waiting to find me in a vulnerable moment. It was Christmas Eve, and my three sons and daughter-in-law (in their twenties and thirties) were at my home. We were all catching up, relaxing, and as the evening went on, we became engrossed in a Star Trek marathon.

The hours passed and I became very tired. Finally, we began to open presents. Someone passed me a gift with a preamble like "I hope you like it; we think you're into this sort of thing." It was a trendy and simple spiritual book. Slouched on the couch, something took hold of me, and I sat up straight and declared, "Oh no, no, no! This is not good. *I* write better stuff than this!" As the words tumbled out, I felt myself posturing as an arrogant, self-righteous I don't know what! Within moments I realized what I had said and attempted to backtrack and substantiate myself, but a chill had already taken over the room. The damage was done! Although I quietly apologize to my son before retiring and told him how mortified I was, I didn't sleep well that night at all and felt the impact of my words for quite a while. And I later apologized to the rest of my family admitting to them that I must not be as spiritually aware as I had thought. It was a humbling experience.

I realized my ego had jumped in to reaffirm its presence, to let me know that I should get off my high horse regarding being so spiritual. I did understand, however, that this was a huge opportunity to practice self-forgiveness. This is a very good example of what *The Course* explains as our egos being suspicious at best and vicious at worst. Our egos can turn around and slap us in the face when we are least expecting it, often when we are vulnerable with fatigue or susceptible for any reason.

Further Understandings of Our Journeys

Our Feelings: A Good Barometer

Our feelings are an indication of the health of our Emotional Bodies and connection to our True Selves. Although we ultimately want to transcend our feelings, until we reach that point, acknowledging how we really feel and discovering why we are experiencing life as it is now, brings understanding that allows us to adjust our attitudes so we can more consciously direct our lives. Here are a few questions from worksheet 22 that help us look more closely at what our thoughts and feelings are really requesting.

- Are my feelings, which influence my thoughts, words, and attitudes, in alignment with what I want or want to become?
- Do my feelings undermine me with limiting thoughts?
- Do I harbor feelings of negativity or jealousy regarding someone else's success?
- Do I *really* feel deserving?
- Do I feel that there is enough love, success, or goods to go around, or do I believe in scarcity and limitations?

Worksheet 22: Lurking Negative or Limiting Thoughts or Attitudes

If we still harbor any of these negative thoughts, attitudes, or limiting beliefs, we are still undermining ourselves. It can take years for negative or disempowering inner beliefs to completely lose their hold on us. Past familiar and generational attitudes are deeply entrenched within our being, and as much as we may try to avoid the traps our parents succumbed to, we often unknowingly adopt their attitudes and behaviors they sneak into our Life Matrixes, just as I explained earlier how although I hated my parent's attitudes I inadvertently adopted many of them.

Our Journeys: Humanity's Journey

As we continue to call for and embrace society's demands for a more loving and uncorrupted world and as our governments, educators, corporations, and associations start to listen and comply, a lighter, more-positive energy will be infused into our world. Our individual and collective journeys of shifting to embrace higher-vibrational concepts affect each other and work in tandem.

Individually, we unearth and deal with what we have unknowingly buried. Collectively we are calling for what Humanity is still doing that is not of love to be acknowledged and dealt with. Individually, the more we let go of the negativities that drive us, the more positive vibrations we are sending out into the world. Collectively, the more people stand up for compassion, fairness, and equally for others, the more these qualities will manifest in the world. Although most of us witness the worst part of Humanity releasing its negativities from a distance, knowing what humans can do to each other does affect us, even if only at an unconscious level.

At this time of the Shift, we are not only recognizing and letting go of our individual issues, we are also urging others around the world to give up their propensity for judgment, anger, hate, cruelty, greediness, and unfairness. We help in the way we feel guided to, however getting caught up in the drama of it all will have a negative effect on us, as well as on Humanity's progress, as we will invite more drama into the world. We must remember that just like us, Humanity as a whole has also been caught up in its collective illusions of lack, fear, and separateness.

We are often so unaware of the driving forces behind our feelings, attitudes, and behaviors, but the more aware we become of our emotional makeups and the hold our unconscious influences have on us, the easier it is to change our trajectory. It also helps to be aware of where we are on the Emotional Guidance Scale, trust the process, and as Abraham-Hicks says, tell ourselves that we are "doing [our] best to make the best of it."[17]

Points to Staying on the Good Path / Keeping the Process Going

- Keep releasing sessions light: Do not overanalyze or wallow in our pasts—**do not get stuck in the darkness.**
- Stay aligned to your True Self: Continue to observe chosen practice(s).
- Develop a short aligning practice: Develop a thirty second to one minute practice to be repeated several times a day that will calm your being. Nothing formal or esoteric required.

- <u>Tap into the love and joy within:</u> Finding and embracing love, beauty, and joy in everything we see and do is our raison d'être.
- <u>Being present: living in the Now:</u> Attuning to the experience at hand and reveling in every moment as it unfolds helps us discover the joy of just being.
- <u>Stay mindful:</u> Continue to practice conscious mindfulness. Practice becoming aware of when you are misaligned from your True Self.
- <u>Practicing nonresistance; loving what is.</u> It is within the neutrality of allowing, with no judgment or resistance, that we find inner peace.
- <u>Dealing with fear as we change:</u> Changing the inner world we created to protect ourselves *can* be scary.
- <u>Find words to explain to those around us:</u> As our new attitudes may confuse or frighten our friends and family, carefully choosing our words when attempting to explain ourselves can be helpful.*
- <u>Use Visualizations:</u> Visualizations can help us get unstuck from stress, negative influences, or reset our mind-set or path. Chose your own or use those located at the back of the book.*

These 10 points are further expanded upon in article "Points to Staying on the Good Path / Keeping the Process Going" on the book's website.

*At the back of the book under "Meditations, Visualizations, and Other Practices," you will find the above quotes and affirmations in the "Affirmations and Self-Talks" section as well as the link to Inelia Benz's fear-processing exercise in the "Exercises" section. They can also be downloaded from the book's website via the Download link using the codes located on the last page of the book.

~

Our current issues represent what Spirit has deemed is necessary for us to release at this important time of the Shift. Releasing unconscious influences with the intention to live consciously is a huge undertaking, but Humanity was never really ready to fully embrace the shifts before. But we are now primed to do so. It is therefore a *very important* and *sacred* undertaking.

It takes courage to look deep within at long-held beliefs and perceptions and be willing to acknowledge that some of them may be based on false, illusionary premises we unknowingly hold that are destructive to us and to others. To then endeavor to do something about it is the most valuable and sacred mission we can pursue. If everyone on the Planet were to do this, there would be no war, no hatred, no injustice, and no lack.

Although our journey is not about changing the world but about changing what is in our minds, as we do so our attitudes change. These attitude shifts affect others; they in turn affect others, and so on. As we all change, the collective energy of the Planet changes because not only do our individual vibrational shifts affect the world's vibration, our attitudes manifest concrete changes, like bringing more compassion, acceptance, and fairness into the world. And so, with every little attitude shift we *are* changing the world for the better.

While our old self-protection mechanisms supported separateness and the *me-against-you* paradigm, we are now becoming sufficiently confident in ourselves and the world around us to adopt an *us* paradigm. Our attitudes and actions will start to reflect this and altruism will start to override self-centeredness. We start to shift from self-centered to unity-centered and become more attuned to the *good-of-the-all* rather than the *good-of-the-few* outlook.

This allows us to open ourselves up to others and therefore more opportunities. This can greatly expand our life experiences. No longer affected by what others want us to do or be, we have no need to uphold a self-image shaped to conform to society's rules or limitations put upon us by others. We are free to be who we came here to be—in all our glory!

> *The Dude abides nowhere,*
> *which is the same thing as saying the Dude abides everywhere.*
> *The Dude is not attached to some self-image, identity or life narrative.*
> *Since he abides nowhere, he is free to abide everywhere.*
> —Bernie Glassman[18]

Now that we understand more about ourselves and our journeys, in the next chapter we will examine how and why our relationships are so important and intertwined with our return to wholeness.

CHAPTER 5

Relationships

*Relationships are the experiences in which we work out
our false notions, skewed perceptions, fears, and judgments about love.*
—Iyanla Vanzant[1]

Whether with a family member, a life partner, or simply a friend, most relationships are fraught with expectations. Sometimes we are aware of them, but often the expectations we have of others are unconscious and buried deep. These play out as we try to satisfy our neediness, Perceived Needs, and Hidden Agendas. Even expectations that we actually understand may not be properly expressed and thus can cause major upsets. Our misalignments with the Standard reveal themselves in our closest relationships. Unless we understand and work to neutralize our unconscious influences, they will play out in our primary relationships, creating conflict and havoc in our lives, like two out-of-control trains rushing toward each other head-on.

The expectations we have of ourselves and others are rooted in our ideas of happiness. But there is no right or wrong way for relationships to work. Every family, friendship, romantic pairing, social encounter, and work relationship is different. The key to creating harmony in any relationship is to embrace each person in our lives for who they are rather than what we expect them to be. Unconditional love, trust, flexibility, appreciation, and forgiveness are of the utmost importance and will allow relationships to develop into true partnerships or kinships. However, as our relationships develop, they will continue for a reason, a season, or a lifetime, as the saying goes. They are not all meant to last forever—even couple relationships. So when relationships do end it is important to release the emotional attachment so that we can move on to our next phase of life.

Healing Our Relationships Is Our Salvation

Years ago, I heard somebody say that we are here to learn how to relate to one another within our relationships. This statement reverberated through every cell in my body, like an earthquake.

At that time, well before I was aware of the Laws of Attraction and Cause and Effect, most of my relationships were fraught with confusion, inconsistency, and insecurity. I just thought *everybody else* was difficult. Unless a person was feeding my neediness or Perceived Needs, which were in a perpetual state of flux, I was disappointed. In all my familial relationships, my insecurity dictated either a needy or defensive attitude. My Emotional Body reacted to the perception that those around me were not fulfilling me, and I was often frustrated, hurt, or angry with family, friends, and even coworkers for not playing along with me.

Years later as I studied *The Course*, I again came across the concept that we are here to learn how to *relate* in our relationships, but by that time I had enough understanding of perceptions to identify with it. One of the main principles of *The Course* is that we heal our split minds by choosing the auspices of love over fear, and we do this by making peace with our perceptions about all our brethren. However, it is in our closest relationships that we are continuously challenged to choose. Our salvation lies in healing all ideas of fear and separation. Within this separation paradigm, the ego loves the word *should*.

The Big Should

Compromises are necessary in any type of relationship. So long as both parties can speak their minds and sometimes have their desires met, all will be well.

As I explained in earlier chapters, *should* is a very dangerous word and is especially harmful within our close relationships. We all know that we *should* eat well, exercise, get enough sleep, and avoid unhealthy mental, emotional, and physical habits. However, when we tell people that they should or should not do this or that, we are saying that what they feel or believe at this moment in time is wrong. We invalidate where they are on their paths. We are also taking away the opportunity for them to experience how that action or attitude will affect them and to learn from their own mistakes.

In *Change Your Conversations ... Change Your Life*, John D. Knight suggests that we ought "only give feedback and opinions when asked and be mindful in doing it. Telling someone they are flawed does not help them and does not extend the hand of compassion. If someone asks for help or guidance, then you can support them in ways they can feel empowered and useful."[2] We have to check ourselves to ensure it is not our perceptions, projections, or limiting beliefs coming through, but genuine caring, concern, and love, and the desire for the other to find *their* Best Self. I once heard a psychologist say something to the effect that it is almost impossible to correct someone without shaming him or her.

So when giving advice or aiming to help someone we have to check our attitude to ensure we come across lovingly, not critically, and be wary of our true intentions. We must not be invested in their heeding our advice;

138

otherwise we are feeding our neediness or projecting our beliefs or desires onto them.

The Cavern between You and Others Is in Direct Relationship to the Cavern between You and You

We can certainly live happy and fulfilling lives without being completely in touch with our True Selves, enlightened, or fully aligned to Source. In fact, most of us do. This is why some hurt and conflict exists in most relationships. Nonetheless, if we navigate the conflicts that arise with compromise and compassion, keep our disparaging emotions at bay, forgive how the other's misalignments show up, and accept their idiosyncrasies, we can easily live a harmonious life. It helps to be aware of our unconscious influences, or at least make peace with how our misalignments show up, otherwise we are living superficially within ourselves, and thereby can only relate superficially to others.

Superficial relationships develop when our injured inner Selves fear being exposed. Not having dealt with what lies beneath, we are not in touch with our own feelings. We hold others at arm's length and may not be able to experience true intimacy with another. When we have unresolved issues, we may feel any intimacy will expose what is hidden, so we are wary of sharing our true feelings. We are also defensive, as simple comments may feel like affronts to our created barriers, so our Protective Mechanisms are on alert. Unresolved past issues may have created inner anger, resentment, or even birthed selfishness, and we may be ashamed of these feelings and fear they will be discovered. Our relationships are affected by our presumed need to maintain our masks of fear. Any feeling that our cover is in jeopardy puts us into a protective mode and an emotional gap between us and the other is inevitable.

The Way How-It-Should-Bes Undermine Our Happiness and Thwart Creativity

The decision to be happy is our own. We often find it easy to complain about what others are or are not doing or what life has thrown at us. But we ultimately do have the ability to be happy—if we let go of some of our *how-it-should-bes*. We just have to shift from a protective, conflict mode to an allowing mode. For example, many young couples have preconceived ideas of what married life will be like and become jolted by the difficulties that arise when sharing a life together. This can include anything from raising children to salaries and conflicts with in-laws. Ultimately, our notions of what *should be* get in the way of *what is*. When we are under the influence of the how-it-should-bes created by past authority that unduly influenced us or by our unconscious influences, we not only undermine our own happiness, but can also put a damper on the creativity and passions in those around us. You can revisit Worksheet 17: False Perceptions, Their Beliefs, and How It Should Bes.

To be happy, live a conflict-free life, and encourage the passions and spirit of creativity with those we are close to, we can change our attitudes and make compromises much more often than we may think. If we allow things to flow rather than trying to maneuver what we want into being, we can avoid the conflicts that too much pushing and shoving creates.

Communication

Communication is paramount in all relationships, but most of us have never learned to communicate calmly and honestly. Being able to communicate properly is vital to our individual happiness. When we allow ourselves to be open and vulnerable and can discuss what is held in our hearts, our feelings find a voice and are validated, bringing us closer to our True Selves.

However, we must be cognizant of the other person's comfort level and style when talking about intimate feelings or touchy subject matters. Some of us can easily express ourselves, while others are not so comfortable and want to discuss with as few words as possible. We must aim to choose our words carefully, making sure we are addressing only the subject at hand. We must allow others to fully express themselves and not put words in their mouth. Discerning if they are looking for a solution to a problem or just an ear to listen is vital.

Tone and Body Language

In any discussion or disagreement, whether with a romantic partner, a parent or child, a sibling, a good friend, or a coworker or boss, the combination of the words, tone, and body language sets the climate of the discussion and conveys the message. We are all different. We have different personalities, backgrounds (even siblings in the same household often experience life differently), fears, needs, and desires. Everyone absorbs the subtleties of communication differently, so being aware of the *full* impact of our words and tone in our communications with others helps to avoid hurt feelings and misunderstandings. Regrettably, we are all too often unaware of how we come across to others.

Honesty, Timing, and Creating a Safe Haven When Communicating

We must be honest when something is bothering us and encourage others into conversation. Whatever needs to be said or whatever truth we want to unveil, sandwiching something negative with positive overtones is always beneficial. For example, if a friend completely forgets to meet you for a lunch date, rather than bluntly saying, "You forgot about our lunch," suggesting the other person is in the wrong, you can let the friend know he or she forgot without adding more guilt to what he or she probably already feels by saying, "I love it when you take time out from your busy day to meet me for lunch. I would love to reschedule in a few days, if you have time" Using positive words and a nonaccusatory stance will enhance the communication between you and the recipient and thereby enhance the trustworthiness of the relationship.

Timing is also important when communicating with others, and unless there is an urgent matter, sometimes it is be best to wait for a more opportune time. If we try to deal with something without considering our timing, we run the risk of creating conflict. If we catch others when they are distracted, exhausted, or running out the door, they may become impatient, and we may come away with hurt feelings.

We also have to create a safe haven when communicating with our partner whereby each respects healthy boundaries so that both can explore and communicate their true feelings without feeling hurried, criticized, or belittled.

Observing Ego

We are often so unaware of how our attitudes, tones, and body language make us appear. The psychological term *observing ego* is the suggestion that we practice stepping back and looking at ourselves when we are with others, like looking over our own shoulders. We can then see how our egos are projecting themselves. We can also check ourselves after the fact. Observing ego can help us discover the cavern that exists between *who we really are* and *who we are being*. If we have close enough relationships to others and have agreed upon reciprocal reminders, those people can also let us know when we are acting from our misalignments. When we have safe havens of communication with others, they can also help us rise above any of our fears or anxieties that show themselves in the way we present ourselves.

People Can Help Us Get Out of Ourselves

People are in our lives to help us heal and find balance. Some may be there just to pull us out of a momentary rut or to help us relax; other times people are there to support us through difficult times; or to lean on as we overcome deep-set fears and heal our misalignments. However, because people can push us to do things for self-serving reasons, we have to use discernment if we feel pressured to do something we are not comfortable with. Of course, this is not always the case, as the other may have an impulse to offer a suggestion where we extend ourselves in a way that will help us let go of a fear and build self-confidence, but that feels uncomfortable. Being receptive to another's suggestion can sometimes help us *get out* of ourselves.

In my twenties, I suffered from panic attacks. They manifested mostly when I was out of the house, so I avoided interactive or social situations in which I could not easily depart without embarrassing explanations. More than once I remember being convinced to go out and get out of my shell. When I went along with the invitation, I usually found myself having a wonderful time and was able to overcome some of the anxiety that characterized that time in my life. Left to my own devices, I would likely have succumbed to my anxiety and given in to the desire to stay safe at home, further anchoring the fears within my psyche. It is prudent, however, to practice discernment when others urge us to do something that may not "feel right," as they may be projecting their desires upon us. Panic attacks can undermine our ability to feel safe, because when they come upon us, we feel vulnerable and fear a loss of control. I discuss panic attacks more thoroughly in chapter 8, "Health and Healing; Death and Dying."

Balancing Our Male and Female Energies

As we start to align to our True Selves, what are known as our male (dominant, builder, protector) and female (passive, communicator, and nurturer) energies will start to balance out. True equality of the sexes will also emerge. Throughout Humanity's history the negative aspects of our male and female energies have prevailed over the positive ones. Those with the dominant, builder, energy have often been fuelled by aggressive tendencies and wielded control over those with a passive, nurturing, energy, who in turn have fallen into victimization attitudes. This has caused much stress, conflict, and abuse for the passive individual, creating an imbalance that perpetuated itself throughout society and our history.

We all hold male and female energies within our beings, however, they have nothing to do with being in a male or female body. They are energetic vibrations. Over time both genders suppressed the parts of themselves that did not match what society dictated in an effort to protect them. But part of becoming whole is to encourage both to shine forth once again. The Shift is encouraging us to find this balance between these two forces. However, while finding our balance with aggressive and passive tendencies, there may be some fluctuation between both.

I have an outgoing personality, and while I am not naturally aggressive, I have been emotionally forceful when I felt that my back was up against the wall. As my unconscious influences drew me deeper and deeper into frustration, I became loud and interrupted others a lot. Not having a good connection to my True Self and unable to get my neediness satisfied or Perceived Needs met, my frustrations needed to find a voice. In fact, once I started to address my unconscious influences and allowed them to surface, it seemed I got louder and interrupted even more. I sometimes thought of myself as *girl interruptus* and often beat myself up over this. Until we find our balance, when what was buried is acknowledged and we allow it to surface, it often stresses our being and this can manifest in many ways. For me there was a need to continuously express myself as my voice had been suppressed for so long; for others it may be anger that comes up. Following my spiritual practices helped, but it took a long time for this manifestation to abate.

Reconciling Traditional Male Builder and Female Nurturer Energies

Throughout history we have encouraged these qualities within the sexes and most have endeavored to embrace them, as not doing so often created difficulties for them. Traditionally, most females aiming to find their empowerment have had to go against the flow and their efforts were most often undermined, to say the least. Males embracing their more gentle sides were belittled, criticized, and marginalized.

The degree to which the standard male and female qualities manifest within us is influenced by our individual personalities, as well as by our sexual orientation, but not necessarily. Throughout history some heterosexual females' personalities have held aggressive, builder qualities, while some heterosexual males' personalities have held gentle, cooperative qualities. If society had been more evolved and individuals balanced emotionally and spiritually, the different ways males and females expressed themselves would not have created problems for them. And the differences between the traditional male and female energies would have been recognized as complementing each other, and all qualities, however overt or covert, appreciated for their value. Balancing our male and female energies creates a win-win situation.

As we answer the call of the Shift and heal the separateness that our egos adhere to and start to exist aligned to what is held in The Standard, our male and female energies will automatically start to balance out. This will serve as a fine-tuning of the positive aspects of the strengths within each. We will be able to maintain the strong, creative, positive elements of male energies while avoiding a tendency toward aggression or need for control. Similarly, we will be able to maintain the more subtle, nurturing, positive elements of female energies while remaining empowered, but without falling into neediness or victimization. Those in female bodies will be able to tap into the builder, protector part of themselves if they wish to, but without needing to employ aggressive tendencies, while those in male bodies will be able to tap into the communicator, nurturer parts of themselves without falling prey to victimization.

This moving towards more balanced male-female energies than past generations is all part of the Shift we are undertaking. Eventually we will become androgynous, although it will take eons for this to come about. In the meantime, men will continue to explore their inner emotional worlds and feel inclined to engage in childrearing, but may still maintain some of the traditional protector qualities. Women will be encouraged and supported to become educated, be able to support themselves, and find their empowerment, while at the same time many will still fully embrace their deep, nurturing natures. As the concepts of equality become more mainstream and we all move closer to our centers, the balance of male and female energies will become part of our DNA and the issues surrounding our different energetic ways of being or our sexual orientation will disappear.

Eastern religions and many within the spiritual community understand that to attain the required balance to return to the Oneness we have all had lifetimes as males and females, aggressors and victims, heterosexuals and homosexuals. (There is a whole section on homosexuality at the end of the chapter). In the meantime, we still have to manage who we are being. Calling up archetypes can help us to find this balance.

Using Archetypes Helps Us Balance Our Male and Female Energies

There have been times on my journey when I recognized that my emotional patterns were not serving me well. Sometimes I may have been too passive or needy while at other times too aggressive. To help me attain emotional balance, or balance the male and female energies within me, I often used visualization and worked with symbols or archetypes. Calling these up allows our minds to translate and our beings to anchor in qualities we want to embrace that might otherwise get buried within lofty spiritual concepts. To help release passive tendencies that may be limiting us we can use typical strong/warrior role model archetypes, and call up gentle/loving archetypes to release aggressive tendencies that are hurting us and our relationships. When our efforts to access a higher awareness are sincere, whatever we need to help us achieve that will work. I further discuss symbols and archetypes in chapter 6, "Words, Symbols, Rituals, Concepts, and Prayers."

Children

Although children are born into this world totally dependent on adults for their physical and emotional survival, they have far more innate knowledge than most people give them credit for. We all came into this world with blueprints of what our souls wish to accomplish and experience, and if we follow these blueprints we will find our souls' desires and become our Best Selves. However, the influences surrounding us as we grew up often infused limitations into our beings. In *The Four Agreements*, Don Miguel Ruiz suggests that children come here with completely pure hearts and that we actually "domesticate" them by unknowingly guiding them within the framework of what society dictates.[3] However, this is not entirely true.

From a highly spiritual perspective we would not manifest on earth if we did not have *any* lessons to learn or could easily overcome the dictates of others' influences, but we are born with the *potential* to remain pure and stay true to what our soul wants to bring forth. One of Abraham-Hicks' main philosophies' regarding children is that we should just leave them alone. We do this with the understanding that they have what they need inside of them to find their own way in life: they know what they need to be happy and fulfilled. Not only that, we can learn a lot from our children!

As well as being closer to Source energy and not being corrupted as much as we have by society, our children, like each generation before, have shown up more evolved than the last. We should listen to what their hearts want to bring forth for themselves, as well as to the world around us. We may know our children better than anyone, but God knows them best. Because of the atmosphere, influences, and restrictive attitudes most of us unknowingly allowed infiltrate into our Life Matrixes from society, we often pass on limiting attitudes and ideas about how life has to progress that could get in the way of our child bringing forth what was intended for him or her. We still need show them how to live by our good examples, guide them towards conscious choices based on integrity, and provide them a safe and healthy environment to grow up in. With everyday living there is always the necessity for ground rules so we do not live in chaos, but from a heart standpoint we must allow and encourage our children to listen to what their soul is whispering to them and find their own inner power.

Children do not belong to us and are not there to make us feel good about ourselves when they succeed. Children are loaned to us; and we are their custodians. Besides feeding, sheltering, and keeping them safe, we are to love and nurture them, and if we are supportive in allowing them to develop their innate gifts and guide them toward finding *their* lives' purposes, they will thrive. When we push them toward goals *we* believe they should have, we harm their ability to find their true, innate purposes in life. Connecting to our true purposes creates our Best Selves.

Young Children

Healthy Emotional Growth in Young Children

Based on her observations from a tribe in South America, Jean Liedloff's philosophy and article "Who's in Control? The Unhappy Consequences of Being Child-Centered," based on her book *The Continuum Concept*, suggests that the physical touch of babies by the adults as they carry them around until they are ready to crawl is of the utmost importance to the baby's development.[4] In *The Five Love Languages,* Gary Chapman concurs with Liedloff and says that "babies who are held, hugged and kissed develop a healthier emotional life than those who are left for long periods of time without physical contact."[5] However, babies also need to develop a healthy individual emotional growth apart from their parents.

Liedloff also tells us that even though constant touch with babies is vital for their emotional growth, constant fussing is counterproductive. Continual attention to their every whim can reinforce a focus on the Self and their discomforts, which deprives them of being witness to what real living is. She explains that they need to see adults doing regular adult things and that depriving them of this will short-circuit their development. They will lack the inner self-confidence to make their own lives work without being dependent on others.

Keeping to Words of Encouragement as Children Age

As children grow up, we have to be careful that what used to be encouragement does not turn into reproach through our fatigue, impatience or frustration. Chapman suggests that as children reach six or seven years old, the positive affirmations we gave them as they started to walk or picked up their toys for the first time often turn to "words of condemnation." He reminds us that when babies take their first steps, we did not scold them for the times they fall down but instead enthusiastically say something like "Good job" or "Look at you."[6] As they age, we are not usually so impressed with seeing them put toys away, and our tendency may be to focus on what has *not* gotten into the toy box. We only boost their sense of self and accomplishment by focusing on what they *have* achieved. Our critical or demeaning words can strike terror in children who *need* words of affirmation to feel loved. I explain Chapman's love language concepts further in the section on couples below.

Confrontations with Children

We have to tread very carefully when confronting children, as their little hearts are so open they can easily be hurt. In *The Road Less Traveled*, Dr. M. Scott Peck says that we correct our children in one of two ways: we either *react* spontaneously, believing that we are right, or we *respond* to our children from a place of humility. As explained in the earlier chapters, when we react rather than respond, we are answering with our emotions and unconscious influences, not to the singularity of the situation at hand. He tells us that responding to our children with neutrality is a more effective way to create and maintain communications lines, and is less destructive to their self-esteem.[7] Cultivating a neutral attitude requires a genuine extension of one's Self, but the effort is amply rewarded by evidence of the child feeling increasingly free to find and fully express his or her voice.

Importance of Expression for Children

It is so very important to allow children to express their anger, hurts, or frustrations. Otherwise, we risk having them suppress and bury their feelings. They also need the space to convey their opinions and voice their desires.

Although some children will be more vocal and reactive than others and we have to curb any propensity toward temper tantrums, repressed emotions are *so* emotionally unhealthy: they will affect children for the rest of their lives. Shaming or blaming children for their frustrations or angers makes them bury the associated emotions, and this blocks the necessary function of releasing them. These buried, emotions will come out one way or another, so it is better to deal with them outright. Like us, children have different ways of dealing with their disappointments, frustrations, and attempts to get what they want. If we have a willful child, we have to be extra cognizant in dealing with their emotions, outbursts, and tantrums without harshly reacting. This is the only way they will learn to curb their outbursts—by their parents' calm responses and good examples.

We also need to encourage our children to articulate what they think about different situations, and for them to consider solutions. This builds critical thinking and gives them tools to draw from when making decisions. Children must also learn to properly communicate their desires; they must be guided on how to appropriately ask for what they want, and to consider the timing of their requests.

Teens and Young Adults

I once heard an idiom that raising teenagers is like pinning Jell-O to a wall. Most parents would agree. Between their physical changes, hormonal fluctuations, heightened emotions, and willingness to do almost anything to have friends and fit in, it is often frustrating, confusing and heart-wrenching all at the same time for parents to be the bystander of their teen's emotions, attitudes, and behaviors.

Caught between childhood and adulthood, teens need and demand the freedom to explore who they want to be, but also need the acceptance, support, and unconditional love of their parents—if and when they ask for it. Teens often act childlike, but demand to be treated with the maturity of the young adults they are growing into. Parents, confused and frustrated by these conflicting messages and their teens' erratic moods and behaviors, become worried, critical, and impatient, and often vacillate between telling them what to do and enveloping them in smothering love.

In *The Conscious Parent*, Dr. Shefali Tsabary tells parents of teens that it is time to "retreat from your dominance and emerge in your kinship. No longer can you be the ever-present parent, but must instead become an ever-present partner." Although she sympathizes with parents and appreciates that it is often very difficult dealing with teens, she explains that parents have to realize that teens need their privacy, will do what they want anyway, and that it is crucial for parents to step back from controlling their teens and knowing everything about their lives. Tsabary says that it is time to realize that "the parenting experience isn't one of parent *versus* child, but of parent *with* child." For the teen to sense the authenticity of their parent's support, they need to feel we trust them, and unless we show them we trust and believe in them, they will become emotionally distant. Parents can help their teens navigate this difficult time, but teens will not ask for advice unless they know you trust them to know what they want.[8]

Tsabary links our being conscious and present to having our children trust us, and even says that "the parent-child relationship ... constantly presents us with opportunities to raise ourselves to a state of intensified consciousness ... we believe we hold the power to raise our children, the reality is that our children hold the power to raise *us* into the parents they need us to become." She distinguishes between permissiveness and setting healthy boundaries and appropriate household rules, but tells us that teens must know unequivocally we are not pushing *our* agendas on them, but adds that when we do it isn't because we don't love our children enough when we attempt to enforce what we believe is best for them, "rather it stems from a lack of *consciousness* ... They will only come to you when they are able to sit in your presence and feel your unconditional faith in their ability to handle their life ... we have to remove ourselves from any illusion we can control their life ... to trust them is your spiritual discipline."[9]

It is in allowing teens to make decisions that they gain the confidence they need in themselves to become adults, and to learn from any bad choices. And although we must still guide our children, we now do so by demonstrating maturity in showing respect, forgiveness, and by allowing for good, open, and honest communication with them, and with those around us. This encourages the development of character, skills which James W. Goll tells us in "A Radical Faith," promote the wisdom and integrity necessary in order to move into adulthood with maturity and accountability. Goll says that kids can excel in sports, or even get big jobs as adults, but they often lack the character to walk their lives with wisdom. Encouraging them to think things through for themselves can give them the practice they need to live wisely in the future.[10]

The Generation Gap—a Falacy?

As parents, when we look below the surface of our limiting beliefs and possibly outdated values, trust the innate characters of our children, and communicate openly and honestly with them, we can get past the surface issues that stand between us. Although the term *generation gap* suggests that different generations experience the world with different attitudes, beliefs, and values, Neale Donald Walsch tells us in *Conversations with God for Teens*, that the generations have more in common than we think: "The separate generations think that they have different interest and different goals ... and that it is the other generation that is standing in their way of getting it ... All human beings have the same goals ... being themselves, and experiencing that at the next highest level, and the next, and the next."[11]

Conflicts ensue because most of us have not been programmed to focus on the positive. When a teenager asked Walsch why her parents only noticed the things she did wrong, Walsch replied that parents often do notice when their teenager behaves correctly, but they don't acknowledge it and have a tendency to focus on the negative. This has been Humanity's Default Position. When she asked how to get her parents to recognize when she does something right, he suggested that she acknowledge them when *they* do something right. *We* can always start the ball rolling toward the positive.

Communication and Real Listening with Teens

Open and honest two-way communication is vital with teenagers, and *real* listening paves the way for honest communication to develop. As parents we usually think we are hearing and listening, but often we are not. We are only listening on the surface level. Most adults and parents have not learned to communicate honestly and patiently themselves, and these skills are even less developed in teens. However, as parents it is important to be aware of what messages we are and are not giving our teens with our communication styles and how and if we listen. In *Hear Me, Hug Me, Trust Me*, Dr. Scott Wooding suggests that parents often block the flow of good communication with their teens without realizing. He says the four most common attitudes parents fall prey to that block the flow of communication with their teens are:

- Interrupting
- Making Judgments
- Showing Emotion
- Not Understanding.[12]

More details of how these attitudes play out can be found in the article entitled "Most Common Ways Parents Block Communication with Teens" on this book's website.

Encouraging Teens and Young Adults to Make Conscious Choices

Even though we need to encourage our children to listen to what their heart is telling them, we also need to guide them to allow their mind to edit those choices. When they make conscious choices and decisions by considering the effects their attitudes and behaviors have on the life they want, they create a sense of self-empowerment. It is important to impart on them that making conscious choices can help them avoid situations that cause them unnecessary emotional hurt and pain or even life-long circumstances they may regret and have trouble disentangling from.

As well as when making lifestyle choices, part of living consciously is choosing to partner up by taking into account the other's character, attitudes, beliefs, and values rather than succumbing only to the lure of attraction, good looks, charm, money, or security. Partnering up or choosing a life mate affects us emotionally, socially, culturally, and financially. And if children come along this choice affects the parents and the children for their lifetimes, as well as the generations to come. Situations not dealt with in a responsible and mature manner can reverberate through the generations. Considering the attitudes and beliefs of the other about the major life issues makes for happier and healthier partnerships and families, and paves the way for more stable generations to come. We are then using our God-given power to use our minds to ensure that what our heart is telling us will serve us well so we can create the lives we want rather than being at the mercy of weak influences like neediness, impatience, immaturity, greediness, or lust.

This Shift is encouraging us all to raise our consciousness, and there are many near and far who are offering us opportunities to do so. None more so than our own children! As each generation comes into the world more enlightened than the last they have much to teach us. We need to heed their insights. And even though our children are often emotional, confused, and may not always be able to fully articulate what they have come into this world to express, we are asked to rise up to the challenge of wholeheartedly growing up to what our children need us to be to help them bring it forth—for them and for us. In doing so we will become healed! As Tsabary says:

> Parental metamorphosis is the key to a leap in human consciousness.... The road to wholeness sits in our children's lap, and all we need do is take a seat. As our children show us our way back to our own essence, they become our greatest awakeners. If we fail to hold their hand and follow their lead as they usher us through the gateway of increased consciousness, we lose the chance to walk toward our own enlightenment.[13]

Couples

Like two out of control trains barreling toward each other
on the same track, couples often smash into each other
just trying to get their needs met.
—Unknown

While most relationships may be based on love and a commitment to experience life together, it is quite natural to experience conflicts. We each hold distinct character traits and come from unique backgrounds and experiences. If we do not respect the differences these engender or allow space for expression, conflicts will develop. Entering into a relationship offers the opportunity to face misalignments within ourselves. We often enter into relationships driven by neediness, Hidden Agendas, or even conscious agendas. Many of us are also under the influence of Protective Mechanisms, so there are many, many opportunities for conflicts to develop and for one or both parties to feel hurt or misunderstood within our intimate relationships.

Differences that Often Create Conflict Actually Add Value

We are inclined to try to have our partners think, act, and feel the way we do. However, making a partnership work involves accepting our differences and embracing the qualities that each bring to the table. Admittedly, this is easier said than done. Once the honeymoon phase is over and real life sets in, seeing the positive aspects of the other or the relationship often goes by the wayside. As with everything else in life, we have to consciously focus on the positive. When we do this we give the positive aspects of the other a fertile place to grow. During hard times or rough patches, throwing in the towel may seem like the best idea when, in fact, it's only the easy way out.

We often marry or choose partners with opposite personalities, but with many qualities we like and appreciate. However, what we like is only part of his or her personality make-up. For example, the person who is organized and gets the bills paid may annoy us by being more focused on money, organization, or routine than we like. We might be drawn to a person who is more spontaneous and brings excitement to the family, although their inability to keep to schedules annoys us.

We are attracted to each other so that we can balance each other out. Bills have to be paid and budgets adhered to or chaos ensues, while spontaneity keeps things alive and fun. We can choose to focus on the positive aspects of our partner and praise him or her for the valuable qualities he or she brings to the partnership, or we can berate our spouse for the aspects of his or her personality that annoy us. It is easiest to be accepting of our partner when we can see the differences as a blessing, recognizing that as he or she navigates life differently than we do it adds value to our partnership or marriage.

Instead of seeing our differences as sources of conflict, we can see them as sources of healing. Making peace and accepting the differences we share with our partners helps us grow spiritually, brings self-healing, and moves us closer to wholeness.

Couples and Their Misalignments

The Course calls any relationship in which we are asked to heal our wholeness a "holy relationship," and in their highest form, couple relationships are the perfect vehicle for this healing because we are usually relating to someone with very different character traits and misalignments and everyday life provides us many opportunities to witness and thereby heal the misaligned parts of ourselves. We are usually paired with someone with the same percentage of misalignment.

Couples with Similar Percentages of Misalignment

When we are paired with another person who shares a similar percentage of misalignment from his or her True Self, the misalignments can show up as completely different issues, or with sensitivities that complement each other.

For example, one partner may be inclined toward anger while the other is inclined toward judgment. One will hold control within their Default Position and Protective Mechanisms to serve their Perceived Needs, while the other will succumb to victimization fuelled by his or her unconscious influences. Until we understand that the real purpose of our relationships is to help us unearth and heal our misalignments, these different ways of being will bring conflicts into our relationships, unless we are an easy going person able to find peace in everything. The illustration below offers a visual of a couple with a similar percentage of misalignment.

#15: Similar % of Misalignments in Couples

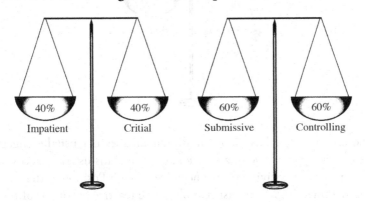

As we can see, each partner is misaligned by the same percentage, but the misalignment shows up in different ways. The healing and return to wholeness and balance lies in acknowledging and understanding the root cause of our behaviors. For the aggressive, controlling partner, we must understand our need to control. Once we do so, we can start to release the negative influences held within our Emotional Bodies, and the aggressive attitudes will start to disappear. Similarly, submissive partners' healing lies in the recognition of their passivity and an understanding of why they succumb to this. They too benefit from releasing what was buried in their Emotional Bodies and can thereby move toward finding their own voices and power bases. Once both parties understand what is happening and are willing to work together, individual healing begins, and conflicts soon abate.

Couples with a Disproportionate Percentage of Misalignment

While most couples may have a similar percentage of misalignments, some may find themselves partnered with someone who has a disproportionate amount of misalignment to them. This, however, is the exception. When this happens, the one living more in tune with his or her True Self is meant to hold the light for the other to see what alignment looks like and what they can eventually aim for.

#16: Disproportionate % of Misalignment in Couples

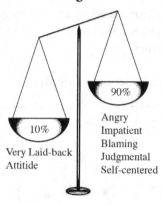

The one with the less % of misalignment does not usually engage in or pursue conflict, nor live in a reactionary state. This usually causes much frustration for the one living from a negative Default Position as they usually have many Protective Mechanisms at play. The reactive partner is often very frustrated with the peacemaker. I was like this. With the exception of the immediate family I grew up in, I spent most of my life surrounded by people who did not engage in conflict. I found this very frustrating. I felt my way of cajoling, pushing, and demanding was how to go about life. When they refused to engage I was further angered and when they questioned my tactics I got defensive. I saw their easy-going attitude or non-aggressive approach as disempowering.

Most Relationships Are Preset Soul Contracts

Whether we are equally or disproportionately misaligned, our main personal relationships are usually preset soul contracts with the purpose of healing our wounds and moving us toward wholeness. Joyce and Dave Meyer are a good example of an obvious preset, disproportionately misaligned soul contract. While he held the light with his easygoing, accepting attitudes, she was slowly shown how her Default Position and Protective Mechanisms kept her in anger, frustration, and unhappiness. She had been guided to read and study her Bible every day and let it speak to her. She connected the dots between how her attitudes were related to past buried hurts, confusions, and conflicts resulting from the sexual abuse by her father. As she was working from within the Christian umbrella, she then gave these up to Jesus. Meyer eventually started to convey her new understandings of how we can bring our brokenness to Jesus (the symbol for unconditional love in Christianity) with her books and programs. Over the last thirty-five years Joyce, with her husband as the organizer, has built up a ministry that has helped millions of people to heal, as well as donated millions of dollars into the poorest areas of our world.

Power Struggles, Honesty, Clues to Trouble

Power struggles often occur within couples because each is trying to appease his or her misalignments. As each party tries to satisfy the neediness and/or Perceived Needs of their unconscious influences and attempts to offset falling prey to whatever he or she is trying to avoid, Protective Mechanisms come into play. As explained in chapter 1, our efforts to satisfy and defend these unconscious influences create an inner pull-and-push.

We yearn for intimacy, but the playing out of our unconscious influences drives us apart from our significant others. We want to feel whole and independent, but our neediness keeps us feeling dependent on the other for our emotional needs. In *Getting the Love You Want: A Guide for Couples*, Dr. Harville Hendrix explains that "husbands and wives push against an invisible relationship boundary in an attempt to satisfy their dual needs for autonomy and attachment."[14] The individual pulls-and-pushes create conflict because they are derived from individual rather than joint considerations, and because these come from unconscious influences that aim to protect us, power struggles ensue as we perceive our emotional survival is at stake. As well, in our unconscious state, we often think we are being honest when we are not.

Many people who marry or enter into a romantic partnership have a healthy self-concept and an understanding of the role of relationships. Past hurts do not shape their expectations about giving and receiving. They recognize the need for honesty, sharing, understanding, forgiveness, and compromise. Most people with this deep awareness can be happy and survive life's adversities. However, our unconscious can often deceive us.

Sometimes we are tripped up by the *honesty* part. We may think we are being honest, but our unconscious influences can rewrite the truth without our awareness. We may be living in denial of the extent of our neediness, Perceived Needs, or Hidden Agendas. We may truly believe what we say and be completely unaware that we actually created our beliefs about how we are or how life should be from a misperception or need that we have to fulfill. For example, we may tell someone we love him or her and fully believe that we do when, in truth, we do not; we actually just want him or her to love us and to validate that we are worthy. This unconscious dishonesty will eventually show up in their attitudes, as there are always clues to potential problems.

A good indication of Hidden Agendas and Protective Mechanisms at play would be people who do not share ample details of their future plans, such as their hopes or dreams, or if they do share a bit, they are vague, get uncomfortable, change the subject, or leave the room if further discussion seems imminent. Although this could be because they are unsure of themselves, it could also be because they are somewhat aware that they exist from within unhealthy influences, self-lies, or half truths.

An example of this may be the avoidance of talking about taking a relationship to the next level when the couple has been together for years. For example, John avoids the subject because he is fearful to enter into this discussion as he knows that his partner Susan wants children and he does not. He now realizes that to not have children would be a deal breaker, but he does not want to lose the relationship because he does love her and it is satisfying his current needs. John does not have a healthy enough self-concept to face this, because he does not think he could find another partner. One of the easiest ways to recognize if someone is working from unconscious influences is to notice how they treat others, react to situations, and if they have the need to always be right and voice their opinion.

How does he or she act when they become frustrated, are criticized, disappointed, or put upon? Do they respond calmly, or with impatience? How does the person treat those close to them, strangers, or even people that serve him or her? Are they critical or accepting of others or events? Do they monopolize conversations? Years ago when I was completely wrapped up in myself and my frustrations, I remember at least a few times when my family called me out on my treatment of the waiter or waitress. I was not being rude on purpose; I was just so completely self-involved. Anyone who is that self-involved is not easy to live with. I was allowing life to be heavy, and those around me suffered.

On the other hand, sometimes we even go out of our way to be nice to strangers and are not so nice to our families; it is those closest to us who can best push our buttons so our defense systems are always alert. Unconscious influences and unhealthy self-concepts can affect our relationships in many other ways, like idolizing our partner, or even love itself.

In our intimate relationships, our love can actually be a type of idolatry. We idolize the other because we think he or she will fill the void of what is lacking in ourselves. The romance part of the relationship reminds us of the unconditional love that we are missing because of our perceived separation from our True Self. However, another cannot fill this lack. We can only satisfy it through our reconnection to our God-selves and the confidence this brings with it.

Making It Work

There are as many ways to make relationships work as there are relationships. And there are many commonalities to happy relationships where both parties are contented and fulfilled.

Focusing on Positive Aspects, Finding Joy, Keeping it Light

While focusing on the negativities of our partner or the life we have created drives us into a downward spiral of negativity, focusing on the positive aspects invites our relationships to spiral in an upward, uplifting direction. We can witness this in others. For example, this is what is at play when we observe a family locked in negativity and discord or a family who exists within a paradigm of peaceful harmony. Positive attitudes and mutual support create synergy and an upward and uplifting spiral of positivity which benefits the couple, as well as the entire family.

Joy, laughter and a light-hearted attitude keep us aligned to our True Selves. These attitudes also keep the spark alive in our relationships. It is so easy to fall into negativity with the responsibilities of adulthood, and even more so when navigating and balancing life with children. In my search for peace and happiness, every book, philosophy, guru, and master I have encountered encourages us to lighten up and find joy. With all that our modern day world demands it is hard to be light-hearted and find time to cultivate joy. If this does not come naturally within the relationship, we have to *make* the time and *consciously* create an atmosphere for joy and light-heartedness to flourish within the relationships and family.

Communication in Couples

Communication is paramount to all happy and healthy relationships but is especially crucial in couples. We need to be able to communicate in a way that is conducive to us being able to share our dreams as well as voice our fears and frustrations without being ridiculed or shamed. We also need to learn to listen to what our partner is saying, without interruption or insinuating our thoughts or ideas into the issue until, or if, they ask for our input. In *Boundaries: Where You End and I Begin*, Anne Katherine suggests that the type of communication we need to improve intimacy in a relationship "presumes contact with and acceptance of feelings and a special quality of listening."[15]

For good, healthy, open communication, we need healthy boundaries, as they create a safe haven that encourages sharing, whereby we can allow our fears to find a voice and our vulnerabilities to come through without fear of being scoffed at for having our feelings. Otherwise, true intimacy will elude the relationship as we will close off vital parts of ourselves to the other. It is also important for our children to witness us talking out issues calmly, as this sets a fine example for them in their future relationships. It shows them that conflicts, misunderstandings, and working out different opinions or ways of going about life are a normal part of sharing lives with others and can be dealt with calmly and respectfully.

Conflict was a huge issue for me during my marriage. Shortly after my marriage ended, I entered a new relationship that was also fraught with conflict. After that one ended, I realized that a lot of the issues that came up in this new relationship were the same as the ones in my marriage, most notably my defensiveness. I recognized that I was the common denominator and asked for understanding. I was shortly led to Christian Carter's program Communication Secrets, in which he and his many guests explained in many different ways how and why couples misunderstand each other. I spent a couple of years listening to several of his audio and video presentations regarding couples and their issues. See List of Recommendations for details.

Really Hearing What the Other is Saying; Getting Heard; Being Present

Even though we may listen attentively to the words and even the emotions and body language our partners use, sometimes we still do not really hear what they are saying. In *Getting the Love You Want*, Dr. Hendrix suggests that a barrier to real communication is often "denial" or that we "simply refuse to believe what [our] partner[s] [have] to say."[16] He recounts the story of a man in his forties and a woman in her twenties. During their therapy sessions, it became apparent that the man was frustrated because he was ready for children and she was not. However, she had explicitly told him that she did not want children for a while. The man said he had heard this but had not believed her, thinking he could change her mind. We often do this. We hear, but often the meaning of the words does not really sink it: we cannot accept or face it.

When we are frustrated or constantly feeling disempowered because our partner can't or won't hear us, sometimes we simply have to state our "bottom-lines." In *Marriage Rules*, Dr. Harriet Lerner tells us that "sometimes we need to challenge the status quo by saying "Enough!"—and really meaning it." She also explains that we need to decide which issues we can easily let go and which need addressing now. She warns us that although we have to make our point clearly, calmly, and confidently—not to go about it aggressively, as this would show a weak stance and alienate our partner. Dr. Lerner says we have to declare our "bottom lines," and speaking firmly, but calmly, we can start with phrases such as, "I like," "This is what *I* think," "This is what *I* feel," "These are the things *I* can or can't do."[17] Although non-aggressive, these are empowering phrases.

Showing the Other That He or She Matters

On her visit to Montreal in April 2013 while giving a live inspirational talk, Oprah said, "It seems to me that we all just want to matter." Although not a profound statement on the surface, it reflects that showing our partners they matter is important. One of the best ways to show this is to give others our time and *really* listen to them. Oprah also said that "human beings walk this planet asking: Do you hear me? Do you see me? And does what I say matter? Do your eyes light up when I enter the room?"[18] No matter what has happened in our day, we want our partners to hear us, to see us, and to acknowledge that what we feel and have to say matters. We also want them to be happy to see us.

Building Trust

Many of the ways we build trust with our partners is with our everyday attitudes, actions, or inactions by:

- Being open;
- Being honest;
- Speaking from the heart;
- Listening with open hearts to our partners;
- Allowing ourselves to be vulnerable by forgiving; Accepting forgiveness;
- Saying what we mean; Meaning what we say;
- Keeping promises we have made.

Holding to these attitudes keeps the partnership strong, and in our discussions we may profess to our partner that we will honor them. Our True Self whispers to us who we want to be and we often propose attitudes and actions to match these. However, as our unconscious influences play out they can thwart us actually keeping to them, as well as give the other mixed messages. For example, we may say we will be more attentive to our partner, but our requirement to answer to our Perceived Needs may override this intention. We may say it is ok for our partner to be out with his or her friends, but the next day berate them for never being home. To keep the partnership strong, we must address the hurt feelings that come about, while at the same time forgive the other for hurting or confusing us. We must remember that our partner is doing his or her best, but is likely working within the confines of at least some unconscious influences.

Respecting Our Different Ways of Navigating Life

Respect is paramount in keeping our relationships in a positive, loving, upward spiral. Couples are often composed of a doer and a quieter one, and these personalities will experience and express their emotions and feelings differently. We need to respect these differences. Speaking with regard to traditional male-female couplings, Dr. John Gray tells us in *How to Get What You Want and Want What You Have* that "taking reasonable risks and pushing to his limits helps a man to feel his emotions ... [and] sharing her feelings in a supportive context assists a woman in feeling her wants."[19] This also holds true for same-sex partners when one is more inclined to be the doer or go-getter and the other more quiet or nurturing.

People who are doers and achievers need respect for all that they are and encouragement in all that they do or attempt to do. At the same time, the quieter, sensitive party needs respect for all he or she is, space to voice their feelings, and love and appreciation for the more-subtle aspects he or she brings to the relationship.

Expressing Our Love

If we were completely aligned 100% of the time, we would not need any specific expression of our partner's love for us. However, we are all here just doing our best to deal with our inner worlds and their unconscious influences. Within this context, how love is received and expressed is different for everyone.

In Chapman's *The Five Love Languages*, he tells us that learning our partner's love language is paramount in understanding how to show our love. Listed below are Chapman's Five Love Languages, with more detailed explanations found in article "Our Love Languages" on this book's website.

- Love Language 1: Words of Affirmation
- Love Language 2: Quality Time:
- Love Language 3: Receiving Gifts
- Love Language 4: Acts of Service
- Love Language 5: Physical Touch[20]

We must also understand that any attempt or gesture to show our love to our partner should be appreciated as such, even when it is in ways that do not fulfill our particular love needs. When living at our highest potentials we would not need *any* outward signs of our partner's love for us as we would be getting that from our connection to our True Self. However, since most of us are not there yet and have been programmed to get our love cues from the external, until we find our way back to wholeness it is important to recognize how our partner feels our love. At the same time, we must show appreciation to our partner for any effort he or she makes to show their love and appreciation, no matter how feeble their attempt seems to us.

When we maintain a strong connection to our God-self true intimacy can flourish more easily. In the Alpha course, Nicky Gumbel suggests that when each person in the relationship is closer to God, they are closer to each other. He depicted this with an illustration of a triangle, like the one below.[21]

#17: Couple Closer to God are Closer to Each Other

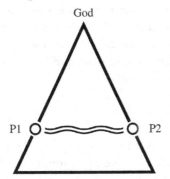 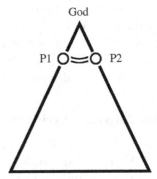

Romantic Love vs. Genuine Love

Even though we say that being in love *feels* so wonderful, Eckhart Tolle tells us in *A New Earth* that what we call "falling in love" is usually just an amplification of "egoic wanting and needing."[22] We become obsessed with the other person, with what our egoic mind then conjures up of that person, and how it seems that he or she can fill our needs. This is why we often say another completes us. This is not true love, as there is no wanting or needing in true love. When we are whole, we don't need completion.

When we run into conflict in relationships, we often feel that maybe what we thought was real love actually is not. We start doubting our earlier feelings of romantic love. Dr. M. Scott Peck explains in *The Road Less Traveled* that because many of us have bought into the "myth of romantic love," when the euphoria disappears, we are disappointed. We now face a dilemma: remain doomed in our misery without love for life or split up. He further explains that many of us get lost in the confusion of the myth, trying desperately to mould our realities into the unrealistic version of the myth of romantic love, and that the more we believe in this fairy tale, the truer it will be for us and the more we will be disillusioned.[23]

Peck continues to explain that what we really feel when we say we are in love is the effects of putting all our energies into our partner and making him or her our "love object … [but] genuine love … implies commitment and the exercise of wisdom."[24] When we truly love someone we must be committed not only to their happiness and general well-being but also to their spiritual growth: we must support them in their quest to become their Best Self. Dr. Peck defines true love as "the *will* to extend oneself for the purpose of nurturing one's own and another's spiritual growth. Genuine love is volitional rather than emotional. The person who truly loves does so because of a decision to love. This person has made a commitment to be loving whether or not the loving feeling is present."[25]

When we understand that our partnerships are the vehicle that can help us grow the most spiritually, we can forgive and extend love to our partners more easily. We can choose to make conscious choices that show love to the other—even if we do not feel the love at this point in time, as doing so is out best option. Love is a decision rather than a feeling.

Love and Anger Are Decisions

One of the first books I read in the '90s on my journey was *Love Is a Decision*. Although I do not have that book anymore and cannot even find any information about it, it had a deep and profound effect on me because it helped me realize that love is a conscious choice, something we can decide to give. Holding on to anger can also be a conscious choice.

Condemning Words That Turn to Anger, Can Turn into Hate

In *The Five Love Languages*, Chapman tells us that a patient once asked whether or not it is possible to love someone you hate. This caused him to reflect on the beginning days of his marriage, and he remembered that he and his wife had often experienced feelings of hate. He says that the condemning things they had said to each other had brought on hurts, which then turned to anger. He explains that "anger held inside becomes hate."[26] Chapman says they found their way back to a loving relationship because they understood that love was a choice. They endorsed that choice by following four steps:

1. Talking out disagreements without reproaching the other;
2. Coming to conclusions without undermining their united purpose;
3. Giving productive proposals without being forceful;
4. Learning to speak the other's love language.

Attraction to What Is Missing in Us; Allowing
for Vulnerabilities and Inadequacies

For most of us, what we originally found fascinating and exciting about our partners is usually what eventually annoys us most about them. We are originally attracted to those qualities because they are missing in us, and in our souls' desire to heal the wounds that keep us from our True Selves, the wisdom of the Universe prompts us to choose partners who have what we need to find our emotional balance. However, as our partners attempt to bring these qualities out in us (usually unconsciously), they come up against our Protective Mechanisms.

For example, if a man's soul's journey dictates that he embrace patience, in everyday life with his partner opportunities to uphold this virtue will come about. The partner may be more laissez-faire than he is, and this will annoy him. If he cannot surmount the challenge to find patience or is unaware of this learning opportunity and does not understand its purpose, hurt feelings and conflicts will likely ensue. These relationships enamor us because we feel connected to what the other person has that is missing in us. However, as time goes by, this brings up old, unmet inefficiencies in us, which creates internal stirrings and conflict within as we have to either face our inefficiencies or continue to react in ways that create conflict.

It is so important within our relationships to express our hurts and frustrations so we can share our vulnerabilities, as well as have a safe haven to express any feelings of inadequacy. In *Love Without Hurt*, Dr. Steven Stosny explains that if we "continuously numb or avoid our core hurts" we deny our true feelings and they cannot find the voice they need.[27] Innocent remarks are then often taken as critiques because we do not want to show how vulnerable we are (we get hurt easily), or any inadequacy (we are forgetful), so we become defensive. For example, one partner may remind the other that something needs to be done by a certain day, which is just a fact. But if the other has denied and buried feelings of past criticisms, this is translated into disapproval, and he or she will become angry or defensive. By facing our hurts over past criticisms we would become less defensive. In coming to terms with the inadequacy of being forgetful we could become motivated to remember next time, and thereby feel more adequate.

Dr. Stosny also explains that most of us are *inadequate* in making our relationships work and feel frustrated that we cannot navigate relationships perfectly. This frustration then triggers us to act in ways that create more hurts, conflicts, or frustrations. Talking about our frustrations about not being able to create a stronger relationship or sharing our feelings of inadequacy about not being loving or available enough is very helpful.

Marriage Crises: Breakdowns, Breaking Points, and Healing

A marriage breakdown occurs when there is no longer a unity of purpose, when communication and respect have been lost, when one in the partnership has given up trying or is simply overwhelmed and exhausted in life. Couples who were once happy often stop putting each other first and listening to each other as family, career, or other interests take precedence. Breakdowns are also sometimes fuelled by the shoulds in our minds, can be influenced by our extended families, social circles, or communities, as well as by our jobs or careers.

Dr. Stosny also tells us that when a relationship has suffered "chronic resentment, anger or abuse, reestablishing a connection is not a fifty-fifty proposition." He explains that in the beginning, it may be as much as a "ninety-ten proposition" with the perpetrator doing most of the work.[28] This is because it is easier for the one who was the aggressor to heal than the one who was subjected to aggressive attitudes and behaviors. Listed below are Dr. Stosny's steps to healing a broken relationship, with more detailed explanations found in the article "Steps to Healing a Broken Relationship" on this book's website. [29]

1) Building Deep Connections;
2) Keeping Lifelines Open;
3) Four Steps to The Power Love Formula:
    a) Acknowledge that our partner is important to us;
    b) Give six hugs per day;
    c) Contract to love our partner;
    d) Embrace the four Rs when we slip up:
        1) Recover; 2) Repair; 3) Receive; 4) Reconnect.

Even though Dr. Stosny concurs with spiritual concepts that we are all ultimately responsible for our feelings and our happiness, he also puts forth that when one partner's attitudes have not been loving or compassionate, the relationship itself has suffered. Being an entity in itself the relationship needs healing, hence the necessity for steps to repair it.

Forgiving Our Partner; Confronting Our Partner

Within the highest levels of understanding there is no right and wrong, only the playing out of duality. However, most of us are not living at those highest levels and often act from and experience emotions influenced by our misalignments. As such, the attitudes and actions we put upon our partners are not always coming from a place of love and compassion. And as our emotions may be dictated by our misalignments we may feel hurt or disappointment when our partner's attitudes or actions do not meet our expectations, or are not what they promised. Forgiveness is *essential* in fostering happy and healthy relationships, and having these understandings can help us forgive more easily. It is also wise not to let things stew because by the time the issue comes to a head the road back is longer and more arduous.

We have a right to be happy and fulfilled and feel nurtured and appreciated within our couple partnerships. Since many of us did not come from loving or nurturing families, we became accustomed to living in mediocrity. Spirit does not want us to live in mediocrity, but many of us do. We may often think we are the only one in the partnership who feels unfulfilled within it, but if we are not really happy it comes out in subtle ways. The other usually feels the rift—they just may not acknowledge it, and they too live in mediocrity. Addressing what is bothering us is the only way to keep a lifelong partnership healthy.

On his talk based on his ministry work with couples, the late Leo Godzich explained that in the same spirit as the steadfast love God has for us, we should confront our partner when something goes awry, and then forgive them. Just as when we have done wrong, God usually makes us aware of it, either through another, our conscience, or by the repercussions, but we also know we are always forgiven. We have to draw awareness to what the other has done wrong, according to the life plan we have discussed, and forgive him or her. If there was no life plan, we have to tell our partner now what we want. However, it is very important to pick an appropriate time, discuss the issue, and always end in love. Godzich reminds us not to let the light go down on the issue: do not go to bed mad. He tells us that when we address our issues, we honor the "covenant with the spouse, like God's covenant with us," and we then *will* be able to work it out.[30] Couple relationships have many challenges, but those who work together face more than usual.

Couples Living and Working Together

Couples who live and work together, like those who share a business, have particular challenges as they are together almost 24/7. Many who teach spiritual or religious concepts do so with their spouses, such as Audrey and Bob Meisner (their ministry focuses on couples and families), Esther and the late Jerry Hicks (of Abraham-Hicks), Joyce and Dave Meyer (they run a large Christian ministry), and Gary and Cindy Renard (who promote the philosophies of *The Course*). In these cases the support of the spouse is vital as they travel around the world teaching their messages. And although Jerry Hicks has now passed on, he was a vital part the process for many years. Gary Renard, author of *The Disappearance of the Universe*, and Cindy have shared that as they spend so much time together, any misalignments they hold often converge. Understanding that the purpose of our relationships is to uncover and heal our misalignments, the Renards practice the forgiveness *The Course* suggests when issues crop up. To help navigate it all, they have developed meditations to help them connect to the unity and connectedness intended within this holiest of relationships. They have now made these meditations available in CD form, and the link is at the back of the book under List of Recommendations.

We Are Sexual Beings

A vital part of being human is expressing our sexuality. However, our sexual energy has been misunderstood. This has caused Humanity much unnecessary confusion and pain throughout the ages. Our sexual energy is part of our life-force and is how we express our inner-love. To become our Best Selves and develop into all that we can be individually and collectively, we need to better understand our sexuality, embrace it in positive ways, and make peace with all that it entails.

As we fell deeper and deeper into duality, the darkness within us needed to find an outlet. We projected this outward into judgment, cruelty, and various types of heinous acts. Not connected to the love within us we distorted our sexual energy.

Rather than a giving expression of pure love, it became a vehicle to satisfy heightened physical urges, the result of the darkness within us needing an outlet. We then deemed our sexual urges as evil, and projected that negative energy into sexual assault, rape, gender discrimination, and judgment of sexual orientation. As we denied, suppressed, and projected this important life force, we further entrenched it as negative within us. We then used our normal sexual desires to play out our hatred and to control others. This flowed through all aspects of society, and certain religious notions promoted the idea that our sexual urges were sinful and ungodly. These ideas came from misconstruing concepts that the masters had taught us. We superimposed our misperceptions onto our normal human sexual urges.

All the masters would have taught some variation of us not having sexual desires when we are connected to the highest part of ourselves. This is because we would not need to express ourselves with physical sexuality, as we would be engulfed in such high energies and continuously experience bliss and rapture—much more than sexual acts could ever offer. We then judged ourselves for not being in those high spiritual states. So, rather than embrace the messages that we were loved no matter where we were in our spiritual growth, we went about projecting our inner guilt about not being at the highest levels by inflicting upon others the judgment, hate, and cruelty

166

regarding our own desires. Within our history, both men and women have used their sexuality negatively.

Throughout history, men have sometimes been chastised for their sexual urges, while at other times they have been encouraged to feel entitled to impose them on whomever they please. Women have often used their sexuality to get what they want—sometimes for selfish reasons but at other times out of desperation to gain control over their lives or destinies. Both men and women have also projected their confusion and guilt over their sexuality and sexual desires by blaming women for the sexual misconduct of males. Women are still often made to feel it is their fault for being sexually assaulted, abused, and raped. A woman can be blamed because of how she was dressed or because she was walking alone or at night. The real problem is the lack of respect within society regarding each other and our differences, and the lack of education to help us eradicate this.

Throughout the ages, it has been a common tradition for some yogis, mystics, nuns, monks, and other serious religious and spiritual seekers to practice celibacy. For some, this was so they could focus solely on spiritual matters. For others, it was because they had attained that higher awareness and no longer needed sexual physical expression. Sometime around the eleventh century, the Catholic Church decreed that its religious figures must practice celibacy and renounce marriage.

Although this decision was partly due to irresponsible and out-of-control, rampant, unhealthy sexual conduct that had plagued Humanity which had created pain and suffering and often resulted in disease, it was also because the Church did not want to share its wealth and property through patrimonial inheritances. Clearly this ruling only served to bury normal sexual desires, which is sadly evident in light of all the cases of abuse that have been uncovered within the Catholic Church.

Sexual misconduct is not only a symptom of the Catholic Church; it is a human transgression unchecked within many religions, spiritual disciplines, and throughout all facets of society by people in power positions and those who are looked up to or are sought out for guidance. Although this is not likely within those existing at the highest levels of awareness!

It is commonly known that yogis, or more evolved beings existing within a higher consciousness, regularly experience physical sensations akin to orgasms, which is just a physical manifestation of the love within us all but that they are tuned into. This can also happen spontaneously to anyone when he or she prays, meditates, or is immersed in spiritual material. As I explained in chapter 4, this happened to me one day when I read some advanced spiritual material—my whole body started to feel orgasmic. Not understanding these feelings I could not control, fear crept in, and I had to discontinue reading and engage in a mental activity to override the feeling. Most of us are not attuned enough to these high vibration manifestations to be able to handle them.

As we continue to raise our vibrations, we will no longer feel the need to deny our sexuality, and as its projection in negative ways disappears, it will become a less-taboo subject. In the future, the need to express our sexuality physically will eventually decline as we become more in tune with the love within and around us. And as we become more open to that love, we will start to express it in many other loving ways. In the meantime, we have to accept and deal with our sexual desires, needs, and urges, and any conflicts they engender within us appropriately.

Dealing with Our Sexuality and its Conflicts

A highly sexual person has to accept his or her high sex drive without guilt, but must deal with their sexuality with maturity, respect, and a full understanding of the consequences on all others involved. This is not always easy. If we are not, we should get help, because unless we have a healthy, positive approach regarding our sexuality it creates a negative energy around us that brings with it unconscious guilt, which affects us in many ways, and can create conflicts with others and chaos in our life.

In the Dalai Lama's Global Conference on World's Religions gathering in Montreal on October 7, 2011, one of his guest speakers, Professor Tariq Ramadan, was asked by a young man how to deal with his inner conflict about wanting to respect women and his sexual desires toward them. Ramadan answered, "Good luck with that." Facing anything that brings with it inner conflict is what this Shift is urging us towards, so there is no shame in acknowledging conflicts surrounding our sexuality and sexual needs and dealing with them—in fact, it is a vital part of Humanity's current evolution.

Having a medium to low sexual energy can also create conflicts within us. We have to accept ourselves without any guilt for not being as sexual as others, which can be a challenge against the backdrop of a society that views sexuality as the most important aspect of our existence. We must also ensure that we do not hold any negative attitudes toward sex in general or those who do have a higher sexual energy than we do.

Denying our sexual natures, allowing for guilt or shame within us— whatever our sexual energy level, or having negative attitudes towards others' sexuality in any way creates a low, negative vibration around our sexuality which perpetuates itself. We will then be in danger of falling further into low-energy sexual attitudes and actions like demonizing ours and others' sexual natures, homosexual bashing, or even rape or sexual perversions. Our sexuality is not the problem; it is our attitudes around it and our denial, rejection, and misunderstanding of it as part of a healthy, normal human experience.

One of the reasons early religions—and many religions today—encouraged marriage was so our sexuality could be satisfied within that safe and sacred bond. It is only when we allow our confusion and conflicts regarding our sexuality and its urges to be at the surface of our awareness that we can deal with them effectively.

As We Continue to Evolve Our Relationships Will Improve

Sometimes we are drawn to another so that we do get together and play out what our soul contracts dictate, and sometimes the chemistry we feel does not necessarily have to end in a long or even short-term relationship. A heart connection with a strong chemical attraction may be a left-over energetic pull from a past-life association. We may have an unfinished lesson to learn with the other and we are only to get together for a time (a reason or a season), learn the lesson, and then move on. It may also be that we are not meant to act on the connection we feel in this lifetime, and the lesson to learn through the energetic pull we feel towards the other is to rise above the chemistry and use discretion in choosing a partner. Relationships create emotional entanglements and the unravelling from those based in neediness or left-over energetic pulls usually carry unpleasant drama and emotional pain.

As the effects of this Shift continue to encourage us to release our unconscious influences, all aspects of our relationships will improve. Current relationships will become healthier, as the conflicts that have their roots in neediness, Perceived Needs, Hidden Agendas, and Protective Mechanism will begin to dissolve. As we start to become more mindful, those of us entering into new relationships will choose our partners more consciously. We will feel empowered enough to seek out people whose character, lifestyle, and values complement and align with ours. These pairings will have many less conflicts than those based in unconscious influences, but when conflicts do arise they will be resolved with calmness and integrity. Children will benefit greatly from these attitudes. Many young parents today are already parenting consciously and embrace many of the concepts in Shefali Tsabary's book, *The Conscious Parent*, that I noted above.

Partnering up Consciously/Separating Consciously

The more we evolve, the more we will be able to easily trust that our hearts are showing us a true picture when choosing a life-partner (or even friends or a business partner). We will no longer need to be so wary of our unconscious influences luring us into bad situations or have to be so vigilant at continuously examining our emotions, desires, or motives. Nor will we have to be so cautious of others' motives. As we will be working at high vibration capacities, our radars will be well attuned to the vibrations of others and if something is off we will cue into it quickly.

The greater our connection to our True Self the more we feel guided towards partners based on true soul parings where we encourage each other to be the best we can be. And because our strength and self-confidence comes from within we are not invested in changing our partner or making them acquiesce to our desires. We also understand that our partner gets his or her strength and guidance from their True Self, and if that guidance is calling them to move on from the relationship we will not be so inclined towards drama, anger, revenge, or the plethora of negative responses breaking up has caused in the past. As well as partnering up consciously, we can also break up consciously.

In our most recent history an intact family provided the foundations we needed to grow emotionally healthy, and when divorce or separations occurred, even if the family life was not perfect, the children felt like the rug was pulled out from under them. This sense of loss is somewhat due to changed circumstances, but much of it is due to the way we separate and divorce. The sense of security children feel when surrounded by unconditional love when growing up is like God's unconditional love for us.

As we become more evolved individually and are more closely connected to our True Selves, our separations will occur without the dire effects of the past fuelled by hurt, anger, rage, revenge, and blame. As we are already encouraging our children to look into their hearts and trust their inner guidance, their connection to their True Self is stronger than in past generations and this gives them a strength and self-assurance that follows them everywhere. And as couples are inspired to separate or divorce with integrity, they will honor the promises made and will be able to agree on shared childrearing duties, day-to-day obligations, and fair distribution of finances. The children then will not internalize the effects of the break-up and pass on the effects of their unresolved issues onto their own children.

Homosexuality

Some religions today denounce homosexuality as a sin that goes against God's plan for us. However, most on a spiritual path believe that being loving, compassionate, and *accepting* of ourselves and others, with all our differences, is the *most* important aspect to aligning with God. They also believe that embracing our sexual tendencies is part of accepting who we are to express ourselves in the world, as resisting our inherent nature actually goes against God's plan for us. Acknowledging the Oneness we all came from by making peace with all others regarding our differences and ways of expressing ourselves is what makes us whole and is the reason we exist.

I once asked Spirit for clarification regarding the Old Testament and what it says about homosexuality and it being a sin. What came to me was that people were told to *populate the earth*, and therefore heterosexual relations were necessary. There are varying thoughts regarding who told us to populate. The Bible says it was God; however, many today believe that our origins are from other planets or the stars. I delve more deeply into these ideas and aim to reconcile them in chapter 7, "Science and Other Related Topics," and chapter 9, "The Planet and Abundance."

From a Christian viewpoint, Jesus' message was of love and *complete* acceptance toward *everybody*. If we experience conflict with how people are, we should ask for understanding, and perhaps a new way of looking at the situation will emerge. The account of Jesus' acceptance of the prostitute washing his feet (Luke 7: 36-9) can be seen as a metaphor for accepting *everybody*, as washing another's feet in those times was a reverent, loving act, so allowing her to do so was full acceptance of her, especially since she was perceived as wayward at that time and in those circles.

I believe that homosexuality in our society provides an opportunity for spiritual growth and offers us a chance to use Jesus' message of complete acceptance to bring unity and reconciliation toward others. It is especially important to address these judgment issues that we learned from our upbringing, society, or our religious circles. Any perceived conflict is an opportunity to grow spiritually. Any judgment stalls our growth. Any ideal or belief based on *I-am-right-you-are-wrong* promotes ideas of separation; not unity; not unconditional love.

Our religious and spiritual communities can offer us much comfort, however our best guides are our hearts. Listening to what our heart knows, rather than adhering to what others are trying to tell us about how to express God's love, is what Jesus taught. When we are sincere and void of unconscious influences, or dogma imposed on us, only love and acceptance of *all* others will come through—not criticism, judgment, or condemnation. Nor will pitting one against another, or groups against each other.

When we experience a conflict with another or a group, it is actually a gift from Spirit for us to move closer to our wholeness and embrace our godliness by making peace with all our differences and the resulting judgments. For those of us with issues toward homosexuals, we have an opportunity to forgive ourselves for judging and for not seeing them as Jesus intended us to see our brothers and sisters, namely, as children of God. For those of us who are homosexuals, we have the opportunity to forgive those who judge, condemn, or create the inequalities we have had to endure.

When our beliefs come solely from the interpretations of any scriptural writings without including love, acceptance, and compassion, we are not actually practicing our godliness or really adhering to the core message of religious teachings. In the *Tao Te Ching*, we are told that we *all* came here in harmony from Oneness, *all* perfect, to be loved and nourished, and will return one day unconditionally loved, just as we are. You can find some of Stephen Mitchell's translation of the *Tao Te Ching* as it relates to us and the Universe in the article entitled "The *Tao* Birthed Us and Looks After Us" on this book's website.

Homosexual Experiences and Our Souls' Journeys

In our souls' journeys, homosexual experiences are often necessary to help balance out our male and female energies so that we can become fully aligned energy beings on our way back to the Oneness we emanated from. In his message "North Korea; Pope Francis; the Vatican; Visualization; Homosexuality," Matthew Ward, through his mother, Suzanne Ward, tells us:

> ... any balance within a lifetime is desirable. However, since sexual energy is one of the most essential aspects of the human psyche, the balance of male and female energies is probably the most desirable ... *homosexuality is an advanced stage of spiritual growth wherein feminine and masculine energies are more balanced than in heterosexual persons....* [Asked] *Why is homosexuality a necessary experience?* [Ward answered] ... how better to learn balance in the two extremes of male and female sexual energy than on an integrated basis?"[31]

Ward further explains that earlier in earth's history, we held this idyllic state of unification of the male and female sexual energies (which he explains is *not* just about "having sex"), but as Humanity fell deeper and deeper into its dualistic systems this became "contaminated." He explains why we will all eventually move toward androgyny:

> The ideal is androgyny, which has nothing whatsoever to do with human sexual nature, but rather with the two opposites of human sexual *energy* attributes. Androgynous souls are far more spiritually advanced because of the male and female sexual energy balance they have achieved ... [this] levelling out most assuredly is part of the divine plan, because feelings of prejudice and hatred and the infliction of emotional and physical cruelty are impediments to spiritual growth.[32]

Ward explains that our past history created the distortion of the purpose of our sexual energy, and that most of the abhorrent behaviors perpetrated on earth (sexual and otherwise) came from the "perversion of the sexual energy stream." This also distorted our view of our sexual natures, and abuse and misuse of our sexuality happened within both heterosexual and homosexual contexts.

At the highest levels our sexual energy and the sex act, whether heterosexual or homosexual, is not about our physicality. It is a joining of soul energies. Telling us that we have misunderstood homosexuality, Ward explains that it is actually "an evolutionary stage of the spirit ... [and that] a loving homosexual partnership is NOT a perversion of sexual energy." However, main-stream society rejected homosexuality, and the Catholic Church supported this notion, which further perpetuated itself. According to Ward, neither heterosexuality nor homosexuality is better or worse than the other, nor one a more important aspect of our soul's journey than the other.[33]

Ward further sheds light on the fact that today those who have a strong disdain for homosexuality may still retain an energetic attachment from a previous life's experiences. They may have had terrible experiences as homosexuals, either being criticized, insulted, or belittled by family, friends, and coworkers, or even tortured or killed, and those who hid or denied their homosexuality carried the weight of their deceit. If in the next lifetime they choose to be heterosexual, their souls may still hold some pain and confusion regarding their treatment in that past lifetime, but rather than now feeling compassion for other homosexuals, their leftover pain and hurt has turned to hostility, and they feel contempt. We would have no recollection of the past-life experiences, adding to our confusion and inner conflicts regarding homosexuality.

No Need to Demonize Others; Work on Our Own Errs

If we look closely enough within ourselves, we will usually find some aspect of misalignment, be it full-out judgments of others or unloving or even cruel tendencies birthed from our unconscious influences. Rather than focusing on what we *believe* is wrong in another, it is more beneficial for us to work on our own misalignments.

In his broadcast *Bringing Up Spiritual Children*, Rabbi Shmuley Boteach questions why we put up roadblocks for gay couples to adopt when there are so many children in orphanages around the world. He suggests that rather than focus on gay issues, we could work on reconciling the other 613 commandments within the Jewish laws. He also suggests that there are many negative things we can focus on in life and that "Proverbs also says that lying, having a proud heart, and being deceitful are abominations. So why do we demonize gays?"[34] Focusing on the purported sins of others is only an attempt to project our inner guilt or misalignments outward. We can adopt Byron Katie's philosophy and look after our own business, not others' or God's. It is helpful to ask ourselves the purpose of our judgments or condemnations.

What is the Ultimate Purpose of Our Choices and Judgments?

When we judge another for their differences, especially when we promote condemnation or it escalates into a fervor of ridicule, it is our egos (Satan) tempting us to point out our separateness. With our thoughts and attitudes, we are either undoing unconscious guilt by upholding ideas of love or reinforcing it by upholding ideas of separation. From a standpoint of *The Course*, homosexuality itself is a nonissue, but like everything else, knowing the purposes for our choices gives us clues to our real issues. Do our choices and attitudes promote harmony, unity, and love, or conflict, separation, and hate?

Anti-gay rallies with their condemning attitudes and demeaning rhetoric not only advance homophobic attitudes, but encourage divisiveness among God's children. They do not promote harmony in the world. I once went to the gay pride parade in Montreal. I had been told I should see it, if only once, and one day a friend suggested we go. What I noticed the most was that it was peaceful. Large gatherings like parades can be rowdy and even disruptive, and most I have attended are characterized by a coldness and sternness between the police and the bystanders in their attempt to keep everyone safe. However, at this parade, the police were walking along with those in the parade laughing and talking with them and stopping to talk to the bystanders. It was all very light and casual. I mentioned this to my friend, and he said that it was always like this. The absence of aggressive energy was palpable! It was a harmonious atmosphere based on acceptance. Anti-gay rallies are based on judgment and making others wrong and push *against* what is not wanted. This invites more confrontations regarding homosexual issues to us and into our world.

Attitude Changes Happen Slowly

Just like with all other negative or divisive attitudes, it will take time for our attitudes toward gays and homosexuality to completely shift toward the positive and filter through all levels of society. Most of us have only known, and thereby believed, what we have been told and what society and our religions have advocated throughout history. These ideas are ingrained into our cellular memories, and will take time to undue. The duality we have existed under promoted biases and judgments, with homosexuality being one of the major focuses, and as we sought to come to terms with the darkness and sexual confusion within us we projected it outwards—homosexuality became a major scapegoat.

As discussed earlier, our sexual energy has been misunderstood. Rather than being an expression of inner-love extended into the world or towards another, it became about the physicality of it all and of having sex. This, combined with the judgmental attitudes Humanity has been beholden to, created and perpetuated the bias towards homosexuality. Our past mostly encouraged us to live in our little bubbles, unaware and ignorant of how the rest of the world lives, what they believe, and why. I know I grew up sheltered from worldviews in a Catholic environment and lived in a town with no mosque or temple. Sexuality, in any sense of the word, was never discussed. I would likely have picked up on my parents' ideas of homosexuality (being Catholic it was considered wrong), if the subject ever came up. So I was neutral with no opinion, but remained ignorant of the truths. Others out in the world were influenced by what society, their culture, and religions believed and propagated.

A few years ago I saw a documentary on the Kennedys where Jackie, when she was probably in her 20s, said something to the effect of "oh those homosexuals." Spoken in her sweet voice, it still held a tone of judgment. I remember thinking that she was probably influenced by and repeating what those around her and the media said, but that by the end of her life had likely changed her opinion.

Although society is not yet fully accepting of the many differences between us, including sexual orientations, we have come a long way in the last half century. We *are* coming out of our ignorant fog and breaking down judgmental and divisive barriers left, right, and center.

Just as with all judgments, we can ask ourselves, what is the purpose of our thoughts, words, or actions regarding homosexuality? What will their ultimate consequence to us be? Do they uphold the ideas of God's love and the Oneness we all emanated from, or do they uphold ideas of our separateness? Do they help us align with God, reach our Best Selves, or become spiritually aware? Do they create attitudes that create harmony within our beings? Do they create a cavern between us and God's love within us and thereby with others? Do these thoughts and attitudes promote harmony with all others? Will they generate divisive attitudes and create barriers between people, or engender unity and break barriers down to help build a more peaceful world?

Most relationships, whether life-partners, siblings, parents towards their children, children towards their parents, family members, in-laws, friends, and even business partnerships, often bring about hurt feelings and frustrations because of differing personalities and unmet expectations, so are thereby fraught with conflict. This happens because most of us bring some sort of unconscious influence into the mix and these often collide, like the head-on train wreck I used as a metaphor earlier.

At the highest level our relationships give us opportunities to heal our misalignments, but since we have been mostly unaware of this we experience them as emotionally painful. We manifested on earth with those to be in our lives with the higher purposes of healing, helping each other in life, and/or helping each other with our life purposes. However, we were all born into this world of duality playing itself out, as were our parents and all others who influenced us, so these higher purpose ideals have often gotten lost in the shuffle of life. For example, rather than sticking it out in a marriage willing to accept the other's personality traits, truly understand their feelings, be willing to compromise, or discuss, monitor, and hold onto long-term goals, we often bail out. Or, we may have come here with the intention of being a good parent and raising a loving family, but as our unconscious influences played out based on what we were exposed to growing up we were unable to do so and created a family life filled with hurt feelings, unmet emotional intimacy, and conflict.

Although scenarios like the two mentioned above bring with them much sadness, emotional pain, and/or anguish, once they have played out our new highest purpose is to make peace with whatever situation has now arisen. And if we are brave enough to do a little introspection and recognize our part in whatever transpired (like being too needy, demanding, or not making ourselves heard) and aim to adjust our attitudes we can grow both emotionally and spiritually, having learned valuable lessons. This is what relationships are all about.

It is only possible to do *our* part within any of our relationships, as we can never force others to change. They have their own paths to follow and are on their own timeline. However, *we* can offer love, acceptance, compassion, and understanding to any relationship—even if it is not reciprocated, and we can bring mindfulness and a consciousness to it by acknowledging when *we* are being needy, acting from other unconscious influences, or holding underlying judgments of the other. However, as we endeavor to bring love, acceptance, compassion, and understanding to those around us, they *may* then be inspired to change. The most important question regarding all our relationships is: do *my* thoughts, attitudes, words, and behaviors aim to create unity and harmony? If they are not, you *can* change them and get the ball rolling.

> *Conscious relationship is truly an immense power*
> *that all of us can use to navigate life and the unknown*
> *that often accompanies it.*
> —John English[35]

Now that we understand our frustrations and unhappiness are a result of the operating systems we unknowingly function under and are beginning to understand why this came about, we can aim to alleviate what is holding us from our True Selves for our own peace and happiness, and create harmony in all areas of our lives. In Part II, we will now consider our personal and spiritual development and growth seen through the lens of various other related topics.

PART II

---

*Other Subjects Related to Who
We Are, Our Journeys, and the
Oneness We Are a Part Of*

CHAPTER 6

Words, Symbols, Rituals, Concepts, and Prayers

I am a Muslim. I am a Hindu. I am a Christian. I am a Jew—
and so are all of you.
—Gandhi[1]

Section 1: Words

Words are but symbols of symbols.
They are thus twice removed from reality.
—*A Course in Miracles*[2]

The above quote from *The Course* indicates that words in themselves have no real meaning— they are simply a tool to communicate something. Along with their dictionary meaning, they express whatever intention, energy, or vibration the speaker gives off, and we further interpret them with whatever associations they hold for us. If we are not aware of this we can misunderstand what the words spoken are meant to express, which can cause confusion and even conflict with others.

Words' Vibrations

Words and the tone in which they are said and the attitude and body language of the speaker, hold vibrations. We can sense all this. If spoken or read to us with open, loving, and positive vibrations, this energy will permeate the meaning of the words, as will harsh, judgmental, and negative vibrations. When continuously exposed to words with strong vibrations, we will tend to connect the positive or negative connotations with the words, regardless of the dictionary definition. When later used with the original intentions and within their proper context, we will still carry over any past associations.

The Three Rs in Christianity

My Catholic upbringing was colored by an atmosphere of strict, brooding severity, which led me to have negative associations with three words in particular: *repentance*, *righteousness*, and *reverence*. My parents' beliefs were rooted in a severe approach to religion, and with my father being authoritarian and judgmental and my mother meek and submissive, along with the cold and strict attitude of the nuns who taught me, I developed a general negative perception of Catholicism and the Church. My father loudly and firmly extolled the virtues of an all-powerful God who could "strike me down at any minute," while my mother sheepishly tried to impart her understanding of humility, which was all about strict self-sacrifice without any explanation of why. Both my parents' attitudes reflected the judgments and limitations of their take on religion. There was no love, joy, or sense of peacefulness in the mix. The individual was to be disempowered, and their gifts and talents suppressed rather than promoted, as any achievement was seen as going against the grain of humility.

However, in recent years, as I was guided to make peace with Christianity, my curiosity and explorations led me to uncover the true meaning of these words. They were not intended to hold the negative connotations I had assigned to them, but were expressions of the higher ideals that help us along our journey.

Repentance

Until a few years ago, the word *repentance* evoked a mental image of fearful people hiding from God, as depicted in much early Christian artwork. It meant punishment from a judgmental God. Joyce Meyer, a Bible teacher, author, and speaker changed this for me. I realized that when she used the word *repent* it had nothing to do with judgment. She was suggesting that we offer up our sins to Jesus (the Christian symbol of unconditional love) for forgiveness. This is akin to many spiritual tenets whereby hurts, angers, shame, or guilt are released to Spirit, the Universe, or however our practice suggests. The idea is the same: when we wholly give up whatever concerns us to a higher power, its effects on us are eliminated.

In his article "Repentance: Oh, That Nasty Word … Or Is It?," Dave Schmidt, a former pastor, tells us that while in seminary school he saw "how cultural perception eroded a word's true meaning and concept, denying us the power that certain words could have in our lives," especially with words like repentance. He explains the true meaning of this word from its Greek origin, *metanoia*, as "a transformative change of heart, especially in a religious conversion … [whereby] *meta*; means to change or turn around and *noia*; meaning the mind or a way of thinking."[3] So one of the original intentions of repenting was to guide us to use the mind (the decision maker) to change our way of thinking and thereby our attitudes and life experiences.

Righteousness

Righteousness is another word that held negative associations for me, evoking memories of pious, long-faced nuns, standoffish priests, and severe-looking church attendees.

My later understanding that we emanated from love and *are* love led me to realize that all we need do is align with that love: with our True Self. We do so when we are happy and joyful and emanate light, loving, positive vibrations. We misalign when we are unhappy and stern, which yields heavy, judgmental, negative vibrations. My experiences of those who claimed to be righteous were of people not aligned with the love within their True Selves or the qualities of the Oneness. At any moment in time we all have the potential to be *righteous; we* just have to align with its precepts.

Reverence

It was not until I understood the real purpose of reverence and was exposed to a type of humility free of harshness from those professing to be reverent that I could accept and make peace with the term. Reverence is not about worshiping anything or any being. It is about opening up to the love within our self. We have been taught to revere the masters who walked the earth, but there is no real requirement to do so. We *can* open to the love within ourselves by joining with the energy of another who is connected to or represents that love, like a guru or master, or by opening ourselves up to our True Self by *being present.* Just moved around

In "Delinking Religion and Politics," Sadhguru Jaggi Vasudev tells us that "in the East, the purpose of worship was to create a reverence, and that it's not what you worshiped that was important, but that it brought reverence into your life."[4] He explains that if we go about our daily lives bringing an attitude of reverence into our activities, whether tending our fields, fishing, painting, or doing whatever brings us the most pleasure, as long as we relate to it with loving abandonment, our mind clears and we can connect to the higher part of ourselves.

Understanding how energetic vibrations affect us, it is easy to see how tapping into the energy of a master, an enlightened being (dead or alive), or anyone who is passionate or working on an enlightened cause can touch us deeply, even to the point of awe or reverence.

Understanding Other Words and Terms

Master: Ascended Master; Ascended Being

What is a Master?
A Master is a man like you. Each one of us has the same potential.
The difference lies only in that although God resides in every heart,
in the heart of a Master He is now manifest.

—Kirpal Singh[5]

Ascended master is a term used for a soul that has completed its final lifetime by overcoming the duality of our three-dimensional world. Through spiritual transformation, the ascended masters were able to transcend fear and separation to embrace love and Oneness. Because of this they were able to ascend above third-dimensional living, no longer identified with the body and its concerns.

The terms *master* and *ascended master* have been fraught with confusion over the years, as they appear to suggest one who reigns over another. However, the terms were intended to signify the virtues of those who have come to this plane of existence and transcended the ego Self, which believes itself to be separate from its Creator or God. Also referred to as an avatar, a master is believed to have descended from the highest realms, functioning on the earth plane as God's messenger and manifesting His qualities, or those of the Standard and Oneness.

Masters, such as Buddha, Muhammad, Jesus, Rama, and Krishna are all said to be incarnations of God or Brahman, who chose to enter our lower realm as humans for the purpose of showing us how to break free of our dualistic, linear, third-dimensional thinking, enabling us to reconnect to the peace, love, and power of the Oneness. In his article "The Process of Self-Awareness," Dr. Maurice Turmel says, "To be a Master is to truly ascend past the lower vibrations, to take control of your body and spirit complexes and to overcome the darkness that prevails in the lower dimensions. True Mastery involves enacting disciplines, becoming the Light you wish to be graced with and standing up for the Light while saying 'No!' to the distractions and manipulations of the lower vibrations."[6] He explains that the term *master* is not considered a term of endearment, nor is it intended for the ego to play out its concepts of me-better-than-you. It is simply stating a fact that these beings have *mastered* thoughts of the separated ego. We will all eventually attain that level!

Vasanas

Vasana is the Hindu term for deep-seated hurts, pains, abuses, and traumas that block our ability to access our True Self. In his article "Vasanas vs. Fears and Beliefs," Steve Beckow explains that a vasana is a composite of "memories, beliefs, decisions, or reactions" weaved together in a complex set of mixed emotions that can be triggered by anything evocative of the original hurt, pain, or trauma. He further explains that any ordeals of this nature not properly addressed can have such a hold on us that we may react to anything with even a hint of a reminder of the situation with an "automatic and habitual round of acting out." He adds that these fear-based behavioral reactions can become so entrenched that our responses to life are colored by our vasana and its protective devices, limiting our ability to live spontaneously.[7]

While everyday hurts and pains may only require being released once, deep-set vasanas may necessitate several efforts before they lose their hold on us. It may even take years! Traumatic situations have many layers to them, and once we decide to embark on our journey to peace Spirit will slowly peel them away, only ever revealing what we are ready to face or can handle at that moment in time. And as the layers melt away, we come ever closer to accessing our True Self. For deep-set vasanas professional help is often advisable or even necessary.

Chavruta: God, Our Intended Friend and Companion

In his article "Yeshiva Lessons," C. J. Chaput states that the word *chavruta* is the Hebrew word for God in the Torah, which means friendship or companionship in Aramaic.[8] We may revere the masters, but they are only symbols pointing us to God's loving energy. They intercede as symbols because as humans caught in our three-dimensional existence, we really have no concept of God and the unconditional love inherent in the Oneness we are still a part of. God seems remote to us, so masters, enlightened beings, sages, and gurus serve as translators between us and the truths of the Oneness.

Section 2: Symbols

Just like words, symbols also hold the vibrations we have assigned to them. The use of symbols has been extensive within the scriptures and practices of all religions and spiritualities. They can give us comfort by helping us to connect to our heart-centers and the higher parts of ourselves.

The Nature of Symbols

Even though throughout the ages many of the symbols used today have held various meanings, most belief systems and religions came to be represented by specific physical symbols. The Star of David now represents Israel and Jewish identity, while the Christian cross is recognized and used as a symbol of Christ's death and resurrection, which erased our sins. The crescent moon and star is now associated with Islam and is on the flags of many Muslim countries, but it is not a widely used symbol and many practitioners do not associate it with the religion. Symbols are also often used as a source of protection, like the Eye of Horus, an ancient Egyptian symbol believed to bring protection and good health. Similarly, the *hamsa* is a symbol common to many Arab and African nations, but is recognized as protection from the evil eye. Because we assign qualities to a symbol, its intention and our belief in it gives it validity for us.

Using Physical Symbols

An object or shape only becomes a symbol if and when we give meaning to it. Thus the power of all symbols lies in the meaning we instill in them. While certain symbols carry centuries' worth of meaning, every person has the power to add their own interpretations. For example, a friend explained why she believes the cross she wears around her neck has always brought her love and protection. When she was a young girl in Catholic school, her teacher, a nun who was leaving the school, gave her the small cross on a chain. At the time, my friend was living in an abusive household, so she believed that the nun was somehow aware of her situation. The nun said the cross would protect her and to turn to it when in need of comfort or love. My friend wore the cross around her neck ever since, and told me that whenever she feels anxious, worried, or frightened, she touches the cross and it brings her a sense of peace.

Choosing Our Own Symbols

We can choose anything we want as our symbols. In her presentation, "Fire the Grid," Shelley Yates tells us that the Indigenous peoples' respect for the Planet allowed them to use symbols from the earth. We may choose a rock, shell, or crystal. Yates states that if you put your symbol in your pocket and say something like "I am a spiritual being living my path, and I invite you to join me," the symbol will then impart a comfort to you, as you have given it that power. She also suggests that you touch it during the day to help center yourself, get back on your path, or calm your self, and that when you take it off or out of your pocket at night, place it on the night table and thank it for the day.[9]

Without realizing it we often choose our own symbols and give them power. When we pick up pebbles or shells from the beach and bring them home, we do so in the spirit of bringing something back as a reminder of our relaxing beach time. Any symbol can work to help or comfort us, but when we choose symbols from the earth and infuse our intentions on them, they help us align to our true nature, because as I explain in chapter 9, "The Planet and Abundance," our earth is a living, breathing being that holds a vibration akin to the universal creative force we emanated from.

Spirit as Different Symbols

Spirit can come through to us in many ways, but will communicate with us in the way with which we are most comfortable, be that as the symbols of our belief system or how it will be most helpful to the given situation. This could manifest as an inner knowing, an insight, a revelation, or an aha moment. Spirit may come through to us as a voice we hear, appear in our dreams, or as a male or female being showing up as a past master, angel, guide, or helper to give us comfort, a message, or our answer.

Spirit's Ability to Come through in any Voice, Form, and in Dreams

Our religious backgrounds or beliefs bring with them symbols for Spirit to communicate with us. We may say, "God told me …, or wants me to …," "Spirit is guiding me to …," "My angels (or guides) are telling me to …" It was Jesus' voice that Helen Schucman, *The Course*'s scribe, heard as she was guided to write, so he is referred to as the teacher of its concepts. However, the voice was also understood as being a symbol of the Holy Spirit coming though in a way that was comfortable for her, because while Helen was not a practicing Christian, she always felt a great love for Jesus. Most of *The Courses'* students also consider Jesus to be their guide and teacher as they study and practice its concepts, but I did not. I had already learned to simply listen to an inner knowing and to Spirit's urgings and insights. I used my own internal guidance system when doing the lessons of *The Course*.

The messages of Spirit can take on many forms, such as an etheric, formless energy. About five years ago, as I was starting to sense that what I had been learning in my spiritual undertakings may have been similar to what Jesus (and all the masters) had taught, I had an experience that urged me to continue to reconcile all this. As I sat peacefully and quietly in a darkened room after a yoga class, the energy of Jesus showed up right beside me. This came out of the blue and greatly surprised me, but what I sensed was so clear and unmistakable, I actually looked over. There was no form, and I even looked around to see whether anybody else had sensed this. Nobody seemed to have. Later, I recognized that this was Spirit expressing itself to me in this way to encourage me in my investigation, and that the message was given to me when I was in a very calm state so I was sure to recognize and understand it. Spirit can also appear in angelic form or as flesh and blood, just like us.

Physical appearances of Spirit were common occurrences in early biblical times, and people of faith believe they really happened. These appearances still occur from time to time, but we are inclined to question their validity. Gary Renard explains that his teachers Arten and Pursah appeared to him in the flesh at various times from 1992–2001 as they guided him to write his first book, *The Disappearance of the Universe.* They also told him they were the essence of two "ascended masters," appearing in third-dimensional form.[10] Throughout their visits they explained that they were the Holy Spirit appearing to him in these forms, as separate entities within the illusion, so that as they answered Renard's questions about spirituality, life, and our everyday issues, their messages would come through as normal dialogues and in a current vernacular. However, one does have to be prepared spiritually for something like this to happen. For quite a few years prior to his teachers appearing to him, Renard had led a very quiet life and meditated regularly, so his connection to Spirit was very strong.

In the scriptures of most religions, angels, light-beings, and the masters are commonly referred to as either being seemingly etheric, flying, taking on human form, or appearing in all their winged glory. The Bible tells us of the angel Gabriel appearing to Mary, the mother of Jesus, and that winged angels also appeared to Isaiah. The Qur'an tells us that Gabriel also appeared to Muhammad to tell him of his missions, and the Hindu epic *Mahabharata* tells a story of Krishna presenting himself in human form to Arjun.

I find it interesting that we believe accounts of past angelic and non-angelic appearances and in profound dreams but are skeptical of these events happening today. One has only to read Renard's book, see him in a workshop, or listen to him on audio or YouTube to see that his message comes from a higher place and that it is his calling to act as messenger. Although we are less skeptical of accounts of profound dreams, it is all just Spirit showing up in ways fitting to the nature of the messages.

Twelve years ago and a few days after I moved into a house and lived alone for the first time in my life, I had a dream that unequivocally showed me that I was being protected. As I was in an almost waking state that first morning, I perceived a tall Rambo-looking warrior by my bedside who declared in a powerful voice, "I will protect you for one month." I understood the message but was confused about the one-month time period. I had not yet set up the alarm system in the house, and as it turned out, it was eventually activated exactly one month to the day of that dream. Only later did I make the one month connection.

Dreams can also guide us, and inspire us to help others. I heard Paul McCartney tell Oprah on one of her shows that his song, "Let It Be," came about because his mother, Mary, appeared to him in a dream and told him to let go of his angst over the Beatles' breakup. The lyrics "Mother Mary comes to me, let it be, let it be" emanated from that dream. The higher realms hold many types of more evolved beings.

Angels, Light-Beings, and Extraterrestrials (ETs)

Scriptural texts report the appearance of esoteric beings, often referred to as gods, descending from the sky in flashes of light and smoke. If you refer to illustration 3, "Levels of Consciousness Within the Different Realms" from chapter 1, you will note that within the realms, or dimensions, the archangels abide in the highest realms, light-beings like Abraham (of Abraham-Hicks) and Oasis are a bit lower, while the extraterrestrials who have visited us can exist from the middle realms down to the lower ones.

Angels, or light-beings, are androgynous in nature, but can manifest with feminine or masculine qualities and appear in whatever form is appropriate. Gabriel likely appeared to young Mary and Sarah, Abraham's wife, in a gentle, possibly feminine form but would have appeared differently to Muhammad to tell him of his mission.

Light-Beings

I usually refer to what some call angels as light-beings. These are the etheric beings who currently reside in the upper echelons of the realms. They have either returned there by overcoming the constraints of duality or chose never to take form during the creation of the Universe. The four energies that spoke through JRobert and called themselves Oasis, and the beings that speak through Esther Hicks and call themselves Abraham (as in Abraham-Hicks), are light-beings.

When the Universe was created and the world of multiplicity emerged, some of the energies chose to take form while others chose to stay in the spiritual realms to serve as behind-the-scenes support for us and the Universe as a whole. The light-beings known as Archangels Gabriel and Michael abide within the highest realms, with Michael being the protector and comforter and Gabriel, God's messenger. The masters who came to earth, such as the Buddha, Rama Krishna, and Jesus (known as Yeshua, then) also came from these highest realms.

In *Meetings with the Archangel*, Stephen Mitchell writes of his encounter with Archangel Gabriel, who appeared to him in all his winged, magnificent glory. At first, Gabriel appeared in a masculine form, dressed in kingly garb, but when Mitchell questioned (in his mind) the dress, the archangel changed into a "seven-foot-tall ellipse of light" and asked Mitchell, "Does this suit you any better?" When Mitchell asked him why he had come, he said that he was answering an inner call from Mitchell's being and that he was just a mirror of Mitchell's consciousness, which had manifested to help him overcome his judgments of those who derive comfort from angels.[11]

Mitchell tells us that in an earlier book he had dismissed the use of angels as guides and for comfort as nonsense, but he now believes that the purpose of his meeting with Archangel Gabriel was to give him an understanding that Spirit, or any of God's representatives, can appear in any *form we are comfortable with* to offer love, comfort, reassurance, or to deliver messages. If our religious backgrounds taught that angels with wings love and protect us, this is how we will feel the protection of Spirit.

Extraterrestrials

I believe there are a few premises at work concerning the ancient gods. Spirit has and can show up in an etheric or human form, be that light-beings from the higher realms such as the archangels, or manifesting as ascended masters, like Arten and Pursah to Gary Renard. Extraterrestrials have also appeared on earth throughout our history.

Some ETs came to communicate with us, to bring messages of love and hope, and to guide us on our spiritual paths. Others came here to help us in our evolution, both as a race and spiritually. Some who came from a lower-dimensional reality—who, like us, could still be strongly under the influence of dualistic concepts of lack, greed, and fear—may have had good intentions but fell prey to self-serving objectives when here, while others may have come to earth with self-centered intentions or simply to cause mayhem.

This is no different from priests, ministers, or gurus whose original intentions were to guide us, but act in ways that deviate from their mission. The more spiritually advanced ETs from the higher dimensions were simply more attuned with the plan of helping us to evolve than those from the lower dimensions.

Because the ETs hail from lower realms than say, the light-beings or ascended masters, they are in a more solid form, so coming here was less of a vibratory adjustment for them. This is why most of the visitors who guided us in the past in solid form and were considered to be gods were beings from other planets. And because they were not the original creative force fully embracing the Oneness paradigm, or the *real* God, they were prone to the lure of dualistic attitudes. This is one of the reasons for much of the confusion and many of the ensuing conflicts regarding God, as the offering of unconditional love while at the same time being judgmental are contradictory concepts.

The beings who visited us also brought knowledge, expertise, and possibly even equipment helpful to our evolution on earth. Some of the sites now being discovered are clearly markers meant to be seen only from the air and may have been intended to ensure the extraterrestrials could find their way back to us. Many of the sacrificial altars recently uncovered may have been for offerings to these gods in the hope they would return—either to continue to help us in our evolution or to bring back their advanced technologies.

Whether seen in physical form like an ET, ethereal form like an angel or light-being, or we are witness to an ascended master appearing in the flesh, all the beings that come from the higher realms to help us evolve are here directly or indirectly by divine decree, as they are part of the Universal Matrix that is guiding us back to the Oneness.

Many believe that extraterrestrials have always guided Humanity and that there are numerous spaceships surrounding the earth at this time, helping us with this Shift and our and Gaia's Ascensions. All scriptures speak of guidance we had from more evolved beings, and we are now realizing that at least some of this guidance was from beings from other planets. ETs and their connection to us are more thoroughly explained in the next chapter. Our and Gaia's Ascensions are elaborated upon in chapter 10, "Ascension."

The Cross

The cross is a symbol that has been used with differing meanings throughout history in various mythologies, religious beliefs, rituals, and practices. And although it is now widely known to represent Christianity, the Celts used the sun cross as a protective device long before the cross was adopted by Christ's followers as their symbol.

In her article "Confusing Signs," Carolyn Sayre states that for more than five thousand years, the hooked cross, also known as a swastika, was associated with the Hindu religion to symbolize peace, long before Nazi Germany adopted it as their national emblem. The literal translation of the word *swastika* from its Sanskrit root, *svastica*, means well-being, good fortune, and luck. Sayre further explains that the Native Americans of the United States were the first in the Western hemisphere to use the symbol of the swastika on their pottery and blankets. Later, American merchants and manufacturers adopted this sign, using it on packaging, wrappers, and in advertising. It was considered a symbol of good luck.[12]

In *An Illustrated Dictionary of the Gods and Symbols of Ancient Egypt*, Manfred Lurker reports that the Egyptian ankh, a cross with a looped top, was a symbol of life. It suggested eternity and as such, was a representation of an everlasting force. Because of this, the ankh was a common feature in the purification rituals for the Egyptian kings.[13] Today, however, the cross is most commonly known to represent Christianity.

The Cross as the Christian Symbol of Forgiveness

In Christianity, the cross is the ultimate symbol of forgiveness. However, the tenet that Christ died on the cross for our sins can have a morose undertone and elicit feelings of guilt. This was how it came across to me as the idea of full forgiveness was never explained. However, the Christian ministers I have recently come across, including Dr. Jim Richards, Joyce Meyer, and the Meisners, embrace this symbol's true power as God's unconditional love and his full forgiveness for all our sins. The current belief is that when Christ died on the cross, our sins died with him, so we are completely forgiven and our sins are erased. This is the real power of the symbolism of the Christian cross.

We really need to believe we are completely forgiven because we are so far removed from the concept of God's unconditional love for ourselves and towards others, because guilt and blame have been the cornerstones of Humanity, having even been promoted within many of our religions. Their power and hold on us is insidious, so our belief in and the call upon of a supernatural being and/or force helps us to overcome them. When we truly believe that we are completely forgiven, we are in effect, resurrected. So the cross also symbolizes *our* resurrection through Christ's.

The Cross and the Resurrection: A Symbol of Rebirth

In Christianity, the cross signifies our sins being absolved through the death of Christ thereby wiping the slate clean, and that him rising from the dead symbolically means we rise *renewed from our past* through the absolution of our sins. This is a huge realization for those harboring guilt and shame from past attitudes, actions, or inaction.

In his talk "Miraculous Probabilities," Dr. Jim Richards testifies that it's been his experience in working with young adults dealing with heavy issues, that they must first believe that they are "raised up in Christ" and can be reborn, before they can free themselves of guilt.[14] The symbol of the resurrected Christ helps us to believe we are completely forgiven for all that we have or have not done—that we are unconditionally loved and forgiven—no matter what.

Dr. Richards also explains that we may not immediately feel different nor perceive evidence of the renewal in our lives right away because our negative emotions and underlying guilt and shame may obstruct us *feeling* changed, possibly stalling the process. So we must claim the change—and do so over and over again. Only by repeating that we want to be renewed can the idea penetrate our being with its barriers. He suggests we declare to ourselves something like, "As of today the real me is in Christ and dead to the old one: the real me is resurrected with Christ." This affirmation (or any other we choose to use) signals our intention to rid ourselves of the effects of our sins, which is in alignment with current spiritual tenets.

Other interpretations of the resurrection can also be helpful. *The Course* suggests that the resurrection can represent the rebirth of the mind. As we understand the concept of Oneness and practice the forgiveness as taught by *The Course*, our mind is renewed and resurrected from judgmental tendencies about ourselves and others.

Further Understanding the Symbolism of the Crucifixion

I never did understand what the cross—especially the suffering on the cross and the Crucifixion—really meant. However, even if we do not understand the symbolism found in the religion we are born into, they can still speak to us. Todd Burpo and Lynn Vincent's book *Heaven Is for Real*, is the true-life story of Colton Burpo, Todd's little boy who almost died of a burst appendix at the age of three.

The book focuses on the experiences he had while unconscious and close to death. Although Colton's father was the minister of a small-town church, he explained that at the time of the incident Colton was too young to understand any of the symbols or concepts of Christianity. Nonetheless, during his near death experience many of the Christian symbols appeared to him.

In the years following his near death experience, Colton began to reveal many things he had seen while in the coma to his parents. He said he saw Jesus, even sat on his lap, and had witnessed him go up and down like an elevator, whereas everyone else needed wings to fly. He mentioned having met Jesus' cousin, John the Baptist, and said "He was nice."[15] When Todd asked his son to tell him more about what Jesus looked like, Colton said that "Jesus has markers." Later when he was able to gently revisit the issue, Todd asked what colors the markers were, and Colton replied, "Red, Daddy. Jesus had red markers on him." When asked where the markers were, Colton stood up and pointed to each of his palms and then bent over and pointed to the top of his feet.[16] With no actual knowledge of the cross and all it represented, this innocent child had seen red marks in the spots corresponding to the nails in Jesus' hands and feet during the Crucifixion.

Some may have difficulty believing these events, but I do know Spirit will show up in our awareness how, when, and where it is comfortable for us, and how the message will be most helpful—for us or for others. I believe this story of a young boy who innocently tells of his experience helps us make peace with the value of the premises of the Crucifixion today.

Many are skeptical about the particular facts of the Crucifixion, and some don't believe it took place at all. I am not really concerned about the details or whether it happened. However, I did notice during the few years I recently attended churches how many people benefited from the belief that Jesus died on the cross to exonerate us of our sins. They felt absolved and relieved of shame and guilt. Believing that Jesus died on the cross for our sins and that we are forgiven and have risen with him allows us to align to the unconditional love of our Creator.

Colton Burpo and William Young's experiences encourage us to adopt those parts of our belief system that allow us to embrace the love within, and the compassion, forgiveness, and unconditional love available to us. (Young's story of emotional and spiritual healing after the brutal murder of his daughter also happened while he was in a coma-induced, dreamlike state, as told in the book *The Shack*). Putting our focus on the positive aspects of our belief systems takes it off those we cannot reconcile that do not serve us, like God being all-loving but also vengeful.

Section 3: Rituals

Your daily life is your temple and your religion.
—Khalil Gibran[17]

Archaeology and scriptures reveal that rituals have been part of cultural, spiritual, and religious ceremonies since the beginning of time. The various ceremonies employed have been to worship or pray to our gods; for purification of our bodies, minds, and spirits; for atonement of our sins; for rites of passage; and for dedications. It is normal that some rituals will resonate with us more than others, however within the different types of rituals throughout the world, many have universal themes or aims.

Opening Up through Rituals

One of the main purposes of rituals is to open our minds and hearts by allowing us to expand our consciousness beyond our usual sensual perceptions so we can connect to our higher Self, God, or the cosmic energies.

Worship

There are many kinds of formal and informal worship within the different religions and spiritual thought systems. Through worship, our being becomes centered, so we can connect to and align with our God-selves. In "Delinking Religion and Politics," Sadhguru Jaggi Vasudev describes what worship means in the East: "A farmer worshipped his plough, a fisherman worshipped his boat; people worshipped whatever aspect of life they related to most."[18] Whenever we do our tasks with a sense of joy, passion, excitement, or quiet peacefulness focusing on the chore at hand, we bring worship to our every day lives.

Singing

When attending churches again a few years ago what kept me going back was the singing as a form of worship to open and close the service. It transported me to a very peaceful place. There were really only two aspects to the Sunday morning service: worship and a sermon. It took a long time to get my head around the *idea* of what they called worship, but I eventually realized that part of the task I had chosen to undertake was to understand that while the rituals we use may differ in form, they are similar in purpose.

I eventually understood that the intention of the worship during the service was to still the mind to allow our heart centers to open so the subtleties of the sermon that followed could get through to us. This has value. It can also allow for a deeper connection to Spirit, as was my experience. The uplifting music often brought me to such a still place that once the service ended I would sit there quietly with eyes closed, basking in the beautiful energetic feeling I had connected to while everyone else got up to chat with those around them. My training with Oasis allowed me to open to energies around me.

Many religions embrace choirs or singing to praise to God. Muslim practices do not usually include music or singing in their worship, but sometimes add a rhythmic quality to the prayers. The Jewish form of worship is usually in the recitation of their prayers. Though their practice does not include singing, they sometimes have a cantor lead the prayers, so the quality of the sound is rhythmic and pleasant. Hindus often use song and music in their worship through Indian classical music called *bhajan*.

Chanting

Chanting is a common tool of Eastern religions, mystical branches of Western religions, and Indigenous cultures. It is used to calm the mind, center the being, and helps connect the participant to higher planes of existence. In *Our True Nature*, Marc-Joseph Chalfoun says that the Universe responds to sound and its vibrations and that "the subtle vibrations of sound take us higher, from the gross physical reality to the finer spiritual dimensions ... [and that] repetitive chanting serves as a tool to break us out of our habitual mental conditioning."[19]

In her article "Chanting," Lori Smith maintains that chanting heals our entire being. She reminds us of how children are calmed with lullabies and of how we relax when listening to beautiful or peaceful music. She explains that practitioners may focus on keeping the same tonal sequence, the repetition of sacred texts, or on the rhythms to bring about the desired effect. Many use "long sustained notes" like chanting om, while others focus solely on the "pure vibration of wordless tones and overtones." Some practitioners use only voice, while others include rhythmic or harmony-inducing instruments.[20]

Sufi Whirling

Sufi whirling is an ancient ritual originally practiced by the mystical Sufis of the Islamic faith. When I witnessed it in a workshop, I learned that the practice aims to quiet the participants' minds so they may either feel closer to God (as a preparation for meditation) or be receptive to a forthcoming sermon, religious sharing, or narration. In The Shambhala Guide to Sufism, Carl Ernst explains that the Mevlevis, a branch of the Sufis also known as the whirling dervishes, made this practice famous. The ritual is performed as a form of dance, with or without music, and sometimes while chanting and reciting poetry. In the ritualistic dance of the Mevlevi order, the participants perform circular motions ranging from "spontaneous trance-like movements to coordinated ceremonial motions." As one continues to practice the mind is quieted, allowing peace and joy to filter through our being as the pathway to our God-self opens up. And although the dance is a Sufi tradition, one need not be a Sufi or a Muslim to become a whirling dervish.[21]

Speaking in Tongues

Speaking in tongues is a Christian practice going back to ancient times and is still practiced today. Glossolalia, a word with Greek origins, is the earliest known term, defined as "ecstatic utterances usually of unintelligible sounds made by individuals in a state of religious excitement." Speaking in tongues appears ritualistic but is considered by Christians to be more of a gift of the Spirit.[22] In Biblical days when the apostles and prophets travelled to distant lands where different languages were spoken, they would automatically start speaking the language of the land. This was considered a gift from the Holy Spirit that allowed them to communicate Jesus' teachings.

The Time magazine article "Speaking in Tongues," tells us that this current term originated with Pentecostal Christians, who believe that to speak in tongues is to be overcome by the Holy Spirit itself. When the Holy Spirit consumes you, you may "utter sounds of another language that might sound like gibberish" but is actually a "soulful outpouring." According to Father Bennett, "the gift of tongues is a freeing of the personality in expressing one's self more profoundly, particularly toward God, even though the symbols are not understood by the speaker. It does not happen in a trance. The person is releasing something deeper than the ordinary symbols of language."[23] In spiritual terms, when we speak in tongues, Spirit comes through, as it has overridden the ego.

These rituals and other not well known practices may seem esoteric in nature and appear odd to anyone not accustomed to witnessing them, but the outcome is not that different from coming home and changing into comfortable clothes, putting on headphones, and listening to favorite music to unwind. Our being understands any ritual we use, and the more we employ it, the more readily we feel the benefits. I now need only sit in the chair where I meditate or read spiritual material to immediately feel calm and centered.

Connecting to the Earth

All spiritual practices I have encountered encourage us to connect to nature in one way or another. The energy of nature is most closely aligned to our spiritual nature, and we can benefit from that connection just by being near or around it. I have even heard ministers finish off their sermons by suggesting we go sit by the lake and take in its peace and beauty. However, few are more drawn to nature than the Indigenous peoples. Dronda Gardner, a friend of mine who is of Native American descent but also draws on Buddhist philosophies, told me that she once witnessed a simple ritual on a quiet unassuming piece of land that peaked her curiosity. Having received her introduction to Buddhism with Ram Dass in the early '70s, it was during those first years that she was guided to practices that helped her let go of what kept her in a state of unhappiness and dysfunction. As this ritual endorsed her strong connection to the land, she felt an urge to partake in it.

It involved lying in a long box she described as being "built half underground and half above ground," and which made her "level with the earth's surface." Unceremoniously she climbed into the box, and as she lay there, small cutouts allowed her to see far along the earth's horizon. As she continued to lie there in stillness for twenty minutes or so and gazed out of the small cutouts, she began to *feel* her connectedness to the Planet and her place within it. This further anchored her already-strong connection to the earth at a deeper, cellular level. In her words, she "seemed to become one with the earth." When we allow ourselves to become one with the energy of the earth, we are connecting to the higher vibrations it holds. This raises our own vibration, enabling us to connect to the higher parts of ourselves as our lower-vibration worries, thoughts, fears, and attitudes dissipate.

Ritual Use of Water

Most religions include rituals involving water. In his article "A River Runs through Them: World Religions: How Water Shaped Our Beliefs and Rituals," Jeffrey Weiss explains that the ancient religions recognized all four earth elements in their esoteric beliefs but that water held an exceptional role in their spiritual practices.[24] Typically, water rituals have served as symbols of mental, physical, and spiritual cleansing.

Weiss tells us that in Judaism, the ritual connected with water is mikvah, a ritual bath. The mikvah is usually only done by men for special occasions but is also performed by both sexes during ceremonies to convert to Judaism. The ritual bath has a special requirement in that it must have at least two hundred gallons of fresh "living water," which is water received through natural, earthly means. In the Islamic tradition the *Wudhu* is a water ritual performed before prayer and again, only with the purest water, and the Koran states that before prayer you must wipe water over your entire body.

Water is also an important aspect of Hindu history, with water rituals tied to the rivers of India, and many Buddhist sects use water in many of their rituals, most commonly in initiation ceremonies. Baptism is Christianity's main water ritual where water is sprinkled on the participant, who may be completely submerged in the Church's baptismal bath. Some are now returning to the use of a natural body of water, like a river, for their baptisms.

Hand Gestures

Hand gestures were and continue to be used in many religious and spiritual ceremonies. Although purely symbolic, once we appropriate meaning to hand gestures, our being comes to recognize the cues they send forth. They can evoke Spirit and help us to become centered or focused. In her article, "11-11-11 The Cosmic Moment is Now," Patricia Diane Cota-Robles offers an explanation of why hands are so important in spiritual practices:

> We receive and transmit energy through our hands. Every acupuncture meridian is represented within the acupuncture pressure points in our hands ... The Light we receive through our hands flows through every acupuncture meridian and helps to unblock the areas in our body that are having trouble receiving and assimilating the electronic Light substance that is our Gift of Life, our Lifeforce, from our Father-Mother God, the Source of All That Is.[25]

In *The Everything Guide to Meditation for Healthy Living*, Drs. David Dillard-Wright and Ravinder Jerath tell us that in the East, hand signs or gestures regarding spiritual practices are called *mudras*. They suggest that our hand positions make a physical link to a state of mind that helps align the physical and mental, helping us to focus mind and body for the practice to come. The universal gesture associated with prayer, with hands flat and palms together, is known as *anjali mudra* in Eastern practices and symbolizes honor for others and sameness of all.[26]

Our hand gestures give signals to our energetic beings based on whatever intentions we have appropriated to them. In the worship time at the Church services I attended, I noticed that many people held out their cupped palms while singing. By the end of the worship, there was a palpable energetic shift in the room, and I realized this open-hand position not only invited spiritual energy to the individual it also enveloped the whole room.

Fasting

Fasting is used in many religions and spiritual practices for various reasons and with different observances. Full fasting may be required for a certain period of time or from daylight to sunset, or certain foods, drinks, or habits may be given up for a specific time frame. The associations with fasting I grew up with were entirely negative. I viewed it as a silly practice because all I was told by my mother was that it was for sacrifice, with no explanation of *why* to sacrifice. However, I have since learned that when done with a sincere heart and to honor one's belief system, fasting, like other rituals, can provide a spiritual boost.

Fasting can also provide true spiritual cleansing when the intention is understood. Most Jewish fasting traditions commemorate historical events for their people. Fasting is also part of Yom Kippur, which is observed as a day of repentance. Active Christians, who honor Lent, commemorate Christ's forty days in the desert by fasting to a certain degree, with most participants giving up certain foods, drinks, or habits. The annual Muslim holy time of Ramadan also holds to a forty day fast, where participants are only to eat or drink before sunrise and after sunset.

During the Dalai Lama's September 2011 visit to Montreal to promote the Peace through Religions Second Conference, Tariq Ramadan, the speaker who represented the Muslim faith, explained that he regards fasting as a physical discipline and that when we achieve discipline over the body, we can more easily achieve discipline over the mind. This I understood! When fasting is done with sincerity, reverence, or for spiritual growth it has value.

Loving Touches, a Symbol of God's Love for Us

Touch is very important to expressing love or compassion to another. It is also a common aspect of religious services or spiritual practices and is often used to seal a ritual. Physical touch, like shaking hands at a church service, can represent our inviting God's peace and love to be bestowed on the other. Many formal and not-so-formal rituals end with touch.

Every week as the sun sets on Friday evening, the Jewish celebration of Shabbat (Sabbath) begins. Lasting until the sun sets on Saturday, this day of rest is dedicated to family, community, and spiritual renewal. In her article "I Am a Child of God," Audrey Meisner explains that: "Traditionally, the father blesses the children by laying his hands on their heads and reciting the priestly blessing. Taking time to bless the children on Shabbat is a great way to reinforce the fact that they are loved, accepted, and supported by their families. In many homes, these blessings are followed by hugs and kisses or words of praise." Meisner goes on to explain that God created family, and that one of the most beautiful aspects of Judaism is its focus on family and dedicating time to be together, as well as the "significance of the Father's blessing."[27] I believe that the intention of promoting loving, supportive families within Judaism, as well as in the other religions, was to mirror how God loves us, and this sacred day of rest reminds us of this.

Whether we embrace any of the rituals I have mentioned, observe any other type of centering practice, or simply attune to what calms us, the experiences derived from them are as individual as the participants allow. With any conscious intention to calm the mind; align closer to Spirit, God, or Source; or be in communion with others, the benefits of even the simplest rituals can be far-reaching. So long as we do not interfere with another's well-being, adherence to our practices, rituals, and the rules within our religious or belief systems is valuable. I believe a compassionate respect and acceptance of other beliefs, rituals, and laws is the only path to a peaceful existence on both an individual and planetary level.

Section 4: Concepts

In this section, I will try to explain some of the concepts from within different religions, spiritualities, and belief systems to alleviate some of the misunderstanding and confusion that come about as we aim to reconcile their apparent differences.

Grace

Grace is often referred to as divine protection. Grace can be bestowed upon us, but we also invoke a state of grace when we align with the qualities of the Standard and attune to the universal energies. While writing this book over the past seven years, especially while surrounded by the reading material I had immersed myself in to prepare for this undertaking, I often felt infused with grace—as if in a bubble of complete peace and serenity. Even when I was working longer hours than I ever had or thought I could manage, I felt peacefully energized when working on the book.

Grace gives us the wisdom to navigate life, the strength make peace with or surmount difficult situations, and the courage to make necessary changes. It can manifest as *aha* moments that allow us to shift our attitudes or give us clarity for the direction we need to take. It can also manifest in more tangible ways, like being guided to a book, program, or person(s) that will help, support, or comfort us. Grace can also be defined as the ability to deal with what we must in a loving way.

Leonard Cohen explains grace and navigating life beautifully in the documentary *Ladies and Gentlemen ... Mr. Leonard Cohen*. When asked what his daily habits were, Cohen replied that if he woke up feeling in a "state of grace," he would continue on with his day, and if he did not awake in that state, he would go back to bed. When asked what he meant by a state of grace, Cohen said it was feeling able to transcend the situations that the day would hold. He said that if we strive for the world and everything to be perfect, we will always struggle, but if we aim to go with the ebb and flow of daily life in a peaceful way we can surmount any situation that may surface in our life.[28] Although some may view this attitude of going back to bed as avoiding life and its difficulties, I see it as a mature, conscious approach. If we attempt to deal with difficult situations and fail, we often amass guilt and/or create conflict or negative karma and thereby bring about more difficult situations. Avoiding what we know we cannot handle at any moment in time is being honest with our self and simply smart.

Archetypes

An archetype is a commonly understood representation that expresses certain qualities. Archetypes are often drawn from our mythologies or religions. They are only symbols but can infuse us with the energy they represent.

We can draw on archetypes from symbols, people, and spirits, and who or what we chose to invoke may shift as our needs change. Early in my journey, when I felt discouraged by not yet being all that I knew I could be, I would try to infuse myself with the energies of women I admired. During meditations and prayer, I reached out to women who exemplified qualities I knew were latent within me. I prayed to Mother Teresa to help me find my selflessness; I called in the energy of Lady Diana to help me access her unconditional love and devotion to her children; and I turned to Linda McCartney for her ability to be so content and peaceful. When I needed nurturing or lapsed into self-pity, I would call on Mother Mary, the Christian archetype of motherly love, for support.

Miracles

Miracles are usually associated with healing or manipulation of the elements, such as a yogi being able to bend spoons with his mind or Jesus turning water into wine. Events that defy reason or probabilities are also considered to be miracles, such as surviving a horrific accident. Miracles are also used to describe any happening that cannot be explained by our linear, third-dimensional laws of nature, such as finding the energy to swim to and save a drowning person when we cannot even swim very well. However, when accessing higher levels of consciousness, we connect to the universal forces, and the laws of time, space, and form are easily overcome. As we engage our higher, supernatural God-selves, we become more attuned to the organic, quantum makeup of the elements.

When we are *completely* aligned with our God-selves we are at one with the elements. Just as we can direct our hands to move a book, in these advanced states we can manipulate the elements with our consciousness. Enlightened yogis and the masters have all attained states enabling them to do this. I believe that when the masters performed their miracles, one of their key objectives was to demonstrate that when we tap into our God-selves, we can overcome what prevents our accessing our latent inner powers and help us recognize that there is more to our existence than we can see with our eyes. I address this more fully in the next chapter.

Miracles We Cannot See

When speaking about his book *The Anatomy of a Miracle*, Dr. Jim Richards states that our limited perspective does not permit a behind-the-scenes glimpse of nonphysical miracles. Spontaneous healings, a person showing up when we need him or her most, or the answer to an impossible request are all miracles. Nothing in our physical world can explain how they occur. Dr. Richards says that when making requests, we must rely on faith because we often do not have evidence of anything happening. He further explains that miracles are "not for the deserving, they are for the believing" and suggests "anything is possible if a person believes."[29] I address faith and our requests more fully below in Section 5, "Prayers."

When we partner-up with Spirit, or invoke the ascended masters or those who have attained those higher states in our prayers, we are not under the laws of the physical world. Because those in higher states are not working within physical laws, they can make what seems impossible happen. However, not all miracles are physical; some are mental or emotional, such as having a change of heart or attitude.

Based on its main premise, the word *miracle* in *A Course in Miracles* proposes that every second of every minute of every day, and with regard to anybody and within every situation, we *can* shift our attitudes from those based in fear to those based in love. (Illustrations 4, "Aspects of Love," and 5, "Aspects of Fear" depict many of these qualities). These shifts are considered miracles, as each little positive shift in attitude raises our consciousness and changes our trajectory. As our changes in attitudes manifest as more loving and compassionate behaviors, we influence Humanity's evolution in a positive way. Every shift to a love-based attitude helps to alleviate the fear-based paradigm that is keeping us all tied to the limitations of third-dimensional living.

The Rapture / Ascension

Some proponents of "the rapture" theory in different sects of Christianity believe this will take place just prior to the one thousand years of peace. Within the time frame of the Shift and our Ascensions we may experience what some are calling *rapture*. The physical ascensions of Jesus, Elijah, and Muhammad occurred because they had completed their missions here, but also had passed their earthly tests by overcoming the limitations of third-dimensional existence. With their bodies lighted enough for them to exist in the vibrations of the higher dimensions they ascended physically into the sky, whether on their own because of their higher states of being or beamed up into spaceships holding a higher dimension energy, a sense of rapture may have ensued as they met with the full energies of the higher dimensions.

The current understanding for us at this time of the Shift is that when we overcome the influence of our third-dimensional existence and become more aligned with the qualities and vibrations inherent in higher dimensions, our bodies become infused with enough light for our being to be ready to ascend. It is common among those who discuss Ascension within the Shift to suggest it is a slow process characterized by a spiritual rise in awareness that aligns with the higher dimensions rather than one momentous event or a physical lifting up. Nonetheless, within this there may be moments of significant spiritual growth bringing with it feelings of euphoria and unparalleled joy experienced as the kind of "rapture" depicted in our scriptures.

Some suggest that physical Ascension may be a possibility for us within the time frame of the Shift, as Gaia exists on a higher plain than during biblical times, but it may not be as we expect. Some recent findings suggest that Jesus, Elijah, and Muhammad did not ascend into heaven as is the common understanding, but were beamed up into spaceships that hailed from the higher dimensions. Some do believe that this type of physical Ascension could happen—if at all, but most likely a sense of peacefulness, joy, and/or euphoria—a sort of *rapture*—would accompany a jump in spiritual awareness.

Within the past few years some of us may have already felt a sense of euphoria or experienced a wonderful sense of well-being that seemed to come out of nowhere—most notably around December 2012, astrologically significant alignments and dates such as 11-11 or 12-12 of any recent year, as well as during the full moons and blood moons of the past few years. This is because the cosmic alignments around this powerful time in our evolution bring with them much light that aims to penetrate our beings.

Leading up to December 2012, many believed part of Gaia's Ascension would be that only those who had assimilated enough light into their beings with their attitude shifts would remain with her in her heightened state—with many experiencing the *rapture* of her elevation. Those who had not raised their vibrations enough to assimilate sufficient light into their beings to join Gaia in her Ascension would now occupy an alternate reality of earth. Those who did ascend with Gaia would simply experience them as just *gone*. However, it did not happen like this.

Various sources suggest different reasons, most notably that at an unconscious level we knew that the collective was making attitude changes in leaps and bounds, so we wanted to give more people the opportunity to make the required shifts and ascend with Gaia. Nonetheless, we do not have forever to align with Gaia's current vibration. There may still be a momentous occasion, so sometime in the near future we may still experience a significant "rapture." I speak a little more of the time frame given to anchor in the fifth-dimensional qualities in the next chapter under sub-section "Limited Time Frame to Anchor in the Shift" within the main section "*The Shift*."

Whether we experience the *rapture* or not, and however we experience Ascension, we are being helped all the time—especially when we forgive or make peace with others or situations. We are simply not aware of the organizing that goes on behind the scenes with our guides at the ethereal levels. Chapter 10, "Ascension," gives more detailed information.

Reincarnation: Past Lives

Within full Oneness there is no awareness of duality, or of its ideas of separation: of me-versus-you or us-versus-them, and therefore no need for life lessons, so within that reality reincarnation does not exist, being unnecessary. However, as we do not exist in full Oneness and have bought into the illusion of separation, reincarnation does exist for us—our souls or essences keep coming back. We do so because it is through our different lifetimes and their varying scenarios and life lessons that we are given opportunities to realign with the unconditional love and unity of the Creator and Oneness we emanated from so we can eventually reemerge with it. However, each reincarnation is intended to be a stand alone and when we are born a veil is drawn over the experiences of previous lifetimes.

A mentor once told me that we have so much trouble dealing with our current lives that delving into past lives would confuse us. Focusing on or trying to figure out past lives would only have the effect of taking our focus off what we need to learn or reconcile this time around. Eastern religions and many spiritual belief systems accept the concept of past lives, but the hazards of focusing on them may be the reason that the religions influenced by the Bible do not support their existence. Spirit, or the wisdom of the Universe, placed us here and now with close associations to those who are to assist us with the lessons we came here to learn in this lifetime—lessons which have nothing to do with our past lives. However, if we do not learn the lesson in one lifetime the same issue will crop up in our next lifetime(s), but the circumstances and relationships would be completely different.

Our current life circumstances can be explained not only by the life lessons we chose this time around and the playing out of karma (explained below), but also the rebalancing of experiences gone wrong in the last or a recent lifetime. Sometimes the life we had chosen or the life lessons we were to complete were interfered with by negative forces like war, cruelty, accidents, disasters, etc., or something that happened through negligence or on purpose. Our guides or angels cannot always protect us, and the Universe does not usually interfere as free will must be observed (except in rare and special circumstances). So, in our next life plans, we may be allowed to choose a life of ease and comfort to compensate for the extra suffering we endured. Our life lessons would then be in simple, everyday issues. We would have no conscious memory of this nor of the choices made before we incarnated this lifetime, but we would be at ease with our circumstances. As well, our souls may sometimes need to make up for having ignored past life lessons, even choosing exaggerated circumstances this time.

Understanding how past lives and life lessons work can help us appreciate the value of our current issues as well as make peace with the discrepancies between our life circumstances and those of others. Overcoming current life lessons is our soul's journey on a micro level. Overcoming all concepts of separateness and eventually *completely* aligning with the Oneness is our soul's journey on a macro level.

Even though most of us do not have conscious past-life memories, it is possible that we catch glimpses or feel emotional shadows of a past life event—especially if we had not made peace with it in that lifetime. Furthermore, as we continue to raise our consciousness and move beyond third-dimensional awareness and linear time, the veil that was erected between our past and current lives may start to lift and we would have more glimpses or déjà-vu of past events that seem real but wouldn't make sense in our current life. However, these would not upset or cause us emotional turmoil because of our more evolved state.

It is also possible that a terrible experience from a recent past life that we did not reconcile *may* have the effect of weighing us down in this one. Uncovering these can help in our emotional healing. Past-life regression has recently gained growing interest among practitioners of various facets of psychology and is sometimes offered as an adjunct to traditional methods, if deemed helpful. However, this is not a common practice and should always be done in a professional setting with a doctor certified in this type of psychology—and only when deemed necessary and for a specific purpose. For most of us, it is sufficient to understand that our various lifetimes offer opportunities to grow spiritually through the life lessons we chose to undertake, as knowing this can help us to reconcile ourselves with issues we face now. Reincarnation and past lives are further explained in "Understanding Reincarnation and Past Lives" found on the book's website.

The Prophets and Disciples of Old Are or Have All Been Here to Help With the Shift

I believe that in the time leading up to and throughout this Shift, the essences of the disciples have been or are here now, seeking to bring Jesus' message to us more clearly, along with the prophets, teachers, gurus, and holy ones who worked with the all the masters.

The ascended masters Arten and Pursah, who appeared to Gary Renard to guide him to write *The Disappearance of the Universe*, revealed to him that in one of their former lifetimes over two thousand years ago, Pursah was Thomas and Arten was Thaddeus, two of Jesus' disciples. They also said that at that time Gary had been the apostle Thomas, and his wife, Cindy, had been Thaddeus. As friends then, they worked together to help spread Jesus' message, and are now working together again to bring concepts of *The Course* (which came through its scribe, Helen Schucman, in a voice and energy she recognized as that of Jesus) to the world. *The Course's* concepts are in effect what Jesus was attempting to teach so long ago. These phenomenons may seem bizarre to many, but with an understanding of reincarnation, past lives, and the holographic nature of the Universe, it is not so far-fetched. I explain the holographic nature of the Universe in chapter 7, "Science and Other Related Topics." The Renards are a good example of a soul pairing.

Soul Groups / Pairings

Souls manifest together time and time again to help and support each other as they learn their life lessons and/or carry out their life's purpose, and we have different associations within these soul relationships each time. If in one lifetime we were the aggressor, we will be the victim in the next, as the Law of Balance aims to center itself within our beings and our karmic bonuses or debts aim to be settled. Our relationship roles also change in our various lifetimes. For example, if in the last lifetime one party was the mother and the other the child, these roles may be reversed in the next one as karma and life lessons merge in the hope that both find peace and forgiveness with whatever issues or situations arise in the relationship.

It is often said, "People come into our life for a reason, a season, or a lifetime." Within this context, the people in our lives are here to help us or us them with some aspect of the soul's journey. This is why our closest relationships are often experienced as painful, as their purpose is to show us our misalignments, so we may heal them. Regrettably, we all too often fail to understand this.

Joyce Meyer's relationship with her husband, Dave, is clearly a soul pairing. As explained in chapter 5, he, the calm one, stood by her as she worked through her life issues brought about by years of abuse from her father. In addition, their pairing clearly also helps Joyce fulfill her life's purpose to guide others with their healing. Over the last forty years or so, her ministry has helped millions of people find their way back to wholeness, funded millions of dollars in outreach programs across the world, and birthed dozens of books, all under the Christian umbrella.

Because we have not been taught the reasons for our relationships, our soul pairings are usually emotionally painful. However, this is where most of our personal growth happens. Not only do all our relationships offer us opportunities for growth and support, they also offer opportunities to work out any karma we may have accumulated with the other.

Karma

Even though karma does not exist within the auspices of complete Oneness, within the illusion we live under karma exists, and as such offers an explanation of how the laws of the Universe play out for us. Karma is the term used by most Eastern religions, and the Law of Cause and Effect and the Law of Balance that I have put forth (in chapter 2) are really just a different or more specific way of explaining karma. Many have confused God's revenge with the karmic Laws of Balance and Cause and Effect playing out in our lives.

There are various understandings of karma within the different traditions, but most agree that as we live our lives, we accumulate either good or bad karma. Good karma accumulates from what is held in our hearts made manifest by showing love and caring to others. Bad karma, on the other hand, is an accumulation of our negative attitudes and their subsequent behaviors that inflict any harm or cruelty on others, either physically or emotionally. Whenever we deal with any situation peacefully without succumbing to any negative attitudes or behaviors or falling into victimization, we are either creating good karma or clearing away bad karma.

Adding to our bank of good karma can neutralize the effects of bad karma, which can affect many aspects of our lives. In *Divine Transformation: The Divine Way to Self-Clear Karma to Transform Your Health, Relationships, Finances, and More* Zhi Gang Sha tells us that "to clear your bad karma is to remove the root blockages to transforming every aspect of your life."[30] We are transformed because we have erased a dark cloud on our soul that would have kept us distanced from our True Self and continued to undermine this life's peace and happiness.

Karma is also played out within our many lives through reincarnation. If we accumulate bad karma within one lifetime, at some point these debts will have to be cleared. If we accumulate good karma in any lifetime, it will be reflected in one of the next ones. Karma is further explained in the article entitled "Understanding Karma" located on the book's website.

Collective Karma

Throughout history we have all been perpetrators and victims and it is important that we acknowledge what we have done collectively. Even though we realize that most of us have come a long way from where we were, we can now see the limitations of our ancestors. Our awareness of having been birthed from a history filled with ruthless attitudes can help us better understand Humanity's more recent deficiencies.

This may be the reason that books like The Pillars of the Earth, A Song of Ice and Fire (Game of Thrones), and Outlander along with their popular recently broadcast TV productions have such large cult-like followings. Having all been written around the same time leads me to believe they came through because of the energy of the 1987 Harmonic Convergence, which is discussed below. Coming face to face with our past allows us to acknowledge and thereby release any guilt over it, and can also inspire and propel us to do better. Our heightened understanding of karma, past lives, the need for rebalancing, and the known repercussions of the dualistic systems we have lived under allows us now to face the more primitive attitudes of our ancestors. We are ready to make peace with our collective past.

Now that we have the understanding of and awareness to make peace with Humanity's past, we have to deal with what is happening in the world, taking into account what we now know of duality, our collective past, and the required rebalancing. Our collective karma is still playing itself out. And as with our individual bad karma, if we want Humanity's Life Matrix to shift we have to address any negative situations in the world without hatred or revenge. While we do what we must to protect ourselves and people suffering at the hands of those still acting under the influence of duality and its dark forces, we must keep our focus on helping rather than blaming. Understanding free will can help us do this.

Free Will, Our Soul's Journey, and the Big Picture

As explained in chapter 1, free will is a principle within the Universal Matrix we live under, and for the most part we get to exercise our free will. However, depending on what our soul's journey dictates, our free will can be overridden. Furthermore, we are not utilizing true free will when we act under unconscious influences.

At the human level, we do have free will to learn—or not learn—the lessons put before us at any point in time. However, in the long run, we do not have free will regarding these lessons. For example, if part of our soul's journey in this lifetime is to learn patience, we can choose to exercise patience at a job that requires it, or choose not to. Should we decide not to and leave the job without learning the lesson, other situations will show up in our life where we are given opportunities to exercise patience. And should we be way off track from what we chose to learn, there may be an intervention. Unfortunate mishaps, relationship breakups, loss of a job, and even illnesses may be our soul's way of urging us onto the paths we chose before coming into the world but are not adhering to. And not all lessons on our way back to Oneness need be learned while in physical form.

In his same book, Mitchell tells of another experience that Archangel Gabriel showed him (in his mind) of one of the lower realms of heaven. Mitchell witnessed a "crowded city … [whereby] hundreds of spirits were walking past us in orderly lines," all going in the same direction. Mitchell says they were all smiling, their journey seemed purposeful, and they all looked the same—"sheeplike." Gabriel explained that this group of spirits had chosen to do the exact same things in unity and as a group and had actually "agreed to become spiritual clones of one another." They had become so distracted from the truth of who they were in previous lifetimes that they had chosen this exercise in this nonphysical realm to help reconnect to that now-distant memory of unity of the Oneness we all share.[31] Reconnection and the lesson of unity has to be learned—one way or another, at one time or another.

Unconscious Influences at Play with Free Will

We have free will in that we can choose to do what we want, be how we want, and want what we want. However, we often undermine ourselves. When unconscious influences tap into our emotions and sensory systems, our intentions can be derailed and cause us to act in unintended ways.

For example, you may decide to be kind to your mother or father even if you have a strained relationship, but when you get together you blow up or give him or her attitude. You may decide you want to get healthy, but succumb to unhealthy choices. In the first instance your unconscious influences override your decision as your Default Position comes into play, and your free will and its power for conscious decision is unduly swayed from being nice to your parent. In the second example, you are answering neediness, attempting to fill void, or acting from an addiction, and unconscious influences have derailed your choice to get healthy, thereby overruling your free will.

When we are under the influence of unconscious influences, we may *feel* we are exercising free will when making choices, decisions, or acting upon an impulse, but we are not truly utilizing the gift of free will at all levels. However, sometimes our attitudes and actions are caused by dark forces at play.

Dark Forces / Powerful Energies

Because there is no right or wrong in the Universe—only the playing out of duality, Humanity has been plagued by what we can generalize as "dark forces" since the beginning of time. The Biblical story of Satan is a good example of this.

In the past it was also common to blame what we did not understand, such as mental illness or an epileptic event, as a dark spirit taking over the person. It is true that sometimes dark spirits did take over or enter people as it did happen in those days, but this was not always the case. And in the not so distant past, exorcisms were performed to rid people of uninvited spirits. Oasis used to tell us that at one time there were no rules in the Universe that forbid spirits from bothering people, and my understanding of this is that sometime within the past forty to fifty years that changed. This seems to be one of the occasions free-will (which also exists in the spirit world) was overridden.

The spirit world is filled with many different types of energies and powerful forces with some bad, some good, and many just neutral. Throughout history there have always been some people able to manipulate these powerful forces—for good and bad intentions, from Moses parting the Red Sea, to Jesus (or priests, ministers, and gurus today) healing the sick, to galvanizing dark forces like the Nazis attempting to overtake the world. Most of the time we will not be bothered by any dark forces or spirits, however, we can unintentionally evoke forces that we do not want, or simply do not know how to handle. This is why it has been recommended to involve a guru, minister, psychic, spiritual councilor, or at least someone trained in a specific technique, like a yoga teacher, when delving into any new spiritual undertaking, as they know how to distinguish energies and control powerful forces.

We evoke the darkest part of ourselves when we allow our minds to get stuck in the negative, and we can even invite in dark forces if we get bogged down in our own, another's, or the world's darkness, as the Law of Attraction is always at play. This happened to a friend of mine many years ago as he tried to figure out the darkest part of himself, and he told me it took a *lot* of work and outside help to override it. We can also unintentionally evoke powerful energy forces we cannot handle or get rid of.

I know someone who went to study a new way to approach her osteopathic practice in the Philippines a few years ago, a seemingly harmless undertaking, but came home very tired and lethargic. She eventually had to see an energetic healer to help her overcome this, because although her approach with her clients improved, the energy she worked with when in the Philippines affected her in ways she could not handle upon her return in her every-day life.

Enlightenment

The term *enlightenment* has been used to denote many different states of awareness. Many truth seekers, especially within Eastern thought systems, believe achieving full enlightenment, or complete alignment with Oneness, is the reason we are here. The masters all attained this state.

In the meantime, we may have an enlightenment experience, which is a fleeting glimpse or moment of clarity revealing the Oneness that pervades everything. In his article "When Time Stood Still," Steve Beckow relates his eight-second glimpse into that Oneness, which he says concluded with the understanding that "enlightenment is the purpose of life."[32] An enlightenment moment such as Beckow's affects the way we see the world, as we are then experientially aware there is more to it than what we perceive within our third-dimensional awareness.

Being enlightened is also used to describe a moment of clarity with regard to a certain situation, like an aha moment. I suggest that being somewhat enlightened means that we have some awareness of the cause and effect of our thoughts, attitudes, or actions, and of our interconnectedness.

Climbing up Mount Sinai: A Journey of Enlightenment

In another article, "Everywhere Are Clues about Life," Beckow offers the example of Saint John of the Cross, who interpreted Moses trip up Mount Sinai as a metaphor for letting go of our lower, chakra-based issues in the aim of fulfilling our journey of enlightenment. He cites Exodus 34:3 of the Bible: "When God ordered Moses to climb to the top of the mountain … He commanded Moses not only to ascend alone, and leave the children of Israel below, but to rule against the pasturing of beasts on the mountainside." Explaining that there are many layers of meaning within the metaphors in the Bible, Beckow suggests that this passage contains an "encoded enlightenment teaching" that our journey toward enlightenment requires that we renounce our ideas, beliefs, and attachment to things: that we need to leave them behind. He believes it also warns that even when we *think* we have relinquished our attachments, our journey will be fraught with temptations, and we must both discipline ourselves as well as guard against being passive toward them.[33] True enlightenment is also referred to as Christ consciousness.

Christ or Cosmic Consciousness: The Christ

Christ consciousness and *cosmic consciousness* are terms commonly used within different spiritualities and some of the Eastern belief systems to denote the state of awareness we attain once we have transcended the illusionary constraints of the lower dimension, have come to experientially know our true reality, and are completely attuned to the Oneness paradigm.

Linda Dillon explains in her book, *The Great Awakening*, that when attuned to the level of Christ consciousness we are in a "state of being in perfect balance, of simply being." She maintains that Christ consciousness is the seventh dimension within twelve realms (as depicted in illustration 3, "Levels of Consciousness within the Different Realms" reprinted below), and that we could think about the seventh dimension as "a place of still point where all energies anchor and flourish … the place of intersection" of the other dimensions, with some being more active and others more passive. Dillon also tells us that as humans we are most attracted to this dimension because of that feeling of complete balance.[34] It is because of this energetic interweaving and its state of complete balance that the masters, who were aligned with this seventh-dimensional Christ consciousness, were able to control the elements and create what are known as miracles while still in physicality.

In *The Holotropic Mind: The Three Levels of Human Consciousness and How They Shape Our Lives,* Stanislav Grof explains that cosmic consciousness, or this creative principle, has been written about in many religious scriptures throughout history and is known by different names: Brahman in Hinduism, Dharmakaya in Mahayana Buddhism, the Tao in Taoism, Pneuma in Christian mysticism, Allah in Sufism, and Kether in the Kabbalah.[35] According to Grof, the message is the same across all these religions, and not only can we connect with the creative principle, but in a sense we *are* the creative principle.

He says being able to connect to and become this creative consciousness makes sense when we look at the boundaries found within the physical universe. He relates this to quantum principles, because it shows us that physical boundaries are arbitrary, illusory, and can therefore be transcended. It is in our enlightenment moments when we transcend these boundaries and experience the cosmic consciousness that we are forever changed. I further discuss these scientific principles in the next chapter.

#3: Levels of Consciousness Within the Different Realms (Reprinted)

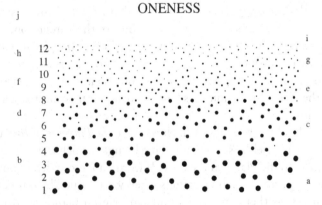

a) 1st 4 dimensions, world of form, separation is manifest
b) all life form, including humans and lower level ET's
c) 5th – 7th dimension, more ethereal, less awareness of separation
d) evolved live forms, higher level ET's, lower level Light-beings. Can take form
e) 8 -10th dimension, completely ethereal, concept of separation foreign. Rarely take form
f) highly evolved light-beings who run the Universe.
g) 11-12th dimension, completely ethereal, no awareness of separation. Very rarely take form
h) highly evolved light-beings that supervise the running of the Universe. Domain of Archangels and Seraphim. Almosy never have taken form.
i) No conscious awareness of Self, separation, its creations or us.
j) 13th - Original creative force we emanated from: God

Third, Fourth, and Fifth Dimensions

We may think of the dimensions as having a starting and stopping point, but they are really states of being or awareness. There are no barriers or lines between them. When we say we exist from or move to a new dimension, this means that we raise our consciousness to a higher plane by the vibrations emitted by our thoughts and attitudes. However, to characterize the differences between the levels of consciousness, we have used the idea of twelve dimensions with twelve levels within each. Humanity has lived in the various levels of the *third* dimension for eons.

Third-dimensional existence is ruled by the mind and characterized by form, linear space, and time. Until recently, Humanity as a whole had been stuck in the lowest rungs of this dimension, where fear, lack, power, control, and inequity reigned. This is why our past was so ruled by brutality, as these qualities engendered it. However, in the past few centuries and especially the last twenty-five years or so, we have shifted to the middle and higher rungs of the third dimension (and into the fourth and even higher). Most of us now consider greed, control, unfairness, and all forms of inequality and inhumanity towards our fellow man wrong. When we embody the higher levels of the third dimension, we feel lighter, happier and can more easily deal with life.

The fourth dimension, partner to the third, is its feeling dimension and is characterized by emotions rather than the mind. In this dimension, concepts of lack and fear can still be awakened in us, and other people, situations, or group energies may influence us to succumb to negative attitudes. Nonetheless, we are ruled by our hearts rather than our minds, so it is a better place to exist from than the third dimension—as long as we are well grounded within our physical reality.

Barbara Hand Clow explains in *Awakening the Planetary Mind* that the earth and its energy fields "support all living beings," which is why it is so vital that we connect to the Planet and nature. If we are not grounded in our bodies or protected by positive earth vibrations when we are ruled by our emotions, we are open vessels that can be manipulated or even maneuvered into fear scenarios or actions that are not aligned with who we are. This is because we can pick up on thought but are not adept at discerning exactly *what* it is or *where* it is coming from. Hand-Clow continues to explain that if the energy of the place we reside is in a balanced state and upholds the concepts of the "Tao, Asa, or Maat … the individual is profoundly grounded." The fourth dimension is also the realm of alchemy and transmutation that sages and shamans can easily access, because existing there means we are not ruled by the denseness of the mind and so are able to commune and communicate with the more ethereal beings in the higher realms.[36]

Shifting to the fifth dimension, we are no longer ruled by false emotions, neediness, or are able to be manipulated by others. In "The 5th Dimension Is Not a Location It's a Creation" Inelia Benz explains that it is easier to create *our* own realities in the higher dimensions because in the "more subtle dimensions, core material is there as a more subtle physicality," so as we raise our vibrations and become "less 'dense' ourselves," we are more aligned with the "subtle and pliable" characteristics of it and can therefore create there more easily. The truth that "we can create our own reality" has been hidden from us because being unaware of the power we hold kept us "spiritually unawakened [and we could and have been] led to create someone else's reality by the use of fear, persuasion, and created illusions of reality." As we become more conscious and in tune with our own "nature [and] reality," we are less influenced by others who would want to push their "created illusions of reality" on us.[37]

Manipulators and those with nefarious intentions have preyed on our trusting natures and openness as well as our fear. Their ideas can be so strongly promoted that they override our good sense, so we cannot see these ideas are unreal and not coming from us. Prejudices that are promoted or acted upon against certain people like gays, Indigenous people, or African Americans, or hate against groups like the Jewish people and the Holocaust, are all examples of fear and hate that people have been lured into. As there is no right and wrong in the Universe, highly evolved psychic powers that can influence people are accessible to many—not only those holding a higher spiritual purpose.

Being spiritually awakened is not a prerequisite to having a psychic ability. It may be a leftover gift from a past lifetime, the person may not have evolved as much or as quickly as was intended in this lifetime, or they strayed from the original purpose to do good with it. This is why we have often been lured to follow those with wicked intentions.

When we are spiritually unawakened and living within third dimensional realities, we buy into fear and hate more easily and cannot see how it embodies judgment, unfairness, and the lack of unconditional love God asks us to offer to *everyone.*

Many of us have already or are at least primed to move from the third and fourth into the fifth dimension, but this usually happens slowly. Although we may attempt to give up judgements or negative habitual responses, the two-step forward one-step backward scenario usually plays out causing us to vacillate back and forth between the dimensions until we fully anchor in the attitudes of the higher dimension.

Most children and young adults today came into the world highly evolved to help us anchor in the qualities this Shift requires and should barely touch the third dimension. However, if their surrounding circumstances do not embrace the qualities of love, the conflict created within their being between what they inherently know and what is in front of them may cause some to behave badly or fall into dysfunction.

Chakras

Within Eastern religions, the chakras are seven meridian points in the physical body that represent an unseen energetic flow, like a life force, which relate to our physical, emotional, and spiritual natures.

The seven main chakras (there are other more subtle ones) are situated from the lower spine up to the crown of the head. The lower chakras reflect our connection to physicality, the middle chakras relate to our emotional natures, and the higher chakras are indicative of our higher consciousness. All our emotions are recorded in our chakras. This means that any negative emotions, conscious or not, block this energetic flow. This keeps us in limitation, unable to access our full potential. Positive emotions unblock this flow. Illustration 18 depicts our chakra system.

#18: The Chakra System

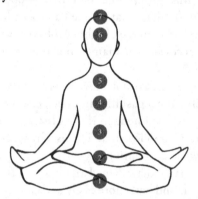

First chakra: located at the base of the spine, relates to material concerns; affects our limbs.
Second chakra: located a little higher up, relates to our sexuality; affects our sexual organs.
Third chakra: located around the naval and solar plexus area, relates to our personal growth and self-esteem; affects our digestive system and our metabolism.
Fourth chakra: located near the chest and heart area, relates to our emotional nature, affects our breast and heart and their functions.
Fifth chakra: located in the throat area, is related to our communication and expression in the world; affects our voice, throat area and thyroid function.
Sixth chakra: often called the third eye is located on the forehead, is connected to the intuitive parts of ourselves; influences our imagination and insight.
Seventh chakra: located in the crown of the head, is related to our higher consciousness and pure enlightenment.

We can use the chakras for healing, as they are either open or blocked and are associated with certain issues. This can be done for anything that is keeping us in limitation, unhappiness, or dysfunction. There are links to chakra information and a little chakra test in the List of Recommendations. Meditation 3: "Specific Chakra Meditation: Fifth Chakra, Communication" is on the book's website. You can access it using the "Download" link by keying in the code for this meditation found on the last page of the book.

The Kundalini

The kundalini is an Eastern term to describe the awakening of a spiritual force brought on by an expansion of consciousness into higher levels of awareness. Often described as a coiled energy located at the base of the spine, the kundalini can awaken gradually after years of spiritual focus, during a deep meditative practice, or as a spontaneous event. Not everyone's life path will include the awakening of the kundalini. Even many serious spiritual or religious practitioners may never experience the kundalini rising, as it is a process that requires many lifetimes of practice and must be in alignment with what we are to achieve spiritually or to teach in this lifetime. In the big picture, we all bring forth different energies and have varying purposes, just as the different masters did whose teachings all come through with a different slant.

When our souls' journeys have primed us for the awakening of the kundalini and as we let go of the lower-base needs and attitudes that block our chakras in this lifetime, the dense energies are replaced by lighter ones, which allow the kundalini energy to move about. Then as we continue to release emotional attachments associated with the middle chakras, the kundalini will start to rise up through these chakras. In *Farther Shores: Exploring How Near-Death, Kundalini, and Mystical Experiences Can Transform Your Life*, Yvonne Kason writes that when the kundalini is awakened, the spiritual transformation of our consciousness is accelerated as an electrical current travels up from the lowest chakra at the bottom of the spine and through the remaining six chakras, ending at the top of the head.[38]

Rising of the Kundalini and Powerful Spiritual Practices: Serious Business

In the Eastern practices, attempts at kundalini rising is a serious matter, and the tools are only offered to serious students of meditation and self-cleansing. A mentor is always involved. A spontaneous awakening of the kundalini can be frightening. Around 2002, when I was working on acknowledging and releasing my unconscious influences and boldly making statements to Sprit, I had a frightening experience that was later explained to me as a spontaneous rising of the kundalini. For a full recap of this experience, see article "My Spontaneous Kundalini Rising Experience" on the book's website.

There are profound experiences in other religious practices, for example, receiving the Holy Spirit in Christianity. This is likely why a priest or minister oversees this process. I was once witness to a ceremony to receive the Holy Spirit. The participant was asked whether she wanted to invite the Holy Spirit in, and the attending minister made the request, saying that she was prepared and ready to receive. While making a gentle gesture over her head, he asked that the Holy Spirit calmly come upon her.

Many yogis and teachers of meditation and yoga believe we should not attempt to raise the kundalini—that it should not be awakened. They believe that we came into this world with it closed and that awakening it is an intense esoteric practice that can have detrimental effects, as some may have difficulty getting along in the world afterward.

While I do believe we should be very careful and engage quality mentors, teachers, or those deemed qualified for any type of serious spiritual practice, I feel that experiences like my own can shake us out of the craziness of the world we are engaged in, just as we are forever changed when we are diagnosed with a serious illness. I never consciously sought out to raise my kundalini, but do believe the experience changed me forever, for the better. We were not meant to be running around with our mind going in a million directions completely out of tune with the moment and unaware of the subtler parts of ourselves. If we do not make these shifts ourselves, we are sometimes shaken out of them by illness, a major life crisis, or by a spontaneous spiritual experience that changes us forever.

Any powerful spiritual practice, such as raising the kundalini or doing the lessons of A Course in Miracles, need to be given appropriate consideration. Although seemingly simple from an outside perspective, as there are no physical signs that anything is changing, they evoke potent spiritual forces that aim to undo the way we perceive ourselves and the world around us, which can have at least a temporary destabilizing effect. Although in the long run the changes are beneficial, in the meantime we have to live our lives without too much interruption. For some, like those of us whose soul life plan is to teach new and profound spiritual concepts to others, we do need to go through powerful transformations which will likely somewhat derail us. This is necessary to free us of our unconscious influences so we can bring forth pure messages. However, for most who are embarking on a spiritual practice, it will simply involve shifting attitudes, recognizing important *aha* moments, and adopting life changes that will support being our Best Self.

If during any self-discovery process, we start to feel depressed or the changes are too difficult to manage, it is recommended to take a break from it all and focus on light-hearted activities that uplift us and bring us peace and joy. Peace and joy is the ultimate goal of any spiritual practice.

Virgin Births

The idea of virgin births was not an uncommon concept in ancient times. Not only were well-known masters who walked the earth in the Middle East and the Far East such as Jesus and Krishna purported to have come from virgin births, the Iroquois tribes of North America also tell of a virgin birth for one of their masters.

In *The Iroquois Book of Life*, Paul Wallace tells of the prophet Deganawidah, known as the Great Peacemaker, who brought many tribes together to form the unified Iroquois nation. Deganawidah lived sometime in the twelfth to fourteenth centuries. It is said that a messenger sent from the Great Spirit, their term for the Holy Spirit, visited the child's grandmother before his birth and told her, "It is the will of the Master of Life, the Holder of the Heavens, that thy daughter, a virgin, shall bear a child. He shall be called Deganawidah, the Master of Things, for he brings with him the Good News of Peace and Power. Care for him well, thou and thy daughter, for he has a great office to perform in the world."[39] As he lived before Christianity reached America, this tale could not have been inspired by the story of Jesus Christ.

The Trinity

One of the main symbols within Christianity is the Trinity, and even among ministers and the clergy, many still cannot explain it. The Trinity represents the Father, the Son, and the Holy Spirit. The Father refers to God, the Creator; the Son refers to Jesus, who is God manifested as man as the savior; and the Holy Spirit (also referred to as the Holy Ghost) refers to the energy that guides us and speaks to and through us. Those who adopt the concept of the Trinity believe in One God (the One original creative force), as they maintain that the Son and Holy Spirit are at one with God but interpreted as three different aspects, hence the mystery of the Trinity. The Oneness of God is all there is, as nothing else really exists. However, within the illusion and the world of multiplicity that is our current awareness, the Son and Holy Spirit do exist and are separate entities.

Different aspects of the Trinity are also evident in other religions. After studying the various religions for years, Steve Beckow explains in his article "Christianity and Hinduism Are One," that the Hindu and Christian religions both similarly acknowledge the different aspects of the Creator and its extensions.[40] So does Taoism and some Indigenous tribes. Taoism asserts that first there was one, then there were two, and then there were three, and so on, and that we all emanated from there. The one relates to the original Creator, the two is synonymous to Spirit, and the three to everything else that came after. Indigenous people refer to the Great Spirit while also acknowledging the Creator aspect. However, within other religions such as

Judaism and Islam, the Trinity is not recognized as the Trinity implies God is dualistic and they hold to pure monotheistic beliefs.

The importance of adhering to the concept of *only One God* and pure monotheism may have developed because of the understanding that in reality all that exists is the Oneness (God). It may also have been to protect us from having to distinguish between the many light-beings in the Universe and those from other planets whose complete focus was to help us from those less committed and/or more susceptible to falling into dualistic attitudes and able to use and/or abuse us, which clearly some did in the past. The potential is always there for any being within the illusion to forego the concepts of unconditional love and unity of purpose. However, at this time of the Shift as we are raising our vibrations we are way less susceptible to negative outside forces, so the *necessity* of adhering to the concept of *only One God* for our own protection is waning.

From an outside perspective the Trinity may appear to be dualistic, but Christianity believes itself to be monotheistic in that it adheres to the belief in only One God. With the understanding of the mystery of God as all-encompassing, the different aspects of God are still recognized. Leslie Stevenson and David Haberman tell us in *Ten Theories of Human* Nature that one of the main principles of the Upanishads, a Hindu text, is that "there is a single, unifying principle underlying the entire universe."[41] It is the Oneness, or creative force of the Universe I speak of. We call this God, Source, the Creator, and many other names.

God, the Creator

> *[When asked] "How many gods are there?"*
> *Yajnavalkya responds first: "three and three hundred,*
> *and three and three thousand."*
> *... "Yes of course, ... but really ... how many gods are there?"*
> *"Thirty-three."*
> *[the same questions is asked four more times, answered as]*
> *"Six."... "Three."... "Two."... "One and a half."*
> *"... but really ... how many gods are there?"*
> *"One."*
> —Yajnavalkya and Vidagdquote, *The Upanishads*[42]

This conversation between the sage Yajnavalkya and his student Vidagdquote attempts to clarify the mystery of the many so called gods that we can perceive who run the Universe. There really is only the *One* original creative force (which in the story *Yajnavalkya* calls *Brahman*) and the light-beings, archangels, or masters are aspects of the One. As shown in illustration

2, "The Creative Universal Force Extending Itself," and explained in chapter 1, that original creative force extended itself, but maintained its Oneness while still encompassing all its creations. Hence, we are all still One with it as the interconnectedness was never lost. Within the Eastern religions, they call these expressions of the One *the world of multiplicity*. We are all extensions and expressions of the One. Stevenson and Haberman also tell us that in Hinduism the term *Brahman*, considered to be that original creative force, is "derived from a Sanskrit root that means to 'grow,' 'expand,' or 'increase.'"[43] So we grew out from the original One.

There has been much confusion over who God really is, and the term has been bestowed upon many beings throughout history and used in many ways. In many cultures, gods embodied the symbols and particular beliefs of a given group of people or tribe. Some prayed to specific gods for the protection of crops, troops, or even the birth process. The ancient Greeks were conscious of many separate beings within the Universe and referred to them as gods, just as many do with the archangels. Many cultures, like the Egyptians and Indigenous people, depicted gods through the images of animals. These depictions may be how the different light-beings who took on certain responsibilities within different groups of people chose to represent themselves. It may also be how some of the extraterrestrials appeared or chose to appear.

Some say that Buddhists do not believe in a God. The teachers and practitioners may suggest that all the confusion about a God external to us distracts us from doing our own inner work to attain *our* higher states of consciousness and connect to our God-selves. Most faiths and even the Western religions are increasingly focusing on our spiritual growth and relationship to God—our connection to our higher Self or Spirit, instead of adhering to dogma or concerns about the terms used.

Today, some never use the term *God*, while others continuously throw it around. New words like *Source* have become popular for this reason, and many, including myself, will sometimes use the word Universe as an all-encompassing term to acknowledge the One God-energy and those working on the higher realms for us, but mostly, I use the word Spirit, synonymous with higher Self, who works with and guides me. This is akin to the common use of the term Holy Spirit in Christianity. Using the terms God, Source, Spirit, Holy Spirit, Great Spirit, Allah, Brahman, Universe or any other word common to our culture is not a problem. Creating conflict over which is the correct term to use, further perpetuates the idea of our separateness by focusing on our different beliefs, instead of encouraging the Oneness that binds us.

God's Representatives: The Council and Its Helpers

Within the layers of the Universe there was at least one, or possibly many higher-dimensional beings assigned to oversee and be responsible for it and Humanity. This would account for the various names like God, Yahweh, Allah, etc. it was suggested we call them. Oasis called those who were set up to run the Universe *the Council*.

The various light-beings on the highest ethereal levels (including the archangels) have different tasks, and in their own way (energetically, telepathically) they consult with each other. They also have many helpers, with the lesser evolved beings reporting to those in the higher realms. Spirit, Great Spirit, Shakti, Holy Spirit, or what I call "the Great Translator" etc. is our connection to the creative universal force—the One *true* God—who does not interact with us (or the world of form at all) and even has no awareness of it or us. This is the Oneness, our Source, from whence we came, and it is its unifying principle that the Council represents and is charged with having us all align to, so that we (and they) can all one day reemerge with it.

The various gods of old and many were the extraterrestrials we called gods were helpers. However, all these beings were and still are within the illusion and working under the auspices of duality, and thus had the *potential* to use whatever means to get and keep Humanity on track. As such, some may have swayed from the qualities inherent in the Oneness.

Knowing all this it is still ok to say "God wants ...," or "God asked ...," etc. when we feel inspired or are aiming to align ourselves with the goodness of whatever we believe is God and when our intentions are pure. It is also ok to use "Spirit" or "Holy Spirit" as these terms refer to our link or personal connection to our origins; to use "the Universe" as this encompasses Spirit and also acknowledges the helpers and our guides (or guardian angels); or to use "Source" as this refers directly to our origins. Knowing that the God of the Bible who sent the flood but who is also said to be all loving, all powerful, omniscient, and omnipresent was not that same *original creative force* of the Universe—the One *true* God who endlessly embodies all those qualities, helps to dispel some of the confusion over apparent inconsistencies in the popular use of the word God and in our Holy Books.

The Son

Within the Trinity of Christian belief, the Son represents Jesus. He is also referred to as the only Son of God, and it is also sometimes said that God sent "his only Son" to save the world. I once heard Joyce Meyer say that Jesus came from, and still abides in, the highest realm. This means that he came from one of the earlier extensions either before or shortly after awareness arose of the separated Self (extensions were explained in chapter 1). Jesus was an aspect of God—hence the term *Son of God*—who took form for a specific purpose, to help show us the way back to Oneness. The *only* Son implies that he was the only one who came from this highest realm. However, all masters or avatars are purported to have come from the highest realms, so there is still some confusion here. If we are all aspects of God, albeit further along the line of the extensions-of-extensions-of-God, but still aspects of God, we are all therefore the Sons of God.

The Sonship: the Son Represents All of Us

The Son, which usually refers to Jesus, has also been referred to as the Sonship, meaning that we are all extensions of the original creations, and so all Sons of God. *The Course* uses the term *Sonship* to help us recognize that we are all sons and daughters of the Father, the original creative force. This allows us to fully comprehend that our relationship with God the Father is akin to the ideal loving, caring relationship between a father and his child. Part of the confusion about God, also known as God the Father, may also be because our history has not always produced loving, caring fathers. So again, the intention of the words used to describe the loving, caring God were misunderstood because we projected our own ideas and experiences of fathers onto the metaphor given us.

Jesus is an example within the Sonship of being connected with our God-selves and completely aligned with the Oneness, so he encourages us to follow his lead. In John 14:6 he says, "I am the Way—yes, and the Truth and the Life. No one can get to the Father, except by means of me." He was suggesting that he was anchored in the Oneness and that by calling on his energy and light we can be encouraged and uplifted, and by following his teachings we too can become completely aligned with our God-selves and the Oneness. Any of us can reconnect to Oneness, but Jesus is a brother we can look to who surmounted the task of overcoming the lure of the ego and its thoughts and attitudes of separation while in physical form and was able to completely realign with the Oneness. He overcame his temptations, is now anchored in the light, and so can we be.

Holy Spirit: The Great Translator

Spirit or Holy Spirit is considered to be the communicator between us and God. The American Indigenous peoples call it the Great Spirit. For Hindus it is the Shakti, and for Taoists it is the Tao. Some today call it the Mother, which goes with the Father metaphor of God. I call it the Great Translator, as it acts as a translator between us and God. The *Tao Te Ching describes* this Spirit energy as:

> The Great Mother:
> empty yet inexhaustible,
> it gives birth to infinite worlds.[44]

While the original creative force has no awareness and is characterized by stillness, the Holy Spirit, Great Spirit, or Shakti is characterized by movement. The use of the metaphors, the Father as the original creator and protector and the Mother as the patient, loving one who is continuously creating from that original template of God-energy and who guides all her creations, was to help us understand what was beyond our comprehension. However, our inability to really grasp the meaning of these metaphors created one of the many "it is likes" that we took literally and misconstrued over time, leading to the confusion of a strict and judgmental God as we superimposed our ideas and experiences of fathers on the message.

God, the Creator; Holy Spirit, the Overseer / Communicator / Translator

Although God is the One and original creator, with the advent of the first separations, this Spirit energy emerged to link everything together in an intertwining matrix and became an overseer/communicator for and between everything that emerged from the original energy, keeping alive the pathway to the bridge between the Creator and its creations. It is the translator between us and God. Those on the highest realms, such as the archangels and light-beings, are its representatives and managed all the creations, as they still do. Within the original creation, our Universe is not and has not been the only one. However, for simplicity, I refer only to us and our Universe. This Tao, or Spirit energy, is all-pervasive. It is in everything and envelops everything. The *Tao Te Ching* says the following about this Spirit energy, or the Tao:

> It flows through all things,
> inside and outside, and returns
> to the origin of all things.[45]

Spirit Speaks to Our Heart

Spirit, Holy Spirit, or Skakti speaks to us in our hearts. When someone says, "God spoke to me," it is really Spirit, as God is a nonparticipant in the Universe. Spirit is always encouraging us to remember our connection to our Source. Spirit is the Great Translator of all we need to be and align with to embrace the love within. It is always speaking to us and encouraging us to overcome what obstructs us accessing that love. It communicates with us through our intuition, dreams, and our conscience; through people on TV, the radio, books, podcasts, or any other commutation device; and it speaks to us through our scriptures and any other uplifting material. It translates to us how we need to be and what we need to be aware of to align with our God-selves. Many of the ancient parables still apply because their themes translate through the ages and Spirit uses them to convey what *we* now need to know or understand to become our Best Self. Joyce Meyer has often said in her broadcasts that she went to the "school of the Holy Spirit," meaning that when she read and studied her Bible she evoked the Holy Spirit to allow it to speak directly to her.[46] Spirit can also speak to our hearts through music, art or nature.

The reason we call the Trinity or other metaphysical precepts a "mystery" is that within our third-dimensional, linear reality, it is difficult to comprehend the concepts put forth. How can God or Brahman and its representatives such as Atman, Jesus and us, as well as Spirit, the Tao, or Great Spirit all be One and the same, but separate and different? How could God or Brahman be the origin—the Creator, yet have all of its sons and daughters within it? In *Ten Theories of Human Nature*, Stevenson and Haberman explain the pervasiveness as well as the remoteness, of the God energy:

> *Brahman* is not only *in* the world,
> it *is* the world;
> there is also a dimension of *brahman*
> that is completely beyond the world of multiple forms.[47]

Scriptural Writings: Sutras

There are writings to support all the ancient belief systems and religions. In the West we call them *scriptures* or *Holy Scriptures*. In the East they are called *sutras*. They offer accounts of the lives of prophets and masters and their messages of love and hope. They describe people's issues and struggles and how they overcame them with prayer, faith, and shifts in attitudes that embrace the Universal Laws. These writings also describe what happened to those who did not follow the laws of the land, which were originally developed to keep us aligned with the Universal Laws. However, because these accounts were written when we were still very deeply entrenched in third-dimensional attitudes, much of what was intended was lost to us.

Many of the messages concerning our empowerment were edited and misrepresented by those in authority, as the political atmospheres in ancient times were based on power—they wanted to control the general population. So much of the inherent power within us was withheld from us as the editors put together the Bible. At other times scriptures were challenged. In *The Complete Life of Krishna*, Vanamali Mataji explains that during the British conquest of India the missionaries wanted to convert the masses, so they denied the importance of the Vedas, the original Hindu text. The Vedas along with the Puranas, which told the history of the Hindu culture, were dismissed as primitive mythology.[48]

The ancient teachings were further undermined as human thoughts, beliefs, and ways of being were transferred onto the original messages and metaphors, which caused misunderstandings about their meaning. This happened because the more evolved ways of thinking and being were so foreign to the lives and beliefs of our ancestors that they could not, or would not, grasp them.

Because of the conflicting messages of many of the scriptures, taking every word at face value has created strife and divisive attitudes. We are told God offers unconditional love, but is judgmental. So unless we reconcile these conflicting concepts how can we offer unconditional love to all others void of judgment? This cannot help but pose a dilemma and create internal conflict in those who wholeheartedly give themselves to their belief systems, as our True Selves know the *intended* truths. This is one of the reasons for so many conflicting interpretations that have led to judgment of the others' understanding of the texts and pitted different sects against each other, even within the same religions. But no matter how misunderstood, misused, or denied, the intentions of the original messages are still held within sacred texts, if we let them speak to us directly.

Scriptures' Ability to Speak to Us when We Are Sincere

In his interview with Oprah on her second-to-last show, James Frey explained that he read, reread, and meditated on the *Tao Te Ching* and let it speak to him and that it worked through him and allowed his inner healing to begin. As mentioned before, Joyce Meyer allowed the words in the Bible to speak to her heart, and help her understand and then overcome her propensity to react negatively. She now brings those healing messages to the world.

Vanamali Mataji also tells us that although the missionaries in India discounted the Hindu texts, great inventors from Europe and the United States saw through to the truths they held, suggesting that the Vedas were the "greatest scriptures in history." These inventors were at the cutting edge of Humanity's understanding of its physical laws and claimed that the Vedas, which held "glorious revelations regarding divinity," were the most important pieces of information known to man.[49] These great scientists and inventors understood the connection between our divine potential, science, and the Universe and its laws.

Section 5: Prayers

You pray in your distress and in your need;
would that you might pray also in the fullness of your joy
and in your days of abundance.
—Khalil Gibran[50]

Always Praying

We now know that our thoughts and attitudes give out vibrations and that these vibrations give off requests. So in a way, we are always praying or requesting by means of our vibrations. When we make conscious requests, whether through formal prayer or in our meditation or quiet time, our vibrations and intentions work in concert with one another. If our unconscious beliefs and their energetic alignments agree that we feel deserving of what we are requesting or that it is possible, our prayers will usually be answered.

I say usually, because sometimes we pray for things that are way off base from our soul's journey, and they may not come to pass. Some soul lessons that we came here to fulfill cannot be overruled, and if a certain request is not congruent with that, it will not happen. We never know God's full plan for our lives, and from our limited perspective we may feel we want something that will not ultimately serve us or that plan.

In our conscious prayers or requests, patience is vital, as the various pieces surrounding what we are asking for may not be in place yet. Still, most of our requests can be answered because our soul's plan does not include the minor details, just general guidelines, such as making peace with difficult life situations.

Are Our Prayers / Requests Coming from True Desires?

To ensure that what we request will *ultimately* fulfill us, we must ensure that our desires do not stem from neediness or any unconscious influence. We must ask ourselves whether we are answering the call of a pure, heartfelt desire that will ultimately bring us peace and happiness in the long term. While it may seem difficult to distinguish between true desires that run parallel to our soul's journey and those that come from unconscious influences, it is our *true intention* that is important.

For example, if we ask for our immediate yearnings to be met, such as finding a specific partner or a higher-paying job, we may actually be working from neediness, a Hidden Agenda, or trying to fulfill a Perceived Need. If so, we may be granted a new relationship or that great position, but there will eventually be conflicts. If we are needy for love, the partner who will surface in our life will likely have a controlling nature, as this is what we will draw toward us. The perfect job may suddenly appear, but perhaps it brings with it extra stress, and we develop issues with our loved ones. It is important to stay mindful of our innermost heart desires that will fulfill and bring us joy rather than those that satiate any neediness, ego ramblings, *desire to prove ourselves*, or attempts to meet society's standards.

Sincere Prayers / Practices Emit Vibrations

A few years ago, I was at an airport in the late afternoon waiting for a connecting flight. Nearby, a group of Muslims was waiting for the same flight. Over a period of twenty minutes or so, four or five of them quietly went over to a corner, laid down their small prayer rugs, and did their obeisance, all facing the same direction. Their religious observance was discrete and subdued. As I sat reading my book, glancing up occasionally with the normal distractions of the crowded area, I started to notice that the deep fatigue that had plagued me all day had suddenly lifted. Putting my book down, I looked around and became entranced by the worshipers gentle obeisance, and then aware that the beautiful, peaceful stillness that had come upon me emanated from them. The atmosphere generated by their worship had infiltrated my being.

My years of spiritual opening with Oasis, as well as my understanding and acceptance of others' rituals had created an alignment in my being that made it possible for my heart to open during their prayer time, so I could then share in the energy they were creating. I had no inner blocks in place.

I like the idea of a five-times-a-day small practice to center ourselves. I know it would have been helpful to me all those years I was living in frustration. I believe that if everybody took five minutes five times a day to say a prayer, do a small meditation, simply shut the office door and take a few quiet breaths, or gaze out the window at a beautiful tree, the lake, or children playing outside, we would all benefit on individual and world levels.

Anchoring in Our Intentions When Praying or Meditating

Whatever the form of request or prayer we use, we are answered in accordance with the quality of the vibration we create around it. If we undermine our prayers with doubt, our faith is not strong, nor is the vibration around the request. When including appreciation for what we have in our prayer time or to simply feel gratitude for what we have, more of the same will be returned to us in accordance with our state of mind, the vibration this creates, and our sincerity.

In "Miraculous Probabilities: The Science of Faith," Dr. Jim Richards confirms that it is our faith, confidence, and clarity that create the "electromagnetic fields" which in turn affect the degree to which our prayers and requests are answered. To create the electromagnetic field that will bring about our desire we must *fully* believe that we are deserving of it, confident that it is possible, and be clear in our message. Wishy-washy requests or negative and/or limiting attitudes concerning what we want affect our vibrations and the electromagnetic fields that can bring it to us.[51]

When our requests are clear and we are not undermining them we only need to make them once, and then let them go. This is so Spirit can get to work on making them happen, without our interfering with the conviction of the original request. However, because we are often not completely aligned with the *belief* that they *will* come about and our vibrations may not be *fully* in alignment with allowing our desires to come into our lives, we create a kind of static in the requests that undermines our requests, as shown in illustration 9, "Static in Connection to the Universal Powers." So reaffirming them is often necessary, but only to clarify with confidence what we want, not to hurry them up or try to manipulate outcomes.

Praying, meditating, or gathering with other people for a common purpose or any spiritual or uplifting event also has great value, and we are encouraged to do so in times of disaster or for those in need within our communities or all around the world. We need not be of the same faiths or hold all the same beliefs as those we pray with because it is what is in our hearts—our *intention* to join with others in spirit or with a common purpose that matters—not the form or words in the prayers. As the energy of the Shift continues to inspire us, we will feel more inclined to rise above that which separates us for the good of all. In the early months of 2016 Pope Francis, a Jewish rabbi, and a Muslim leader demonstrated the importance of banding together no matter our different beliefs, as they prayed with their heads bent together for peace and for people suffering throughout over the world.

Doing Our Part; and the Make Me, Not Give Me Attitude

As we have uncovered the truth of the power we hold that was hidden from us for eons, we can no longer play the innocent victims! We can no longer blame others, our circumstances, or the world for how we experience life. Nor can we blame God. And if we do want help, rather than always asking for things or our circumstances to change, we can ask for the qualities that will make us happy with what we have and help us make peace with our circumstances.

Byron Katie's *loving-what-is* philosophy underlines the importance of having an accepting attitude, no matter what the circumstances. This is really where our peace of mind lies. We can also endeavor to shift to the notion of *make me, not give me.* We can ask for help with an attitude shift. We can ask for compassion, understanding, and patience for ourselves and with others. We can ask for acceptance of others if we are judgmental. We can ask for humility if we have a tendency towards arrogance. We can ask for any qualities or virtues we know are latent in us but are aligned with God or the Standard. When we embrace the concept of *make me, not give me, not only do we become more* peaceful, because we are not resisting or pushing against what is, we are creating a lighter vibration that does not obstruct or block the flow of the Universe.

All Roads, Their Symbols, and Practices Guide Us to Our God-selves

Once I became focused on looking at the similarities as opposed to the differences in the various religions and spiritualities and saw how many of the precepts aligned with psychological teachings, I discovered new insights that pulled everything together. The Law of Openness requires that we not only have open hearts but that we are also open to different ideas and approaches. We must be receptive to the fact that our individual perspectives are not the only ones, and that they even may be misguided. It helps to remember that over our lifetime most of us have changed our minds about things we once believed to be true.

It is vital to let go of judgments regarding the various words, symbols, rituals, practices, concepts, and different types of prayer or worship characteristic of the various belief systems, as they all create different paths to help us connect to our God-self and reach our wholeness. When done with sincerity, all legitimate spiritual and religious practices lead to the universal experience of Oneness, and the symbols within them are simply tools to help us reach or retain that state. They have simply spoken to various cultures and within different time frames. Having emerged through the various rays of consciousness when the Universe was created, they all hold a different slant with the same purpose of helping us realign with our God-self.

Whether from the culture we were born into or adopted at some point in our lives, all these aids were given to help us and are sacred, so long as they promote the aspects of love. Because Humanity has been so occupied with worry, fear, blame, judgment, conflict, and anger, a wealth of practices and tools are available within psychology, religions, and spiritualities for us to clear the channels to access the peace within. We are all seeking to connect to our

True Self and find our Best Self, no matter what our cultures' histories teach us as the best way to do it.

> *A universal theology is impossible,*
> *but a universal experience is not only possible but necessary.*
> *… What all genuine spiritual and religious teachings share*
> *is that they are leading to an experience*
> *of oneness and love, which is universal,*
> *since such an experience is not dependent on symbols or words,*
> *and in fact transcends anything specific.*
> —Ken Wapnick[52]

Now that we have a better understanding of these different symbols of our belief systems, in the next chapter we will look at the connection between our existence, spiritual journeys, and science.

CHAPTER 7

Science and Other Related Topics

Existence without form isn't imaginable,
yet at the same time it's the ultimate reality—
this includes both yin and yang; the unmanifest and the manifest;
the formed and the formless; the seen and the unseen;
the temporal and the timeless.
—Dr. David R. Hawkins[1]

The relationship between science and our spiritual journeys became quite evident to me in recent years and captured my interest. In this chapter I will address those areas that relate to our individual, collective and universal journeys. In doing so, I will touch upon a wide array of topics and cite many different people and sources so that you may further investigate anything that sparks your interest.

For centuries, the convictions of the Church and scientific world have been in opposition. However, in ancient times, the great thinkers, engineers, astrologers, and astronomers were revered by the philosophers, truth seekers, holy people, and those following sacred journeys. They recognized that scientific findings and our personal and collective journeys were connected, and that on a broader level they were all connected to the cosmos and the universal forces within it. Is it possible that the "one unifying principle" physicists are looking for is the same unifying principle that ties us all together spiritually—the Oneness I and others speak of? Could the unity within the Oneness and the love held within it hold clues or have commonalities with the energy scientists still seek? They may! Either way, I believe we are getting close to again acknowledging the connections between science and philosophy/spirituality/religion.

All Matter Is Composed of Energy / Vibration

JRobert and Oasis often said that within every cell of our beings is a whole Universe. All matter is made up of the same thing and matter is organic. Everything is part of the macrocosm, is in a constant state of flux, is interconnected, but still unique. In his October 2012 message, Matthew Ward characterized our uniqueness and interconnection within the Universe:

Each of you is a unique, independent and inviolate soul self, in the infinite and eternal interconnectedness of All … Our universe … whose beginnings were what you call the "Big Bang," and from that moment onward, no thing exists only unto itself and anything that happens anywhere affects everything, everywhere.[2]

Within this microcosm, everything, including us, is characterized by vibration.

We Are Energy / Vibration

Those within spiritual circles have understood that we are energy (or vibration) for years, and many religious teachers are also now realizing the impact of shifting our attitudes. Although they may not all use the same terminology, their teachings are geared toward us shifting our thoughts, attitudes, and their associated vibrations to line up with the Standard, or what Joyce Meyers calls right standing with God.

Shifting our energies and vibrations to higher, lighter-vibrational thoughts and attitudes is how we realign ourselves to the creative intelligence of the Universe. Within the third-dimensional experience from which we are emerging, Humanity existed within the lower, denser vibrations.

In *Power vs. Force*, Dr. David R. Hawkins explains how our emotions, attitudes, and their vibrations affect what we attract to ourselves, and emit to the world around us. He offers a numerical value system that corresponds to our approach in navigating life. According to Dr. Hawkins, the vibrations we emit create "attractor energy fields [and he assigns] levels below 200 as destructive of life in both the individual and society at large, and all levels above 200 are constructive expressions of power."[3] The lower-level expressions are considered *force* because since they push *against* universal flow they do not produce positive outcomes. The higher-level expressions are derived from *power* because they are aligned with the flow of the universe and thus do produce positive outcomes. Below are Dr. Hawkins's numerical values for certain attitudes and how they affect us and the world around us.

Energy Levels below 200

Shame = 20; Guilt = 30; Apathy = 50; Grief = 75; Fear = 100; Desire = 125 (not pure desire from the soul but from longing, neediness, etc.); Anger = 150; Pride = 175.

Energy Levels 200 and above

Courage = 200; Neutrality = 250; Willingness = 310; Acceptance = 350; Reason = 400; Love = 500; Joy = 540; Peace = 600; Enlightenment = 700–1000.

Dr. Hawkins further explains that we operate at different levels in various aspects of our lives, and that these all influence our general level of consciousness. He also explains that even minor increases in our vibrational energy levels have a huge impact on our accessing true power and raising our consciousness, as the scale is not based on simple mathematical calculations but on "a *logarithmic* progression," whereby the new number reflects an increase in the energy we emit to the nth degree.[4]

According to Hawkins, for hundreds of years Humanity's *"collective level of consciousness"* was stagnant at 190, just below the neutral point of 200, but in the '90s it rose to 207.[5] This jump was surely a reflection of the energy of the Harmonic Convergence of 1987, which I address later in this chapter. With all the energy and impulses leading up to and within our current Shift as we go through its final push, we are encouraged to further distance ourselves from the lower-vibrational attitudes we held. Our collective number now must be much greater than the 207 noted from the '90s.

Creating with Our Vibrations

Oasis, Abraham-Hicks, Inelia Benz, Dr. Jim Richards, and many of the spiritual and religious teachers today suggest that we have to raise our vibrations (through our thoughts and attitudes) to match what we want. We do this by focusing on what we *do* like and want, *not* by thinking about what we do not like or want. Believing with every ounce of our being that it will come about; imagining and dreaming about it coming about; and conjuring up the *feeling* of it already manifest in our lives is what invites what we want it into our sphere. Successful people do this automatically, without realizing that it is a spiritual tenet. And even though manifesting through our vibrations is a universal tenet that is 100% effective, it only works for us when *we are 100% attuned* to what we want, which we often are not. I explain this further in the "Abundance" section of chapter 9, "The Planet and Abundance."

Electromagnetic Fields Created from Our Current Beliefs

The laws of the Universe operate under the principle like that of a boomerang. It will return to us what we send out with our vibrations. So if we wish to make changes in our lives, we must create different vibrations, thereby creating a basis for different creations.

In the broadcast series "Miraculous Probabilities: The Science of Faith," Dr. Jim Richards explains the connection between our heart, or inner beliefs, and the scientific foundation of how the energy we impart through these beliefs creates electromagnetic fields saying "You're always functioning from your current beliefs, and those current beliefs are always creating an electromagnetic field, and in that electromagnetic field you are organizing energy to accomplish the beliefs of your heart."[6] Real, lasting changes come about when we alter our heart's electromagnetic fields rather than using pure brain or will power. This is because the strength of the heart's electromagnetic field is far greater than that of the brain.

Dr. Christiane Northrup writes In *Women's Bodies, Women's Wisdom* that the electromagnetic fields we create from our heart chakras are forty times stronger than those created from our brains. Some say even much more so. When we embrace lighter, more-positive attitudes, like forgiveness, we shift energy away from the brain, where resentment resides, to the heart, and when our energies move to the heart area, or the fourth chakra, we activate this strong electromagnetic field that aligns more closely with the loving forces within the universal matrix.[7]

Subatomic (Universal) Laws and Probability

In his same broadcast series Dr. Richards also points out that Einstein said that even though there are laws at the subatomic level, probability also plays a role. This means that although we exist within a matrix (individually, collectively, and cosmically), the potential exists for various possibilities: this sacred geometry system we exist under is organic and at the beck and call of all vibrational shifts, including those of our thoughts, emotions, and attitudes. It also affects the trajectory of the Planet, which I address more fully in chapter 9 "The Planet and Abundance."

In *The Holotropic Mind: The Three Levels of Human Consciousness and How They Shape Our Lives*, Stanislav Grof explains what physicists uncovered as they explored the "subatomic realms of the micro world and the astrophysical realms of the macro world." They discovered that the things we had believed up to then about what we considered to be the material world was in fact, only a surface view. Their findings showed that the basic and static "building blocks of the material world" were in fact made up of "hundreds of subatomic particles" that did not always behave in the same static manner. Grof explains that in some experiments, some particles behaved as if they were solid "material entities" and some behaved with "wavelike properties." These inconsistencies conflicted greatly with the then current Newtonian principles.[8]

Grof also tells us that when physicists further explored the micro world, they concluded that what "appears to be made up of solid objects" is actually an interweaving "complex web of unified events and relationships." He says that we can then conclude that "consciousness does not just passively reflect the material world; it plays an active role in creating reality itself."[9] If consciousness can affect form and solid objects, we can then affect our forms—our bodies and our health.

Creating New Blueprints for Better Health and Aging

In his 2011 talk in Edmonton, Kryon, who speaks through Lee Carroll, explains how we can influence our health and aging process through the messages we give our bodies. As a cell divides, it will take its blueprint from what is already there—what we already believe. If we are sick or believe we will get sick, we are creating a blueprint supporting that idea, and that cell will replicate that belief unless it is given a new blueprint. Kryon further explains how the "dividing cell" tells the "stem cell" to do as it always does, *unless there is a request to do otherwise.*[10] Therefore, we unknowingly direct requests to our body through our ingrained beliefs. When we are sick, we need to tell ourselves we are healthy or at least getting better. If we maintain our current beliefs regarding illness or aging, the messages we send to our cells will further entrench those beliefs.

Everything, including us is energy/vibration. To make any changes to our life we must send different messages out into the Universe. For better health, or with regard to how we age, we must send messages that support these ideas to our cellular bodies. Inelia Benz's Ascension 101 course includes an exercise, "Meet Yourself in the Future; Successful and Healed," whereby we bring back the new "vibrational signature" of what we want to become.[11] This creates a new blueprint for our cells to work with. A recap of this exercise is located at the back of the book in "Meditations, Visualizations, and Other Practices" under Visualization #4.

Connecting to Everything in the Universe through Higher Vibrations

When we learn to become fluid in our consciousness,
we have the ability to tap into this vast ocean [of infinity]
and literally become one with the universal holographic fabric.
—Ronald L. Holt[12]

As we embrace thoughts which hold higher-frequency vibrations, our emotional makeup, physical bodies, and sensual perceptions will shift. As we raise our vibrations, we may start to see, hear, and sense that which vibrates at the higher levels. We may be able to communicate telepathically with those on this plane and connect to beings that occupy the higher levels, including light-beings, archangels, the masters who have returned there, mystics and saints who once walked the earth and now abide in the higher realms, those who have passed on, and the higher level ET's who are nearby helping us with our Ascensions. We will also be able to tap into all that ever was, is, or will be. This is because our Universe is really like a holograph, as time and distance are illusions.

Holographic Universe

Many metaphysical thought systems, such as *The Course*, recognize that the Universe is holographic, and as the above epigraph from Holt explains, all we need do is raise our consciousness to tap into it. He defines a holograph as having "the maximum symmetry of all fractal planes or geometric faces within the system to which it belongs. So if we take a cell, an atom, or a molecule, we would have all the necessary requirements in that tiny object to see the entire holographic matrix to which it belonged."[13]

JRobert and Oasis and scientists now agree that all the cells in our bodies are made up of the same stuff as the entire Universe. Holt brings these two concepts together. He says that a "Geometric Holographic Matrix creates the model for all creation in the physical, and that because it is holographic, even the smallest portion of this matrix provides the code for the entire reality itself."[14]

Because of our limited third-dimensional view of reality we do not sense this connection to everything: to the All. Holt explains this as our limited views "compressing and fragmenting" our realities. Our sense of separation and all of our issues stem from the fear that comes out of this illusionary separated view of ourselves from the All. Holt suggests that we need to move beyond the limitations we have erected and "embrace the entire holographic reality." We break through those limitations with our seemingly inconsequential micro attitude shifts that promote unity, while the culmination of these eventually leads to us recognizing the macro Oneness that pervades everything and its holographic reality.[15]

Seeing and Sensing Those in the Higher Realms

Scriptural accounts suggest that there have always been people who were able to see and sense angels (light-beings) and the masters dwelling within the higher realms. This experience of seeing/sensing was not available to most of us as our energetic vibrations were too dense within the limitations of the third dimension we occupied. This is changing. In Matthew Ward's September 2011 message, he compares our energetic vibrations and ability to perceive with the metaphor of blades of a fan on different settings.

You can't see us even when we are standing beside you because our etheric bodies vibrate at frequencies that third density vision cannot detect, just as you cannot see blades of a fan on its highest setting. But indeed etheric bodies have a degree of mass that lessens in density as souls continue to evolve spiritually.[16]

Many of us are now primed to be able to see, hear, and feel those on the higher realms because we are raising our vibrations by releasing the lower-density attitudes. With the exception of those who came here with the gifts of seeing, the rest of us were not attuned to the higher frequencies. This is changing. A recent example is of Gary Renard, who as I explained in chapter 6 had raised his vibration/frequency high enough to be able to see, hear, and have conversations with the ascended masters Arten and Pursah. He had been meditating regularly and had also chosen to forgive a certain individual and make peace with the situation that had developed between them. Any sincere spiritual or prayer practice can help raise our vibration. So can making peace with difficult situations because our nonresistance to them creates a higher vibration within us.

Communicating Telepathically

Once we let go of the constraints of our third-dimensional limitations, telepathic communication becomes more of a possibility. We are all interconnected within the Universal Matrix, and since we are vibration all our thoughts also carry vibrations. When we remove the constraints and exist at a higher vibratory frequency we have the potential to tap into the thoughts around us. While this is just an impending quality for most of us, we may get hints of its potential. I myself once heard words that a friend thought, without them having been spoken.

Early in my spiritual journey, I was sitting peacefully with a friend when the words "I think I will get up and get a snack" suddenly buzzed into my mind. Their sound held a vibration and it felt as if they were transmitted on an invisible wire cable between us. It seemed somewhat bizarre, but I asked my friend to get something for me, as well. She looked at me, mouth gaping and asked, "Did I say that out loud?" She had not.

The lines of communication between us were open and I was in a very peaceful state, so my connection to the Universal Matrix was open. I believe events like these are a result of being aligned at the moment or are *gifts* from Spirit as proof of our progress. For me, it was a validation that the recent work to release the constraints of my thoughts had expanded my mind beyond the limitations that had previously held me down, opening the door to higher levels of consciousness. I never experienced a repeat of this experience, but it led me to believe that we can expect many types of small, inconsequential experiences beyond our third-dimensional restrictions once we raise our vibrations by letting go of our lower-density limitations. The reason we can tap into another's thoughts is that within the holographic nature of the Universe, there is only *one mind* masquerading as many, through our separated bodies.

One Mind: The Collective Mind

A premise of *The Course* is that there is only one mind posing as many, which Buddhists define as the world of multiplicity. As we raise our vibration from the denseness of the third dimension we are able to tap into that one mind because we are better aligned with the malleable universal frequency. This one mind is also known as *the collective mind.*

The concept of a collective mind, that we are all part of one mind, has been around for a while in philosophical and psychological study. Eckhart Tolle recently brought this concept of the collective mind to the public in his book, *A New Earth,* where he explained its effect on us as individuals and on Humanity as a whole.

The collective mind explains why our thoughts affect more than us individually and that the collective thoughts, say of a group, affect us all. In *Quantum's Little Book of Big Ideas: Where Science Meets Spirit,* physicist Dr. Fred Wolf explains that our thoughts may seem to be personal and self-contained to us, but are actually being thought everywhere by everybody, at some time, in some form, because "there really is only one Mind."[17] We may not all think in exactly the same way, but the collective consciousness holds all the intentions and vibrations we emit. Our cells also carry Humanity's collective history.

In *Women's Bodies, Women's Wisdom,* Dr. Christiane Northrup discusses how our bodies carry our personal histories through our cells and tissues like "little data-banks," as well as the histories of everyone and everything.[18] This is because every thought affects our cells and all our thoughts are connected in an organic interweaving pattern within the Universal Matrix. Everything about the collective is within and around all our cells. All this knowledge is called the Akashic records.

The Akashic Records

The Akashic records are like a memory bank. They hold the vibrational imprint of every thought. Everything that has happened, is happening, and will happen in the Universe, including the records of Humanity's life journeys and the information of all other life forms in the Universe since its beginning is held in the Akashic records. They have often been referred to as a computer filled with information or a universal data-bank of knowledge.

This holographic body of information does not follow the third-dimensional law of linear time. This is why when we tap into it, we can see the past, present, and future. New discoveries are usually made by accessing what is held within the Akashic records. Psychics accessing the past or future are also seeing what is held within these nonlinear, holographic records. Our ideas and insights often come from within this knowledge base. When two people in completely different parts of the world come up with an identical invention or idea at the same point in time, they are both accessing what is available within these records. Their timing may coincide because as a collective we asked for it as the discovery is part of the cosmic timing of our evolution.

This collective mind that we tap into exists because of the original spark we all came from. The Oneness that pervades us all was never broken. We may not recognize it because of the illusions in which we have been entrapped since our descent into duality, but it is there and available for us.

All in Harmony with Each Other Whether We Recognize It or Not

Everything in the Universe and our essences exist in harmony, although we find this difficult to recognize. In a 1988 workshop, Abraham-Hicks said:

> You have more harmony points with every person on the planet than you have disharmony points, because there is much more of you that is in harmony with your Core than you realize or that most of you allow. The closer you come to being in harmony with your Source Energy, the more in harmony you are with each other.[19]

Abraham-Hicks also tell us that if we want to be happy, we need to think things about those in our lives that will bring us happiness. Since all thought is organic and we are all connected, what we think of others influences how they will be around us. Constant positive thoughts about others can help them change their moods and may even change their life trajectory.

The Beginnings of the Universe Was Not Clearly Defined; Nor Are We

In her article "Bang Goes the Theory," Amanda Gefter reminds us that in the '80s Stephen Hawking was the first to combine quantum physics with cosmology. His findings suggested that the beginnings of the Universe were organic and not entirely defined—what he calls the "no-boundary proposal." This concept suggests that every universe begins with many possibilities and beginnings. Each universe is a mishmash of quantum space and time "undistinguishable" from the other.[20]

This means that the Universe had no definable map of creation in its distant past. Since we live under the laws of the Universe and its beginnings were not purely defined within its creation potentials neither are our creations. Our thoughts are powerful. They allow us to create within an organic process, where there is no definable map. Our large, life-changing creations as well as our small, everyday ones are all under this organic process whereby we can influence the outcomes. Be they conscious or unconscious, with every thought and attitude we can and do create, because all thought processes are organic. It is to our benefit to consciously direct our thoughts.

Organic Nature of Our Brains and Their Thought Processes

Our brains and thought processes can be shifted and swayed. On a recent TV broadcast, author Robert J. tells us that our brain is malleable and doesn't calcify, allowing us to change our beliefs about things. We just have to look back at what we believed years ago. We no longer accept as true many of the same things, individually or collectively. He explained that it takes only one person to have an idea, and it then catches on. For example, at some point in time, someone had the idea that women should have the right to vote; others soon also believed the same. Sawyer explained that these new ideas were brought forward through our thought processes, which eventually manifested as actions, and ultimately changes came about that aligned with the original idea.[21]

Effects of Our Thoughts on Matter

Affecting matter, such as bending spoons with our thoughts, is often dismissed as hokum, but yogis have been known to do it. When we believe that Jesus changed water into wine as a real event rather than a metaphor, it is described as a miracle. What allows these phenomena to occur?

We now know that we are vibration. We also now understand that most of Humanity has been vibrating at a dense, low frequency for eons and that this low vibration has restricted our focus to third-dimensional form and its solid attributes. It was inconceivable that we could overcome the solid boundaries of form and matter, or that pathways actually exist to allow matter to become malleable. Most of us may not vibrate at the levels required to bend spoons or turn water into wine, but we do affect matter to some degree even in our current medium-vibrational levels.

Scientific findings now suggest that thoughts and their vibrational stimuli can have an impact on matter, such as changing water molecules. In his experiments, Dr. Masaru Emoto exposed water to different words, symbols, and energetic patterns. What he found was that the water picked up on the vibrations from the words and symbols. When plain water from a dam was examined, its molecular structure had no particular design. Under close examination, it still looked like a puddle of water. However, after receiving a blessing from a Buddhist monk, the structure of the same water was reexamined. It had remarkably formed into a beautiful crystal pattern. Dr. Emoto explained that all thoughts and intentions can affect matter and that "giving of love is vibration," which is what the blessing was.[22]

This is really no different than when people talk to their plants, encouraging them to flower and grow beautiful and healthy—and they do. Plants don't hear words but the intention and vibration is imparted. I believe studies such as Dr. Emoto's offer valuable scientific legitimacy to understanding how our physical, emotional, and spiritual makeups are intertwined.

Illusionary Nature of the Universe and All Perceived Realities

Our reality is merely an illusion, albeit a very persistent one.
—Albert Einstein

Not only are our limited, five sense-based perceptions about life illusionary, but the whole Universe and everything in it is actually an illusion, although as Einstein says, "a very persistent one." This is because we are so entrenched within the illusion of separation and form that we cannot conceive of beyond it. Nonetheless, the only true reality is the Oneness we are all a part of. All form (including our bodies) and all concepts are illusions. *The Course,* as well as other highly spiritual teachings, suggests that the scope of the illusion we live under is so great that we *believe* we exist when in fact we do not. In *The Collected Works of Ramana Maharshi,* Maharshi tells us, "In our natural state, actions, cause, the result of such actions and all the various other theories put forward (in the scriptures) do not exist. In fact, even the diverse world does not exist. As such even the worldly individual who is attached to (the various attractions of) the world is also non-existent."[23] Science is starting to be able to prove this.

All this talk about the Shift, our awakening, and the forgiveness and other practices required to undo false illusions take place within the illusion. We exist, but only within the illusion. I am speaking to you, from within the illusion. Reincarnation exists, within the illusion. Our solar system, the Universe, and all the other universes are, were, or will exist only within the illusion. Our star brothers and sisters (the extraterrestrials), the light-beings, the archangels, and the masters are all real, but only within the illusion. Even the Mother, Spirit, Holy Spirit, or Shakti are all real, but only within the illusion. Once all of us within all the realms finish the lessons we need to learn to fully embrace the Oneness from which we all emanated, there will be no more use for the Universe. It will disappear, much as the Bible describes in 2 Peter 3:10: "The heavens will pass away with a terrible noise, and the heavenly bodies will disappear in fire, and the earth and everything on it will be burned up." However, this will only happen within the illusion, as none of it really exists, and none of us will be around to witness it, as by then all our consciousnesses will have reemerged into the Oneness as the purpose for form will no longer be needed.

However, while we are experiencing existence within the illusion, we must use concepts within its third-dimensional, linear reality to help dispel the parts of the illusion we are ready to let go of. For example, reading this book from within the illusion and understanding some of its concepts or using some of the suggested tools will help dispel some of the illusion. Within the limited third-dimensional constructs of the illusion, we understand time as linear. However, that is also an illusionary concept.

Time: An Illusionary Third-Dimensional Concept

Our perception of time, within our earthly existence of form, is not perceived in the same way as in the higher realms, or what some call heaven. This is because within the holographic nature of the Universe, time is an illusion. There is only the present moment. In his poem *On Nature*, the ancient Greek philosopher Parmenides expressed his views on perception, truth, and how it relates to time by saying, "there is not, and never shall be, any time other than that which is present, since fate has chained it so as to be whole and immovable."[24] The only time there really is, is the *Now*, and within that Now, everything that ever was or will be exists. Everything is based on perceptual awareness, and since everything finite is an illusion, so is time. Some who meditate and enter the state of complete Oneness attune to this. They experientially understand that there is no past and no future. These are linear, third-dimensional perceptions.

Science has made the connection between the nonabsolute nature of time and the organic nature of our thoughts. In Dr. Fred Wolf's study on time in *Quantum's Little Book of Big Ideas: Where Science Meets Spirit*, he explains that time stretches for the objects in motion:

> The theory of relativity tells us that time is not absolute. Fixed time intervals, say one-second units, are not equal for a moving clock and a clock at rest. As a thing moves faster and approaches the speed of light, a one-second time interval stretches, covering longer and longer time intervals as determined by the clock at rest. At the speed of light, time slows so much that it completely stops. Or, to put it another way, any time interval, no matter how

short, stretches to infinite time measured by a resting clock. And so it is when we enter thought.[25]

In the second half of the 2010 movie *The Genesis Code*, the writers give a scientific, non metaphoric explanation of the seven-day creation. They explain that since the creation scenario was written about the beginning of the Universe, at the time of the big bang, time was much shorter than we now experience it. As the Universe expanded from that moment on, time became longer. So what would have been seven days, fourteen or so billion years ago, would now be experienced as much, much longer. Put another way, the fabric of the Universe has stretched since that original moment and so has the concept of time. Illustration 19 gives a simple visual of how the fabric of time has stretched since the big bang.

#19: Time and the Big Bang

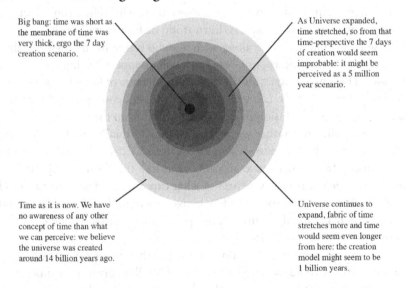

Big bang: time was short as the membrane of time was very thick, ergo the 7 day creation scenario.

As Universe expanded, time stretched, so from that time-perspective the 7 days of creation would seem improbable: it might be perceived as a 5 million year scenario.

Time as it is now. We have no awareness of any other concept of time than what we can perceive: we believe the universe was created around 14 billion years ago.

Universe continues to expand, fabric of time stretches more and time would seem even longer from here: the creation model might seem to be 1 billion years.

(Time frames given are just for explanation purpose; they are not scientifically based).

Within our limited third-dimensional awareness of the Universe as we experience it, we still hold to the concept of time. However, one day the whole Universe will disappear, as dense form and time will no longer be required.

The Disappearance of the Universe

Our current Shift sometimes referred to as the New Age or the Golden Age of Gaia, has also been referred to in Revelation 20:1–4 as one thousand years of peace. It states that Satan (which has similar attributes to how I use the term "ego") as anything that supports duality and separateness) will be locked away for one thousand years but will be released again for a short while after that. This time of peace will be only one step on our way back to complete reemergence with the Oneness.

This one thousand years of peace will also be within the illusion as it is not our raison d'être. As explained in chapter 1 regarding our beginnings, our Universe was created to play out the duality we originally generated from our choice to do it on our own, apart from the Creator. We are now ushering in a period that will be marked by peace and harmony. This means all humans will live peacefully together, as will the rest of creation—humans to animals, animals to animals, as well as our relationship with the Planet causing its weather patterns to even out.

Even though we are primed to enjoy approximately one thousand years of peace on earth, this is not our ultimate purpose. Since the Universe was created to play out the duality we had chosen, there will come a time when we no longer want or need to express, learn from, or forgive within the auspices of dense form. The Universe along with all who reside in the higher realms and even Spirit, Holy Spirit, or Great Spirit will disappear, having served their purposes. These metaphysics are the reasons for the title of Gary Renard's book *The Disappearance of the Universe*, which introduces concepts and practices that aim to undo the illusion of the separated Self from the Oneness.

At one point or another we will all transcend duality and its illusions and return into the Oneness, where no awareness exists. We will return to the Godhead from whence we all came, and like the Eastern philosophies suggest, will be within the Oneness of what can only be described as "'God Is,' and then we cease to speak."[26] The Universe will fold back into itself, and all its components in all realms will disappear. I have often wondered if this has something to do with black holes.

I am excited to see manifestations of the positive changes we are bringing about on earth with our shifts in attitudes. This will happen quite quickly; it has even started. We just have to look at how more open and accepting many are starting to be, and how we are demanding this of others, organizations, and governments. The world will soon be a *very* different place—not perfect yet but very, very different from the previous one hundred years.

Usefulness but Eventual Dissipation of Symbols of Love

In her article "Reclaiming Your 12-strand DNA," Julianne Everett tells us how aligning with higher frequencies is how we may become aware of any of the twelve masters who have walked the earth, as they represent the twelve rays (see my illustration 20 below) of consciousness of our original twelve-strand DNA that we lost but are now regaining.

This is what is meant when we say, "Jesus will return." Whether he returns in physical form or not, he can be in our awareness anytime we are aligned with the higher frequencies. I believe Jesus meant he would return *when we* will have understood and embraced his lessons of unconditional love and forgiveness and attained those higher frequencies where we can perceive him. Everett also explains that the twelve masters will also dissipate the more we integrate the higher-consciousness attitudes saying, "These radiant guides, however, are simply fields of divine intelligence that will dissolve into all that you are when you merge with your soul at the heart and your Presence is firmly established within what is referred to as the Holy of Holies in the center of your skull [the pituitary gland that is being reawakened with this process]."[27]

Illustration 20 shows how each of these rays manifested outward separately but were still connected to the Oneness. Therefore the masters who came forth conveyed to us slightly different aspects of the Oneness. The different slants in their teachings affected the focuses of the religions that emerged later. My explanation of the masters and the religions is but a simple overview to show the subtle differences. I believe this may be helpful to our understanding of the different concepts highlighted in the various religions or by the followers of prophets and philosophers, and it elucidates how and why people can find personal and spiritual guidance from all of them.

Masters Came to Us as Different Aspects of the Oneness

#20: 12 Rays Within the Illusion

Different religions, ways of being, and their inclinations emerged to bring us back to the Oneness we emanated from.

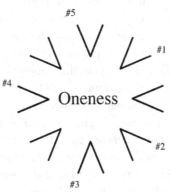

While masters like Lau Tzu, Krishna, Jesus, Muhammad, and the philosopher Confucius and any other being we invite to help us only serve as *symbols* of love and the highest levels of consciousness, it is still recommended that we use them until we no longer feel the need to do so. As we increasingly embrace higher-vibrational attitudes and begin to access the fourth, fifth, and higher dimensions, we will no longer feel the need to call upon them as much, as we ourselves will *feel* the connection to the love they represent and are guiding us to find within ourselves, without the need for them as symbols to access it. For more detailed information regarding the five above-mentioned masters, see article "Masters and their Different Aspects" on the book's website.

In the same article cited above, Everett tells us that to get the most from this recalibration of our DNA, we must reconcile the lower aspects of the self-centered ego with the compassionate God-self and unlock the lower-level, body-focused aspects of ourselves. This opens up pathways for the encoding of our original twelve-strand DNA so its energy and intrinsic wisdom can be translated to all parts of our bodies. With this new recalibration more light will penetrate our bodies, so much so that it will change their physiology.

Our Bodies Are Changing from Carbon to Crystalline

Because we exist within the illusion and are still in form we have to align our bodies with the energy around us. As we raise our consciousness and shift into the higher dimensions and this recalibration of our twelve-strand DNA takes hold, more of the light from our original Source will penetrate our now less dense forms. This absorption of light happens automatically and helps us in all areas of our lives, as well as in our Ascension process. It actually changes our bodies to how they need to be for us to comfortably exist at these levels—from carbon, the dense physical characteristic of the third dimension, to crystalline, the lighter form inherent in the higher dimensions.

This crystalline nature is powerful as it holds and *intensifies* energy. We will increasingly find it easier to choose the lighter, higher-vibrational attitudes and feel guided to embrace physical habits that align with our new energetically lighter bodies. This crystalline energy can also help us feel wonderful physically. Most who embrace high-level spiritual tenets look far younger than their years. On the negative side, however, if we are not attuned with or ignore the nudges toward higher-vibrational attitudes or our new bodies' requirements, we will *greatly* feel the effects because of the intensity of this crystalline nature. In *The Lemurian Science of Immortality*, Almine tells us that dense bodies tend to be more susceptible to disease and premature aging as they are inconsistent "with the fluid unfolding of Cosmic Life."[28]

Cosmic Timing

Many seek a new story of archaic human history,
because the latest information suggests that human
ancient cultures were globally connected and advanced.
—Barbara Hand Clow[29]

Within the matrix of our Universe and throughout Humanity's evolution, there have been many eras of great spiritual awareness, which were brought on by cosmic timing, ushering in impulses for change.

Tens or even hundreds of thousands of years ago, two evolved civilizations, Lemuria and Atlantis, are thought to have existed. Although they were very spiritually and possibly even technologically evolved, power, control, and corruption must have prevailed as they eventually self-destructed. The exact dates of the existence of these societies are debated, but range from one hundred thousand to ten thousand years ago, and they may have even coexisted for some time.

Some believe that their eventual destruction and disappearance underwater was the result of clashes in focus and attitudes. Others believe it was caused by a natural cosmic disaster. In *Awakening the Planetary Mind*, Barbara Hand Clow tells us that the last great planetary disaster that forever altered life on earth took place in 9,500 BC. In her research, she draws from D. S. Allan and J. B. Delair's book *Cataclysm: Compelling Evidence of a Cosmic Catastrophe in 9500BC* and summarizes their proposal that it was at this time that the earth's axis was "pulled into its [current] tilt by fragments of a supernova." She further postulates that whether or not we believe a cataclysmic or human event brought about radical climate changes, there is clear evidence that 11,500 years ago "*a radical shift occurred in human culture.*" From that time forward we adapted to climate changes by implementing farming practices and our interactions with Gaia was forever changed. Hand Clow also proposes that this time may be connected to the account of the great flood in the Bible, before which we existed in a golden age.[30]

Many are of the opinion that the Lemurians and Atlanteans continuously communed with extraterrestrials and that the survivors of these races continued to do so later on. According to some accounts, the survivors of Lemuria found their way to areas in the Pacific like Hawaii and Peru, while surviving Atlanteans established themselves in ancient Ireland, Sumeria, Egypt, Mexico, and South America—all bringing their spiritual knowledge with them. We now know that five to six thousand years ago advanced spiritual knowledge was practiced by the Sumerian and Egyptian civilizations.

Approximately 2,500 years ago another wave of spiritual understanding occurred. Around 600–500 BC, ancient philosophers such as Socrates and

Plato made great strides in understanding Humanity and the cosmos and aimed to pass those on to us. The Buddha also appeared around this time. Jesus' time some two-thousand years ago was an era of great potential, with an actual portal opening (see below), when we were encouraged to love and forgive all, but regrettably the political climate undermined his message. Around the middle of the 6th century the prophet Muhammad was sent to us, but as before when the masters appeared, divisiveness grew within the ranks of his followers, which undermined his teachings. It took almost a thousand years for the next great wave of enlightenment to surface.

In the Renaissance period, there was a push to embrace love and beauty to awaken the subtler parts of ourselves—however, most of society didn't catch on, not having sufficiently evolved to sense the Oneness we all shared and we continued to project our fears and their judgment, greed, hate, and cruelty onto others. It was still not yet the cosmic time to see our way out.

More recently, in the wake of the atrocities of World War II and with the advent of the atomic bomb, we hit rock bottom. An inner cry went out to the Universe from the generation which lived through the world wars and/or witnessed or were aware of the hatred and inhumanity towards the millions of souls who suffered cruel deaths. This cry, coupled with the development of the technology that could destroy all of Humanity, was answered through the next generation. The baby-boomers' pleas for "Peace not war" and all of the literature and music of the 60s and 70s that urged us towards love, compassion, and fairness created enough stirring of consciousness for us to usher in the current Shift, which actually began twenty-five years ago with what is known as the Harmonic Convergence.

1987–2012: The Harmonic Convergence

Beginning in 1987 and culminating sometime between the end of 2012 and first months of 2013, the Harmonic Convergence was a cosmic event during which planetary alignments with the sun triggered energetic impulses that created the impetus that has given Humanity the momentum to replace the third-dimensional qualities of fear and embrace the higher-dimensional qualities of love. This convergence was part of a cosmic timing, or divine decree, having been deemed the time for Humanity to start its *final* push toward its Ascension.

In *The Great Awakening*, Linda Dillon explains that although this process of awakening and Ascension started eons ago, 1987 ushered in a "conscious collective awareness" that something was shifting and changing.[31] Individually, this encouraged us to start to remove what had previously blocked our access to joy and happiness, to embrace our limitlessness, and live in greater harmony with those around us. Collectively, we have been guided to make changes that support a shift toward a more loving and just society, as evidenced by our insistence on equality, fairness for all from our governments, corporations, and associations and by demands for transparency. Our recent interests in doing what is best for our bodies, for the animals that share the Planet, and for keeping Gaia healthy are also manifestations of this more gentle awareness that we are beginning to experience.

The fall of the Berlin Wall in '89 and destruction of portions of the Great Wall of China over time have been interpreted as physical manifestations of the shifting energies of Gaia and her inhabitants. The unearthing of all the abuses inflicted at both micro and macro levels and the uncovering and disclosure of the corruption that has plagued our governments, corporations, religions, and associations are other results of this influence. The exposure of all the unfairness presents opportunities to address the injustices.

As this momentum snowballed, the economic upheavals, the uprisings in the Middle East, the equality demanded for women, and fairness for those in minority like gays, immigrants, the Indigenous peoples, and those of a different color, creed, or race have all been a part of this influx of energy unearthing what is not of love, compassion, and fairness so we can turn toward and demand compassion and fairness for all. Now that the horrific ways in which we have treated one another and our Planet for control and greed have come to light, more and more people are demanding governments, big businesses, our health industries, and world organizations to make the necessary adjustments.

Within the past few years extra energies have surrounded our Planet to further uncover what has gone on—to the extent that we can no longer ignore the inequality and unfairness insidiously imbedded in society. This final push has brought with it the impetus to *fully* address our societal issues, as well as for Gaia to take her rightful place within the higher realms of our Universal Matrix. This is all part of what is called the Shift.

The Shift

There was much controversy and fear regarding December 21, 2012 because this was considered to be a time of reckoning. However, it was more of a cosmic cutoff date, where Humanity was challenged to transform the vibrational levels of the Planet as a whole to harmonize with those we were programmed to enter within the cosmic timing laid out for Gaia and our evolution. There were so many prophesies of destruction surrounding this date because throughout history and even within the twenty-five years from 1987 to 2012, it did not always look as if we would embrace enough of the higher qualities and attitudes required to help raise the vibrational level of the Planet to where it needed to go. This is what the doomsday prophecies were about.

As I explain in chapter 9, "The Planet and Abundance," our Planet, or Gaia, is a living, breathing organism. The physical and environmental abuses we have subjected her to as a result of our greed and ignorance and the accumulative hatred and our collective, misguided negative energy have affected her. This is similar to how the effects of sustained emotional abuse shows up in our bodies. As a living, breathing organism, Gaia had to shrug all of this off. This explains many of the climatic disasters.

Our personal and collective choices mostly fall under the law of free will. Seers, prophets, and psychics only see *potentials*. Those who prophesized doomsday scenarios that we would not make it were picking up on a moment in time, the collective vibration at that time, or only a portion of it. They can never really get a 100% accurate view of the future, as free will is always a factor; they see what energy is at work at that moment in time and extend it forward in time. They also pick up on energies present possibly influenced by one group of people or another. But as it turns out, in the last few years, sufficient numbers of us followed our impulses and changed *enough* of our separate and conflicting agendas of hate, judgment, greed, control, and blame on all levels. If we had not, there could easily have been planetary devastation. However, we had raised our vibrations enough individually and collectively to absorb enough of the light and love energies that were available during that crucial final push of the Shift and thereby averted a major catastrophic event.

We Skimmed Through

As our existence is organic, prophets, seers, and channels receive their information from the fabric of our cosmic matrix and the energy that is prevalent at that moment in time surrounding the subject at hand. This explains why their messages are not always accurate, or we get differing messages. But why all the doom-and-gloom prophesies surrounding December 2012?

What they saw or sensed regarding the time surrounding December 2012 was in effect, a projection of our prevailing collective energy. It is not that they were wrong or frauds, but that what they saw was where we appeared to be heading, given the energy of the collective and/or a moment in time they picked up upon. And while in most cases the intention is to give a pure unbiased reading, their filter is rarely 100% clear. In being open to the universal energies of non-linear time, the projections of some may also have been colored by their own past-life experiences. Below are a few examples of what some highly sincere and dedicated light workers sensed about our future within the recent past.

In *The Great Awakening*, Linda Dillon tells us that at the beginning of her interactions in the mid-'80s with the higher beings she channels who call themselves *The Council of Love*, their predictions regarding the time period around the Shift "were quite dire."[32] In *Fearless Love*, a CD series from a few years ago, Gary Renard said that it *looked* as if we would make it, but he did encourage us to keep practicing opportunities for forgiveness.[33] Joyce Meyers also mentioned in one of her talks a few years ago something to the effect of "Get this now—2012 is coming" when teaching about replacing our negative attitudes with more positive ones. This comment just appeared to slip out, and she didn't further address it. The December 2012 date was not a subject that was focused on under the Christian umbrella. However, our higher Selves are attuned to this Shift, so concepts beyond our chosen area of study may seep into our messages. The Holy Spirit must have deemed it necessary for some who were listening then, or through later rebroadcasts, to understand the connection between *getting it* now and the much-talked-about, approaching December 2012 date.

Limited Time Frame to Anchor in the Shift

December 2012 passed without any major worldwide disasters, but we still need to strive to embrace all that this Shift requires of us. There is a time-limited window of opportunity to anchor in the qualities inherent in the higher dimensions, but we *are* making headway in aligning ourselves to its higher precepts, as *many* are now choosing to replace judgment with acceptance, hostility with harmony, and power and greed with compassion and fairness. Cosmic events are also helping encourage us to dislodge negativity that is still part of our world.

The blood moons and solar flares of the past few years have brought many influxes of energy that encourage us to release what is not of love by bringing issues to the forefront, and to shower extra light and love on us and the Planet. In "Activating the Andromedan StarGate at Lake Louise, BC," Sananda speaks through Elizabeth Trutwin and tells us that this activation which took place on April 17th, 2015 ushered in a huge surge of energy aimed to propel the dismantling of the stronghold the cabal has on all areas of our existence, while at the same time ensuring that the perpetrators of greed and injustice will be held accountable for their actions, on this as well as on the ethereal planes.[34]

I cannot presume to foretell what the future may hold; none of us really can. Just as with the many differing prophesies and projected scenarios regarding December 2012, our future is influenced by the vibration of the

Planet as a whole, and its vibrational energy has an ever-changing, organic composition. Our current mission is to cultivate the qualities that will support and collectively contribute to usher in the one thousand years of peace promised in our scriptures and marked in the stars.

Just as December 21, 2012 served as a guideline date, other dates have been offered as deadlines for us to fully align with the required higher vibration qualities. Many, like Inelia Benz, have predicted that the end of 2017 will bring another powerful wave of energy to propel our Ascension process, requiring us to fully align with the energy of the Planet in the 5th dimension. Others convey vaguer dates, like 2020 or 2025. The projected time frames may be fluid instead of exact dates and times, but cosmic dates are relevant because the energies they bring with them are part of the cosmic cycles that govern us. For this reason and because of our recognition of and energy we give them, these cosmic dates do create portals with energetic openings, whereby we can benefit from, or feel their effects, and more easily align with the powers held in the Universe.

Portals / Vortexes / Gateways

Portals, vortexes, or gateways are energetic openings. They can be created through solid forms such as with powerful artifacts, megalithic structures, or high-level energetic stones, crystals, or technologies. Certain places can act as strong energetic gateways, and portals can open in areas where a sacred event was held. Cosmic alignments can cause gateways to other dimensions to open during certain time frames.

Some portals remain open, such as at Machu Picchu, which can be felt by those who are at all sensitive to energetic waves. The energy structures of our ancestors such as Stonehenge in England and the pyramids found in many countries once held great power, and their transformative powers may have been used for healing and/or energetic and physical transportation to other dimensions.

Scriptures in the Bible tell of artifacts such as the Arc of the Covenant and King Solomon's ring. Their powerful alchemic energies likely opened gateways or portals to other dimensions, and are believed to have given godly attributes to the owner/user, JRobert talked about once being invited into the bowels of the Vatican where the ancient Holy Books are kept, and he told us that he sensed the strong traces of the original energy imparted onto them they still hold. Ancient artifacts do still hold great power. We will not have access to them until we have the spiritual awareness to use that power wisely and for good, not destroy ourselves with it.

Portals or vortexes can also be created through a concentration of positive energy during a gathering. The energy that is created and uplifts us from an inspiring speech, sermon, or spiritual gathering, at a great music concert, the perfect sports move or performance that awes us, or an event that brings us together for a good cause like the annual Terry Fox run in Canada, all create portals or vortexes from the accumulated energy of the participants or spectators. Through the experiences these bring us we are reminded that our hearts can expand to feel more than what our every-day living allows. For examples of portals/vortexes created I have witnessed see article "Created Portals and Vortexes" found on the book's website.

Throughout history and more specifically since the Harmonic Convergence, many portal openings have been given to us to take advantage of the creative energy of the light being infused onto the Planet from higher realms to help us with our Ascensions. All the impulses we have recently had to overcome what is negative within us individually and as a collective are a response to this. As we embrace these changes in attitudes, we are infused with even more light, and our vibrational signatures change.

Recent Portals

In recent years, many date-specific portals have opened up, providing us with pure light energy and bringing with them impulses to let go of any of lower, third-dimensional attitudes we may still retain. When we take advantage of these specific dates parts of us that were previously dormant are reawakened. I participated in several group meditations in 2011 and 2012 that used the portals in conjunction with certain dates preparing for the Shift of December 2012. By honoring these dates, such as 11-11-11 and 12-12-12, with quiet time or meditation, I was able to take advantage of the extra light or energy available during those specific times. Doing so left me feeling a little lighter, brighter, and calmer, and these feelings stayed with me. Comments such as "You look different, but I just can't put my finger on it" and curious looks were common around that time. These subtle, but visible changes are physical manifestations from these light-filled energetic boosts and are similar to the palpable changes that occur when we consciously make attitude or behavioral shifts with our inner work. I am certain that participating in these events also gave me the extra impetus to help bring this book to fruition.

Many other portals or gateways have opened or been created since 2012 such as with the full blood and blue moons of recent years and the star gate activation at Lake Louise, B.C. Canada in April 17th, 2015. Although powerful energy is created during specific time frames, these energy boosts also help create momentum to keep us moving on a positive upward spiral. Since the portals usually remain open or can easily be reactivated, they can continue to influence us long after the specific dates, like with Machu Picchu.

Recent Portals Brought Impulses to Release the Old and Allowed for New Ideas

The portals that have opened within the last few years brought healing energy with them. This enabled our vasanas (old, buried hurts and pains) to resurface so that we could release them and opportunities to rise above our third-dimensional attitudes, habits, and protective devices— all to allow for the light to penetrate us. This light and love these portals bring also encourage us to find joy in the present moment and in all we do. However, to access it we need to embrace nonresistance, create harmony around us, and find peace and joy no matter what is happening in our lives, otherwise the light and love cannot get through our dense energy form: it is as if it hits an impenetrable wall. While it is next to impossible to avoid any conflicts, all negative or fearful thoughts, or never worry about difficult situations, it is vital to not allow them to overwhelm us or penetrate our hearts.

Many of the recent portals are and will remain open for some time, so we may still be faced with emotions that well up. As they arise, simply allow them to do so. This is an internal cleansing. Make peace with issues that come about that usually anger you or of changes thrust upon you. While the Shift is drawing the emotions out of you for release, it also brings with it loving, universal God energy that nurtures us throughout the process of releasing, helps us through unplanned upheavals in our lives, and supports us during any changes we feel guided to make or that are put upon us. Portals also bring about synchronistic events.

Leading up to the Shift and during the final years of it, portals opened around certain months or time frames that brought in ideas and guided people who didn't even know each other to bring similar themes to the world. Between 2003 and 2004 long-held beliefs about traditional Christian history were challenged. Gary Renard's *The Disappearance of the Universe*, Dan Brown's *The DaVinci Code*, and Elaine Pagels's *Beyond Belief: The Secret Gospel of Thomas* were all published within a year of each other. While different in scope, these books all offered ground-breaking theories challenging beliefs that have pitted man against man and held us hostage within the false paradigm of separation.

Open Portals Are Conduits To God / Universal Energy

In Ronna Herman's article "The Mystery of the Vesica Picsis," she explains how portals create a "pathway between the spiritual and material worlds."[35] She uses the term *Father* for God or the original creative force—the stillness component, and the term *Mother* for Spirit—the active component.

Herman writes that portals are the active and aware Spirit that brings the original and unaware God energy to us at a point where we are still immersed in time. God and Spirit are both similar and different. The Father aspect is stillness, expansive, and *unaware*, whereas the Mother aspect is movement, expansive, and *aware*. We need the Spirit or Mother's movement to bring the Father or God's stillness to us. When this happens, a portal is created.

The time surrounding December 2012 was a major portal and brought with it much love and light energy. During this cosmic event, Humanity made it through without major worldwide catastrophes, notwithstanding the violent weather patterns of the last few years. We may be over the hump, but the anchoring in of the energies of the Shift is a process. This Shift has often been compared to a birth, with some pains, the birth, and then an adjustment period for both mother (Gaia) and child (us). This Shift is actually the culmination of a twenty-six-thousand-year cycle.

The Yuga, the Twenty-Six-Thousand-Year Cycle of Time

The period surrounding December 2012 brought one cycle to a close and opened up another. Many speak today about the year 2012 as an alignment of stars and the halfway point within a fifty-two-thousand-year cycle. In her article "Reclaiming Your-12-strand DNA," Julianne Everett writes of the Yuga.

> A Yuga is an East Indian term for a 26,000 year cycle of time. Each Yuga is divided into 2000 year dispensations that are given to Avatars for bringing humanity into higher and higher levels of God Consciousness. Our present dispensation was activated nearly two thousand years ago by the Beloved Lord Jesus the Christ, also known to some as Sananda. His cycle has been centered at impulsing the Christ Flame within every heart that is receptive to the love, the wisdom and the power of God.[36]

She continues to explain that in the final years leading up to the end of this twenty-six-thousand-year period, we had grown on all levels so to be able to respond to what is held within of the "frequency" it brings with it. The major portal that has opened at this time of the Shift offers a huge potential to reawaken in us important human genetic patterns that Humanity lost as it descended deeper and deeper into third-dimensional density.

Reawakening Our Original Twelve-Strand DNA

The Ascension of Gaia and her inhabitants out of third-dimensional constructs is a huge undertaking, and as we raise our individual vibrations towards that goal, we start to recover our original twelve-strand DNA. In her same article as above, Everett further explains that within Humanity's recent experience, only two strands of our DNA were operational while the other ten remained inactive. As these inactive strands are being enabled, our DNA is evolving to higher levels. This is because we have acted upon the impulses to release lower-dimensional attitudes and lifestyles and our beings are now more aligned with what they originally were.

Everett states that "beyond the suffering of the ages which is recorded within each of us, there is much great news that has also been stored within the higher octaves of the self both externally and internally ... [and reigniting] our 12-strand DNA creates the blessed re-weaving of our Higher Self." She explains that this will affect all the meridians of our bodies within all our chakras and we will feel the positive aspects of this on a both the physical and emotional levels, and that when we completely unlock our twelve-strand DNA much "joy and bliss" that was latent within our beings will be unblocked. Everett also tells us that as we shift our vibrational levels all those working with us on the etheric levels can begin to intertwine this new DNA into the different energetic parts of our bodies. She suggests that to get the process going to receiving this higher DNA that we call on our higher Selves to help us, no matter what symbol we use to do so.[37]

Innate Understanding of the Cosmos and Peaceful Concepts

There have always been great historical figures and thinkers who appeared to *know* significant and essential things. It is said that Galileo envisaged the solar system in his mind's eye. There have also been those who paved the way for safer, more egalitarian societies. Those who worked for women to have the right to vote and promoted the abolition of slavery and racism were the light bearers of recent past generations. However, during the last couple of decades, there has been an influx of young people and children with exceptional innate knowledge for us and for the Planet.

In the fall of 2012, Malala Yousafzai, a young Afghan girl who bravely encourages and promotes education for girls in her country, was shot for her initiatives and incurred severe injuries. This cruel attack brought awareness to the need for girls and women to be educated in her country and for greater equality among the sexes in the hope of a fair and safe life for the females of Afghanistan. Following her recovery, Malala took it upon herself to courageously promote her ideas around the world, paving the way for a better circumstances and chance in life for girls and women, wherever they are marginalized.

Severn Cullis-Suzuki, daughter of David Suzuki, addressed a group of people during a UN meeting on the issue of the environment in 1992 and again in 2012 regarding the healing and protection of our Planet. Severn has bravely stood up in front of the world to challenge us to become more mindful of the Planet so she and future generations can live in a world with clean air, water, and healthy soil.

Confident and gifted young people from mainstream society to civil servants and potential political leaders have emerged at this time of our evolution to defend the rights of people, animals and the Planet. In contrast to previous generations, such as those of the 60s when the voices of forward thinkers were too muffled against the backdrop of the establishment, these young people have come forth with such a sense of self-assurance and awareness that we have no choice but to rise up and meet their expectations. They are on the cusp of becoming our leaders, and some of them already are. With their gifts, insights, and confident but quiet unassuming ways and sense of fearlessness and limitlessness, this generation is primed to anchor in the necessary changes this Shift requires. We need to heed their advice and address their concerns. This time around, the idealism of youth will be met.

The Quantum Connection

As science continues to discover more about us, the earth, and the Universe it is becoming increasingly evident that everything is indeed connected and in a continual state of flux.

Quantum and Matter

In his article "What's All This Talk about Life Being an Illusion," Dave Schmidt reminds us that the Newtonian physics of the past maintained that "everything is made of matter coming from energy. Matter is solid, real, and makes up all of the stuff in our universe. The bodies, cells, molecules and atoms are all parts of matter. Matter does not change." Within this paradigm, energy does respond to its environment but does not change its basic structure. Based on Newtonian physics, particles and waves behave differently. Because we are living a third-dimensional existence, the laws of matter (particles) apply to us, but as we are also energy beings so do the laws of waves, which are not so rigidly defined. The quantum concept suggests that reality is bound up or exists within potentials. Schmidt says that "energy can change whether in the form of particles or waves. And it changes based on the perception of the observer."[38] The potential then exists that we *can* influence form, as well as make thoughts and ideas manifest.

Schmidt tells us that this idea of potential and creation can be traced back as far as Aristotle's time, when the Latin word *potentia* was used to describe a potential reality that could be influenced by an idea. Ideas come from thoughts, and we already know we can consciously direct our thoughts giving us the potential to create new realities. It then follows that by engaging the quantum potentiality we can even unlock the pathways to changing our DNA for better health.

Quantum, Our DNA, and Our Consciousness

Because quantum is organic it is always in a state of flux and therefore can be influenced. In the Edmonton lecture mentioned above, Kryon tells us that as much as 90% of our biology is quantum and that looking into the organic "random patterning" of the 90% portion of our DNA would be beneficial to our health. He explains that the quantum fields "are filled with potentials instead of absolutes, and they vary depending on many factors ... including Human consciousness."[39]

Kryon concurs with Dr. Wolf that consciousness must have a role to play regarding quantum. He explains that even as physics works within its laws and relationships, there is still that missing understanding of how wave and particle can be influenced. He concludes that it can only be explained by consciousness. God, Spirit, or the creative force of the Universe has a consciousness, which can be directed, as in the Creation story of the Bible. We also have a consciousness that can be directed. Thus we can create and influence our life and our health.

Kryon also tells us that this 90% of our DNA holds all the information about us, from the beginning of our souls' journeys, and that our individual souls all hold a "mark of the creator energy held within our DNA." He further explains that the knowledge that we had access to this powerful creator energy was held back from us and not allowed to surface because we had not reached a high enough level of consciousness to avoid annihilating ourselves with the information within it. However, we are now on the threshold of reaching the minimal required level of wisdom. As we delve deeper into the quantum function, Kryon says that we may "discover a new kind of physics that is always benevolent in its attributes ... you're about to open a door and look at something that is not linear and that has a bias—the bias of benevolence."[40]

The Universal Matrix

The Significance of Numbers; Our Cosmic Veneer

While the Universe may well be within the illusion, there is an overlapping matrix of numerical relationships written out in its cosmic veneer. Scriptures give evidence of this, as we see certain numbers expressed over and over again, such as 3, 4, 7, 12, and 144. These numbers came though the messages, metaphors, and symbols given to us as they relay the connections within the matrix and their interrelationship to our existence within the Universe as it was first mapped out. Even though there are many numerical connections, the basis of our Universe consists of ones and zeros, much like a computer program.

The Universal Matrix of Ones and Zeros

I have heard it often said that the Universe is a matrix of patterns of ones and zeros, and I have had some direct experience of this. Computer programs are made up of ones and zeros, and early in my journey I was told to make my requests clearly and concisely, as if I were giving information to a computer. Around that time and for just a few moments during a meditation, the numbers zero and one flashed continually across my awareness. It looked similar to a computer programming code. A few years later, with the knowledge I had acquired, I realized that this incident was the result of tapping into the Universal Matrix, without translation from Spirit. Spirit can offer us words, pictures, and insights, but occasionally we may spontaneously tap into a natural and pure flow of energy that appears in patterns. My experience was of ones and zeros. I did not sense an intrinsic message, but I found the event momentous.

Astronomy and Numerology: Cosmic Roadmaps

In ancient times when science, spirituality, and religion were considered intertwined aspects of our existence, astronomy was clearly paramount in the understanding of our continuation and evolution. As we discover the celestial alignments of ancient structures such as with the Pyramids at Giza and the large stones at Stonehenge we are realizing that our ancestors had a far greater understanding of the connection of the cosmos and our existence than we do now. In *Awakening the Planetary Mind*, Hand Clow tells us our ancestors found the "stars were living data banks" of knowledge and understood that "the cycles in the heavens mirror the cycles on earth ... there are hidden and influential time cycles, such as the precession of the equinoxes and the

261

cycles in the Mayan Calendar, that guide human metamorphic processes."[41] Numerology was also important in our past.

In *Helping Yourself with Numerology*, Helyn Hitchcock tells us that long before any alphabet existed, the ancients used the "science of numbers" to help them in their everyday lives. She explains that numerology is valuable "because the numbers or symbols have a metaphysical value holding a definite meaning within them denoting inner dynamic characteristics shaping one's destiny."[42]

We cannot base our whole lives on astrology, numerology, and the like, because inner wisdom is our best guide, but the influence of these cosmic elements is clearly more than coincidental.

The Significance of Numbers in Our Past and Scriptures

The number *3* has been an important aspect in all religions, as in the depiction of three aspects of Oneness: God, the Son, and the Holy Spirit within Christianity and Brahman, Atman, and Shakti in Hinduism.

Even though the numbers one and zero make up the underlying matrix of the Universe, in ancient times, the philosophers and builders of the megalithic structures considered the number three to be vital to their understanding of our connection to the Universe and paramount in the expression of form, like at Giza.

The power of three is dually expressed physically at Giza. The three pyramids each hold the inherent triangular geometry of the three sides. This could represent the perfect alignment of body, mind, and soul. The three sides meet at the apex of each of the structures, which may represent the apex of our existence, which is the balancing of our three aspects. Although it is becoming increasingly evident that the pyramids housed potent energetic power and were possibly built as portals to other dimensions, we can also create portals or vortexes with our own energetic alignments in moments of complete balance of body, mind, and soul.

In Eastern thought systems, it is in the balancing of our three aspects, the body, mind, and spirit that helps us be in touch with our divinity. It is when these three aspects are in continual balance that we reach the state of enlightenment—the apex of our existence. We are then the portal. The masters had all achieved this state, and became portals who could guide others to reach higher states of being. Those portals remained open, and this is why we have been encouraged to call upon the masters and why we are helped or uplifted when we do so, even while simply looking at their picture.

In Christianity the influence of *3* is represented by *God the Father* and its power with the *Holy* Spirit as the translator between us and that power, and the *Son represents Jesus and us*. Jesus is the redeemer but he also demonstrates

262

our potential. It is in the perfect balancing of these three aspects that we can reach our potential—our apex. Through our faith we can create a portal to work through.

The number *4* is a common number within many belief systems. Indigenous peoples consider the four elements to be of utmost importance celebrating and depicting them in various forms. Stephen Knapp tells us in "Lord Vishnu" that within Hindu writings Lord Vishnu has dominion over the four corners of the Universe.[43] In the Bible, Revelation speaks of etheric beings protecting all four corners of the earth.

The number *7* represents our chakras, the Eastern concept that depicts the main subtle energy meridians within our bodies. In the Bible, Revelation repeatedly mentions the number seven. For instance John must send the message to seven churches, and he sees seven golden lamp stands. In Hindu mythology, Vishnu is often represented as having seven heads.

The numbers *12* and *144* are also common numbers in religions. From Zoroastrianism, to Judaism, to Christianity and Islam the number twelve represented the divine. Each of these religions put forth that their associated divine incarnation on earth had twelve disciples. The Greeks also believed in twelve gods from Mount Olympus. Within spiritual and religious beliefs, there is an understanding that there are twelve levels of consciousness (as depicted in illustration 20) and twelve levels within each of these twelve levels, which total 144. There are twelve signs of the zodiac and in the Old Testament there were twelve tribes of Israel. In Revelation 7:1–8, we are told each of the twelve tribes of Israel held 12,000 individuals and the four angels who guarded the four corners of the earth and its weather would still everything until all these 144,000 people were given the seal of protection from God.

Existing and Moving Within the Different Dimensions

As explained in chapters 6 we call the different vibratory energetic levels within the Universe dimensions, so our third dimensional linear minds can better grasp how the non-linear, energetic patterns within the Universe work. As such, we say there are twelve dimensions, with each having twelve dimensions within them, for a total of 144 dimensions. And these dimensions or energetic patterns are fluid. They do not have clear demarcation lines separating one from the other.

All beings whether light-beings in the higher dimensions or those of us in form in the third dimension, regularly move within the main dimension we occupy. Within the third dimension Humanity has inhabited for eons, some have lived all their lives on the highest levels, others on the lowest, with many fluctuating between various levels.

On any given day we can move through the various levels of the main dimension we occupy. We can wake up feeling great and be on the highest echelons of the third dimension, and then if we allow something to upset us and remain angry or go into a revenge or victimization mode, the vibrations these attitudes emit bring us down to the mid or even lower levels of the third dimension. However, we now have the potential to move into the higher dimensions.

In the past, we may have briefly shifted dimensions in a moment of clarity of how an issue unfolded and adjusted our attitudes, but our habit has been to fall back into old responses, like in a two-step-forward, one-step-backward progress, as the issue that angered us would then anger us only *less* often. However, as the energy of the Shift brings with it the potential to release unconscious influences and more compassion and a deeper understanding of issues, we might make a two-step forward leap and not slip backward, as now the issue or person that usually angered us may *never* anger us again. And because we maintain our new attitudes, we move to and stay within the higher dimension our energetic shift allowed for.

Although Dr. Hawkins does not talk about dimensions in his Energy Level chart I discussed at the beginning of the chapter, in the example above our better responses and attitudes would move us from below the 200 negative impact level to above it to the positive impact level, and even though every momentary shift in consciousness is beneficial to the overall energy level of Humanity and the Planet, until we maintain or continue with the attitudes of the positive impact level, we would not greatly impact Humanity's energy levels.

As our Energy Level continues to rise above the 200 level and we reach into these higher dimensions, we truly become creators of our own realities since these higher levels are characterized by the quantum factor which is greatly influenced by thought, attitude, and intention. This is a powerful cosmic power we can hone that benefits us, Humanity as a whole, and Gaia.

Gaia: Almost Completely Anchored in the Fifth Dimension

Because of Gaia's recently raised vibratory level and her decision to ascend (more fully explained in chapter 10, "Ascension)," Gaia has now almost completely anchored within the fifth dimension. Giving a linear perspective to a nonlinear concept, if we could see this, we would see something like her top 20% anchored within the seventh dimension, her middle 60% anchored within the fifth, and her bottom 20% still anchored within the third dimension. See illustration 21.

#21: Gaia Anchored in Different Dimensions through Time

Middle Ages

10% of Gaia anchored in the higher
levels of 3rd dimension
90% anchored in the lower levels of the
3rd dimension

Rennaissance

25% of Gaia anchored in the higher
levels of 3rd dimension
75% anchored in the lower levels

1960s

50% of Gaia anchored in the higher
levels of the 3rd dimension
50% in the lower levels

2013

75% of Gaia anchored in the higher
levels of the 3rd dimension, and reaching
into the 5th and 7th
25% of Gaia still anchored in the lower
levels of the 3rd dimension

Although Gaia is now mostly anchored in the fifth dimension, she too can vacillate between the three dimensions she touches, much like we do. When major chaos erupts in the world, or when she is shrugging off physical or emotional hurts with severe weather, she may be shifting dimensions slightly. Because Gaia is now akin to the higher vibrations, she returns quickly to her usual higher levels. As do we!

Part of a Greater Family: The ET Connection

Once we have freed ourselves of the limitations of third-dimensional realities, we can begin to recognize our reality as multidimensional beings. The Shift also brings with it the potential to remember that we are all part of a larger, cosmic family. Many already do. Some have come to this Planet with this knowledge at the surface of their consciousness, while others will easily recognize this truth with just a few hints as the awareness lies just beyond their conscious awareness. Others will have little interest in accessing that part of their existence and be ambivalent about it, while some may retain strong blocks to remembering. All of these variations are fine. Our personal journeys will guide us toward what we are meant to remember and align with. However, there is still a prevailing fear of extraterrestrials.

Some people may have been influenced by the confusing and conflicting evidence as well as the negative reports of ETs from our distant and recent past. Others may even hold past life associations in cellular memories of negative experiences with them. Our history shows that we mostly lived under the influence of hate, anger, greed, blame, control and judgment, characteristics of living at the lowest levels of the third dimension. This may have left us open to attracting ETs from the lower dimensions. Some abuse may have taken place, but if so, we may have allowed it to happen, not having been sufficiently evolved to be confident in ourselves or to practice discernment and disengage with the ETs who wielded power over us. Now we do!

We have not only raised our collective vibrations high enough to no longer attract the lower-level ETs, within this cosmic time frame only the extraterrestrials helping us with our individual and Gaia's Ascension are permitted to interact with us. In "Activating the Andromedan StarGate at Lake Louise, BC" Sananda also tells us that at this time in our Ascensions process "only Extraterrestrial Craft at least 15 million years advanced of current Earth have access in or out." He adds that at the time of "disclosure" (see below) any lower level extraterrestrials and their crafts in close proximity to earth will be removed.[44]

The idea that accepting our connection to those from other planets is part of our spiritual evolution is new for most of us. It was for me. However, it is important to dispel fears of those who may one day, possibly in the not so distant future, make themselves known to us because fearful attitudes will only serve to encourage more conflicting information to flourish. We now know that science and the other universal understandings are related to the unmasking of our false illusions. It lifts the veil to the truth of who we are within ourselves, and it also illuminates who we are within the Universal Matrix.

Our Origins: The Garden of Eden or the Stars?

Some people believe Humanity evolved from the apes. Many are of the opinion that God planted us here in the Garden of Eden, and others suggest that we were sent here from other planets thousands of years ago. Over the years I have heard theories that we came to earth as an experiment from different planets because the races that we came from had lost the ability to evolve. I have also heard that humans are the link that can bring the Universe back to the Oneness it emanated from, hence, the specialness of Humanity. However we came to be here, evidence is being unearthed that beings have visited from other planets or dimensions. Many call these our star brothers and sisters, extraterrestrials, or ETs.

Our Star Brothers and Sisters

Five or six years ago, before I had any knowledge of this connection, I attended a conference where I happened upon Dr. Lynne D. Kitei's talk on the Phoenix Lights. She spoke eloquently, seemed genuine, and my interest was peaked so I bought her DVD *The Phoenix Lights: We Are Not Alone.* In her presentation and on the DVD she described sightings that she witnessed over a few years, culminating with a major sighting on the night of March 13, 1997, in Phoenix, Arizona. She recounted her experience as well as those of the many citizens she had interviewed who witnessed this event. All the witnesses remembered feeling peaceful and awe-inspired as they watched the huge spaceship pass overhead, and said that it traveled in complete silence. They spoke of their experience as being positive and extraordinary! They all truly *felt* that any visitors who were aboard had come in peace. She also discussed her investigative work since that event.[45]

Dr. Kitei draws on the ancient stories of the Ojibwe natives living in the area as evidence to support the existence of alien life having visited the Phoenix area. To study, investigate, and promote this event and its importance to Humanity, she quit her successful medical practice to work with those around the world investigating this type of phenomena.

I believe that many if not all of us came from the stars, and that our earliest ancestors came from many planets. However, except for those already living on earth, most of them exist in higher dimensions than we do. However, they will not present themselves to us until we have raised our consciousness enough to no longer be confused or fearful about their existence and not attack them. Here is what Kryon said in his 2011 Edmonton talk regarding our star brothers and sisters:

> Some day you'll meet the star seeds, your Pleiadian sisters and brothers. They're even here now, since they are quantum. You've got Pleiadian ancestors who lived a very, very long time in a graduate situation in a planet that went through the test just like yours. And it developed a quantum factor. They have benevolence and they have quantum energy. That's how they get here instantly and return, and they'll never interrupt your free choice. That's also why they don't land and say hello. Instead, they sit and cheer on the sidelines for what you've finally done.[46]

It is clear that many ETs are around us now as the sightings have significantly increased in recent years. In his article "Manitoba UFO Sightings Up in 2012," Kevin Engstrom reports on a Ufology Research finding that in

Manitoba the number of UFO sightings more than doubled in 2012 from that of 2011. It reported "1981 sightings ... more than twice the number of reports made in 2011 and nearly double the previous all-time national high of 1,004, made in 2008."[47] It is no news that this phenomenon of extraterrestrials nearby and watching us is met with a combination of fascination, skepticism, and fear. But if they do exist and are nearby, the ETs are not attacking us, despite their clear technological advancement. This fact should alleviate some of our fears.

The ETs, the Masters, and Their Vibrational Levels

As shown in illustration 3 (reprinted below), ETs can exist within our third-dimensional realm, in dimensions just higher than ours, and even within the higher realms. Like everything except complete Oneness, they still exist within the illusion and under the auspices of duality, and can exercise free will. Those who appeared in the past and created havoc were from a lower-dimensional existence but were more technologically advanced than we were, while those who came from the higher realms came exclusively to help us evolve and did not have self-serving agendas.

#3: Levels of Consciousness Within the Different Realms (Reprinted)

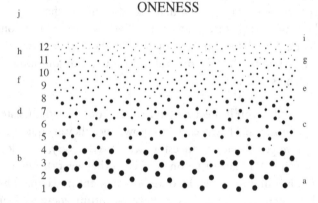

a) 1st 4 dimensions, world of form, separation is manifest
b) all life form, including humans and lower level ET's
c) 5th – 7th dimension, more ethereal, less awareness of separation
d) evolved live forms, higher level ET's, lower level Light-beings. Can take form
e) 8 -10th dimension, completely ethereal, concept of separation foreign. Rarely take form
f) highly evolved light-beings who run the Universe.
g) 11-12th dimension, completely ethereal, no awareness of separation. Very rarely take form
h) highly evolved light-beings that supervise the running of the Universe. Domain of Archangels and Seraphim. Almosy never have taken form.
i) No conscious awareness of Self, separation, its creations or us.
j) 13th - Original creative force we emanated from: God

Accounts of the prophets and holy people ascending into heaven may well have been of them ascending into the spaceships of the spiritually advanced ETs, as they had overcome lower third-dimensional attitudes and aligned with higher-dimensional vibrations of these beings and their ships. They may have been able to physically levitate as they had transcended the laws of the physical, or they may have been beamed up, but either way it was understood that they could withhold the higher vibrations within the ships. These would have been momentous occasions, for them and any witnesses.

Within Humanity's history there have been more visits from the ETs because they are closer to us vibrationally than say the archangels and masters who exist in the highest realms. It would be very difficult and possibly detrimental for those on the highest realms to acclimatize to our lower-vibrational levels, so the lower we sank into our third-dimensional attitudes, the less those from the higher dimensions could easily come here. It would be akin to someone from a loving, peaceful family and country being thrust into a cruel family and warring society. The intention was that the ETs from these realms closest to us were to act as intermediates between us and those light-beings who represent God, or the original creative force, and support and steer our journeys back to the Oneness from which we emanated. Many of the accounts of God punishing Humanity may have actually been the actions of lower to mid-level ETs who got frustrated or impatient with our inability to change and unleashed punishment on us, or lost sight of their original mission and acted with cruelty.

Those visitors may not have all been spiritually advanced, but then again, neither were we, having lost our way. As we fell deeper and deeper into third-dimensional ways of being, we got caught up in various efforts to reconnect with the gods or to ensure our afterlife. Sacrificing ourselves, others, or our loved ones was a common practice in our past. However, it may not always have been because we were instructed to sacrifice by the gods—we may have made the decision on our own to demonstrate our earnestness regarding our evolution.

It is a common understanding in spiritual circles that within the higher realms all that really matters is our return to the Oneness. From this perspective, we, our lives, and how we accomplish our return is not relevant. Our lessons can be learned in this lifetime, in another, or on the ethereal levels. In ancient times this may have been communicated to us and we may have taken it upon ourselves to sacrifice humans to the gods to prove ourselves, or so they would return to guide us further and/or with their technologies.

Whatever the underlying motives, history reveals we did much to appease the so-called gods. We worshiped them through idols, built huge temples and pyramids to please them, and we may have even sacrificed ourselves for or to them. We were clearly visited by many different types of ETs in our past, and they may have greatly influenced us.

The ETs Who Have Visited Us

According to Germane, as spoken through Lyssa Royal in "ET Civilizations," throughout history many ET groups have interacted with earth, including the Lyrans, Sirians, and the Pleiadians. The Lyrans were an authoritative group that played the role of strict, dogmatic parents who humans both loved and feared. During their active time on earth, they commonly used the symbols of birds and cats to depict their kind. The Sirians, however are said to have been zealous and devoted to serving and saving mankind, much like crusaders. Their representative symbols were usually serpents and dogs. The Pleiadians had a very deep love of mankind. They are genetically and emotionally connected to humans and have often throughout history been drawn back to earth to help us. Their love for humans is like parents who both love and fight over their children. They were symbolically represented by the seven stars of Pleiades.[48]

Germane also explained that the ET groups often fought with one another, leading to territorial disputes over the land and people of earth and the eventual division of the planet into different sections. So even though these groups were more advanced in many ways, they were still within the illusion and fell under the influence of greed and a warring mentality. Maybe we just carried on their warring tradition. The specialness of Humanity may be our potential to overcome the warring mentality with its hate and greed, and thereby affect the whole Universe positively. This would be huge! We are at the pinnacle of making that choice now.

Focus on Messages of the Masters

We may have been off about certain aspects of our origins and who/what the gods of old were, but these are just details and neither discount what the masters taught nor the good intentions that our scriptures hold. When we are sincere in embracing the love, forgiveness, and compassion our scriptures point to they will still have a positive and uplifting impact on us. As we continue to uncover all about who the gods of old really were, we must be careful not to allow defensiveness about our beliefs to overshadow the true intentions of the masters and the intrinsic value of the belief systems that blossomed in their wake.

Because of all the myths, stories, and supposed truths regarding our past it is very hard to distinguish fact from fiction. However, this really only affects the details, because the ET connection was and still is indirectly by divine

270

decree. In the grand scheme of us all ultimately returning to the Oneness, these more highly-evolved beings from other planets (whether they were more advanced spiritually or technologically) were to help us advance and release lower-dimensional attitudes to attain a higher consciousness, even though, like us, they sometimes lost sight of their purposes.

Where Did the ETs Come From?

Many of us are enthralled by the growing evidence that points to our extraterrestrial connections. However, we must also ask ourselves, where did they come from? What are their origins? Illustration 3 shows where the ETs abide within the different dimensions and how they too emanated from the Oneness we are all a part of. They do not exist in a vacuum. The extraterrestrials are but one strata of the original creation of form (the big bang and our Universe)—they are not the "be all, end all" of existence. The purpose of every being within every realm of our Universe, whether ethereal, an ET, or in human form, is to eventually align with and reemerge with the Oneness we all emanated from.

Importance of Bloodlines / Keeping DNA Pure

The leaders, prophets, kings, and pharaohs of old strongly advocated the importance of keeping their bloodlines pure. Whether they were human, ETs, or the offspring of ETs, pure bloodlines were considered to be of such importance at that time that in some cases the siblings of a king or pharaoh married and incestuously procreated. In these cases their effort to keep the lineage strong may have actually backfired, as the close genetic matches may have resulted in overly ambitious, cruel, and even depraved offspring, who as leaders would have perpetuated injustice, greed, and cruelty keeping us in further fear and darkness.

There is also much evidence that extraterrestrials of the past mated with humans to produce more-highly-evolved offspring. We do not yet know whether this was for our benefit or theirs. Was their intention to retain and not dilute the DNA of the more-highly-evolved beings who had recently mated with humans in order to keep the rulers more closely connected to their evolved states so they could guide Humanity, or was it for their own selfish purposes? Throughout the ages, it is possible that all of the above occurred. Today, we still maintain the concept of bloodlines within royalty, although it is not clear whether this is now for practical reasons such as ensuring that descendents adhere to certain norms, to keep the power within families, or to keep the DNA pure.

We Attracted Lower-Vibrational ETs with Our Lower Vibrations

Even though we may have been somewhat spiritual in ancient and biblical times, we were also barbaric in many ways, and as such became hosts for negativities as we drew beings with selfish and cruel intentions to us with our vibrations. We just have to read our history and early scriptures to see how cold, cruel, and unloving we were in many ways. Because of these accounts of many negative interactions with the ETs, it is understandable that we would be wary, confused, and fearful of them now.

Our fears and confusion is also based on the more recent tales of alien abductions and accounts of experiments done on humans. We do not know yet whether this was for their benefit, out of curiosity, or to check on how we were evolving. It may have been for all these reasons, at one time or another. We must remember that we have only recently understood that the use and exploitation for our benefit of what we consider lower life-forms, like with animal testing, is questionable or even wrong. The ETs who have conducted experiments on us are also still within the illusion and may similarly have been unaware of how others interpreted their actions. It is important to point out that *we* still use, manipulate, and even create animals for our own purposes, like with animal testing and the raising and slaughtering of animals to eat. With this Shift and Ascension we are all becoming more evolved and connecting the dots between our actions and their effects on who and what is around us.

Because it is our cosmic time for this evolution, we are protected from any negative beings. The extraterrestrials that are nearby are waiting to reunite with us as old friends. However, as a collective we must set aside our fears before what is known in many circles as *disclosure* happens on a worldwide scale.

Disclosure

You will start to hear the term *disclosure* more and more. It relates to the ETs that are nearby revealing themselves to us. Many eagerly await what they foresee as a momentous occasion—when all the ETs who have been helping us with our Ascensions will reveal themselves to the world. Those who joyfully anticipate this event already feel the connection to their star brothers and sisters, as they have a soul remembrance of past life associations. Others just feel the excitement of it all. However, because many others are apprehensive not only because of past events, but also because they do not yet understand the connection the extraterrestrials have with us at this time in our evolution, we are getting help to overcome our fears. In the same article mentioned above, *Activating the Andromedan StarGate at Lake Louise, BC*, Sananda also tells us the activation of April 17th, 2015 brought with it powerful crystal energy to help pave the way for disclosure to come about.

It is important that we continue to unearth the truths about our past relationships with the ETs, the whys and wherefores of the apparent abuses they inflicted upon us, and the reasons for the obvious cover-ups that have gone on since the 1950s and earlier. Then when it is time for us to welcome them, we can do so knowing the truth of what transpired in the past. This coupled with our understanding of why we succumbed to their influence and the knowledge that unlike the needy people eons ago who were at their mercy, we can welcome them confidently, but with appropriate prudence. And they do have much to offer us.

The extraterrestrials who are nearby helping with our Ascensions are also more technologically advanced with equipment and powerful energetic knowledge that could help us—especially to clean up our Planet—and which could also help lessen the effects of cataclysmic disasters. Some believe they already have. There have been many reports that shortly after devastating events such as Chernobyl and the 2011 tsunami in Japan, more UFO sightings were reported than usual in the affected areas. Those who study these phenomena believe they were helping to reduce the damage and human suffering.

Even if the ETs that are nearby have benevolent intentions, this does not mean there will not be *lots* of negotiation involved when we do welcome our star brothers and sisters into our world again, be that three, thirty, or one hundred years from now. There will be many factors to consider. There are links about the ETs on my List of Recommendations.

Except for a few throughout our history we have perceived from within the limitations of our third-dimensional existence. However, we have recently been sensitized to many of the concepts in the field of science and their inherent relationship to our existence through books, movies, articles, YouTube videos, and interviews with forward thinkers and channels who have come forth with messages for us. We can now at least understand if not believe that we are multidimensional beings living within an illusion even though our current reality is that of form. We actually chose to come here in form within the illusion of the third dimensional realities.

Inelia Benz tells us in "The 5th Dimension Is Not a Location, It's a Creation," that "all physical reality is multidimensional and an illusion, but we create them to have an experience of singular individuality.... at the same time, we choose to be aware of only a tiny little spectrum of that all encompassing reality," and that tiny spectrum dictates what we experience as "real."[49] So, it was our choice to come here and experience life in singularity and from within the limitations of the third dimension, while at the same time our ultimate purpose was to rise above these limitations, and recognize our connection to the Oneness and each other.

Within the illusionary Universe, we are all connected to each other: humans to each other, humans to ETs, humans and ETs to those in the higher realms, such as the ascended masters, light-beings, and archangels—and all of us to the Oneness. As we come to adapt to and increasingly accept the changes this Shift brings with it and open ourselves up to our True Selves and our God-selves, the blinders will drop and we will be better able to embrace all that we are individually, collectively, and cosmically. Universal cosmic truths will be uncovered, understood, and eventually accepted.

> *The fact that we exist imposes constraints*
> *not just on our environment but on the possible*
> *form and content of the laws of nature themselves.*
> —Stephen Hawking and Leonard Mlodinow[50]

In the next chapter, "Health and Healing: Death and Dying," we will explore the connection between our journeys, return to wholeness, and our health, as well as discuss the importance of our approach to death and dying.

CHAPTER 8

Health and Healing, Death and Dying

> *Our civilization is coming to equate the value of life*
> *with the mere avoidance of death.*
> *An empty and impossible goal, a fool's quest for nothingness,*
> *has been substituted for a delight in living what lies latent in all of us.*
> *When death is once again accepted as one of the*
> *many important parts of life, then life may recover its old thrill.*
> —David Ehrenfeld[1]

This chapter draws on the works of many experts with regard to mental and physical health and the healing of our bodies and minds. It also covers death and dying, our attitudes toward these, how best to deal with death—both our own and others'—and what dying, or "laying the body aside," really means. Even though I bring these concepts to you with all sincerity, I am not a medical or mental health professional. Any information here should not replace professional consultation.

Section 1: Health and Healing

> *Creating health means accepting that there are events in everyone's life*
> *that cannot be explained or changed,*
> *and at the same time realizing that each of us has conscious input*
> *into our state of health through choosing relationships,*
> *thoughts, foods and activities that support and nourish us fully.*
> —Dr. Christiane Northrup[2]

We are now really starting to understand that there is a powerful connection between our thoughts and attitudes and our health and wellness. At our core, we are programmed to be vibrant and healthy in a mental, emotional, and physical way. However, a complex set of influences affects both our physical and our mental health.

Our soul's journey may deem that an illness is a good vehicle for our spiritual growth and/or for the growth of those around us, and this illness *will* show up at a certain point in our lives—no matter what we do. We may hold a genetic predisposition to certain diseases, but they may or may not manifest, depending on exposure to outside toxic influences and/or how we emotionally navigate life. Apart from DNA predispositions and influences we have no control over, at the deepest level most forms of disease are energy blocks that we create either by burying our anger, frustration, or disappointment, or by weakening our immune systems through unhealthy lifestyles or subjecting them to too much stress. And even though we cannot always pinpoint why we got sick, if we honestly investigate our inner world, we may find a mental, emotional, or physical connection that threw our energy system off balance, and to which our body responded with an illness.

Positive Vibrations Keep Us Healthy: Understanding the Mind–Body Connection

We are creating our physical and emotional condition at every moment, whether we are aware of it or not. It is like breathing. We breathe automatically, without conscious thought. Just as polluted air and water will damage our physical health, emotional pollutants (such as fear, worry, pettiness, anger, blame, revenge, jealousy, hate, cruelty, dishonesty, etc.) will damage our spiritual and mental health, which then affects our bodies. Once we grasp that everything is vibration, it is easy to understand that surrounding ourselves with positive vibrations is the healthier choice. We know that when we are with people or in an environment that emits positive vibrations we feel good, and when we are surrounded by negativity, we feel bad. Although not so obvious, these vibrations also affect our physical bodies. As mentioned in the last chapter, our cells carry all of our emotions.

Unaddressed Emotional Pains Are Open Doors for Ailments

Internalizing our pains and hurts is the real problem, and until we learn to change this, life stresses from the past will affect us now. On a broadcast of *It's a New Day*, Joan Hunter tells us that traumatic situations are held in our cellular memories until we deal with them. They sit there like open doors for ailments. She tells us that emotional traumas affect our autoimmune responses, as they induce stress hormones that bring us down physically.

Hunter also explains that these traumas weigh us down emotionally and that in her workshops she puts heavy books in people's hands to represent the weight they carry from past situations not dealt with. She says that we are born to be healthy and vibrant and that God wants us to thrive. All we have to do is believe this with 100% of our being and take hold of it.[3] However, as noted above, there are exceptions that can override this, such as a predisposition or our soul's journey, as some soul lessons are to help us make peace with everything that having an illness might entail, for us or our loved one.

In *The Alchemy of Illness*, Kat Duff explains that our experiences in life become imprinted onto our bodies, because our immune systems are programmed to carry the memories of our emotions. She draws on the work of Deepak Chopra, who explains that every negative emotion we experience affects our well-being. He compares the emotions we accumulate throughout our life to grains of sand piling up to form discomforts and health issues.[4]

Stress, Its Purpose, and How It Affects Our Bodies

Stress is a normal response to perceived stressors. It causes us to constantly feel emotional and psychological pressure, which in turn causes higher levels of adrenaline and cortisol to be produced. However, as with all our deeply ingrained attitudes and habits, we can retrain ourselves to react to stress in a positive way by being conscious and mindful of our reactions to the stressors. This new way of looking at stressors and processing stress helps us to understand what we have done with past stressors and how they may have affected us.

Biology of Stress: Cortisol, Metabolism, and Illness

The hormone cortisol rises as a natural response to stress or perceived threat, and so long as we are not subjected to sustained stress, our body chemistry returns to normal. However, if stress becomes more of a constant in our lives, our cortisol levels will remain high, affecting our overall health. In *The Complete Doctor's Stress Solution: Understanding, Treating, and Preventing Stress and Stress-Related Illnesses*, Naturopathic Doctors Penny Kendall-Reed and Stephen Reed tell us that cortisol, the hormone involved in the fight-or-flight response, adversely affects the human body because it reaches *all* the tissues within the body, and its effects are thereby widespread. So, when cortisol is chronically stimulated, it affects our bodies in many different ways. In the past, raised levels of cortisol offered humans a form of protection. However, it is now the leading cause of hormonal and metabolic imbalances. Kendall-Reed and Reed further tell us that experiencing the continual stimulation of stress not only contributes to creating a condition called the *metabolic syndrome*, but also causes issues with fertility, immunity, and healing. Stress also adversely affects our life force: breath.[5]

Antidotes to Stress: Deep Breathing, Being Present, and Lightening Up

Deep breathing is one of the most uncomplicated healthy habits we can engage in. In *Conscious Breathing: Breathwork for Health, Stress Release, and Personal Mastery*, Gay Hendricks explains that stress affects our most important life-force, breathing. As the body reacts to stress it activates the nervous system, pumping adrenaline to the body's now tense muscles. This includes our stomach, and as it tenses up our breathing rate increases. We then experience short, shallow breaths and begin to breathe from the chest. This chest breathing is restrictive. He further explains that healthy breathing comes from deep within our bellies and sends relaxing messages to all our cells. When our bodies relax, our breath slows down shifting to the belly giving us a deeper breath that is more physically nurturing.[6]

If we allow ourselves to become conscious of when we are stressed, we can reduce it by learning to shift our breathing from our chests to our bellies by taking deeper, slower breaths. Conscious breathing is essential if you are prone to experiencing anxiety or stress, because it creates a general sense of well-being by releasing the tension. It also helps us to focus, clear our mind, and become present. In *A New Earth*, Eckhart Tolle suggests that just bringing awareness to your breath "forces you into the present moment … [and when] you are conscious of the breath, you are absolutely present … You cannot think *and* be aware of your breathing."[7] Conscious breathing clears our minds of distractions and stabilizes our emotions, and at this time of the Shift when its energy and vibrations are affecting our bodies and whole energetic system, it is even more important to monitor our breathing.

In "Reclaiming Your 12-Strand DNA," Julianne Everett explains that if we are to get the most out of this recalibration of our beings, "breath is the key [and that] deep breathing" is recommended. This will ensure that the encoding of our original 12-strand DNA, its energy, and the wisdom held within it can be translated to all parts of our bodies.[8]

Lightening up and not taking ourselves, others, and life so seriously is a tenet common to the all spiritual and religious teachers and practices I have ever come across. Allowing stress to dishearten us or a serious attitude to overtake us adversely affects our mental and physical health. As we become more focused on the issues we are stressed over, take too seriously, or give too much attention to, we are less likely to be able to pay attention to or act upon more promising, enriching, uplifting, or life-affirming possibilities around us or that may cross our path.

However, not *all* stress is bad. Researchers are now realizing that the real problem is more in the way we view, understand, and internalize stressors. In her video *How to Make Stress Your Friend*, based on her research and books, health psychologist Kelly McGonigal tells us that if we befriend our stress, we can use it to our advantage.[9] Using stress properly can *enable* us to take action and move forward in life, empowering us through achievements or better results than if we had not reacted to the stress triggers.

Our Minds, Our Emotions, and Our Well-Being

Even though standard medicine is starting to recognize the mind–body connection, our emotional states play a much larger role in our physical health than is outwardly visible. According to Debbie Shapiro, whose book *Your Body Speaks Your Mind* won the 2007 Visionary Book Award, the role of the mind in relation to health is inseparable from our emotions. She refers to the undeniable and close interconnection between what is going on in our lives, our thoughts and feelings, and the physical reactions that manifest in the body. Our state of mind affects our body physically, in the same way as viruses and colds.

Shapiro explains that the mind and body are not two separate entities that function independently from one another, but they form what she calls "a single bodymind." When something goes awry in our bodies, this is the result of a combination of physical and emotional causes. It is an expression of our mind manifesting itself through our body parts. She says that "happiness, hopefulness, optimism, and contentment appear to reduce the risk or limit the severity of cardiovascular disease, pulmonary disease, diabetes, hypertension, colds, and upper-respiratory infections ... [while] depression—extreme opposite of happiness—can worsen heart disease, diabetes, and a host of other illnesses."[10]

Shapiro maintains that by treating illness as a learning experience, we can direct positive energy toward healing, whereas the belief that illness is beyond our control will not direct any positive energy toward the body. She reminds us that Indigenous peoples know and work with the mind–body connection.

Hurtful Buried Emotions Surface—One Way or Another

Because the mind–body connection exists in all of us, our emotional issues will inevitably surface in some way, regardless of how much we try to avoid them. Even if we deny that something is wrong, they are still alive in our unconscious mind, and affect our weak spots. This could be our sleep patterns; digestive, nervous, or immune systems; or they could heighten anxiety, depression, or addiction. Projected outward onto others they can show up as hostility, aggression, prejudice, or fear. This will then bring chaos into our lives, further adding to our stress which in turn can cause us to become ill. Addictions, as poor substitutes for dealing with buried hurts or confusing and conflicting emotions can also come into play when we have not properly dealt with our emotions, and they further add to the problem. These cycles continue until we deal with the real underlying issues, as well as with the effects of any conflicts we invite in or addictions we have succumbed to.

Panic Attacks

Panic attacks are one example of anxieties, buried emotions, and/or inner fears or conflicts reaching a crisis and needing to find an outlet. They tend to come upon us suddenly, are entirely disabling, and usually characterized by palpitations, sweating, feelings of heightened anxiety, and thoughts that we will die.

I suffered from panic attacks in my mid-twenties. I later realized they were symptomatic of unacknowledged emotions and inner fears and conflicts because of my family dynamics. I had many of the typical symptoms, as well as a feeling of unreality, like I was not there. As the symptoms came upon me, I became fearful because I thought I might lose control, go crazy, or possibly die. The physical symptoms can also mimic heart attacks, and on a few occasions I actually called my doctor in fear. Panic attacks undermine our ability to feel secure. They contribute to agoraphobia, a condition defined as an illogical fear of the outside or of being in crowds. During those few years I preferred to stay inside, because I felt safe there. I especially tried to avoid large spaces, like stadiums, because the idea of loosing control in such a large public place was horrific and the expansive openness stressed me further. I needed to be in my own small, comfy, and safe environment that mimicked the confined world I had created in my mind.

The Spirit–Mind–Body Connection

"Flourishing" in all Aspects of Health

In *Spiritual and Psychological Aspects of Illness: Dealing with Sickness, Loss, Dying, and Death*, Beverly Musgrave and Neil McGettigan tell us that in the last 30 years, the industrialized world has shifted its approach to psychology. Today, a more comprehensive type of psychology called "positive psychology" has begun to address the idea of "flourishing" rather than getting by in relation to mental health.[11]

This new approach is more holistic because it takes into account the idea that being successfully treated is no longer about only treating symptoms, but also about restoring the person to complete wholeness. For wholeness to occur, one must focus on the many facets of well-being. This includes being self-accepting and having emotional vitality, a positive outlook on one's life, a purpose in life, positive relationships, a sense of independence and belonging, and an interest in others. Musgrave and McGettigan suggest that this "flourishing" encompasses the presence of positive emotions, positive psychological functioning, and positive social functioning. We need to translate this philosophy of "flourishing" into the medical profession so that the well-being of the person as a whole—the mental and spiritual, as well as the physical is encouraged.

Treating Our Afflictions at the Proper Level

While there is a strong mind–body connection to our issues and illnesses, when treating anything, we have to employ treatments that match the issue, as well as the severity of the issue. In *Grace and Grit*, Ken Wilber maintains that our diseases or concerns originate from the "physical, emotional, mental, or spiritual" plane and that it is important to focus at the same level for treatments. If we believe the disease originated from a level higher than it actually did, he says we will instill *"guilt"* within ourselves. Conversely, if we believe it originated from a lower level than it actually did, we will create *"despair."*[12]

Wilber gives the simple example of breaking a bone, a physical-level issue, which needs the simple physical treatment of setting a cast. He explains that using a mental-level technique, such as visualization to heal it would be ineffective. Also, if we adhere to the belief that everything that happens to us comes from our thought processes and that we can heal the break with our thoughts, our method would also be ineffective because we are misapplying a high-level concept to a low-level issue. Except for the highly enlightened beings who can manipulate form, most of us could not heal a broken bone with our thoughts.

One day in the not-so-distant future, when we are more attuned to our True Selves and the power that holds, we will be adept at not only preventing most discomforts and illnesses, but also at treating them without the use of medications that often have negative side effects. In the meantime, if there is an indication for the use of medication to relieve pain or counter any physical disease, anxiety, depression, or any other form of chemical imbalance for a while, or even for a lifetime, one should certainly explore these options and adhere to the advice of a trusted physician.

Listening to Our Bodies: Reclaiming Their Wisdom

Our bodies, with their emotions, feelings, and even physical cues are our best indicators of issues that need attention. In *Women's Bodies, Women's Wisdom*, Dr. Christiane Northrup suggests that if we feel sad or if something moves us, we should allow ourselves to cry. If we feel tired, we should sleep. If we feel lonely we should engage in social activities or get out and see people. By feeling and listening to our bodies, we are connected to what is going on inside them, and can often avert more serious outcomes. She says that our bodies are equipped with an "innate wisdom ... we can generally trust our 'gut feeling' ... because the solar plexus, the place in the body where we generally feel that gut reaction, is in fact a primitive brain ... [and] a major intuitive center." We should pay attention to our feelings, what our gut conveys, and not question why we feel a certain way.[13]

Northrup says that if we do not heed the message the first time, our body will speak to us with increasing insistence through cues and discomforts, possibly even a general breakdown or illness. Our body has its own internal wisdom, and sends us signals when something is off. It also knows how to heal when listened to and properly guided. She further explains that understanding comes *after* we have allowed ourselves to experience our feelings.

Compassion Is Always the Answer Regarding Illness

While understanding the body–mind–spirit connection is important, we must be careful not to allow this knowledge to override compassion. No one is perfectly aligned to their True Self, and our misalignments can play out in different ways. Our DNA and soul journey may encompass a certain illness—regardless of our lifestyle or attitudes, so it would be a mistake to assume that we cause *all* of our physical and mental issues, or that other people cause theirs. Making negative or hurtful comments about another's illness is not being spiritually aware. Internalizing within ourselves or expressing to others only love and compassion regarding a diagnosis is the only acceptable response.

Illness or adversity may be part of the journey we, and those around us, are to experience for spiritual growth. They could also simply reflect or amplify how our misalignments are playing out at the moment. In light of what we know about creating our own realities, if someone we know is going through something difficult, be that a life issue or illness, we should take care not to allege that his or her attitude is the cause of their circumstances. Doing so will only serve to worsen a tough situation, already likely surrounded by fear, confusion, and possibly some inkling of guilt. We do so like to show what we now know.

Many of us who have become aware of our ability to create our own realities and of how certain attitudes may heighten susceptibility to developing specific illnesses can easily fall into the trap of alluding to and pointing out that others in dire circumstances must have brought it on themselves, which is not always the case. And talking among ourselves about our perception of the cause of another's illness is really just an ego boost: it is a feeble attempt to validate that we are knowledgeable. It is a judgmental attitude akin to religious dogma.

As all the masters have taught, love, compassion, and kindness are *always* the answer in *every* situation. Instead of in effect condemning someone who is already suffering, our intention should always be of a loving nature with the purpose of being supportive and a source of comfort to those struggling with fears, frustration, guilt, pain, or any other difficult life situation they may be dealing with.

Mind Health and Healing

When we create peace and harmony and balance in our minds,
we will find it in our lives.
—Louise L. Hay[14]

Practicing Mindful Awareness Keeps our Mind Healthy

To live a fulfilled life, as well as keeping our bodies and emotions healthy, it is important to keep our mind clear and healthy. In addition to prayer, meditation, and yoga, the practice of mindful awareness can help to achieve mind health. In *The Developing Mind: How Relationships and the Brain Interact to Shape Who We Are*, Dr. Daniel J. Siegel states that applying mindful awareness to our everyday lives has been shown to improve the health of our minds. It gives us increased mental flexibility and concentration, as well as a general sense of well-being. Siegel further explains that it also enhances empathy and compassion in our relationships. These shifts in our brains also give a greater sense of "resilience" by creating an "approach rather than withdrawal" impulse when confronted with challenging situations.[15] Dr. Ridha Arem tells us in *The Thyroid Solution* that practicing mindfulness during simple tasks, such as exercise, will have a greater effect on our emotional and mental health, as our thoughts then become structured and focused.[16]

Mind Health Creates Physical Health

In addition to looking after ourselves, dealing with genetic dispositions, and following the prescribed healing modalities we have chosen, in her same book as mentioned above Northrup she tells us that "creating health is also based on the following eternal truth: Acknowledging, feeling and then releasing rage, guilt, loss, anger, and grief is the key to all healing." She explains that creating health requires an entire shift in the way we think, relate to our bodies, minds, and spirits, and connect to the Universe.[17]

She also tells us that until we are able to completely make the required mental shifts, we may still have to follow standard medical solutions. In the meantime, we need to accept that some things in life cannot be changed or explained, but that each of us has the ability to make conscious decisions about the state of our health by choosing our thoughts, attitudes, relationships, and activities. And even regarding difficult situations, forgiveness is the key. Very rarely do people maintain or regain health and wholeness until they make this shift. In *You Can Heal Your Life*, Louise L. Hay offers us an affirmation to help us forgive. This quote and the ones below are located at the back of the book in "Meditations, Visualizations, and Other Practices" under the "Affirmations and Self-Talks" section.

> It is easier for me to forgive than I thought.
> Forgiving makes me feel free and light …
> The more resentment I release, the more love I have to express.
> I am learning to choose to make today a pleasure to experience.[18]

Benefits of Resetting Our Mind-sets and Setting Intentions

No matter how we feel, we can always reach for the "better-feeling thought" that Abraham-Hicks talks about. If we wake up feeling tired or unwell, we can either wallow in it, thereby further anchoring the feeling, or we can choose to reach for a thought that characterizes how we want to feel—we invite in that better feeling. For example, instead of saying to ourselves, **"I feel awful and will never get through the day,"** we can say something like, **"I seem to have woken up tired. I'm sure I will feel better once I wash and eat something."** Northrup suggests we say something like this to ourselves when we go to sleep: **"I want to feel good in the morning so that I can start the day feeling energized."** The positive emotional energy produced by these affirmations has the power to draw better health into our lives, and the more we use it, the better it works.

She explains that when we direct our thoughts to the feelings of health that we want, we are "setting up an invisible magnetic field that begins to draw health to you, unless you keep blocking it with other thoughts such as 'Well, I want it, but I'll never get it.'" To anchor our inner guidance and negate negative thinking, Northrup also suggests we set and repeat our intention, for example, **"I am intending vibrant health,"** before going to sleep, for a period of 30 days."[19] As we sleep, our intention to attain or maintain health is programmed into our bodies and minds. We can also do this to attract joy, comfort, and support into our lives.

Usefulness of Understanding Our Illnesses without Overanalyzing

When we succumb to illness, we are sometimes curious and want to know why it happened. Examining if we had a part in bringing our illnesses forward helps to alleviate further errors in healthy choices. However, overanalyzing can be counterproductive! Northrup warns that when we try to control and figure out the meaning of our illnesses, we really only create an illusion of control.

She explains that our "symptoms and/or illnesses ... [come with] messages" and suggests we ask ourselves, "Am I open to listening to them?" When we are open, we are on the way to healing. Northrup adds that being "open to the wisdom of our bodies, means that you allow the illness to speak to you, often through the language of emotion, imagery, and pain." This is for the purpose of understanding, healing, and possibly making life changes—not for an in-depth analysis of why it happened. She quotes the 12-step program's "whying is dying" to give further credence to the idea of not putting too much focus on why we got ill.[20]

Our egos can easily seize upon any over analysis of why we got sick with ensuing feelings of guilt, which would not help our recovery. So if we do become ill, it is better to focus on our healing rather than on the why scenarios.

Depression and Mental Illness

Depression and mental illness share some of the same symptoms, and serious depression can often be a precursor to mental illness. Clinical mental illness brought on by a chemical imbalance is a very serious, life-altering and threatening disease. We have only recently started to fully understand and be able to diagnose and properly treat these chemical imbalances, making it possible for those afflicted to live full and satisfying lives.

Situational and Mild Depression

Most of us suffer from some form of depression at some point in our lives, even if it is mild and short-lived, like situational depression. Situational depression can last for a few days or even a few months, and is the most common type of depression. It is also the easiest to deal with, as it is not caused by a chemical imbalance or genetic predisposition, and is usually not debilitating, as its effects are typically short-term.

In situations over which we have no control, such as becoming the sole caregiver of a sick relative, we must create coping mechanisms and/or get support from family and community. In situations we can control, such as being unhappy with our job, it helps to make a decision to do something about it and then create an action plan. In both these situations, we may feel distressed and experience a great deal of frustration and anger. Should this continue without relief or a solution, there can be a downward spiral from lethargy to apathy, to a loss of joy of living, diminished self-esteem and mild depression, and these *can* be difficult cycles to break out of. We may even need to make drastic changes in our lives or seek professional help to regain our balance. I often succumbed to this type of depression, did get the help, and fully recovered. Serious depression, however, brings with it a plethora of different symptoms and issues.

Serious Depression

In *Happiness: The Nature and Nurture of Joy and Contentment*, Dr. David Lykken writes that serious depression (also known as *morbid depression*) is "the happiness thief ... [and] is not the result of too much negative emotion, but rather the absence of the positive." He states that serious depressions are characterized not only by feeling diminished, sad, and lacking luster for life, but also feeling "*hopeless.*" Lykken explains that the usual life stresses, frustrations, angers, and even thoughts of revenge are at least "compatible with hope," because they hold an element of "what-ifs." Severe depression and its hopelessness not only rob us of the ability to find any joy in life, but is also a "life-threatening illness." Severe depression is genetic and those afflicted are often suicidal. Morbid or clinical depression is a mental illness.[21]

Mental Illness

Mental illness is something we are just starting to fully understand. There are many kinds of mental illnesses with many terms, including depression, clinical depression, mental disease or illness, manic depression, and bipolar disorder—all of which can be debilitating. Mental illness often does not have any real noticeable outward physical signs, but many of the symptoms line up with what society would characterize as a weakness in the person such as lethargy, unclear thinking, inability to make decisions, keep a job, or even look after our personal hygiene. Today, many still shun, criticize, marginalize, and mistreat people with mental illness.

In families with a history of mental illness, some succumb to its effects to differing degrees, while others are not at all affected. As more people come forward and share their stories, we can better understand how this debilitating illness robs the sufferer of quality of life and creates hurt, conflict, and confusion for those afflicted, as well as for their loved ones.

In *Changing My Mind*, Margaret Trudeau, the ex-wife of the late former Canadian Prime Minister Pierre Trudeau, maps out her life with its ups and downs through years of suffering from bipolar disease. Now in her sixties, she lives a satisfying life enjoying her grandchildren and helping others by sharing her story. In her introduction, she says, "The journey to get where I am today has been a long and perilous one (never mind a very public one), but that's partly because I was in the dark about my condition for so many years, as were those trying to help me." She tells us that she is happier now than she has ever been in her life, although she was also able to find some contentment when her children were young, despite her illness.[22]

Trudeau shares that as her frustrations mounted—being a young mother married to a much older man, and public figure as well—her behavior became erratic. Her sister once voiced concerns to their mother and suggested Margaret seek professional help. Their mother gave the common reply of the day: "Certainly not... There is no way that Margaret can see a psychiatrist. He will only blame me. That's all they do: blame the mothers."[23]

After much pain and frustration, trial and error, many hospitalizations over the years, and much love and help from family and friends, who even orchestrated an intervention, Margaret eventually found the right doctor and combination of medications and started to take them religiously adjusting them when needed. In addition, Dr. Colin Cameron, one of her psychiatrists, says that she finally took charge of her own well-being and "set out to change her entire approach to life, including diet, exercise and giving up marijuana." He further explains that Margaret understood that to keep an even keel, she had "to protect her private time and space ... [and] prioritize certain important relationships and let go of others." Cameron also tells us that to bring about her healing, Margaret had to make peace with all parts of herself, including her "twin demons: bipolar illness and pain."[24]

As with any illness, once we accept that there are certain aspects of life we must keep in check, we can gain an infinite amount of self-confidence, freedom, and peace. Like Margaret, those who do heal have made a commitment to want to feel and get better, and took the steps to do so. They engage their will, along with the practical modalities, and do not give up—even if they fail over and over again.

Committing Ourselves to Healing

Healing processes starts with a decision. The degree of healing is, of course, dependent on individual circumstances. Some will remain ill because they are getting the attention and love they crave, afraid that if they were to be healed, they would end up alone and abandoned. However, once we embark on any path of wholeness, be that emotional, mental, or physical, our inner guidance is ready to help us along the path. When we commit ourselves to healing, information and guidance can come from all directions. Regarding healing, Northrup says that when we make the commitment to heal, we engage our will, which in turn gives us the power to turn our thoughts and feelings into a physical reality, just like what Cameron said about Margaret Trudeau's decision to take charge of her own well-being. Northrup states

"There is power inherent in committing yourself to the process of creating health in all levels of your life." She suggests that committing ourselves to healing requires two things: 1) Admitting that we need healing; 2) Opening ourselves up to the flow of information attracted by our commitment.[25]

Replacing—Not Breaking—Old, Unhealthy Habits

There is a saying that old habits are hard to break, but when we take steps to overcome negative influences keeping us from being the best we can be, we are trying to *replace* the old habits, not break them. Say we are addicted to junk food. We don't have to break the habit outright. We can begin by replacing a few of our snacks with healthier choices and gradually increase these exchanges. We may use tools such as visualization and affirmations to anchor new habits, such as picturing ourselves eating more healthfully or looking healthier. A good affirmation might be **"I will *only* crave food that is *good* for me."** Once the decision is made and we stay strong in our conviction, the effect can be dramatic. It's like flipping a switch. We could also tell ourselves something like, "I exist in health" as many times a day as possible. If we feel that we watch too much television, we can gradually reduce the habit by substituting other more physically or mentally energizing activities. When we consistently replace an unhealthy habit with a healthier one, a new inclination develops toward the healthier one.

As noted in chapter 7, Visualization 4 in "Meditations, Visualizations, and Other Practices" (located at the back of the book) is a recap of Inelia Benz's "Meet Yourself in the Future; Successful and Healed." This practice is a useful tool to help us develop new habits.

Benefits of Mind–Body Practices and Programs

As we now understand the connection between mind and body, we can employ various practices to increase the mind's clarity, which can contribute to our physical and mental well-being. This clarity of mind helps us to better hear the whispers of our inner wisdom that Northrup talks about. In *The Thyroid Solution*, Ridah Arem suggests that certain practices, such as meditation, music therapy, dance or movement therapy, yoga, and tai chi help us cultivate a clearer mind. These can also curtail the effects of stress because they "produce a physiological relaxation response that causes a release of nitric oxide, which lowers the effect of stress in our body and mind."[26] They also have a positive effect on our self-image and self-esteem, can increase the quality of life for people suffering the effects of mental disorders, and can even improve the outcomes of medical treatments.

Getting help to deal with any behavior that may ultimately harm us and/ or our families is always recommended. We were created to live in health, and that includes mental and emotional health. Arem also states that people who suffer from obesity or alcoholism usually benefit greatly from self-help groups. Such groups provide an important mind–body experience because they help participants learn better coping mechanisms for their behaviors, thus speeding up recovery time. Meeting as a group helps us to see and feel that we are not alone. It also allows the individuals to express their personal feelings and thoughts and share experiences with others who understand.

Not Succumbing to Society's Ideas about Our Issues or Illnesses

As we are now armed with a wealth of information regarding disease-related issues, how they come about, and the importance of avoiding self-condemnation for why we feel out of sorts or fell ill, we must also refuse to believe in the stigma that our culture puts on some illnesses. In *Grace and Grit*, Ken Wilber reminds us that certain diseases in various cultures and in past eras were tainted with shame and disgrace, as they were associated purely with mental issues which were completely misunderstood at the time. He tells us, for example, that people with gout were judged as having a "moral weakness" and those with tuberculosis as having a "consumptive personality." And nobody ever considered the underlying causes of the so-called mental weakness that supposedly led to the disease.[27]

Even though science has now progressed to understand the origins of many diseases we wrongly diagnosed in the past, we still have a long way to go to reach a full understanding of most illnesses, their root causes, our unconscious influences, and how we need to deal with illness at all levels. While we do have the *potential* to avoid and heal all our diseases, rise above all pain, and overcome our need for medication, *very few of us* are at that level. So we must be wary of imposing idealistic ideas on those who are sick or in pain. Armed with all our newfound information we now have to be careful not to stigmatize our illnesses because of what we *do* know, rather than what we *do not* know, like we did in the past. Whereas before we may have blamed an illness on the person's lack of morality or character weakness, we now have to be wary of suggesting it is their lack of spirituality or godliness surmising that they attracted their illness with negative thoughts or attitudes.

Even mainstream medicine is now starting to recognize the relationship between the body, mind, and spirit with regard to our health. Pet therapy is often proposed as part of a person's overall healing, as is stress reduction and relaxation techniques to someone with a cancer diagnosis. In *Spiritual and Psychological Aspects of Illness: Dealing with Sickness, Loss, Dying, and Death,* Beverly Musgrave and Neil McGettigan suggest a holistic approach to health and illness, taking into account the "living human web" of interconnectedness between the mind, body, and spirit and with the understanding that the integration of these three aspects of our being is the basis to our identities.[28]

The Holistic Approach

What a Holistic Approach Entails

A holistic approach is based on the premise that the body is intended to be healthy, whole, and functioning optimally on all levels and that it holds the wisdom to heal itself when something has gone wrong. Holistic prescriptions encourage the body in that direction. It aims to return the patient to his or her optimal health, taking into account any predisposed genetic illnesses. Incorporating natural cures, such as a homeopathic remedy and good quality vitamins and herbs, while still retaining standard medicines if deemed necessary, a holistic approach may include investigating our diet, our sleep patterns, and the stress in our lives. It will be recommended that we tweak these if they are negatively affecting our health and overall well-being. A health-care practitioner using a holistic approach may also recommend exercise, yoga, meditation, tai chi, acupuncture, extra fresh air, time in nature, and so on. These all hold healing properties that affect our overall well-being on seemingly subtle levels at first but with wonderful long-term effects if kept up, as they encourage the body to find its natural rhythm. A holistic approach can be used in many different healing modalities, such as Mézières, a style of physiotherapy where practitioners treat the body, mind, and soul as one whole entity.

Naturopathic Medicine

Traditional naturopathic medicine deals with the body holistically, taking into account body issues, the mind-body connection, and the soul's need to express itself. It draws on the wisdom of the body and its ability to return to wholeness.

Naturopaths / Naturopathic Doctors

Today there are different certification levels for a naturopath. Some are certified traditional naturopaths with a few years of specific education, while others are certified naturopathic doctors who have studied the traditional natural therapies but also advanced clinical medicine. Naturopathic doctors use both naturopathic concepts and standard medical and clinical knowledge to assess and manage their patients' health issues, and are therefore adept at differentiating between minor and more serious concerns that would require traditional medical interventions. They also refer patients to traditional doctors if deemed necessary. There are now many colleges and universities that offer degrees to become a doctor of naturopathic medicine.

Naturopaths believe in optimal health and consider prevention a large part of maintaining it, often urging their patients to make changes to avoid issues or illnesses before they become a serious problem requiring medication. A few years ago, my naturopathic doctor suggested that I restrict my sugar and carbohydrate intake because my sugar levels were in the upper-normal levels—borderline high. Around the same time, my doctor looked at the same blood work and said that I did not have a sugar issue. This was technically true, as my levels did not bring up the red flag, but they were close to that. Knowing that many of us succumb to type II diabetes as we age, my naturopathic doctor wanted to address the issue now, as a preventative measure, while my medical doctor did not feel the need to address it.

If you want to add a holistic approach to your existing health program for your current overall health, as well as to help you age with general health and vitality, there are many naturopaths and naturopathic doctors to choose from. However, this can be a bit confusing as the certification levels can vary from province to province in Canada and from state to state in the U.S., and recently the lines have become somewhat blurred, as some standard medical clinics are now engaging both naturopaths and naturopathic doctors on their staff. In smaller clinics, naturopaths can even share certain standard medical duties. It is therefore important to find out whether the practitioner in question is legally recognized. Do not hesitate to shop around until you find one you are comfortable with, has the level of certification you are looking for, and is the right fit for you, as each practitioner has his or her own unique approach.

What We Are Putting into Our Bodies: Knowingly or Unknowingly

If you had a million-dollar thoroughbred horse, would you feed it junk?
—Dr. Joel Fuhrman[29]

Toxins, Unhealthy Foods, and Chemicals

Our bodies are equipped to handle and eliminate toxins. This naturally happens if we are in good health, do not put undue stress on our bodies with excessive amounts of refined foods, alcohol, and drugs, and ingest the vitamins and minerals that help our bodies deal with and get rid of toxins efficiently. Keeping emotionally balanced also helps with toxin elimination. Today however, with the prevalence of toxins in almost everything—our food, water and even our air—our bodies are reeling from their accumulative effects.

In *Detox: Cleanse and Recharge Your Mind, Body and Soul*, Christina Scott-Moncrieff tells us that toxins can affect our ability to think, can produce physical symptoms such as headaches and fatigue, and can create heightened emotions, such as anger, frustration, hopelessness, and misery. She explains that there are four main detoxifying organs in the body: the digestive system, the liver, the skin, and the kidneys. Each of these organs eliminates toxins in a very specific and different way, so it is important to keep them functioning optimally. We can help these organs perform properly by ingesting mostly natural, unrefined, hormone-free foods, keeping alcohol and drugs to a minimum. She also emphasizes the importance of exercise as it feeds our cells. Scott-Moncrieff suggests that drinking water is one of the best ways a person can increase the detoxification process of these important organs.[30] I discuss drinking water and its benefits below.

As well as keeping well-hydrated, keeping our body systems alkaline rather than acidic is vital to overall health. We are less likely to succumb to serious illnesses such as cancer when our bodies are alkaline. Most foods that are alkaline are natural and plant-based—and these are also the foods that have a higher vibration, an important aspect as our bodies now require this because of the higher vibration the Planet is now occupying. Keeping foods in their natural state (instead of processed) and eating lots of fruits, vegetables, and legumes is good for the body. The harsh effects of toxins do not only come from drugs and alcohol. There are several common foods, products, and chemicals that we consume daily that may actually be acting more as toxins than nutrients, with sugar being one of the most common and detrimental.

Detrimental Effects of Sugar on Our Overall Health

Although sugar has been a mainstay of our diet for centuries, it is only in the last quarter of the 20th century that consuming sugar has become an epidemic. In *The Sugar Solution*, we are told that an increasing amount of research links more health problems to sugar than just the obvious like diabetes, and that large amounts of sugar consumption can now be associated with high blood pressure, cancer, infertility, Alzheimer's, birth defects, and sexual dysfunction.[31]

It also tells us that the stress we put on our ability to "manage blood sugar" is not built into our structure. Explaining that our biology is set up with the "prehistoric rules designed to keep the mind and body running oh-so-frugally on a sometimes meager supply of glucose," our body's response is to conserve sugar, stock-pilling the energy in our "muscle and liver cells" for when we need it.[32] And it seems that information regarding the harmful effects of ingesting large amounts of sugar has not only been known for decades, but that the information was buried.

Negative Effects of Sugar Buried in the '70s

While attending a conference on gum disease and diabetes in 2007 Cristin Couzens, a dentist, was surprised to learn that sugar was actually being promoted as a healthy option in sweet tea drinks, instead of a dangerous link to chronic disease. When she asked the speaker about this, he told her that "there was no link between sugar and chronic disease." Shocked by this attitude, she actually quit her job and devoted herself to an investigation of this premise. After much searching she discovered that in the '70s the sugar industry had manipulated research to increase consumption and gain profit much like the tobacco industry has manipulated research and denied obvious links to lung cancer in the past. Couzens says her investigation into the sugar industry unearthed "lists of their board reports, their financial statements … names of their scientific consultants … a list of research projects they funded … and memos where they were describing how their PR men should handle conflict of interest questions from the press." A conscious effort to sway public opinion away from the growing evidence of the harmful effects of sugar became apparent as the paper trail revealed "industry lobby efforts to sponsor scientific research, silence media reports critical of sugar, and block dietary guidelines to limit sugar consumption."[33]

Couzens remarked that their method of presenting studies that contradicted other scientific studies created conflict of opinion and confusion within the general public so that making an educated decision about the effects of sugar was nearly impossible. However, where our health is concerned, even if the body of evidence is split down the middle, we need to err on the side of caution, *especially* when some of those giving us the results are employed by those selling the product. She found that today's sugar industry still denies and keeps us in the dark about the adverse affects of sugar on our health

Other Substances / Practices / Choices that Negatively Affect our Bodies

Gluten: In his article "Why Is Wheat Gluten Disorder on the Rise?" Joseph Mercola tells us that the rise in gluten intolerance is likely due to our recent dramatic dietary changes since the '50s. He explains that this intolerance is a condition whereby we cannot properly assimilate gluten and that the "undigested protein triggers the immune system to attack the lining of the small intestine, causing diarrhea, nausea and abdominal pain."[34] *

Wheat: Even though gluten is found in other foods, wheat seems to be the main product now giving us digestive and other health issues. The problem is that our wheat today has been so altered over time from its original form that our bodies have had trouble adjusting.*

Meat and Animal Products: People choose to become vegetarians (or vegans) for many different reasons: for health, the Planet, spiritual motivations, animal-rights concerns, and/or for ethical principles. Although much evidence suggests that a vegetarian and even more so a vegan diet benefits not only us but the Planet and many vehemently promote them, we must remember that our return to wholeness advocates that love trumps judgment. So criticizing or demeaning others for their habits or values—even if we believe ours endorse more spiritual or ethical principles may negate the good our choices provide.*

Genetically Modified Organisms: GMOs are foods or crops that have been manipulated in laboratories to develop supposedly better attributes, such as increased yields, better nutritional content, and more resistance to bacteria and insects. Experts disagree over the impact they have on our health, the Planet, as well as on our socioeconomics. In a recent interview Dr. Vandana Shiva tells us that a huge problem has occurred in India that affects the everyday farmer because there is a controlled monopoly in rice-seed sales, which have all been genetically modified.[35] *

Mercury: Rising mercury levels in the general population are having negative effects on our nervous systems, kidneys, and lungs. The National Research Council of the National Academies found that today the highest concentration of mercury comes from manufacturing and processing which is "easily volatized to the atmosphere where it is distributed on a global scale."[36] *

Fluoride: There is much disagreement among experts about the safety vs. the benefits of water fluoridation to prevent tooth decay. In an interview, "Warning: This Daily Habit Is Damaging Your Bones, Brain, Kidneys, and Thyroid," Dr. Paul Connett suggests we drink filtered water and rather than ingesting fluoride by drinking water we brush our teeth with a fluoride toothpaste.[37] *

*The article "Substances and Practices that Affect Our Bodies" found on the book's website further explains the effect of these substances.

Our bodies all respond differently to the toxins in our air and water as well as to all of the 20th century additions, processing, and modifications to what we put on or into our bodies. Even so, one way or another they still play a major role in many of our health issues. In the short term they can zap our energy and make us feel generally unwell, but in the long term all these unhealthy additions and alterations affect our organs, give us digestive difficulties, and build up inflammation in our bodies—a now known cause of many diseases. They can cause us to succumb to a disease much earlier than our DNA might suggest. And even though past generations approved the changes/additions often deeming them helpful, they may not have considered or been aware of the long-term effects. And let us not forget how the sugar industry buried evidence for profit; so others likely have too. Therefore we must be judicious in examining and questioning what is now considered the norm as well as new products or processes being promoted to us—especially by those making profit from it. And as we continue to raise our vibrations our body's energetic patterning changes and it will more strongly reject unhealthy, non-pure substances becoming even less tolerant of toxins, and low-energy, modified, processed, and sugar and hormone-ridden foods.

Not so far in the future, maybe fifty, one hundred, or two hundred years from now most of us, if not all of us, will likely be vegetarians or vegans, and we will look back on eating animal-based foods with distaste. We will have also eliminated processed foods, chemical additives, and unnaturally sweetened beverages from our diets. In the meantime, until we do make a complete change to lighter fare, we can still impart a more-positive vibration onto what we consume through intention.

Everything We Ingest Holds Vibrations

We raise our vibrations when ingesting healthier foods, as processed and dense foods keep us in a lower-vibrational mode. Natural foods hold a higher vibration than processed and chemical-laden foods. Plant-based foods hold a higher vibration than animal-based foods. Clean water, pure juices, and natural teas hold a higher vibration than alcohol or drinks consisting of refined sugar and its alternatives. In recent years, many people have been inspired to change their eating and drinking habits to consume what holds a higher vibration. Whether they are aware of it or not, this is a response to the energy of the Shift and the changes it brings to our physical requirements. Our bodies will continue to require healthier, lighter choices and we will respond to this by demanding programs that support this from both food producers and our governments. If we continue to ingest lower-vibration foods, we will feel their effects more than before. I know I do.

Raising Our Vibrations with What We Consume

Our different cultures and belief systems have encouraged us to bless, give thanks for, or impart positive energy onto our food and drink. Although the prayers or rituals surrounding meals hold specific meanings within the context of the culture, religion, or tradition, any positive conscious focus we give our food or drink before we consume it imparts a transformative vibration onto it. So, even if we cannot afford the highest quality food, by blessing, giving thanks, or imparting loving, healing energy to whatever we eat or drink we can positively affect it. We can also simply take a few moments, overlay our hands on our plate or glass, and ask it to energize us. Nonetheless, it is better to try to consume foods in their purest form.

In a podcast video "Raising Our Vibration with Food," Inelia Benz takes us to the supermarket armed with two apps called Fooducate and Buycott, which scan the labels and barcodes of products to tell you whether the product is healthy, the likelihood of it containing GMOs, and whether it is boycotted.[38] This can be a handy tool if you would like to know more about (what) you are eating.

Water, Detoxification, and Our Recalibration into Higher Frequencies

Drinking clean, fresh water and detoxifying our bodies is vital today because we ingest and are exposed to many more chemicals and toxins in our food, water, and air than even our grandparents were. Moreover, at this time of the Shift, as our bodies recalibrate to the higher energies around us, drinking water has become vital to our overall well-being.

In her article "Health Benefits of Drinking Water," Nancy Hearn discusses the importance of water for the maintenance of health, explaining that when water is lacking, toxins accumulate more easily, decreasing the ability of nutrients to enter the cells.[39] When our bodies lack water, the first thing to be affected is the detoxification process, which is needed to maintain healthy cells. In her same article as mentioned above Julianne Everett concurs that drinking water is important, and explains that at this time of the Shift as we release lower-level attitudes and buried issues held in our lower chakras it affects our bodies. She explains that: "As you shift into the higher frequencies of the fourth dimension, your emotional or astral vehicle is receiving the biggest jolts of energy since you are basically a water entity that carries electro-magnetic charges through the fluid systems of your body."[40]

Our body is our temple, the vehicle whereby we are able to express all that we are, can be, and could bring forth into the world. However, we often do not treat it as such. We all have the potential to be the million-dollar thoroughbred beings Dr. Fuhrman suggested—emotionally and physically. Why wouldn't we want to reach that potential?

Addictions

Addiction ... has the goal of alleviating suffering,
but invariably perpetuates a cycle of suffering.
—Dr. Lawrence Peltz[41]

Most addictions are the expression of *deeply* buried hurts, pains, conflicts, or anger. However, because coping mechanisms and the propensity for addiction varies from one person to the next, sometimes even minor disappointments, confusions, or conflicts can act as the trigger to someone's addictions.

If we cannot express or address our internal issues, we turn to exterior comforts, which can take a hold on us. The same can happen when we cannot express what our heart or soul wants to convey, either due to our own misunderstandings of it or to society's pressures to conform. Addictions can be attempts to appease this suppression of Spirit wanting to express itself. Whether we are addicted to overeating, drinking, drugs, gambling, shopping, or any type of overindulgence that is counterproductive to our mental or physical health, the addiction becomes the issue once it takes a firm hold on us. The original reason we felt bad is forgotten and the addiction becomes the problem, as the behaviors inherent in the addict perpetuate the problem. So does the guilt and shame that goes along with it.

Addictions—The Great Pain Mask

On a broadcast of *New Day*, Jeff VanVonderen, a world-renowned and sought-after addiction specialist, calls the denial of pain that is acted out in addictions and negative behaviors "the great pain mask." He explains how shame, which is "frozen-up pain," further entrenches the addiction, and that the shame derived from an addiction "creates its own behaviors." The addict often expresses this shame by acting out or doing stupid things. This means that they do and say things that really go against their intrinsic values. The addict then feels regret resulting in more guilt and shame, adding another layer of buried emotions as most of this is not acknowledged, as we are afraid to allow for or show our vulnerabilities.[42]

As a society we have been afraid to show our vulnerable sides and weaknesses. Mary Addenbrooke concurs with VanVonderen that much shame and guilt goes along with addictions making them difficult to treat, and considers this in *Survivors of Addiction: Narratives of Recovery.* Her findings also show that those around us and society as a whole "have a powerful influence" on us. She refers to Carl Jung's findings that people are "restricted by their need to meet the demands or supposed demands of the outside world by presenting a fine *persona* to the world." Addenbrooke explains that these "fine *persona*[s]" have hurt us by sending us into denial and this denial of our feelings or our heart's desire to express itself freely is often played out through addictions. She also tells us that all the recovered alcoholics in her study finally acknowledged and accepted their vulnerabilities, and they no longer felt the need to hide them.[43]

Help for Recovering Addicts

In *The Mindful Path of Addiction Recovery*, Dr. Lawrence Peltz suggests that while in recovery, the patient faces conflicts when tempted to revert to the source of his or her addiction, but that it is usually the fear of losing what is important to them that they are finally able to overcome the temptations. But addictions are insidious. So, even if the addict makes great strides in overcoming the present danger of partaking, the impulse to act may rise again at any little emotional flutter or from a trigger. Peltz says remaining mindful is a vital part of the recovery process as it "develops the capacity to stay in the body, deemphasizing the stories, and allowing the truth of the choice between slavery and freedom to manifest more fully." He shares three steps that help the addict who is ready in their recovery: 1) Get Grounded in the Body; 2) Feel Both Sides of Doing / Not Doing the Drug, or ...; 3) Make a Choice once Cause and Effect is Understood.[44]

Part of recovering from an addiction comes from having a reliable and nurturing support system. VanVonderen tells us it is very important to show love for the addicts in our families, while at the same time not enabling them. This can be especially difficult when dealing with our children. Even if we were good parents, we might ask ourselves what we did wrong, but at this point we can only go so far in helping the addict heal him or herself. VanVonderen says all we can do is pray for them, be a strong support system, and use our discretion when knowing what to do. He suggests that we tell loved ones who are addicted that there is "nothing we won't do to help you get better, but we will not support the dysfunctional behavior."[45]

Health-Care, its Costs, and Our Health-Care Systems

Government-funded health-care systems are becoming the way of the future, as many countries, including Canada, Sweden, Germany, Morocco, Israel, and Great Britain have embraced either complete or partially government-funded health-care systems, while the U.S. recently put a universal health-care system in place that has given many people coverage under it who were not before, but is still going through growing pains. Canada adopted a Medicare system in the mid-'60s. Along with individual and employer contributions, both federal and provincial governments add funding to the mix. Within the countries that offer health-care systems, some are fully government funded, some publicly funded, and some a combination of both. Most have centralized guidelines and standards, but many are decentralized for their budget and administration, like in Canada. Many also have a two-tier system, offering more personalized services for extra fees, while others charge a minimal fee for the use of private services.

One of the frustrations regarding health care, government funded or not, is its escalating cost. Within the Canadian health-care system balancing the budget while at the same time giving good service is an ongoing struggle. Within most countries today where we have modern technology and cures for most health issues, we seem to be overmedicating, over testing, and overspending. Steven Brill's article "Bitter Pill: Why Medical Bills Are Killing Us" in one of Time Magazine's February 2013 issues offers much insight into this problem.

Just as with many issues currently being addressed around the world, we are at the in-between stage with discovering what is not working in our health-care systems and bringing about what will be optimal. As individuals, the best we can do regarding our health and any health-issue is to educate ourselves, insist on finding out what will ultimately suit us best, and encourage and support those who are trying to bring about the necessary changes.

It is beneficial to look after our bodies as much as possible because they are our vehicles for spiritual expression, but as such they are only secondary in their purpose. The more focus we put on our bodies the less we are focusing on personal growth or spiritual matters. And because the Universal Laws are always at play, the more we concern ourselves with our body the more we will attract body issues. The body is a tool; not our raison d'être. I finish this section with a quote from Neale Donald Walsch's *Conversations with God* series, and even though he is referring to happiness, I believe the concept also applies to health (we could substitute the last line with something like "you will never reach your potential").

> *If you live your life as a function of your body and your mind, without*
> *a daily awareness of your soul and even of collaboration with your soul,*
> *you will never be continuously happy.*
> —Neale Donald Walsch[46]

Section 2: Death and Dying

It is easier for a soul to die and to relinquish the body than to be born into the confines of a body and its mind.
—An old spiritual understanding

Views of Death in Different Cultures and Throughout Time

Within different cultures, there are many attitudes toward death and dying. Some are serious and somber, while others take a spiritual view of death as the end of one journey and the beginning of another, while others celebrate death with drinking and merriment. My father told me that when he was a boy in Ireland, he was at a wake in the family's living room of a deceased man, and the singing, drinking, and merriment went on for hours. Eventually someone even propped the body up in the casket to give it a drink. The merriment at Ireland's wakes is likely to evade the morbidity of it all and abate any fear of death.

In *A Brief History of Death*, Douglas J. Davies says that a fear of death is apparent even in the founding story of Buddhism, which "tells how the young Hindu, Gautama, encountered the bitterness of life by seeing a corpse and was launched on the search for enlightenment."[47] He says that Buddhism proposes that the reality of death is a deceptive fear. In Hinduism, karma is the method through which people can make sense of and cope with death. Christianity has largely come to terms with this fear through the resurrection and corresponding belief in life after death.

Throughout time, some have tried to shift our fear of death. Davies tells us that, in 1907, Christian theologian Albert Schweitzer addressed death as a "theological problem." He argued that death was used in Christianity to frighten people, which in turn resulted in numbness. No one talked about death or addressed it. Schweitzer decided to approach death differently. He asked us to imagine living on earth indefinitely, without end. However, this approach did not work as intended because this seemed dreadful to most, as life at that time was a struggle at best and unbearable at worst.[48]

Even though most of us do not talk about it much at all, I have found death is discussed more among older people than young ones. I remember my grandmother once saying, "I hope I have a peaceful death." I don't know if she meant physically or spiritually, as I had no insight into these matters at the time. However, I do believe a peaceful death can be achieved when we have some kind of faith in the after life and/or have tried to live as best we can— given our circumstances and with at least some effort and focus on honesty and integrity. Still, there is much in our history to cause us to fear death.

300

Reasons for Fear and Avoidance of Talk of Death

We all face the unknown when we die, and many of us are also afraid of the pain and suffering associated with death. Much of this has to do with the way death has been perpetrated throughout history. All the talk in our religions about hell and damnation and the misunderstanding of karma, has left many feeling confused and fearful of what will happen to us afterward. It doesn't help either, that history has given us horrific and graphic accounts of death in writings as well as in images portrayed on canvas, and we further commit macabre deaths and their surrounding events to film. This all serves to keep our fear of death alive. We rarely hear stories or see visuals of a peaceful, spiritual death. Because we are not very aware of the spiritual tenets of life— and so fear death so much—we often fight it and thus suffer (both physically and mentally/spiritually as they are connected) as we approach the end of life. Today, most think of death with an unshakable dread. In short, society does not sufficiently prepare us for death, especially in the West.

As much of society has lost its sense of any type of spiritual life, we have no connection to what lies beyond our current existence. We are no longer aware that death is but a release from the denseness of form into the ethereal realm of Spirit. Those we have loved and lost are already there and eventually so will we all be. At the soul's level, we know that death is simply passing on to the next state, but without this spiritual understanding, an inner drive to make our mark on the world is created.

Disbelief in an Afterlife Makes Our Accomplishments a Priority

If we do not believe in a higher meaning to our life or in life after death what we accomplish while on earth is all that we can hold onto and it thus becomes the most important aspect of our life. Without being able to connect to the deeper purpose of our life we inevitably erect false ones. We may be inclined to put our main focus on accumulating, or becoming someone important, famous, or successful. With a lack of connection to any spiritual purpose, we often cannot forge the deep bonds with others or understand the real purpose of relationships. These all further distance us from our True Self, and so we miss the subtleties of the powerful spiritual connection available to us because it is beyond our awareness. Without this connection, we have no real sense of "Why we are here" or of how to reconcile the deep longing this void creates in us, so we deny our spiritual life, as well as the inevitability of death by avoiding the subjects.

Blindness to What Is Beyond Physical Death

Living under the veil of our third-dimensional existence has left us mostly unaware of the realms that exist beyond what we can see with our eyes. We are part of a larger picture, and deep within our consciousness, we have memories of where we came from. Those memories are not from far ago in our distant pasts, as we have all recently experienced the ethereal realms in our in-between lifetimes. However, most of us now have no conscious awareness of this and are unable to be in contact with the energies that exist in the higher dimensions—the beings within them that have passed on, the light-beings who never took form, or the masters who have returned there. There is really no separation between us here in bodies and all those in the higher realms. It is only from within our limited third-dimensional perspective that we cannot recognize it.

Today, there are more and more channels who have been able to clear the paths to those realms and communicate to us what they are sensing, hearing, or seeing. And even though most who do channel are gifted and work to hone that gift, we all have the potential to connect to the spirit world. We just have to break down the barriers that stand in the way.

We also dread the loss of loved ones because we think they will be gone from us forever. An elderly woman I knew told me shortly after her husband had passed on that she talked to him all the time. She couldn't see him, but could feel his presence and his love, support, and comfort around her. She was a very open and loving person, so by the Law of Openness, she was able to have that connection with him. We all can, but we have to place ourselves in the right frequency. When we are open enough, we can feel, sense, hear and communicate with those who have passed on. There are many ways we can connect with deceased loved ones, but spending time with them as they make their transition can bring much-needed understanding and healing.

Spending Time with Loved Ones around the Time of Death

When death is imminent, spending time with the patient has benefits for all concerned. In the final stage, patients become aware that something is happening as Spirit is giving them messages. The more open they are, the more receptive they are to these messages and the less fear they have. We should be there for them at their bedside for comfort and to show them love, but as they are preparing for the profound journey that is between them and their Spirit, we should not interfere with that process or attempt to interject our ideas onto them. Oasis always said that, in the presence of the dying, we should say as little as possible so they can prepare unencumbered for what is ahead. We can hold their hands, make them comfortable, and do anything they ask, but we are not to distract them or interfere with the process.

In addition to spending time with loved ones as they are dying, it is also important to spend time just after their death. It is usually the custom in hospitals or even when people die at home to give the families a few minutes with their loved one before ushering everyone out and moving the body. However, this is changing. When I volunteered in the kitchen of a hospice a few years ago, I discovered that when someone had just died, the family and the minister, if he was there, were encouraged to stay in the room with the deceased for quite a while.

Stephen and Ondrea Levine, who work with the dying and their families, tell us in *Who Dies? An Investigation of Conscious Living and Conscious Dying* that everybody benefits on so many levels when the loved ones get to spend a few quiet hours alone with a beloved who has just passed on. They explain that in the few hours after the death, the process is still going on and even though the body gets cold and loses color, "the facial expression softens. Peace is clearly evident." That is a very important aspect for the family to witness and partake in.

The Levines suggest that as the family members mourn their loved one in such close proximity with the body still in bed, they should each respond in their own way: touching the forehead, holding a hand, or even laying one's head across the deceased's chest. As they do this, the separation between the loved one and those still here on this earthly plane narrows as "death and love meet." And even though the grieving process lasts much longer than a few hours, when it begins with everybody so physically close to their beloved, it has begun with intimacy, love, warmth, and a better understanding that this body is just a corpse and that the person's essence and the love he or she shared lives on, because they have experienced it.[49]

View of Death from the Higher Realms

We fear and view death as the loss of what we know because we cannot sense what is beyond. We see death from the perspective of the body, not from that of the soul. From the soul's perspective, physical death is really a graduation from the school of the lessons of this particular lifetime in its journey back to wholeness. In Taryn Crimi's message from her guides, "Death Is Not the End but the Start of Something New," they tell us that instead of seeing death as a "separation and ending that those in the 3rd and 4th dimensions do," they see it as part of a journey, just as one might celebrate the graduation of a child as the beginning of something new. They even suggest that death is something to be celebrated with joy and excitement.[50]

Of course, this may seem odd to most people, but as Crimi tells us, this is because we are so enveloped in a "veil of forgetfulness," thinking that death is the end, even though in reality we have "died many times before." Her guides also tell us that our souls have an exit option that each of us can tune in to, and that when someone dies, it is "almost always a subconscious decision." This is because in most cases there are no accidents, even if it appears to be so. How it happens is usually a choice of the soul, who has "willingly agreed to the experience." This is also seen as for the highest good for whoever has a strong connection with the dying person, as the soul choosing to exit is in accordance with the lessons to be learned by the souls of all who are loosing the loved one. I have discussed the exceptions in chapter 6 Section 4, "Concepts," under sub-heading "Reincarnation: Past Lives."

Opening Hearts; Positively Aligning With the Process of Death

In an interview with Jeffrey Mishlove, entitled "Conscious Living, Conscious Dying," based on *Who Dies?*, Stephen Levine talks about his experience working with people who are near death and who have come to him and his wife, Ondrea, for help and emotional healing in learning how to face their own death.

Levine tells us that our relationships are usually run like businesses and that in the face of death, we have a tendency or desire to want to "finish business." He says that throughout life, most people live in a tit-for-tat way whereby we tend to make deals, for example, "I'll forgive you if you forgive me, but I'm not going to forgive you *until* you forgive me," and so on.[51]

In the Levine's therapeutic approach with the dying, they noted that many stopped viewing their relationships within this businesslike framework, and realized that this change was made possible by opening their hearts to take others in. Levine further explains that the patient can do this whether or not those keeping vigil takes them into their heart: the other's attitude shouldn't affect this important end-of-life process. When those he was treating did shift to this openheartedness in their relationships, they began to heal emotionally—a crucial step for a peaceful death.

JRobert and Oasis often maintained that we came here to learn how to die. I understand this to mean that to make a good transition we are to be aligned with a positive, loving, vibration so that our passing is as much in alignment with the energies on the other side as possible: a peaceful death, like my grandmother hoped for. The continuance in our soul's next chapter is then not tainted by what transpired in this lifetime. We can only attain this when we have made peace within ourselves for the attitudes we held and with what we have and have not done, with all that has happened in our lives, as well as to everyone we have loved. We will also more easily make peace with the dying process when society develops more humane attitudes and practices surrounding death.

Necessity of Development of Proper Attitudes around Death

Ram Dass, a philosopher and close friend of Stephen Levine, tells us in the preface of *Who Dies?* that we must look at our overall inhumane approaches to death, as we live in an age where our fears of death are amplified by the use of the "technologies and sterile mechanics" so sadly prevalent today. He tells us that Levine's work aims to change our relationship with the dying process.[52] Evident now in palliative care residences, this is carrying over into other hospital units. It is also important to keep the dying patient comfortable. R. Zalenski and R. Raspa tell us in "Maslow's Hierarchy of Needs: A Framework for Achieving Human Potential in Hospice," that when hospice patients are physically comfortable, they are better able to concentrate on important, deeper spiritual concerns that need to be at the forefront of their attention at this stage in their lives.[53] Plato would be pleased.

Dying is a natural process and a progression of living. If we can alleviate the fear and grasp its real purpose, we can feel more peaceful in death. If we can connect to our souls or higher Selves, we can overcome the fear of death. In that same preface to Levine's book Dass also tells us that the root problem of our fear is the denial of the power of our spiritual connection. If we listen to our hearts or intuition instead of restricting ourselves to what we know within the limitations of our third-dimensional framework, we will change our relationship with death.

There is a great example of dealing with the fear of death and our ability to transcend it in Ken Wilber's *Grace and Grit*. Wilber tells the story of his wife, Treya, who was diagnosed with breast cancer ten days after they were married. In his review of the book, John Wren-Lewis tells us that when we are in the face of death, "some kind of transcendence of the physical is the only alternative to despair" and says that Treya's story is the account of her reaching that transcendence before her death by accepting her fate as something she had no claim over.[54]

To come to peaceful terms with death and dying, we must address it. We have to teach people the real meaning of death and help alleviate the fears surrounding it. We can do so within programs in our churches, through community self-help and grieving programs, and by encouraging the understanding of our spiritual natures. We also have to teach our children about death in a way that explains the subtleties of the process without conjuring up fear. When we are completely aligned with our True Self, we can find peace with whatever is in front of us, even our death.

It is a common understanding within many spiritual circles that we unconsciously choose when we will die. Some believe that God or some higher power decides when our time on earth is to be over. I believe that we get an impulse that comes from our souls, Spirit, or God-selves that tells us when our time is near. I also believe that at the highest levels of awareness, we can also consciously choose when it is time to leave our bodies aside, as at these levels we know when we have accomplished all we came to achieve on earth in this lifetime. Having this incredible insight, we may even be aware of the bigger picture and understand that it would be more beneficial for those close to us, or for the benefit of all, for us to work from the other side. After being in the hospital for a few months and being of good cheer on Christmas day, my mother passed away on the following day. We all knew her death was imminent, but I truly believe she chose to hang on until after the 25th because she never wanted to disturb or be a bother to anyone. I had young children at the time and she would not have wanted our holiday tainted or their fun diminished by her death.

Celebration of Life / Grieving / Unresolved Issues

Even though most of us view death and funerals as morose, saying goodbye to our loved one should really be a celebration of the person's life. Without denying the fact that we will miss our loved ones, when our farewell ceremonies focus on the departed's life, with its good times, bad times, joys, and sorrows we can recapture the spirit of the person's time here on earth, and we will feel less sad. Nevertheless, it is appropriate to grieve the loss of the presence of a loved one, as having an open heart that can love and thereby also feel the pain of loss is a spiritual tenet. And we must remember that everyone grieves differently and deals with the loss of a loved one in his or her own way and on their own timeline.

Within many of our religious and spiritual belief systems, we have been taught that our individual tragedies are part of God's plan and that we are not to reason why. From a highly spiritual perspective, we may understand this. Nonetheless, those dear to us who have passed on will always be missed, and often the loss of a close family member or friend changes us and our lives forever. The more we can remember their spirit, the love they brought to us, and any of the other qualities they graced our lives with, the faster our broken hearts will heal. However, sometimes our grief is complicated by unresolved issues.

Many of us have a family member or loved one who has passed on with whom we had quarreled and not mended the divide, so rather than experience true grief we may feel anger or guilt, or even fall into depression. Whatever the unresolved issue, we must forgive the other for their part and forgive ourselves for ours—even if it was us who created the situation or continued the rift. This is easier when we understand Humanity's past and the dualistic system we have all been entrenched in.

Many of us feel strong connections to those who have passed on, and we can feel their presence/essence all around us. And those we have been close to who have passed on are helping us in all areas of our life, whether we sense this or not. However, no matter how much we feel them nearby, nothing can replace hearing their laughter, seeing their smile light up a room, or getting a hug from them. So it is normal to miss those who have passed on and appropriate to grieve the loss. Loving others and missing their presence is part of being an openhearted, feeling, human being. For them, however, death is not the end.

Personal or collective human death or tragedy is often the catalyst for our returning to a sense of spirituality or a spiritual life—whatever that means to us. Even though we often consider physical death the ultimate loss, so is any loss to the connection of who we are. In his talk *A Course In Miracles: Forgiving Relationships*, David Hoffmeister reminds us that at the highest levels of awareness we grasp the "eternal state of mind" and that every thought of judgment, pain, unhappiness, or every frown or even any sense of fatigue is death, because denial of the joy and peacefulness found in that eternal state of mind is the death of what we can experience.[55] If we transcend all these limitations during the dying process, we can experience the peacefulness found within that eternal state of mind.

To prolong life is no more valuable than to prolong death.
Both lose their luster when viewed against the backdrop of eternity,
where existence transcends either state.
—Almine[56]

Now that we have looked at our individual physical and emotional health and have addressed death and dying, in the next chapter we will consider our Planet and its health as well as Abundance and how these tie into our journeys and the Shift.

CHAPTER 9

The Planet and Abundance

> *Modern civilizations have come to truly believe that the*
> *paths to a better life are consumerism and to use our cleverness*
> *to manipulate the "machine of nature" to our advantage.*
> —Thom Hartmann[1]

Section 1: The Planet

> *Think of the earth as a living organism that is being attacked*
> *by billions of bacteria whose numbers double every forty years.*
> *Either the host dies, or the [parasite] dies, or both.*
> —Gore Vidal[2]

Gaia, our Planet, is a living, breathing organism. She is a conscious, living, being. Just like certain parts of our bodies, such as our hair and nails which continually die and grow back, our Planet can be replenished—to a certain degree. However, when we abuse ourselves, we need a period of rest to regain our strength, and we need to cleanse ourselves of built-up toxins.

What we do to our bodies affects us as a whole. If we go out on a night of binging, we may feel under the weather the next morning, day, a few days afterward, but we usually recover. However, if we continually go out on drinking binges, we will eventually become very sick. The same is true for our Planet. She can and has recovered from small abuses to her body and resources, but over time, like with us, the impact of constant mistreatment will cause serious issues to eventually arise. Whatever abuses we have and continue to put upon our Planet will cause a reaction somewhere in the fissure of her fabric.

Some of the changes Gaia is going through are simply part of her evolutionary process. When sitting atop Mount Etna with JRobert in 2008 our group witnessed the effects of this first hand. We were surrounded by miles of desolation, and the heat of the earth was felt beneath our feet as we gazed upon smoldering crevices—all leftover effects from recent eruptions. He explained that "la planete est encore en evolution," meaning that our Planet is still in an evolutionary stage. However, many of the changes on Gaia are because we lost our connection to her through greed, ignorance, and modernization.

At one point in history Humanity lived in harmony with nature and lived sustainably with the Planet's natural elements. The further we fell into duality, the more we aligned with an attitude of lack and greed and our lives became based on acquiring, amassing, and trotting over whomever and whatever to get what we wanted or *thought* we needed to survive. As Thom Hartmann expresses in this chapter's epigraph, we now do this to such an extent that we even manipulate nature to those ends.

The Health of Our Planet

Physical and Emotional Abuses Affect Our Planet

The natural flow of Gaia's energy has been depleted as we have defiled her land, polluted her air and water, dammed up her waterways, and raped her natural resources. Humanity's hate, greed, killing, judgment, and control over each other have also affected her energetic body. Just as mistreatment of our physical and emotional bodies affects all aspects of our well-being, it is the same with our beautiful Planet. In attempting to rebalance her self, Gaia's energy flow has shifted and swayed, often causing violent weather patterns.

In his video "The Engines of Mass Creation," Fernando Vossa tells us that not only does the energy we send out individually anchor and remanifest within ourselves, it also affects all of Humanity as well as the Planet. The energy of any aggression we carry out collectively towards others and our Planet facilitates the creation of violent weather and geological events. Vossa states that "in high stress events of the earth, the magnetic fields of the energy of the earth such as 9/11 send out spikes of energy all over the world and creates earthquakes, etc."[3]

So even though some climate issues are a natural progression of our Planet's evolution, our attitudes and actions have and still do play a major part.

Messages about Our Relationship to the Planet, Its Resources, and Our Futures

Many today are aware of how delicate and even precarious the health of our Planet is, and how this will impact our futures. Over the more recent years messages have come to us from many sources like contemporary scientists such as David Suzuki and foundations such as Greenpeace, but messages about the health of our Planet and future have been coming to us ever since World War II.

The Little Prince, by Antoine de Saint-Exupery, is a children's story from 1943 that follows a little prince as he visits other planets. The story's intention is to reveal all of humankind's weaknesses. Throughout the story as we visit each planet, we find people who are disillusioned in one way or another and not in touch with reality. One claims he can control the stars, but only through the use of strict orders; another one, a conceited man, lives in complete isolation on his planet to avoid competition with others; while another, a businessman, continually counts the stars, obsessed with his claimed ownership of them, but he never considers their beauty. These characters are in contrast to the Little Prince, who, as someone actually connected to reality, lives in a relationship of reciprocal care with the stars and his planet. He cares for the planet, and the planet takes care of him in return. This is a simple story, but it beautifully shows how one can be happy and live in harmony and peace with our Planet through a reciprocal, loving relationship built on care, trust, and appreciation of all she has to offer.

In *The Last Hours of Ancient Sunlight*, Thom Hartmann reminds us that "Kennedy challenged us to think of our children's future before our own, to create change that could be lasting and to build a new world that could sustain itself and yet protect its valuable natural resources." Why is it that some fifty years later, we are still not really *getting* this?[4]

In 1992, approximately thirty years after Kennedy's plea, David Suzuki's daughter, Severn Cullis-Suzuki, along with a group of twelve and thirteen-year-olds raised money to go to Brazil to address a UN meeting on the environment. Advocating their rights to a healthy and livable planet, for now and for the future, she urged the UN group to look at how our global actions are creating environmental devastation. She pleaded that they consider the impact of issues like extinction and pollution and to reconsider deforestation, because at a certain point there will be no turning the clock back to what was. At twelve years of age, Cullis-Suzuki understood the importance of respecting the needs of the generations to come.[5] Our children's futures are about their immediate and future health, as well as having a thriving planet to live on. Twenty years later, many are *still* really not getting it, and pleas are still flooding in from many people and sources.

In January 2014, the singer and songwriter, Neil Young sought to enlighten and mobilize Canadians with his Honor the Treaties tour, by focusing on the harm we are doing to the land and people of the Athabasca Chipewyan First Nation, whose community lives downstream from the Fort McMurray oil sands in Alberta. After visiting the site and listening to the First Nation leaders' accounts and concerns, Young came to the conclusion that the long-term damage in the Fort McMurray area is comparable to that of Hiroshima after the atomic bomb. His comment provoked controversy from politicians and business people, but hopefully it will help to jar the public from its collective denial of the oil sands' long-term health and environmental impacts. During his tour, Young also denounced the proposed Keystone XL pipeline through Western Canada and into the United States as disastrous for the environment. Some of the funds received for his tour were directed to help the First Nations people and their fight against these projects.

In response to a "Got land, thank an Indian" T-shirt that a man was wearing, Young said that this was a fact and part of our heritage. He said we should all be proud of it and remember that Canada came about from the peaceful treaties we made with the First Nations. By breaking these treaties, we are killing their people, decimating the Planet, and ultimately hurting all of us.

While this particular event and reminder concerned an issue on Canadian land, in discounting Indigenous peoples' concerns about the environment, we ignore the wisdom of aboriginal people throughout the world. The tribes and nations who chose to reject industrialization, retained their environmental wisdom and their connection to Gaia so they might educate us in the event Humanity lost its way. We *need* to listen to them, not ignore their messages, pleas and plights. I explain this choice later in this chapter.

What We Allow by Default

Many of us are unaware of how many of the choices we make on a daily basis not only make us sick but also add to the destruction of the Planet. In a 2013 interview with Bill Moyers, about her book *Raising Elijah* and her film *Living Downstream*, Sandra Steingraber explained that many "toxic trespassers" have been infused into our bodies without us even being aware of it, which not only directly affect our health, but that they also have major impacts throughout our food chain.[6]

Among other issues, Steingraber discusses the effects of a chemical called Atrazine used for years to kill weeds that has seeped into our drinking water and how that and other toxins contaminating our food, water, air, and even products such as mattresses are making us sick. She also said that some reports show that toxins have even seeped into breast milk. Moyers's reported that in recent years 40–50% of honeybee hives have disappeared, adding that one-quarter of our diet relies on honey.

Since many of the studies about new and even current products widely available conflict, Steingraber asks, do we really want to take a chance with our health and that of our children? Can we even trust the studies that show no harm? Remember what Couzins' research on sugar found that I noted in the last chapter. When making choices or taking a position, we should ask ourselves what we would do or want done were our children or loved ones to be exposed to a substance with even a hint of toxicity and potential for long-term adverse affects. Most would surely presume they were unsafe until they were 100% proven safe—and not by those who would profit from their sales.

Both Steingraber and Moyers urged us to support the need for rigorous testing by researchers with no ties to the manufacturers of the product(s)—*before* they are ever allowed to enter the marketplace. We also have to question many products currently in the market, as we now have proof that some of what was approved and/or was considered advantageous to us has had long-term and far-reaching negative effects on our health, and/or for the Planet. Nevertheless, Steingraber also advises that even with all the confusing and contradictory information regarding what is harmful and what is not, we must not allow ourselves to become weighed down by apathy or despair over what we now know about toxins and our environment. Nor should we allow ourselves to be derailed from our purpose by the push-back from those wanting to promote their selfish agendas. The interview offered many other statistics to substantiate their claims.

Climate Change

Although many still deny the reality of climate change, scientists from all over the world are in agreement that we have almost reached the tipping point of no return. We have been warned! Are we going to build a boat like Noah did (metaphorically speaking) or are we going to pooh-pooh the warnings of the experts and be responsible for the next generations suffering global disasters of epic proportions? We must remember that God sends messages to us in many ways and through many people. Can we look our children or grandchildren in the eyes and tell them we love them, while allowing this to happen? I hope not, because there is much correlation between climate change and recent disastrous weather patterns, and it will only get worse.

In their essay, "At the Edge of the Roof: The Evolutionary Crisis of the Human Spirit," John Stanley and David Loy tell us that in 2012 the "Arctic sea-ice melted in summer to some 55% of its 1990 extent"—with 2012 being the year the U.S suffered long periods of no rain that wiped out many of its crops, not to mention the effect on people by strict water restrictions. They also note the projection of senior British climatologist Peter Wadhams of Cambridge University who tells us that the North Pole's Arctic ice-cap is now on track to disappear "decades ahead of mainstream projections."[7]

Even though our journey away from living in reciprocity with nature started eons ago, with a major shift taking place with the industrial revolution effectively changing our trajectory, it has now grown to the extent that our own very survival is in jeopardy. As industry and government coalesced to bring about the changes, somehow along the way greed and power became imbedded in our industrial progress. Clarifying that the fossil-fuel industry has now become the worst offender of climate change, Stanley and Loy tell us that they have in effect high jacked our "human rights: the right to food, water, and sanitation, to social and economic development." They explain that this has been allowed to happen because the fossil-fuel industry is "often in collusion with government." Therefore both our governments and the corporations are to blame, and both need to be held accountable.[8]

Stanley and Loy tell us that some pro-environmental activists suggest that "human rights courts should treat climate change as an immediate threat to our rights," and that governments should not only be forced to stop their back-door relationships with fossil fuel companies they also should be obliged to create a "post-carbon society at the scale of a war effort." They argue that this *can*, in fact, be done because the technology is available. They name the fossil-fuel industry as the main impediment to clean energy because it "possess[es] a truly dangerous combination of wealth, power and destructive intent ... spending sums of money to undermine climate science, subvert political institutions, and corrupt governments." Nonetheless, they also caution that we *must* fight to override this seemingly insurmountable problem. They refer to Thom Hartmann (among others) who suggests that "corporate charters should be revoked and rewritten. Why should delinquent corporations have a legal charter to make enormous profits by destroying the public good and the planet?" [9]

Our governments are and will continue to be pressured into making laws with stricter enforceable guidelines regarding climate change. Most of us can see now that harming ourselves and the Planet for personal extravagance or monetary gain is emphatically wrong, and so there is support for more clean energy options. Changes are coming! We *are* moving away from harmful environmental practices. So before they are forced upon us, *we* can start to make shifts toward more ecologically friendly alternatives within our families, farming practices, and businesses so the transitions may not be quite so painful.

~

We need to make wise decisions now about what we are doing to ensure that our children, future generations, and Gaia are healthy, vibrant, and not incapacitated by our actions. We also have to believe we can make this happen, while at the same time face the fact that some of what is familiar to us may disappear. We do this by being open to alternatives. For example, I was always one to love a lush green lawn, but as it became harder and harder to attain this ideal because of restrictions on watering and the products that could help bring it about, I became discouraged.

A few years ago as I was walking around Kelowna, B.C. (a dry, arid area in the Okanagan valley) I noticed that many of the houses' properties were characterized by various decorative alternatives to grass. Using a combination of different colored pebbles, small rocks, mulch, small flowering and cactus-like plants and shrubs, beautiful landscapes were created. I decided that day I would create something similar in my next house. Ideas and insights like this will start to be birthed in us as the Shift continues to inspire us to reach for viable alternatives. We have to recognize that there *is* enough of what we need for all of us to go around, we just have to use what our Planet has bequeathed to us wisely.

The Secret of Enough

As much of Western society is focused on acquiring far more than what we really need, most of us never move beyond physical concerns into the emotional or spiritual needs, which are necessary to keep us balanced. In *The Last Hours of Ancient Sunlight* Thom Hartmann talks about an "enough point … [whereby] a person has security, where their life and existence is not in danger." He reminds us that our current society lives under the myth that "some stuff will make you happy, then twice as much stuff will make you twice as happy, and ten times as much will make you ten times as happy, and so on, into infinity."[10] Although greed has been around for eons, it has only recently extended to such abusive actions towards our Planet as to threaten her (and thereby our) very survival.

In his essay, "The World of Wonder" in *Spiritual Ecology*, Thomas Berry explains that in North America this attitude of acquiring grew as a result of our lack of embracing or understanding the concept of "Earth-based spirituality" when we first came here from Europe. He reminds us that not only did the Indigenous people understand the relationship between heaven, earth, and its people, evidenced by their rituals and ceremonies to evoke the powers of the Universe, most ancient cultures did as well. He tells us that the pillars in India, China, Greece, Egypt and Rome "were established to delineate a sacred center which provided a point of reference for human affairs and bound Heaven and Earth together."[11]

Barry explains that we came here from Europe believing we were religious, educated, scientifically advanced, and able to create our own political organizations. We "saw ourselves as a divine blessing on this continent. In reality we were a predator people on an innocent continent." We saw a land that could allow us to break away from the "monarchical governments … and their world of royalty and subservience," so rather than be in awe of the grandness and beauty of this land, we saw it as a "continent available for exploitation." Although we were searching for new values, our attitudes of greed and control did not really change; not did they reflect the values of the native people already here.[12]

Traditional teachings among most native people worldwide reveal their understanding of the concept of *enough*. Those who live off the land, free of material obsessions, believe the earth will provide them with basic necessities. They love and revere the Planet, and understand our deep connection to it. They appreciate that the earth nourishes us with water, air, and food and understand that maintaining the purity of these is crucial. They recognize the Planet as a gift from our Creator and that every molecule on it lives and breathes. Embedded in their histories is the belief that we are all its stewards. Throughout the world, most Indigenous peoples understand and maintain this reciprocal connection with Gaia.

If mainstream returns to that reciprocal relationship with Mother Earth, we will all have access to its life-affirming energy: we will have enough. As I noted in chapter 6, Barbara Hand Clow tells us in *Awakening the Planetary Mind* that the earth and its energy fields "support all living beings." Embracing the reciprocal relationship with Gaia deems we are protected by being grounded in her energy field and ensures we have what we need to survive, which is why returning to the wisdom of nature at this juncture in our evolution and with our growing population is so vital.[13]

In large part, except for the few who have rejected commercialism, such as the Mennonites, Indigenous peoples, and certain rural tribes, having lost the connection to the concept of *enough* and respect for our Planet, most societies have fallen under the spell of acquiring and greed.

Nearly Getting It Right, Many Times

We were not always like this. In fact, many believe that here on earth Humanity advanced socially, spiritually, and technologically many times, and almost got it right. As previously mentioned in chapter 7, it is widely believed in spiritual circles that Atlantis and Lemuria, as well as many other advanced cities and states, existed where most of the inhabitants lived in peace and harmony—with each other, with Gaia, and with other advanced civilizations beyond earth. Although most were quite advanced in many ways, some still existed under the illusion of duality and that polarity eventually found its extremes: the influence of dark forces prevailed and those civilizations eventually self-destructed. We got *close* to complete harmony, but it simply was not our cosmic time to attain it, as the dark forces within us were more powerful than the light.

The Hopis see it a little differently. While they agree that throughout history there have been many ups and downs in our spiritual awareness and ability to live in harmony, their accounts suggest that our ancestors had to go underground many times to survive what, as a whole, we had done. Whether these understandings are metaphoric or not, their stories suggest we then reemerged, given a chance by those in charge of the Universe to try again. However, each time we faltered then reemerged, we lost a little more of our connection to our Source as our "veil of forgetfulness," became thicker and we dove deeper into the realm of separation and duality.

Existence of Domination and Aggression for Seven Thousand Years

In his same book, Hartmann tells us that around seven thousand years ago an infectious domineering attitude began to infiltrate all of civilization. When a culture that has lived peacefully for thousands of years is faced with a "violent dominator culture," it has no choice but to adopt some of the violent and controlling tendencies themselves in order to survive. He calls this a "Younger Culture" attitude.[14]

He explains that in North America, when colonists or "Younger Culture 'visitors' from Europe" first came here, what began as a friendly relationship based on negotiations and trading soon turned sour when the native people realized the truth about their newfound "friends"—that "these visitors were, instead, thieves and murderers and rapists, stealing the native's lands, animals, and killing their citizens." As the natives tried to defend themselves, they had to adopt those same violent, dominant behaviors as the invaders, eventually becoming "infected with [these attitudes] turning into nomadic warriors and hunters of humans." What began as a survival tactic transmuted into the infectious disease of brutality, and it continued to spread throughout Humanity. It became a way of being. The Universal Laws yielded to the new attitudes and behaviors and they became ingrained in us.[15]

Even though at some point in history most societies have gotten caught up in power, cruelty, greed, and injustice toward each other and nature, many of the prophets have reminded us of the virtues of following the wisdom of our Planet. The *Tao Te Ching* advises us that in keeping with the universal flow, we need to follow its promptings:

Man follows the earth.
Earth follows the universe.
The universe follows the Tao.
The Tao follows only itself.[16]

The Indigenous Beliefs and Our Planet's Healing

Indigenous People's Roadmap to Harmonious Living

Charles Eisenstein's article, "The Three Seeds," answered the notion that had grown in me that the Indigenous peoples' gentle nature and connection to the earth were somehow connected to the healing of Humanity. He explains that maintaining harmony and a connection to nature was a *conscious* decision Indigenous people made as a group, eons ago. He writes about the role they have played in our evolution and how they offer us a roadmap back to harmonious living. Most of us in the industrialized world have somehow lost our way and forgotten the importance of our connection to and reciprocal relationship we once had with nature, but for the most part the Indigenous peoples have maintained that connection. Eisenstein further explains that thousands of years ago when we chose to play the game of "separation" with nature, the prophets at that time suspected we would lose our way and left "three seeds" to help us find our way back.[17]

The first seed was the "wisdom lineages" whereby the lines of transmission were preserved and protected the essential knowledge. The wisdom lineages were the mystical branches of the different religions or belief systems such as the Zen masters and gurus in the Eastern religions, Hasidism or the Kabbalah in Judaism, Sufism in Islam, and the mystical branches of Christianity. The sages and holy men within these spiritual branches upheld the humility and mystical, experiential aspects of their faiths.

The second seed was the "sacred stories: myths, legends, scriptures, fairy tales and folklore," offering recurrent tales crouched in imagery and allegory. These transcend the conscious mind, as they are refined supernatural conduits that convey the hidden knowledge of the ages and infuse us with awe, wonder, and hope, so that however far we wander into the "Labyrinth of Separation," we always had a lifeline to find our way back.[18]

The third seed was the "indigenous tribes" who consciously chose to forgo the journey of separation with Gaia and growth into a technological society that destroyed nature. They instead continued to live close to the land and in harmony with nature so they could eventually provide us with a roadmap back to living in accordance with the "laws of nature." The various tribes hold different aspects of the knowledge we have lost. They can show us how to commune reciprocally with nature and the animal kingdoms; to read and understand dreams; raise our children (as explained through the work of Jean Liedloff noted in chapter 5); and see beyond our limited third-dimensional idea of time.

Eisenstein further explains that although many tribes have disappeared, and most of them and many of us are saddened by this, their assignment was only to continue to exist long enough to show us how we as humans can live in reciprocity with nature and Gaia. As such, their mission has not been to change the world, but to act as a signpost showing us the way.[19] As a whole, they have no awareness of this, but they do feel and have felt sorrow and the unfairness of what we have put upon them and the Planet.

Righting Wrongs / Mobilizing for Indigenous Rights

Before starting to write this book I had little knowledge about the abuses of power concerning First Nations Peoples in Canada. Sadly, what I learned in elementary school was that we did wonderful things for them by setting up communities and schools. However, what I learned could not have been further from the truth. What we really did in effect was steal their land as we did not keep the treaties we signed, imposed Christianity on them through cruel and harsh methods, abused and raped their women, and mentally, physically, and sexually abused their children often separating them from their families and forcing them to attend our schools or those we set up for them that ignored or renounced their culture.

In the '60s government-funded residential schools were set up that were managed by the Church, whose aim it was to replace the influence of Indigenous children's' families and culture, so native students could better be assimilated into the Canadian culture we had created. At least 30% of Indigenous children were forced into this school system, and as these schools were often far from their homes many of the children were separated from their families.

The effects of centuries of abuses upon our First Nations People are far-reaching. Recently, growing numbers of people have joined efforts to correct the past mistreatments of Indigenous peoples here in Canada (and around the world) with hands-on efforts as well as calling on government bodies to meet with them to negotiate fair terms.

One of my editors is Mohawk, one of the six nations of the Iroquois confederacy, as is her mother, now a social worker working with different First Nations communities throughout Canada. Her main objective is to help those in various communities overcome the repercussions from the abuse and trauma they suffered as children when forced into the residential school system, but she also addresses general issues within the communities like self care, lateral violence, and suicide intervention. And her programs are not all restricted to those of native heritage.

As part of a comprehensive response to the charges of abuse and other ill effects for First Nations children that resulted from the Indian residential school system, on June 2, 2008 Canada set up a Truth and Reconciliation Commission to bring to light the truths of what went on in those schools and to make recommendations on how to make amends. The Commission was completed in June 2015 with 94 recommendations, and as of June 2016 many groups are working to bring about the recommendations.

In 2012, Canada saw different tribes band together to peacefully protest inadequate government support for their plights. This movement was called *Idle No More* and essentially countered and fought a bill led by Canada's then Conservative government that would directly affect the First Nations communities by not offering properly regulated protection over the environment, especially when in close proximity to their land. The protest began as a hunger strike moving across all major cities in Canada, then spread to the United States where it became one of the largest protests ever concerning Native American concerns. Many Canadians who were not of First Nations heritage joined in the protests—some to show support and others because the bill would affect the future of the environment and people as a whole.

The movement grew into the US because it addressed longstanding Native American objections to the exploitation of resources and development of lands that affected their way of life—lands they had once owned and were either coerced to sign over or were cheated out of. Even though Idle No More's original intention was to bring awareness to a specific issue, as it caught on, it brought awareness to the general plight of Indigenous people in North America. The plight of Indigenous people all over the world are coming to the forefront and many people are now mobilizing others for their causes on many continents—and they are having results.

Survival International recently took the lead in the movement of a campaign to help the India's Dongria Kondh peoples' struggle against a resources company to prevent a planned bauxite mine that would have had a huge impact on their land and way of life. The organization brought in well-known British stars Joanna Lumley, who narrated a documentary film "Mine: Story of a Sacred Mountain," and Michael Palin to help promote their cause. The film shows the tribe's history and spiritual connection to the land with its forests and sacred mountain and how this project would completely alter their way of life. It clearly delineates that what the developers are proposing to do in the name of what they consider modern expansion will in fact eradicate this autonomous tribe. The Dongria Kondh people are autonomous and actually thrive in the area their people have occupied for centuries, contrary to the popular belief that rural tribes and those living isolated from civilization are all characterized by hardship.[20]

The final decision for the go-ahead of this project was left to the country's Ministry for Environment and Forests, and the proposal for the mining project to move forward was denied. This has set a precedent and will have an international impact for future companies whose intention is to encroach on tribal lands for profit, as it brought to light the necessity of *fully* investigating the effects projects of large corporations have on tribal and native peoples and their way life.

Indigenous people all over the world tap into and sustain their empowerment through their connection to the land and their cultural traditions. We must ensure that projects for profit (or those in the name of progress we want to promote) no longer infringe on rural, native, or Indigenous peoples' health, culture, community, or way of life. By overtaking the lands and forcing our ways upon the Indigenous in the West we disempowered them, to say the least. The effects of centuries of abuse, misuse, control, and marginalization did extensive damage.

It is imperative that we partner with the descendants of the Indigenous peoples throughout the world so their healing from the effects of how we treated them in the past may begin. We must also acknowledge what we are *still* doing to undermine them today. Their welfare must be kept at the forefront of any decision-making that will impact the environment and their lands, so they may begin to regain their sense of empowerment.

We must do this for them, but we also do it for all of us. As a collective society, it is the Indigenous people who have maintained the connection to our Planet, and their beliefs are our roadmap to achieving a good and healthy future for our children and our survival as a whole—just as they intended eons ago. We would do well to *carefully study* and *reflect on* their approaches to nature.

Keeping the Complex, Organic Process Moving Forward

Even with all the denial and cover-ups that have gone on, over the years many have worked to expose what was been done for money and greed or in ignorance or denial of the repercussions on our environment. However, believing what our governments and big businesses tell us is so deeply entrenched in our psyches that the informers, whistleblowers, protestors, and even famous people like Neil Young have to shock us out of our indifference and denial to recognize how what we are doing to our Planet is jeopardizing the futures of our children, grandchildren, future generations, and indeed Humanity's survival. We have strayed so far from the intended relationship we had with nature, that the memory of our appreciation of her gifts and how we followed her cues and gifted others is completely forgotten.

Mother Nature Offers Freely

Our Planet, Gaia, or Mother Nature—an appropriate name in this context, gives to us and she asks for nothing in return. Embracing the idea of giving to others simply because we can and they need it would do much to raise the Planet's vibration, further aligning us all with what the Shift is asking of us. We can take our cues from Mother Nature.

In her essay, "The Koan of the Earth" in *Spiritual Ecology*, Susan Murphy points out the magic in nature. She explains "its gift-economy of ever-evolving life provided the original soil, water, seed, and original plants," and that with our work and resourcefulness we eventually turned seeds into a variety of foods. Our Planet also allowed the animals that helped sustain us to graze on her pastures. And for a while, we followed her gifting philosophy. We gifted her bounty to others in hard times, and traded her offerings and the multitude of goods we crafted from her environment. Later, coins replaced trading, which eventually led to selling for profit, until finally greed and profit totally replaced fair value sales. Although today we have no memory of the choices made ages ago, which grew into us now being ruled by what Murphy calls "the industrial super-magic barrel" that benefits only a few, we are now powerless against those choices and dependent upon this modern industrial machine for our basic needs.[21]

Most of us understand that we have to change our ways to protect our environment and we do what we can, but fully embracing sustainable living while at the same time keeping our mouths fed and our houses heated is a complicated issue; it will not happen overnight. In *The Revenge of Gaia: Why the Earth Is Fighting Back—and How We Can Still Save Humanity*, James Lovelock tells us that we need to understand that keeping our social, economic, and environmental issues moving in a positive direction is an organic process that needs to be continually reevaluated and tweaked— because "sustainable development is a moving target." So, however frustrating or even futile our efforts may seem, especially when looking at the big picture, we have to do our best and engage with the process because, as Lovelock warns, "if we fail to take care of the Earth, it surely will take care of itself by making us unwelcome."[22] With our numbers now over seven billion people, how can we ensure we all have what we need to thrive: how can we deal with over-population?

Overpopulation

Overpopulation is becoming a huge issue. Even though there is enough food to feed everyone on the Planet, we need to adopt smarter choices to make this come about. Our numbers tax our fresh water supplies and energy resources for our necessities, comforts, and conveniences, as well as to support the modern and often extravagant lifestyles many of us have become used to. Our ways are unsustainable and cannot continue without major consequences. The message is catching on, even if slowly, and the Shift brings with it the consciousness to consider and allow for those that will address the issues associated with sustaining our numbers. It also brings with it the impetus to lessen our numbers.

Decreasing Our Numbers

In the Western world we are having fewer children and I believe this trend will continue. More people are choosing not to have children and most of those who do are having fewer children than in the past, while others are choosing to adopt. Although many couples of the same sex who want to have a family choose to have their own children by the methods available, many more than in the general population adopt. Also, our growing collective concern about overpopulation will in turn affect our DNA and there will soon be more people who cannot have children. This will have been a soul choice and therefore not be an issue for those in tune with the agreement. They will have come here for other life experiences than having children. In addition, as Humanity becomes more evolved and attuned to higher-realm vibrations, we will come to have conscious control over childbearing. Birth control is a conscious choice, although many still have a moral issue with it. Not 100% effective, many birth control methods can also pose health risks. In any case, birth control is only a temporary fix until we have full control over our bodies, as we will—once we evolve a bit more.

Years ago I heard that on more evolved planets, the beings who wanted offspring simply made a conscious request within themselves and their bodies acquiesced. Just as I explained in the section on virgin births in chapter 6, at high vibrational levels we would have enough control over our bodies to create a burst of energy to generate life. At these high levels we would exist more consciously, and our desire to have children would be weighed against our ability to care for them as well as all the effects this choice would have on everything and everyone around us. In the meantime, we have to deal with overpopulaion as best we can, while continuing to partner with countries in the developing world that still have high birth rates, even though food, fresh water, and medical care are scant.

Some countries with large populations now have a birth rate of less than two per family, whereas many developing countries are adopting government programs that educate people on family planning. While medical advances help alleviate much pain, suffering, and the loss of loved ones all over the world, they are also increasing our longevity, which in turn affects our global numbers.

One of the reasons many developing countries still have high population rates is because the effects of medical advances are happening at a faster rate than compliance with family planning. Even though in the Western world where there is widespread practice of family planning, medical advances continue to aim to extend life, so within any given year our numbers are still growing, albeit less than in many of the developing world.

The prospect of our population continuing to grow at its current pace is frightening, although this is based on our continuing to replace ourselves as we are now doing. Even with all the medical advances, I believe this will soon balance out. The growing awareness of overpopulation and its issues has affected us on more-subtle levels. A reduced *desire* to produce offspring, a decrease in future fertility rates, and the potential to *consciously* create or not create offspring will all contribute to lowering future population rates. The Shift also brings with it other ways that will help our numbers on earth.

Soul / Life Lessons Learned: No Need to Continue Manifesting on Earth

As we embrace the higher-vibration attitudes of this Shift, we are completing soul/life lessons that we chose to learn while in physical form on earth. Many of us are in our final or almost-final lifetime here.

As explained in the earlier chapters, our Universe, including our Planet, was created for us to play out the duality we had chosen at our beginnings. Manifesting in form on earth is only one way to learn the lessons that help us return to the Oneness we emanated from.

Once this Shift is more fully anchored within us, fewer souls will need to come here in bodies. They will move on to higher-level lessons within the different realms or areas of the Universe. However, this does not mean that no souls will choose to come here. In Italian, the translation of the phrase *to give birth* means *to give to the light*. I see this as meaning that every birth has the potential to help us all return to the light of the Oneness we emanated from. There now is more potential than ever for those souls being born to *give to the light*, as not only are they coming into a world that has grown spiritually by leaps and bounds over the past few years, these young souls have consciously manifested on Earth now to help us anchor in the Shift.

The more we continue to evolve, some who have graduated from this particular classroom of life and form will choose other dimensions or planets to continue their spiritual growth, while others will want to return here to either help those who still have not fully completed their chosen lessons or to simply enjoy what they have been part of creating—a more peaceful and loving environment on earth. As this Shift is encouraging us to embrace the multidimensional beings that we are, in time, other places in the Universe will become options for us to manifest onto.

Living Elsewhere

We are now discovering that we are part of a larger family—our space family. It wasn't even fifty years ago that the astronauts first walked on the moon, and we are now making plans to send citizens into space. I believe this Shift is bringing with it the potential for Humanity to further explore other options of where to reside. This may not be in our immediate future but may be in the not-*so*-distant future as we might think, as we are reaching the level of the exponential function in our research into space, space travel, and the cosmos. Understandably, this may seem daunting to most of us. But remember, it was only a few hundred years ago (a drop in the bucket of our existence on earth) that most people stayed put within their communities and rarely ventured further than the necessary distance to meet their needs. And those who first travelled afar to find a better life sensed there was something better beyond, even though those around them were skeptical and/or afraid.

One Step At a Time, Plus Another, and Another Shifts Our Trajectory

Because many of the resolutions to restore our Planet to its once pristine self involve long-term solutions, we do have to become conscious of how our choices and attitudes affect our futures here on earth. We have to remain positive, be open to the various solutions proposed, and invest in those not yet perfected—even if they are costly. We also have to investigate any that come from unlikely sources. As mentioned in chapter 7, the extraterrestrials nearby helping us with the Shift and our Ascensions are also more advanced technologically with equipment and powerful energetic knowledge that could help us—especially to clean up our Planet, which could also help lessen the effects of cataclysmic disasters. Although this may not be something we will consider embracing today, we can allow for the *possibility* of it in the near future. In the meantime, each small change we make toward sustainability builds on the last one, and each attitude shift towards appreciation for others doing their part, especially when their way differs from ours, alters the trajectory of our Planet and helps its Ascension process.

We Must Value All Efforts

Most of us are doing *something* to help the Planet and Humanity—in one way or another. Some efforts have a large visible impact; most do not. From monks and yogis spending their days in prayer and meditation, to everyday people doing their best to live their lives with joy, passion, compassion, acceptance, and/or integrity, to people working for animal and human rights, to those working in associations and governments for the betterment of us all, to those who rally others into action—all of this positive energy is working in tandem to raise the vibration of the Planet and bring about the Shift. Illustration 22, Different Contributions Back to Oneness, in the Conclusion offers more specific examples of what we are all doing on different levels to help raise the Planet's vibration.

We may care deeply about the Planet, but in our sincere efforts to guide others to where we think our world needs to be going, instead of focusing on promoting what we believe and the benefits of what we are doing and why, we may focus on what we think others are doing wrong, or are not doing. We may even get angry, judgmental, or become aggressive. We must remember that we are all contributing in different ways to bring this about. The negative vibrations of pushing *against* what we think needs to be done, actually risk delaying the advancement of our cause. Any misplaced aggression likely only stems from our frustration that we know our whole society has gone wrong, but cannot even pin-point or articulate the full scope of our frustrations. So we alleviate our feelings of powerlessness by putting *all* our energies into a specific cause sometimes promoting it relentlessly. Although deep down we know the problem is more complex than this one issue, we just cannot make all the connections.

We must not allow apathy, pessimism, or disillusionment to hijack our vision of a better world. In *The More Beautiful World Our Hearts Know is Possible*, Charles Eisenstein tells us that even though many of us in the Western world no longer trust that society is going in the right direction, we *must* give our frustrations a voice; otherwise we may become apathetic. His vision of an emerging world is one of a "Story of Interbeing [meaning] a reunion of humanity and nature, self and other, work and play, discipline and desire, matter and spirit, man and woman, money and gift, justice and compassion, and so many other polarities." He asks us to look at the impediments to making this vision manifest not as "obstacles to be overcome ... [but as] gateways to our fully inhabiting a new story and the vastly expanded power to serve change that it brings with it."[23] Visionaries like Eisenstein (among others) are starting to lay down explanations, connect the dots, and put words to the frustrations we feel regarding our Planet and modern society as a whole.

What Can I Do to Help the Planet?

In addition to doing our own little bit to help our Planet and feel appreciation for whatever others are doing, we can further educate ourselves by really listening to and trying to understand what we are being told. It is important to heed those with firsthand information and with no stake in what they are saying, instead of the politicians and heads of corporations who do. We can sign petitions and vote for those aligned with a strong vision for us and our Planet's future.

We can also join prayer and meditation groups that send light and love to the Planet in general, or to specific areas under distress. (See my List of Recommendations for links to meditations). We need to stay hopeful that we can restore Gaia to her original pristine self. And we must keep alive the dream of what we want for earth and our future by *holding the vision in our minds* of a clean and healthy Planet with everyone experiencing its abundance.

> *The dream of the planet is a collective of billions of smaller,*
> *personal dreams, which together create a dream of a family,*
> *a dream of a community, a dream of a city, a dream of a country,*
> *and finally a dream of the whole humanity.*
> —Don Miguel Ruiz[24]

Section 2: Abundance

> *Money's original purpose is to connect human gifts with*
> *human needs, so that we might all live in greater abundance.*
> – Charles Eisenstein[25]

The above quote illustrates how our perception about abundance, now all wrapped up in money and success, has veered very far from the original intention for which money was created. Later on in this chapter I explain how this came about.

True abundance is experienced when we tap into joy, and we find our joy when we are fulfilled. We feel fulfilled by connecting to our True Self and following what our heart is whispering to us, so we may discover our soul's life path. And even though true abundance does not exclude having material possessions or living magnanimously, it is our attitude about attaining, maintaining, and being grateful for what we have or attained that will bring us joy and allow us to continue to flourish.

Our abundance is not so much about what we have or who we are but about our attitudes regarding the lives we are now living. Abundance also means different things to different people. We embrace abundance when we appreciate having healthy and loving families, good friends, or feelings of happiness and safety. Although abundance is about thriving rather than just getting by, when we live in a safe environment and country and can breathe clean air and have fresh water, we truly are abundant. Until everyone on the Planet is living in safety and has the basic necessities of life, we can work to help make their lives more abundant. Embracing the Abundance Paradigm also means living with a limitless attitude, fearlessly answering the call of our soul's urgings.

Embracing Our Limitlessness; Being Magnanimous

Creating feelings of being abundant is really about embracing a limitless attitude toward life: it is about being magnanimous. It is about appreciating and loving ourselves enough to embrace feelings, attitudes, and things that bring us joy. It is about being able to create all that we want, opening ourselves up to be able to thrive in all areas of life, and embracing all the potential held for us within the Universe—and to see it all as good. Sometimes these potentials are about the people whose lives we touch in very practical ways, as was the case with Mother Teresa. Sometimes it is touching others with our art or music, but most often it is just in the way we go about our lives lovingly and fearlessly. When we do this and don't shy away from what is required of us, enough money and success will follow to fulfill our needs and desires to the extent that our souls' journey dictates.

When We Embrace Our Limitlessness We Are Given What We Need

I was brought up in a middle-class environment, and when it came time to go back to school for some formal English education at the age of fifty-four, I had the freedom to do so as I had fortunately been financially set up in life to follow the urging of my soul to write. I had a business background but no formal writing experience, so returning to school was necessary to acquire the skill to express what was rumbling around inside me that needed to be shared in a professional way—even though at the time I did not know why I was returning to school. I now see that this was all in my soul's plan, or at least the potential was, as I could have shied away from the task at any point in time because of uncertainty, fear of failure, thoughts that I was unqualified to write such a book, or I could have succumbed to suggestions from those who disagreed with my decision to go back to school without any clear plan of why. But I didn't!

If we go forward in faith and answer the call of our hearts' urgings, no matter what others or societal norms say, what we need will be given to us. It did for me throughout the writing of this book. We will also be primed to create abundance in all areas of our lives and engage the universal Law of Expansion. I now feel I have stepped onto that upward spiral of the Law of Expansion and am primed to bring this book to the world and experience all the joy and abundance it will bring me.

Humanity's past attitudes have not encouraged us to fearlessly embrace our limitlessness. We have been programmed to put up barriers of *I can't, we shouldn't, how could we,* or *how dare I?* Our wings have often been clipped by others' *you shouldn'ts.* Thus many of us are stuck in limitation and the fear of embracing all that we could be. Others who have been influenced by Humanity's programming instill judgment and biases onto those around them who are aiming to fulfill their hearts' desires and attempting to become all they can be. Whether these influences come from within us or from others, they can censor things that may come our way to make our lives easier, more enjoyable, or more fulfilling. And although we are to aim high and live fearlessly, sometimes following our hearts is a fine line to walk, as we do have to consider those around us. We also have to continuously check that no arrogance or underlying egoic self-serving wants or needs are slipping into the mix. Truly embracing the Abundance Paradigm never brings with it any guilt; it brings feelings of contentment, appreciation, and joy.

Joy, Appreciation, and Abundance

I once read something a little girl wrote about joy and being "glad" that stayed with me. Her father had died and her mother remarried a pastor. Her stepfather treated her and her mother lovingly, and she recalled him saying that the word *glad* was in the Bible about nine hundred times. So this is what he had based his life and ministry on—being and living the tenets of gladness. He believed that God wants us to be glad and happy. We can live in gladness when we feel appreciative and express joy and happiness and all other attitudes that align with these precepts. Being glad and grateful for opportunities and the small and large gifts the Universe has bestowed upon us is what embracing the Abundance Paradigm is all about. The article "What We Can Be Grateful for" on the book's website gives other examples of what we can be thankful for.

Modern society is so caught up in wanting more, and we are running around so busy that we have lost our ability to appreciate the things that we have. We don't care about or take the time to appreciate them. Myself included! However, in the last few years it has really hit home for me, and probably for many of us, that we have so much to be grateful for, especially in the Western world and in consideration of all the people in the Middle East who have had to leave their homes and communities and live in fear for their safety and futures, subjected to harsh situations, and at the mercy of others. This Shift brings with it the impulse for true appreciation.

One day a few winters ago I walked into my bedroom and suddenly felt an overwhelming appreciation for the heat in my house. In the cold of a Montreal winter, if our power goes off for even a half day, we are cold. I then started to appreciate having a roof over my head, indoor plumbing, and the availability of necessities like food and clean water at my fingertips. Appreciating what we have puts us in a positive vibration and tells the Universe we want more of the same.

Abundance and Our Creativity

Our creative impulses, what is held in our imagination, and answering the call of our dreams and desires are our soul's way of urging us on to bring about what we were created for. In doing so, we also create the abundance our soul's journey dictates.

Abraham-Hicks tell us that when we allow ourselves to imagine and dream about our desires they can become so familiar to us that they fall into the realm of possibility, so that the "next logical step" can only be their materialization. They also explain that if our desires feel unattainable, so are their manifestations. We must remain open and positive without putting up barriers to our dreams, desires, and their successes. Abraham-Hicks suggest we ask ourselves, "Does your desire feel like the next logical step?" If it does, we should follow it. If it does not, then perhaps the timing is off or it is the wrong thing for us and not in our soul's plan.[26]

Our Prosperity and the Ability to Tap into Our Creative Life Energy

So long as we have not erected blocks within our Life Matrixes regarding money, our prosperity is related to our ability to create from our life energies, be that through creating business opportunities, working within our educational system, or creating through the arts. Wherever our interests and strengths lie, we will be guided to do what we came here for. For me it was writing this book and creating the support systems that will go along with it. Spirit wants us to tap into our creative life energy to bring about our abundance.

A few years ago I was considering moving to Vancouver, as my eldest son and his family live there. My other two sons, who still live in Montreal, had also considered the move there. However, Vancouver has the highest real-estate market in Canada, and Montreal has the lowest. To relocate, I would have had to pay more than twice what my house was worth in Montreal to get something far smaller.

At that point with the realities of moving in my awareness, I decided to start buying lottery tickets regularly, hoping I could make up the difference with a win. I knew the Universe would supply what I wanted/needed, as the decision was made to be close to family, not for looking better than the Joneses. Although I was starting to realize that this book would be valuable to many and probably successful, I didn't really connect the two. I was writing it because it was in me and would not let go—I wasn't doing it for money. However, I have dedicated my whole life energy and actually put my life on hold through this process for quite a while now.

Shortly thereafter I had a dream that my website for the book offered all sorts of links for workshops, other support systems, and webinars. The next day I had a meeting with a web designer, and as I explained the book and what I thought I might need to support it, without even using proper terminologies, he sketched out exactly what I had seen in the dream. I realized that Spirit wanted me to create the abundance I needed for what I then wanted in life—our family living in closer proximity and supporting each other—from within my own alignments and life energy. I believe that the Universe could have provided me with a lotto win, and it does for some people, but for most of us, we are guided to let go of what we need to so we can align with our power source to create what we really need in life to make us happy.

Carl Jung suggested that if we investigate that which trips us up the most, we will find our gold. Although not everyone's passions, contentment, and prosperity comes about by overcoming the negative attitudes that have undermined their peace and happiness and then helping others to do so, it is for me.

Modern Society Has Hijacked Our Connection to Our Creativity and Life-Energy

Because our most recent history existed under the lack paradigm brought forward from Humanity's Default Position from years of struggling and living under the control of those in power who were corrupt and greedy, our current society's consensus is that there isn't enough to go around. We are thereby inclined to overwork, stay at jobs we do not enjoy, and our day-to-day duties are most often detached from anything tangible. This all causes our life-energy to become depleted. Sometimes we overwork because we feel we have no other choice having backed ourselves into a corner wanting to satisfy all our desires, needs (real and perceived), the lifestyle we created, and the responsibilities we have taken on, with most of this coming about as a response to our unconscious influences. We might also have unconscious issues about our true worth and be seeking love and validation though our efforts. To tap into the joy true abundance allows and become happy, productive, and feel contented we have to consider the impact our attitudes, actions, and day-to-day life have on our life-energy.

In the past our creativity and life-energy was directly connected to the land. We grew food and crafted products from what nature offered, and we looked after the livestock she permitted to graze upon her land. This created a sense of satisfaction because we had a direct relationship with what our life-energy brought forth. This, along with the fact that we were connecting with nature in our every-day lives energized us. As we exchanged with others what *we* had grown, crafted, or looked after, that connection to nature was retained.

Today most of us exchange our life-energy for money, which we rarely even see or use in physical form, as most transactions are now done electronically. Our work is often far removed from the product, if indeed we are even involved in creating a product. Working hours on end in offices, often in front of computer screens and under unnatural light, we are detached from a direct connection to our efforts, and our life-force is drained. Modern society, with its focus on money, service industries, and electronic systems has in effect stolen from us our sense of satisfaction with the reverent, peaceful, feelings that are created when we connect to the land and its abundance. Stanley and Loy tell us in "At the Edge of the Roof: The Evolutionary Crisis of the Human Spirit," that the machine we unknowingly created has changed society to such an extent that "the dominant institution of our age is no longer religion, government, or academia. It is the global business corporation."[27]

Abundance and Money

Some of us are greedy about money while others are reluctant to even talk about it. It is not a good thing if money is always the most important factor in our decision-making, contracts, and relationships, but we should not brush the subject aside for fear of talking about it, as I did when I was sixteen years old and too timid to ask about my salary in an interview for summer babysitting. Money or compensation should not be a taboo subject.

Our Conflicts Surrounding Money and Our Self-Worth

In our work life we put out our life-energy and we should be appropriately compensated for our efforts given our skills and experience, unless there are extenuating circumstances or we choose to volunteer our time. In our world today we need money to survive, so it is certainly essential that we have a good relationship with money. I did not.

My father was a school principal, and we had a nice house and he drove a nice car, but I was brought up in a strict Catholic environment that espoused humility. My father frequently expounded in a loud and aggressive manner the evil of money and often referred to the Biblical metaphor that it was as hard for a wealthy man to get to heaven as it was for a camel to fit through the eye of a needle. Although he was educated and successful in life my father's attitude was that people should not talk about their accomplishments or focus on or discuss money. To some degree he was right, as money for money's sake is a dangerous attitude, but his negative inferences about money and success were somewhat biased and based on his self-righteous and judgmental attitudes. Because of this, I received conflicting messages. Although my father enjoyed what money brought into his life, he too was conflicted, evidenced by his concept of money being evil.

To make peace with money we have to make it our friend (as Inelia Benz suggests below), own it as a necessary part of living, and allow it to flow through us. Charles Eisenstein even suggests in *Sacred Economics* that if we transform our way of relating to the Planet and each other we could allow money to become "sacred" again as we would be tuned into its ability to reconnect us with the purity of exchange between each other and what nature has to offer us.

Returning to this notion we could actually begin to change our attitudes not only about money, but about our connection to everyone and everything, and as Eisenstein says rediscover "the core of what it means to be human." To transform our attitudes about money from its current inanimate, cold, and evil construct to something innate and sacred, we have to recapture the sacredness of life and living, and embrace our interconnectedness to nature's bounty and to our exchanges with each other. Along with all the other shifts we can make to connect to our True Selves, creating a healthy view of money and the merits of its exchange value will help alleviate unhealthy attitudes regarding our worthiness, as sacred exchanges underline the importance of relationship and increase our self-worth.[28]

Self-worth, Helping Others, and Compensation

Self-worth has been an issue in my life. I now understand that part of my soul's journey is to acknowledge my self-worth, and making peace with earning money for my efforts—even if it is by helping people with their spiritual development—is part of that process. This is not so for everyone. Many people who spend considerable time and energy helping others know deep down that they are not to be compensated for doing so, as somewhere within their being they understand it is not part of their soul's journey, and they live a simple life. Some are okay with this; others not so much. Some who dedicate time, effort, and even their lives to helping others find themselves in dire financial circumstances. Although those who dedicate their lives to helping others are usually looked after by the Universe, for some, poverty may be part of a soul lesson they are to make peace with but have not yet done so. Others may have self-esteem issues like I did, are affected by unconscious influences that undermine their financial security, or are caught between conflicting spiritual principles.

It is a common spiritual tenet that we are not to benefit from or make money when helping others, especially when it is with their spiritual development. It is also a common spiritual principle that we will be looked after and it is our God-given right to create whatever we want in life. These are actually conflicting premises. Many who give of themselves for the betterment of others may not be able to reconcile these contradictory premises and will opt for the more humble approach and not expect nor ask for compensation for their efforts, while others will eventually allow money to become the most important aspect. Those who work selflessly like Mother Teresa did may simply understand that it is not in their life plan to benefit from helping others.

Not all religious and spiritual teachers charge for their help, but many have given up careers to devote their lives to helping others, and need to make a living somehow. We are not all meant to be Gandhis and Mother Teresas. I once heard Byron Katie sum this up perfectly saying, "Some charge; some don't—it's all good," when speaking of the certified facilitators who teach her principles based on her program *The Work*. To help shift any negative attitudes our inner beliefs we hold about money, we must keep our thoughts and words aligned positively.

Aligning Our Thoughts, Words, and Actions with the Abundance Paradigm

If we want to change our financial situations we have to align our *whole* being with the premises in the Abundance Paradigm, including our thoughts, words, and actions. Creating abundantly is our birthright. However, if we have thoughts like "I'll never get out of debt or ahead in life," we anchor that into our Life Matrix; if someone makes a suggestion for an outing and we cannot afford to join in and say something like "I can't afford it," "I never spend money on things like that," or "I'll never be able to afford that," we immediately confirm our lack. These negative declarations confuse any messages we may have already sent to the Universe. On the one hand we may want something, request it, and even day-dream about it, but then the words we utter contradict the desire as the vibration attached to the pessimistic words throws a negating component into the mix. This also undermines in us the belief that the Universe can deliver what we want, thereby further blocking the energetic pathways to the Abundance Paradigm and the likelihood of these experiences materializing.

Conversely, positive affirmations such as "I'm in debt today, but know it will change soon;" "I would *love* to join you but can't afford it right now;" or "That sounds like so much fun, maybe another time" confirms our *desire* to participate, even if we cannot afford it now. This invites in the likelihood of being able to partake at another time. Because we have started our replies on positive, hopeful notes, our vibrations emit the desire to the Universe, the belief it can happen, and so the potential for it happening is then born. Our energetic pathway to the Abundance Paradigm is open.

We can refer again to illustrations 7, 8, and 9 from chapter 2, which show what happens to our connection to universal abundance when our pathways to it are open, closed, or have static. The article "How Being Open, Closed Off, or Creating Static Affect our Requests" found on the book's website gives more details on how our thoughts and attitudes regarding having limited funds affects our desire for an improved financial position.

Monetary Abundance: Cheating; Pitfalls; Flow

Cheating is a symptom of believing in the lack paradigm. It can take on many faces, such as stealing, lying to get a job or promotion, taking credit for work not done, consistently using work time for personal business, going after somebody else's partner or spouse, or any other form of dishonesty.

Some of us cheat because of low self-esteem. We don't feel worthy enough to feel that life will provide us what we want or need. Others may be dishonest or corrupt because their unconscious minds believe that because of past wrongdoings they don't deserve to be happy or have abundance in their lives. Therefore, they punish themselves by doing even more wrong. Guilt, whether conscious or unconscious, is insidious in nature and undermines all our beliefs, including those about what we deserve in life. At a spiritual level there is no such thing as doing right or wrong; there is only aligning or misaligning with Source.

When we cheat, we tell the Universe that we do not think there is enough for us or that we do not believe we deserve what we want or need. We then create a negative set point in our minds regarding abundance. We can even start out with a positive set point, but thwart our good intentions.

Monetary Abundance: Its Power, and Pitfalls

Good intentions can be thwarted. Even though the path to our soul's journey may be clear and we start with good intentions, we may get caught up in situations that derail us. Greed, power, or arrogance may take hold, or we may get lured into corruption. Any of these can make us lose our way. For example, if on our soul's journey we were to be successful and somewhat wealthy, whether for ourselves, to help others, to give our family a good life, or even to help our partner with their soul's life work, be it political, spiritual, or any service to mankind, we may get sidetracked with any of the above temptations and find ourselves on a negative spiral of action—consequence—negative reaction—consequence, and so on. This can cause us to lose our momentum, way forward, or even all of our money. Keeping a vision of the highest ideal of our purpose at the forefront of our consciousness will help keep the pitfalls that monetary abundance and the power it brings with it at bay.

Flow of Abundance When We Release It

Our faith in the Universe or God to deliver must be released. We must embrace the Abundance Paradigm. This means we have to believe and act on the belief that there is enough for us and enough to go around for everyone. If we want a better financial situation, we have to act as if we know the money we need will come to us, but also must not be stingy with what we have or with our time. We should not go into debt, but if we give money to those needier than ourselves and to those who support our spiritual journeys, we are releasing our faith in abundance with our actions. If we have no available funds, then we can give our time or support to others.

A few years ago, I felt guided to embrace this concept. I started to give certain % of my net income to those who have helped me connect some of the dots in bringing forward this book. This is the approach I took, although giving money to those in need also releases our faith in abundance. If our monetary situation changes we can adjust the dollar amount, or even our percentage. It is not the amount that matters as much as our intention to share what we have based on our belief that the God/Universe can provide for us. When we only concern ourselves with our needs (or even just our families) we do not hold to that belief.

Money is not the enemy. In fact, if we treat it like a friend who brings us what we need and what we like, we create a good vibration surrounding it, and will have enough for what we need. If we share what we have without fear or stinginess, enough will be returned to us for what we want in life. In *The Prophet,* Khalil Gibran suggests that when we give with pure intentions, even when we have very little, we will never be without.

> There are those who give little of the much
> which they have—and they give it for recognition
> and their hidden desire makes their gifts unwholesome.
>
> And there are those who have little and give it all.
> These are the believers in life and the bounty of life,
> and their offer is never empty.[29]

Money, Wealth, and Accumulation

Money is not inherently evil; nor is having a lot of money. As society is set up today, money is necessary for our every-day needs, hobbies, education, and it gives us the freedom to travel and experience all the world has to offer. It is our fixation with accumulating money for money's sake and using the power it gives us over others that causes problems.

In *Sacred Economics* Charles Eisenstein points out that our obsession with the amassing of wealth brings with it moral dilemmas and rules to live by. How far can we step over others to become wealthy or successful? How do we reconcile the special treatment accorded to us because we have become part of the elite—rich and powerful?

Eisenstein reminds us that the concept of accumulation only came about as we settled into communities and started to farm. The early hunter gatherers and nomadic people did not amass food or goods since transportation would have been a problem as they moved about. And even though in the past the accumulation of grain and other food stuffs had been a necessity to make up for seasons of poor crops, he says that in general "accumulation is one of the violations of natural law" and is rarely seen in nature for any other reason than for survival.[30]

Although the accumulation of wealth can be used for the good of the many and sometimes is, as Eisenstein says amassing wealth for greed or power and hoarding money goes against the laws of nature. He suggests that we consider "wealth as flow rather than accumulation" When we do so, we are inviting in the powers of Universe to help us create *real* abundance with our wealth—enough that can be used for the good of the many so that all people can have access to what they need.[31]

Money, its Energy Fields, and Reconnecting With It

Money has energy just like everything else. We can affect this energy field positively or negatively and either attract money to us or deflect it away from us. In *Clearing Your Wealth Lines*, Inelia Benz explains how we can tap into money's energy field, and she urges us to acknowledge it for ourselves, but also believes doing so will help to create a healthier collective energy exchange.[32]

If we are having trouble with our finances, we may hold negative attitudes about abundance and money and its purpose within our Life Matrixes. In another practice "Reconnecting with the Spirit of Money," Benz guides us to release any attitudes that stand in the way of our inner acknowledgment that money allows for our basic human needs to be met.[33] The link to the YouTube video of Benz's exercise to reconnect with the spirit of money is in the above endnote and at the back of the book in the "Exercises" section of "Meditations, Visualizations, and Other Practices."

Abundance Is Not Unholy

Many within religious and spiritual circles expound the idea that abundance is unholy. It is not. Throughout the ages, as we played out the duality we had originally chosen, we used money and its power to control and manipulate our brethren. We became greedy. We then judged the money as evil, not the way we used it. We were even able to substantiate doing so because we superimposed our ideas onto the spiritual tenet of humility, making money the culprit rather than the abuse of it.

Within our different lifetimes, we have all been poor, wealthy, have led modest existences, as well as experienced being royalty. In the past, among the monks, the religious, and the druids some practiced poverty and chastity, just as today there are monks within Christianity and Buddhism who still practice these vows. However in the early years, Christianity did not advocate these practices, but at some point in the Middle Ages, poverty and chastity became the required tenets of the Church. Women also ministered in the early church. We know that many of the ancient prophets were wealthy by biblical accounts of their livestock, lands, and large families, but it was not stated that because they owned a certain number of cattle, they were unholy. Their position in life was simply stated without prejudice. This is because in ancient times the having and sharing of goods was considered sacred, and abundance was believed to be a gift from God (or nature).

Gift Culture and Strengthening Human Connections

In *Sacred Economics*, Charles Eisenstein suggests we return to the "gift culture" and its concepts humans once held. He compares this "gift culture" to the reciprocal relationship with nature we once shared and the Indigenous people still believe in.[34] He explains that "gift culture" philosophy highlights the importance of "receiving" gifts but also of "acknowledging" them, suggesting that doing so fosters communal relationships. He explains that we now live in a time of separateness; we don't want to need others or their help and that this has caused us to lose our sense of community connection whereby we look after each other. He says that in reality "to refuse a gift is to spurn relationship," as gifts acknowledge and strengthen connections whereby the giving and receiving of gifts "creates bonds and widens the circle of self ... and to refuse to give or receive says, 'I refuse to be connected to you.'"[35] Some of the premises/advantages of "gift culture" are that gifts circulate, rather than accumulate, and flow toward the greatest need.[36]

Necessity of Aligning With the Abundance Paradigm

We undermine our requests by feeling undeserving, worrying about not getting what we want, manipulating and conniving to bring it about, or having negative attitudes about or being jealous of others who have what we want. These harmful attitudes alter our vibrations concerning the original requests. We can even cancel the requests out by becoming impatient and thinking they will not happen. We do this because lack and limitation are part of Humanity's makeup.

We actually request only tidbits of what is available to us. Abraham-Hicks often say that we would be amazed at what Source "holds in escrow" for us. So when we push, connive, and manipulate to get something we want, or act from any unconscious influence we create confusion surrounding what is held in waiting for us. In his broadcast, "Miraculous Probabilities," Dr. Jim Richards explains that when we try to make things happen in unsavory ways or force a timetable, it is like "trying to *get* something from God and this creates a distortion" and undercuts what will ultimately make us happy. He suggests that rather than trying to get something from God, we should shift our awareness to want to bring forth "what God already has in store for us."[37] We can bring forth what is the right thing for us by staying positive, open, and listening to what our heart is telling us, thereby creating an allowing vibration. Creating mental images of what we want helps bring it forth.

Mental Images and Dreaming Our Desires into Being

As we aim to keep our vibrations aligned with what we want, conjuring up mental images of our desires already being present in our lives helps to instill the appropriate vibrations into our energetic fields. Manifesting what we want or how we want to be in our lives by focusing on active mental imagery of our desired future is a component of Inelia Benz's Ascension 101 program that I mentioned in chapters 7 and 8.[38] I have used this full program often, and a recap of the module "Meet Yourself in the Future; Successful and Healed," is at the back of the book under Visualization #4 in "Meditations, Visualizations, and Other Practices."

When we make mental images of us healed, successful, or at peace with others or our situations, we shift our vibration levels to invite these into our beings. Once the mental images are anchored into our memory banks, they are in our vibratory mix and become part of us and our Life Matrix. Practicing with mental images helps us to *own* what we are requesting.

Leveling Out of Abundance as Humanity Embraces Fifth-Dimensional Attitudes

Inequality in the situations of individuals, financially or otherwise, has existed for eons. Those of us who have been given much in life or are in positions of power, either by hard work, through good luck or opportunities, or from family connections were intended to be guardians of all that is on the Planet. We have been given this so that we can help those in need, as wealth allows us the freedom to do good works and power allows us to get things done. Although some abused the wealth and power they were given, not everyone did. We have to be careful not to let their attitudes and actions misrepresent those who have used their wealth and power wisely and for the good of the many. This Shift and Ascension bring with it the necessity for sharing and equality for all—including the distribution of the earth's resources so that all may live in comfort.

Knowing that in the future many of our leaders would fall prey to greed and abuse of power, the ancients may have even set the fairer distribution of wealth in motion hundreds, or even thousands of years ago. Just like the powerful artifacts (discussed in chapter 6) that will remain hidden until we have the spiritual maturity to use their power wisely, much gold and riches may also remain hidden, to be uncovered only when greed has abated and we are ready to share with everyone on earth. Some who have or will soon inherit family money or royal wealth, or amassed it on their own will start to distribute it (or at least a *much* larger portion than their predecessors) for the benefit of the masses or the Planet. This is already starting to happen as a few are now using their wealth for good, rather than hording it for their own purposes as has been the norm. We are already endeavoring to create equality by crafting and supporting programs that help the impoverished at home and in other countries, and for many, addressing others' plights is becoming paramount in their life. Equality and abundance for all is on the horizon.

~

According to Mark Boyle, sustainability and reducing our dependency on money are connected. Although many of us now view abundance as meaning more than just having money, he tells us in the *Moneyless Manifesto* that we are completely unaware of the impact money has on us "personally, socially, and ecologically." He says that the "monetary economy" we created now owns the whole Planet … it kills our spirit teaching us to consume instead of play

... [money] doesn't serve us, we serve it." Having completely lost the original "gifting" relationship between people and the bounty of nature we lived by when we first started using coin and until we "reconnect in those ways, true sustainability and non-exploitative ways will continue to be something we talk about."[39]

Although we have made some headway regarding sustainability, and we are starting to question our monetary systems because we are now aware that it works for the few, not the many, we have been mostly ineffective in making changes that have major impacts. This is because we are working against what Susan Murphy calls "the industrial super-magic barrel" (which I discussed earlier in the chapter) we unknowingly created that now infiltrates every aspect of our existence. This has dramatically changed our focus so much that, as Stanley and Loy tell us in "At the Edge of the Roof: The Evolutionary Crisis of the Human Spirit," for the first time in human history we no longer believe that *our children are our future,* because we are now ruled by what they call the "global business corporation."[40]

However, we must not become discouraged, because even though shifting our focus and dismantling this "global business corporation" seems like a momentous task, this Shift brings with it the energy and impetus to change: the insights for new ideas, the energy to galvanize to bring people together, and the momentum to make it happen—all for the betterment of ourselves, each other, and the Planet. We just have to follow through on the ideas, insights, and inspirations that come to us, as well as support those who have the power to bring forth change.

Individually, as we start to answer the call of the Shift, without realizing it, we will automatically want to ensure our Planet's healthy survival and to help others live in safety, freedom, and abundance. Feeling closer to our True Selves and Source, our contentment will come from within and we will be able to shift to the "enough" concept that Thom Hartmann spoke of and that the Indigenous people still hold to. We will also feel inclined to extend love and help to others so we can all appreciate the bounty our world offers and live in abundance together.

The scenes of your life serve a story much bigger than your own.
—Kurt Bruner and Jim Ware[41]

In the next chapter, we will consider the Ascension process we and Gaia are undertaking: what this Shift is really all about.

CHAPTER 10

Ascension

Ascension is a great leap of experience on every level of your being.
—Sananda[1]

*A*scension is a term that has been applied to the masters, saints, prophets and sages who in having attained enlightenment overcame the physical constraints of duality and form, such that they rose up into the skies, or heaven, as some suggest. Today, the term Ascension has come to be more associated with the Shift. Humanity and Gaia are in the process of ascending together toward a higher dimension and consciousness. This answers many ancient promises and prophesies of our restoration to the higher realms.

In *The Crystal Stair: A Guide to the Ascension*, Sananda, who speaks through Eric Klein, expounds on the above quote, stating that the third-dimensional reality Humanity has recently embodied is based on our sensual perceptions and what we perceive as solid matter. Our thoughts and emotions are included in this and exist in the fourth dimension, but only as the emotional component of the third.

When we exist in the fourth dimension we are more open-hearted than when in the third, but we are still living according to our sensual perceptions, without an expansion of consciousness towards the All. We expand our consciousness from the fourth to fifth dimension when we can extend the qualities of love to others without the limitations of sensual perceptions. For example, in the fourth dimension we may *feel* compassion for someone and their pain, but may internalize the pain and not be able to rise above it whereas in the fifth we can.

As we raise our consciousness to fifth-dimensional vibrations we become more attuned with the qualities of the higher realms which we could not perceive from the lower third-dimensional limitations, or from within the emotions of the fourth. Sananda adds that nothing has changed in nature or the Universe, but our vision has expanded. It is as if we have taken blinders off. When we raise our consciousness enough to break through the third-dimensional limitations, our perceptions change. We can more easily see the good and light in others and in situations. We are more inclined to feel peaceful and extend love and acceptance to others. Joy is more accessible to us. The world seems more vibrant, nature more alive, and colors appear to be brighter.

As our vision widens, we experience life differently. In *The Great Awakening*, Linda Dillon tells us that as individuals we can experience this time of Ascension as "our chance to be, to live and fulfill our soul mission and purpose, and to complete this phase of our role in the unfoldment of the Divine Plan. It is the gift of life being lived in alignment with the truth of who you are and your place in the Universe."[2]

The scriptures and many other writings contain accounts of the physical manifestations of the Ascensions of Krishna, Muhammad, Jesus, Enoch, and many others. As explained in chapter 6, *ascended master* is a term describing a soul that has completed its final lifetime by overcoming the duality of our third-dimensional world. Through spiritual transformation, these beings who became ascended masters were able to transcend all ideas of fear and separation to embrace only concepts of love, unity, and Oneness.

Lifting into the Higher Dimensions as Promised

Ascension is now also used within the spiritual community to denote Gaia lifting herself out of the dark and dense third dimension into the fifth dimension or even higher up to the seventh. We are collectively invited to ascend with her on this Shift. Our impulses to do our part in embracing higher-dimensional attitudes come from the higher realms and are divinely inspired. Much light and love has been beamed to us from the higher dimensions to help during this time of the Shift with both Gaia's and our individual Ascension processes.

The well-publicized Mayan calendar's December 2012 date was really just a predetermined cosmic appointment for Gaia to make her Shift into this higher fifth dimension. Although her ascent started before that time—as her journey, like ours, is a process—sometime around that December date she was to make a conscious choice to initiate her final push toward this higher dimension. Within the Universal Matrix, our personal journeys are interconnected with hers, so it is also our cosmic time to make this journey into the higher dimensions, if we choose to do so. Gaia has made her decision, and we are invited along. However, our passport to join her requires adopting the lighter attitudes of love and its attributes and embracing the Oneness inherent in the higher dimensions.

At levels beyond our awareness we chose to be on earth at this time to participate in this personal and cosmic journey. However, we need not understand or even believe all the talk about Ascension, we simply just have to embrace and internalize the qualities of love inherent in the higher dimensions. As we release the dense, low-vibrational attitudes, our consciousness expands and our vibrations become more congruent with the higher dimensions. We thereby experience a personal Ascension into these higher realms. However, unlike the accounts of the masters and prophets who ascended to heaven, we do this gradually.

Shifting Dimensions: An Energetic Movement

When we describe our journeys or Ascensions as shifting or moving between different levels or dimensions, this does not mean a movement in a physical sense: the movement is energetic and we shift dimensions through our vibrations when we align with those inherent in that other dimension. There are no lines that depict the levels or dimensions, but we describe them as such so our third-dimensional linear minds can better understand. We could think of it as the different areas of the ocean which have varying qualities depending on where you are, like water temperature and size of waves, and require different skills to navigate but have no linear demarcations on the surface.

In "Ascension the Larger Picture" Steve Beckow helps us further understand by distinguishing between enlightenment and Ascension, telling us "Enlightenment is an event in consciousness; ascension is an advance in dimension ... enlightenment signifies a radical, discontinuous leap in consciousness or experience; ascension signifies a radical, discontinuous jump in dimension or plane."[3] However, shifts in consciousness do encourage us toward higher levels attitudes and behaviors and their cumulative affect allows us to move up dimensions.

Whereas in the past, we may have briefly shifted dimensions in a moment of clarity as we gleaned a greater understanding of how an issue unfolded, our habit has been to fall back, like in a two-step-forward, one-step-backward progress, as an issue that angered us, for example, would then anger us only *less* often. This Shift and Ascension process offers us the potential to advance and stay in the higher dimension, because when we have our moments of clarity its energy brings with it the spiritual vision to dispel our propensity to anger and see through our differences to the light and love in the other. When we accept this vision offered to us it allows us to anchor in the higher dimension as we now embody its qualities.

A Better Understanding of the Third and Fifth Dimensions

These dimensions are not static or linear, but they do embody different qualities. In her article "The 5th Dimension Is Not a Location, It's a Creation," Inelia Benz explains some of these variations, telling us that "the difference between the 3rd, 4th and 5th dimensions are ones of empowerment, subtlety of solid matter, and capacity to do." She says the third dimension is characterized by "tunnel vision" and when we exist under its influence we tend to focus on the one reality we perceive, which is always characterized by form and separation. Even though Oneness is still all around us, it is just beyond our awareness. Benz tells us, "There are no dimensions in Oneness, because there is no singular construct of individuality with 'other, whether 'other person' or 'environment'" and that within the fifth dimension and higher, there is not even recognition of the differences within the dimensions.[4]

Benz tells us that the most exciting and important aspect of existing within the higher dimensions is that we create our own realities through each passing moment. She further informs us that we actually fashion the dimensions ourselves by the "raising of our personal vibration, raising the vibration of the Planet, and being fully aware of our intention and energy behind all our communications with others and self."[5] The degree to which we free ourselves of the limitations we created within our diminished awareness is how the higher dimensions will play out for us.

Our Personal Ascensions

Finding the connection to our True Selves and returning to our wholeness is our personal Ascension process. To be able to live comfortably on Gaia involves being able to endure the vibrations inherent in this new fifth dimension she now embodies. It is ethereally lighter, more malleable, and visually brighter than the third dimension we and previous generations have occupied.

If we do not embrace the qualities of the higher dimension our Planet now almost completely occupies, life will be experienced as difficult—much like looking into a brightly lit room from darkness will hurt our eyes. So it is in our best interests to quickly embrace the qualities of Oneness, exchange all aspects of third-dimensional attitudes based in divisiveness for those of unity, and find peace in our hearts with those in our sphere and with people or groups we do not resonate with within our communities, countries, and throughout the world.

This does not mean we condone past and current negative, divisive, unfair, or cruel behaviors, but we have to forego all ideas of *me-and-you* and *us-and-them* and deal with people or situations calmly and rationally, and with appropriate actions when necessary. It is easier to do this when we remember that we all emerged from the same Oneness and are all on our journeys back, but that not everyone is on the same leg of the journey, or has caught on yet. Therefore, some of the dualistic and fear-based controlling and divisive attitudes and their actions will persist for a while, we just cannot allow them to affect *our* vibrations. We must keep them positive for our and Gaia's Ascensions, so we may contribute to a world of peace, fairness, and equality.

Our Ascensions and Recapturing Our Twelve-Strand DNA

At this time of the Shift and Ascension we have the potential to reactivate our twelve-strand DNA. And we do this by first raising our vibrations. This makes our bodies more malleable and open to high vibration energies. As we choose the aspects of love and hope over those of fear and pessimism, our energetic fields can allow cosmic light through, and the more we do so the more natural it all becomes. As we allow cosmic light through it rekindles the light within us (something we never lost but forgot how to access) and we can then more easily allow the grace that surrounds us help us with our Ascensions at this time of the Shift. This all paves the way to reawaken our original twelve-strand DNA within our beings, but we must ensure that there are no roadblocks.

In "Reclaiming Your 12-strand DNA," Julianne Everett tells us that we are surrounded by so much grace right now that we have the ability to move quickly with Gaia, but that to allow this grace to permeate our beings, we must release the pain that separation and fear have inflicted upon us.[6] This is why we have recently been encouraged to face and overcome the effects of our unconscious influences, as they block cosmic flow. We are then free to take advantage of the grace now available to us which will encourage us to find what brings us joy and/or to fulfill our life purpose—be that embracing our passions, helping others, animals, or the Planet, immersing ourselves in nature, or listening to music attuned to the higher vibrations in the Universe. These all help us to balance our energetic beings with the joy-filled universal vibrations inherent in the nature of the cosmos.

Necessity of Returning to Balance with Nature and the Cosmos

As we aim to balance our personal vibrations, we also have to be able to harmonize with those of Gaia. Mark Torgeson is a music alchemist whose mission is to help us shift our energies to attune with the vibrations inherent in nature and the cosmos. In his talk, "DNA Activation and Music," he tells us that "sound is synonymous with consciousness" and music that is properly attuned to the vibrations of the Universe can help us engage the multidimensional beings that we are becoming through the Ascension process.[7]

In "Nature, Consciousness and Ascension," Torgeson also tells us that "nature is an aspect of the self that is to be nurtured ... it is either in balance or coming toward balance," so we can take our cues from it.[8] He continues to explain that with the amount of light coming into the world from the higher dimensions at this time, it will be "harder for the darkness to flourish." It will be increasingly difficult for us to hold on to old, negative attitudes because if we do, we will greatly feel their effects. We can fight this or surrender to it by abandoning old, third-dimensional attitudes and beliefs, but one way or another our egoic interests will have to be relinquished.

This Shift is happening on Gaia, and *we* have to adjust. She will no longer adjust to our third-dimensional, low-level attitudes and vibrations. So just like a birth, this Shift to higher dimensions will come about, and we can either embrace what it requires of us and the process will be easier, or we can fight it and our lives will feel more difficult. However we go about it, our personal Ascensions are central to Gaia's Ascension.

Gaia's Ascension

Gaia is a sentient being of archangelic stature, with a physical body
we call "Earth—just as we have a physical body—and a soul.
—Steve Beckow[9]

As early as his April 2011 talk in Edmonton, Kryon told us that the positive ramifications of our collective optimistic attitudes and choices had many of us baffled at what was happening to us and in our world. He explained, "It is a benevolence that you have created, and that is new. You now sit in a revolutionary change and some of you are aware of it and feeling it. It is the shift of Human consciousness and it's shifting right into the quantum factor, since you are becoming more quantum in your consciousness … and it is becoming benevolent."[10]

Since 2011 Humanity as a whole has embraced and acted upon even more higher-level attitudes thereby creating further benevolence in the world, and because of this we, and Gaia, made it through December 2012 without major catastrophes.

Even though we are starting to embrace this quantum factor and beginning to realize our creation potential within it, we must still release all tendrils of negativity we hold. So does Gaia. Her Ascension process brings with it labor pains, and we are and will continue to feel them. It takes time for new attitudes to manifest into actions and for actions to fully affect realities. All the unfairness and corruption that was hidden is being brought to light, and it often appears that the entire world is in chaos. But as with our individual journeys to wholeness, what was hidden must be revealed before it can be released.

Gaia has suffered from the physical assaults we have put upon her body, as well as from the negative attitudes and behaviors we have perpetrated against one another, and so she too has needed to release it all to regain her balance for her Ascension. The raging weather patterns of recent decades are Gaia's way of releasing the hurts to her physical and Emotional Body.

However, as we can now acknowledge that the physical and emotional abuses Humanity has put upon Gaia have manifested in severe climate patterns and environmental issues, we must not get caught up in the guilt and negativity of it all. We now understand and are making changes, but it does take time for the ramifications of our old attitudes and actions against her to abate, so we will continue to be exposed to some harsh and changing weather patterns for a while.

Avoiding Getting Caught Up in Dramas of Past or Fear of Future

As this move toward Ascension unearths all that has transpired in our world so that we are no longer living in denial, focusing on any past or current world-wide issue or drama, plotting revenge, or dedicating enthusiastic energy to conspiracy theories is counterproductive to our and Gaia's Ascensions. This is not to suggest that we pretend these didn't happen or aren't still happening in the world, but by investing negative energy in *any* issue we fuel the fires of negativity and its lower-dimensional attitudes upon Gaia and her inhabitants. If we feel inclined to help in some area, we must do so with neutrality and love—to truly help—without any notions of blame, hate or revenge. It is only through the positive vibrations of love, compassion, and understanding that we will create the better world we want.

Those in authority who have been under the influence of dark forces have kept us under their control using fear tactics for greed and power. This kept us feeling vulnerable and powerless, and since the knowledge of who we really are was hidden from us, we could not access our personal power to overcome their influence. If we allow ourselves to be caught up in anger or the drama of it all, we will play into the dark one's hands again and be sucked under like quicksand. In *November Waves and Responsible Creation*, Sandra Walter tells us that these types of responses are part of the "old programs aimed at restricting Human ascension."[11]

Walter writes that by divine decree the dark forces that have plagued Humanity for so long are loosing their power. The doom timelines have now dissolved and we, encouraged by the media's sensationalizing of it all, are now the ones perpetrating most of the negativity of doom and gloom on earth with our fears and constant focus on the bad things that are still happening and *could* happen.

Yes, there will still be evidence of the dark forces at work, and they even seem to have worsened recently as the energy of the Shift and Ascension intensifies what is held within us—the good and the bad—but we must be wary of being sucked into fear scenarios of world-wide catastrophes. They are now unfounded, only delay our progress, and make it more difficult to embrace the higher-consciousness attitudes that *will* help bring forth a more peaceful world. The darkness in our world *is* being displaced—just as when light shines in the dark, the darkness disappears. We just have to look at how many people are crying out for fairness and equality for all, and honesty and transparency from those in power.

According to Walter, enough people have allowed sufficient light to be infused into their beings by adopting the lighter qualities of the Oneness paradigm, and this along with the abundance of light being showered upon the earth at this time of Ascension is helping to dislodge what is not of light. The more of us who focus on the positive, lighter, and inclusive attitudes, the faster those who still hold negative, darker, and divisive attitudes will relinquish them.

Gaia's Ascension: A Cosmic, Universal Event

In *The Great Awakening,* Linda Dillon tells us this is a unique time for Gaia, as the Council of Love (the name for the many light-beings, ascended masters, and archangels she channels) tell us that Gaia has never ascended. This is why at this time "there are beings from all over the galaxy and far beyond who have come to witness, help, and participate in this Great Awakening."[12] The ascended masters, archangels, the light-beings that manage the Universe, as well as many ETs from the higher realms are all assisting us in a myriad of unseen ways to help us make our Ascensions with Gaia. And they are waiting with bated breath! Whether our individual Ascensions happen slowly over time, in increments, or as a rush as described in the possible rapture scenario I mentioned in chapter 7, we are all primed for this to happen. And it is not just us and Gaia!

In his talk "On Ascension," Mark Torgeson tells us that it is not only Gaia but also our sun and solar system that are ascending. In fact our sun is "taking the whole solar system with it ... [and we] are just part of the physical reality that is being swept along."[13]

Not only that, it is actually the cosmic time for the whole Universe to ascend to a higher consciousness, and we are helping it along. This huge undertaking of the completion of Humanity's difficult journey to overcome all the manifestations of duality while in physical form holds enormous value for the Universe. Gaia's Ascension out of duality serves to elevate the vibration of the whole Universe on its journey back to Oneness. So our personal Ascensions and that of Gaia may play a far larger role in the big picture than we could ever imagine, as they will not only benefit us, but the solar system and Universe as well—a vital part of all of our journeys from the illusionary world of form to its complete reemergence with Oneness. The Ascension of Gaia is truly a cosmic event of huge proportions.

Ascension: the Fulfillment of an Ancient Promise

This Ascension is the end of the twenty-six-thousand-year cosmic yuga cycle previously explained in chapter 7, whereby we (Gaia and her inhabitants) are to make a Shift in consciousness from the auspices of duality, its ideas of separation, and all their manifestations. This time has been spoken of in many of the ancient texts. In his article "Ascension Has Been in the Works for a Very Long Time," Steve Beckow reminds us that "Ascension is the fulfillment of an ancient promise," and tells us that SaLuSa said in 2009 that our continued belief in the completion of that ancient promise—that "the end times would see you restored to the higher dimensions" has kept us from completely losing hope for a better future for the inhabitants of earth.[14] This Ascension may well be but one leg of our reemerging *completely* with the Oneness and is still within the illusion of time and space, but the fulfillment of the promise of this Ascension within our time-space reality will start to usher in:

> *the restoration of Love on Earth. The restoration of peace and harmony, where all beings have the opportunity to experience love, joy, peace in physicality and form. It is not about abandoning human form. It is about surrendering the pattern of living from our heads instead of our hearts.*
> —Linda Dillon[15]

In the next chapter, we will look at our individual and collective futures as well as that of the Planet.

CHAPTER 11

The Future

It's never too late to be what you might have been.
—George Eliot (Mary Ann Evans)[1]

Our Futures Will Embody Compassion, Fairness, Equality, Acceptance, and Positive Attitudes

Just as we have the power to become all that we can be, we also have the power to create a beautiful, clean, safe world where everybody thrives. A world in which our futures are no longer characterized by the fears and limitations of the negative associations we unknowingly allowed to filter through to every aspect of our lives.

The dark forces within some of those who manifested on earth not only withheld from us the knowledge of the power we hold within, they used their power to control and engender fear in us, luring us into a fear-lack paradigm. This kept us vulnerable, powerless, and victimized, affecting the full spectrum of Humanity's existence. However, we now understand their moves and have caught them at their game.

We now know that we are powerful beings, have learned how to develop our sense of empowerment, and understand that we can create the life and world we want by being positive, hopeful, and standing up for ourselves and the disenfranchised.

Armed with the knowledge that there *is* enough to go around, we no longer buy into the fear-lack paradigm we had been manipulated into. We are taking back our power. In her article "November Waves and Responsible Creation," Sandra Walter addresses the dark forces that have kept us down by undermining our power saying, "Clever move, dear dark ones. Well played."[2] I say, our turn. Checkmate!

Horrific things are still going on in the world as the dark forces continue to lure us into fear scenarios but thankfully, most of us not in their clutches avoid falling prey to their tactics. Many individuals who have been directly affected by hate crimes, like Malala Yousafzai and Scarlett Lewis, are courageously facing the injustices put upon them without yielding to feelings of revenge or fear. Groups of people, like those living in Paris at the time of the terrorist bombings in November 2015, and the LGBT community after the brutal Orlando shooting in June 2016, refused to allow fear to overtake their lives, as evidenced by Paris's immediate return to its outgoing, vibrant self, and the LGBT's continuation of pride month. Most of us are dealing with what we have to, head-on, while embracing the qualities of compassion and hope inherent in the light of the Oneness. We are no longer yielding to fear based in attitudes of darkness and its divisiveness. More of us are cultivating our personal power, our connectedness to each other, and to the Oneness paradigm.

This Shift we are in the process of anchoring in is encouraging us to become one with ourselves, one with others, and one with the All. In *A New Earth*, Eckhart Tolle tells us that "underneath the surface appearance, everything is not only connected with everything else, but also with the Source of all life out of which it came."[3] Nature is the closest manifestation on our Planet to which we can align ourselves. This is why Siddhartha tells Govinda that the river spoke to him. This is also why the Indigenous people honor all of nature: in doing so they acknowledge the embodiment of Creator, Source, and the Oneness within it. Tolle writes that even when we acknowledge this Oneness by honoring our connections or commune with nature, we are but scratching the surface of the Oneness we are all a part of.

In our human capacity, the best way we can *fully* embrace the light of the Oneness within us is by extending its qualities to others. However, we have to first cultivate the qualities of love within ourselves, as this allows us to more easily see them in others. We can then focus on the commonalities we share instead of on our differences and separateness. We are then more inclined to extend love's qualities to everyone: our loved ones, those in our communities, and finally the world. This not only further anchors the love within us it sparks the remembrance of it in those we offer it to. Knowing of our individual power as well as our ability to connect to and extend the light and love within us, Humanity is finally ready to overcome its negative programming, become accepting of all others, and grow into who we were meant to be.

Many Attempts to Overcome Humanity's Programming

There are many stories and legends in ancient history that show how Humanity failed in its efforts to overcome the auspices of duality's hate, greed, control, and brutality. Inevitably, the many steps forward were repeatedly followed by more steps back. Recently, we have been on a positive trajectory with more steps forward than backward.

Everywhere we turn people are calling for fairness, justice, and equality for all, transparency from those in power positions, and reconciliatory measures for individuals or groups of people whom we allowed to become disenfranchised. Soon, our future will hold only steps forward! We can refer to illustration 10, "Our Exponential Function," from chapter 2 to see how steps forward coalesce to gain momentous energy and then take a sharp turn upward. Recognizing that we are approaching the sharp turn upward can encourage us when we see or hear of unfairness, inequality, cruelty, or chaos still manifesting in our world. It has been a long road to get from the brutality of the past towards the masses to this forward momentum of compassion and fairness for all. I think it is helpful to map out the ups and downs in our history that brought us to this place of only-forward motion.

Ancient History; the Masters of Old

Hopi historical accounts tell us that we lived a quiet, peaceful existence for a while, but then were forced to go underground because the world had become uninhabitable as Gaia adjusted herself to the negativity we put upon her. Their traditions report that this happened many times, and that each time we reemerged, we were further alienated from our origins. Whether we take this literally or metaphorically, the message is the same.

Many believe Lemuria was an ancient continent occupying the area that is now the Pacific Ocean and that like Atlantis, it now lies buried beneath the seas. Some believe that many from these civilizations were more advanced spiritually than we are now. Whether through the misuse of advanced technology or simply by the polarity of the divisive positive and negative forces within the people, they destroyed themselves before they could finish their journeys of Ascension.

Ancient Egypt was a highly spiritual place, but as duality played out, somehow true knowledge was lost, as evidenced by their focus on the body as being crucial to the afterlife. Many efforts were made to return Egypt to its glory days, but as their territory was invaded and they attempted to defend their land, they fell into a defensive, combative mentality. This disrupted the "Maat" of the land (the ideal balance, harmony, morality, and justice the leaders aimed for) and the people became fearful and dissatisfaction set it, which drove the country as a whole further away from a true connection to the Oneness paradigm. Pharaoh Akhenaten attempted to rebalance his people, but was denounced as a heretic and dethroned.

Later on many masters were sent to us, but much of their teaching was misconstrued, ignored, or misrepresented. Ideologies were created in their name, but a great deal of it served to divide rather than unite their followers. Buddha sought to undo dualistic mind-sets by encouraging people to completely embrace compassion. Then Jesus came and exemplified the concepts of Oneness with his teaching of unconditional love and forgiveness for all. Muhammad followed and tried as well to encourage the people to share, be compassionate, and be kind. Unfortunately, many of the intentions behind their lessons were lost.

We then fell into centuries of spiritual darkness as our duality continued to play out through greed, control, cruelty, warring mentalities, and our need for power. Among other ways, this need for control and power played out through the ideologies we had created and paved the way for the Holy Wars and the Inquisitions. Glimmers of light were scattered throughout this era, as with the 13th century Sufi poet Rumi who through his writings answered the longing of our hearts for its connection to our Source, and the brutality we lived under created cries to the Universe demanding a gentler and fairer society. A deep spiritual awareness was rekindled.

The Renaissance Created a Glimmer of Hope

Following the Dark Ages and late Middle Ages, the writers, poets, and artists of the Renaissance period spoke to the core of people's beings. Their work illustrated human frailties and evoked emotions that touched our very souls. Shakespeare and Da Vinci reminded people that they could still marvel in awe, and later, Victor Hugo's writings gave a voice to distress while at the same time evoked a spirit of hope.

This era also birthed scientists, like Galileo and Copernicus who unlocked mysteries of the Universe that were misunderstood. Martin Luther challenged the rigorous rules of the Church, and the mystic Teresa of Avila advocated contemplation and Christian meditation practices that brought one to an exalted state, synonymous with experiences of Eastern meditation practices. However, many of these forward thinkers were feared by those in power and were jailed or killed for heresy as their beliefs deviated from those of the established rules of church and state.

The same enlightened energy of the Renaissance sparked the urge to leave Europe and search afar. Even though this impulse was likely brought on by the desire to make a fresh start on new frontiers and escape the atmosphere of hatred and brutality that had recently rocked Europe with its witch hunts and the Inquisition, the support for these voyages was based in power and economics and sanctioned by politicians and the church. And not everyone was ready to embrace gentle, fair, and peaceful behaviors. Even if the individuals who inspired these expeditions had pure intentions, the cruelty that had characterized many at that time followed, and European explorers imposed it on the Indigenous people of the new lands. By the middle of the twentieth century after the two world wars, the impulse to demand a gentler and fairer society came through once again.

The Twentieth Century and Those Who Inspired
Us to Fulfill the Promises of Old

In the earliest part of the twentieth century, Gandhi promoted nonviolent civil disobedience among his people to help eradicate poverty for the masses and to attain fairness and equality for all in India. During this same period, Mother Teresa became known to the world for her compassionate and selfless work tending to the sick, starving, and poor. Nelson Mandela emerged about the same time, with his legacy being that he influenced the end of apartheid in South Africa.

Since World War II the inner and outer pleas to replace cruelty and brutality with compassion and fairness brought forth charismatic leaders such as John F. Kennedy, Robert Kennedy, and Martin Luther King Jr. to help guide us to more enlightened attitudes. They were all assassinated. However, their messages were not completely lost as they have inspired many to carry on their work towards fairness and equality. This era also brought out others, and with popular slogans such as "Make love, not war," the energy, speeches, and words put to music of those who came forth during the '60s touched hearts and souls and encouraged people to think about practical as well as spiritual matters. Over time, however, the movement lost its force, as the social systems in place were resistant to change. But the general spirit of the '60s was never completely snuffed out.

Today, truth seekers who represent social justice and spiritual, religious, scientific, cosmic, and psychological areas are bringing together the concepts that were birthed in the earlier parts of the twentieth century and the '60s, by tying everything together in a way that now offers concrete substance and practical applications. As we are giving form to esoteric concepts and clearing up misconceptions that have created conflict within our religions, these new ways of understanding are gaining more-widespread support. After many, many tries, Humanity is now ready to embrace the equality and fairness for all that we have so longed for. We are ready for our Ascension out of third-dimensional living.

At the Pinnacle of Our Evolution

At this time of the Shift we are all *awakening* to the truth of who we are, the truth of who our brothers and sisters on the Planet we share are, and are starting to embrace the concrete changes all this brings with it. We are all primed to become the best and most empowered expressions of ourselves. The Adam of the Bible, who represents all of us and who fell under a great sleep, is awakening! Humanity is awakening from the illusions of who and what we are!

While it may not be apparent in all areas of our world today, most of us are primed to embrace our shared connection to the Oneness we emanated from and extend its inherent qualities to others. We are starting to manifest what will bring about a safe, fair, and egalitarian world, where everyone has what they need to survive and thrive and is free to live in alignment with who and what their soul wants to bring forth.

The children of those born since the enlightenment era of the '60s, especially those birthed from within the bubble of energy following the '87 Harmonic Convergence, simply *expect* a peaceful, just, and equitable world, and they are here to help us firmly grasp the ideas of compassion, fairness, acceptance, and equality necessary to bring it about. They reject ideas of inequality and prejudice. They don't accept that people should be taken advantage of by business, bullied by government, or be talked down to by religious hierarchy. They embrace ideas that align with practices that help our Planet thrive. They are not in denial of the consequences of actions and do not buy into the illusions that past generations did. They will be the leaders of the new era we are ushering in.

We now understand it is more beneficial to work with others in relationships: personally, professionally, and for the betterment of our communities and the world. In his article "Lifting The Veil; The Forming of Sacred Partnerships," Steve Beckow recounts Archangel Michael's message— that we will start to see the light in one another, be able to overlook our apparent differences, and join with others for personal and world-related issues. Michael says this is "happening at an unprecedented rate, and it is happening in terms of union of friendships, of groups, of what we would call partnerships or sacred unions ... Even strangers across the lands, across the continents, are realizing, 'I need to be working. I need to be talking. I need to be playing. I need to be in a form of relationship with that person, or with that group of people.'"[4]

Acknowledging that many of us have feared to speak up and talk about the way we feel about the world around us, which has kept us at arm's length from others, Michael explains that joining with others at this time of the unfolding of our True Selves and Ascension is not only part of the plan, "it *is* the plan ... [which] has always been one of union and reunion."[5]

People, especially the younger generation, are yearning to do something with their lives—to make a difference. In a discussion on Oprah's "Super Soul Sunday" broadcast, Marie Forleo told us that in her consultations with young people they seem to "have a sense of urgency, especially women. They yearn to show up and to make a difference, not just to have a paycheck."[6]

Those within different cultures, religions, and races will start to work together. Almost fifteen years ago in the Alpha DVD series (basically a

Christianity 101), Nicky Gumbel suggested it was time for the different branches of Christianity to work together and focus on their similarities.[7] That is a good start, and I believe to some degree they have, but we still need to aim higher. To bring about the loving, peaceful world we all want, just as we have to reconcile our differences within our families and those around us to have peaceful lives, we have to make peace with the differences between the various religions instead of trying to prove which one is better by focusing on their differences.

Reconciling Our Present Realities While Creating a Better Future

While we aim to create better lives for ourselves and a better world, we must also acknowledge and work within the present realities. As we build confidence in ourselves to feel and give love and treat others fairly, we will feel empowered enough to make decisions that create harmony and only positively affect our families, communities, and the world around us. We will start to embrace the concept of "the good of the all, rather than the good of the few," and our actions will align with and reflect this precept. As we will have the awareness to connect the dots between our actions, their outcomes, and the repercussions they could have on others, we will make conscious choices that will not generate negative consequences.

Ripple Effects of Dysfunctions and Past Actions Take Time to Disappear

Whether in our personal lives, regarding others, our communities, or the environment once we become aware of and change our personal dysfunctional behaviors or negative attitudes toward others or actions that harm our Planet, we will still see the ripple effects for a while. The repercussions will not fade away immediately.

Shifts we make regarding our individual or family issues will not always bring about huge immediate changes. It takes time for decades of dysfunctional behavior to heal once we shift our attitudes, for the effects of a lifetime of unhealthy habits to abate, or for years of irresponsible spending to turn into financial balance. Even when we become aware of and change unfair or prejudice attitudes toward others, the fall out from years or even centuries of unjustness takes time to heal, as ripple effects often pass down through the generations. And urgent as it is to get the processes going, changes we make toward our environment and the Planet will not bring about many immediate results. So we must not get discouraged if we do not see any instantaneous effects of our efforts.

Sustainability, Energy Issue, and the Future

Most of us are not out in the world promoting sustainable living as our life-long mission. However, in our everyday lives we can make small choices to minimize the impact of our footprints on Gaia. We can recycle diligently, choose more-energy-efficient transportation, and buy more local goods and food supplies. And we can continue to uphold concepts of sustainability while still embracing other cultures and their tastes. Chef Michael Smith, of *Chef Abroad* and *Chef Michael's Kitchen*, supports sustainability, and I once heard him say that we should think universal but buy local when shopping and planning our meals. This encourages us to adapt the goods we have locally while still enjoying the flavors of the many fine cuisines from around the world.

Energy-efficient solutions are increasingly being adopted, but at the moment most of us are still at least somewhat dependent on oil and gas to heat homes, drive cars, and travel. And even the governments who support fossil-free living have to balance this without throwing millions of people out of jobs. We have the technology for the change over to happen; we just have to invest in the projects. So we have to support and vote in those who can and will do it. It won't happen overnight, but Gaia's Ascension is encouraging us towards cleaner energy and inspiring us to develop even better, safer, and cleaner energy sources than we have already discovered.

In his June 3, 2014, message, Matthew Ward said we will slowly "forsake fossil fuels as renewable energy sources expand" and that when Gaia has raised her vibrations up enough, "when Earth is within energy planes where photons are more numerous than electrons, [we] will be using 'free energy' only."[8] Ilie Pandia concurs that we will one day have access to free energy. In his article, "Free Energy," he asks us to imagine a world where free energy is abundant through the access to "unlimited clean Energy and devices to convert that energy to various useful forms for us: electric, thermal and mechanic." However, he maintains that we have to fully *believe* in this world and bring it forth by our alignment with its possibility. He says that this *is* possible, and free energy will change our lives dramatically, but we have to reprogram our minds to believe it.

Explaining that our political, socioeconomic system has been based on the control and power those in charge have wielded over us to the point that we unknowingly created a "collective agreement to 'not even imagine abundance,'" Pandia tells us that it will take collective optimistic vibrations to bring the world we want into our sphere of possibilities and overrule the lack paradigm that remains firmly entrenched in our unconscious minds. He suggests that much could be done if we were to use our imaginations in the opposite way they have been programmed—to reach for and therefore bring forth abundance instead of lack. The huge profits for the few at our expense could become obsolete, and instead of the exploitation of funds, quality would remain.[9]

The availability of free energy is in the realm of possibilities. However, *we must believe in this potential*; this will help Gaia align herself to the higher dimension from which we can more easily bring it forth.

The State of the World and Doing Our Part

Even though most of us won't be able to make major changes in the world, we can all change our thoughts, shift our attitudes, and make small choices that are better for everyone. Even small shifts in attitudes affect those around us, and they then affect those around them. This will then affect *all* the generations afterward. We can also learn to connect the dots between our actions and their consequences and thereby affect the quality of life of those around us.

We *can* educate ourselves as to how to leave a lighter footprint on the Planet. We *can* demand and support government programs to uphold these concepts. We *can* be cognizant of the effects of our consumer choices on our health, the environment, and the economies of our countries. We *can* make more energetically sound choices. We *can* embrace dialogue and mediation of conflicts with those around us. We also *can* encourage conciliatory solutions at all levels of social and governmental systems, both at the micro-and macro levels, for the small and larger issues—all for the betterment of the people of the world.

We know what to do and have the expertise to fix the inequalities and inadequacies in our world, but as Bernie Sanders tells us in his speech at the Vatican on April 15th, 2016 "our challenge is mostly a moral one, to redirect our efforts and vision to the common good."[10] Every little redirection of our efforts helps the whole cause. However, we must remind ourselves that major changes come about slowly, and not allow ourselves to become apathetic because of what we still see going on in the world nor be discouraged by how slowly social, economic, and environmental changes come about. We must be hopeful about our futures.

Hope: Encourages Us, Holds Our Dreams Together, and Keeps Our Efforts Moving Forward

The most important thing to remember in wanting to create a better world is to maintain the positive and uplifting vibrations congruent with creating what we want. We must dream of the world we long for, believe we can bring it about, and keep the dream alive by directing our vibrations to where a brighter world may flourish. Hope is the harbinger that will keep the dream alive and help us create the world we so long for. Hope keeps the door open to bring about our dreams.

Feeling discouraged by what we see going on in the world is not an option as we continue to challenge our governments, businesses, and associations about all issues that will affect us in the near and distant future and hold accountable those who profit at the expense of everyday people. And while demanding changes and compensation for those who have been mistreated, it is important to do so with confidence and conviction, always maintaining integrity and holding to positive vibrations.

We cannot afford to get caught up in drama and blame scenarios or focus our energies on the many conspiracy theories that abound, as this creates static and blocks in our energetic patterns. Even though we have had to unearth, acknowledge, and work to fix what is wrong in the world—just as we do individually with ourselves, getting caught up in anger, revenge, or blame thought patterns or scenarios hampers our Ascension process. No matter how dire things may appear at times, or how discouraging our movement toward a better world seems, we must never give up hope.

Having hope at the forefront of our thoughts also helps keep people with negative energies away, while attracting to us those who are on the same wavelength as we are. Although the affirming people we do attract won't necessarily have the same habits, exact values, or spiritual or religious beliefs, nor the same approaches or energy levels that we do, they will have integrity and a positive outlook about what we are all aiming for. As we attract more like-minded people into our sphere this will boost our confidence as we continue to go forth, creating an upward spiraling movement toward our goals for a better and fairer world.

The Powerful Multidimensional Beings We Are

Our newfound heart openings will start to unblock all our chakras helping us feel lighter and better and improving our relationships. It will also allow us to connect to our God-selves, which will help us uncover our life purposes and bring forth our Best Selves.

Many among those teaching within the religions and spiritual communities are now encouraging us to listen to our little inner voice, because whatever we call it— innate wisdom, our higher Self, God, Spirit, or Holy Spirit, this divine guidance we can all connect to will whisper to us what we need to hear. This will become the norm in the future. As we connect to our God-selves, we move away from needing to go to a minister or priest to get our answers or have a guru to help us grow spiritually. We will all start to recognize that *we* can connect to the God part of ourselves and step into the power it holds;

we can become the creator beings we were meant to be; *we* can bring about what we want individually, for those around us, and for the world as a whole.

No More Fear In Hearing Divine Guidance

As the limitations of our third-dimensional existence fade away, we will be able to sense and communicate with those beings in the other dimensions that we have an affinity with, beings we worked with in other lifetimes, or who simply speak to and through us in this one. We may have been guided by or have a strong connection to an archangel, ascended master, or light-being who speaks through us to help us individually and/or to inspire us as how to help at this time of planetary awakening. This is all just part of the veil of our forgetfulness lifting as we break through the limitations we all unknowingly erected.

Even though we easily quote the words of the prophets and sages of old, in our past or more recent history hearing divine guidance has not been accepted. Only a few centuries ago all too many were denounced as witches or accused of heresy, and today anyone claiming divine guidance is often looked upon suspiciously, scoffed at, or even accused of insanity. In her talk "Becoming High Frequency," Shelley Yates, who has been guided by light-beings since her near-death experience, explains that her ex-husband tried to have her committed for hearing voices; but the Supreme Court of Canada did not uphold the ruling, going so far as to state that the world could benefit from more people who share her worldview of love, fairness, empowerment, connectedness, and unity.[11]

As we continue to learn about the Universe and our place in it, start to adapt to the new energies around us, and open up to all that we can be, our fears about our individual divine connections and ability to communicate with those in the higher realms will diminish. And as we continue to open up spiritually, the veil of forgetfulness drawn over our connection to the cosmos will fall, and we will be able to connect to the multidimensional beings that we are.

Embracing Our Star Brothers and Sisters

As explained in chapter 7, many believe that at least some of us (we are still figuring this part out) originated from other planets, and although most have no sense of this, some have, and more and more people will start to feel a connection to their origins.

One day soon, be it three, thirty, or three hundred years from now, communing with those on the higher planes will once again become the norm. To get there however, we must be ready to relinquish our third-dimensional attitudes and fears. The masters will return as they said they would, but not until we have learned the lessons they left us with.

Also, even though most of us are not aware of it, many believe that thousands of spaceships currently surround our Planet and are infusing us with light and positive energy, and that many high-vibration beings from other planets are even living here among us now and are some of the way-showers guiding us and Gaia with our Ascensions.

Although in the past some extraterrestrials who visited earth had malicious intent, this is no longer true, as Sandra Walter already told us in her article "November Waves and Responsible Creation," which I talked about in chapter 9. It is by divine degree that we will no longer be bothered by the dark ones who plagued us in the past. We have now embraced our power.

Whether three, thirty or three hundred years from now, our future *will* include us inviting those from other planets—on our terms for camaraderie and possibly to assist us with issues concerning our Planet—if we have not yet figured them out on our own. Just as did many of our ancient civilizations, we will one day return to the mutually advantageous and friendly relations with the more spiritually evolved extraterrestrials.

Awareness of Cities of Light

Many believe that there are cities of light existing in parallel realities and that we can see and have access to them when we are attuned to their higher vibrations. We cannot see them from within the density of our third-dimensional awareness as time and space are part of its illusion, but within the holographic nature of the Universe they exist now, just within a different reality than that which most of us are still experiencing. Once we are more fully aligned to the higher vibrations in the Universe, even more help will be made available to us, as these cities of light can provide physical and spiritual healing. However, we will only be able to see them and benefit from what they have to offer once we have released enough denseness and allowed enough light to permeate our beings.

These golden, crystalline cities of light just beyond our awareness are in proximity to areas that are known for having spiritual strength such as Sedona, Arizona; Mt. Shasta, California; Machu Picchu, Peru; and Mongolia, China. They are portals to other dimensions. In her article "Crystalline Cities of Light," the now-deceased Amorah Quan Yin tells us that on one of her journeys to Mt. Shasta a lighted being that presented itself as Jesus told her that at some point in the future the whole of the city of Mt. Shasta and its adjacent areas would be "anchored as a living City of Light" and that it would be the first one to function on earth adhering to the higher universal principles.[12] When this happens, we will be able to take advantage of its healing modalities. Although it was Jesus who appeared to her, it could have been any of the masters.

These cities of light are spoken of in our various scriptures and may be what is referred to in Revelation 21:10–11: "In a vision he took me to a towering mountain peak and from there I watched that wondrous city, the holy Jerusalem, descending out of the skies from God. It was filled with the glory of God, and flashed and glowed like a precious gem, crystal clear like jasper." I believe the author of Revelation was given a vision of the potential for this powerful energy center, or portal, located in Jerusalem and of how this beautiful city beaming with the light of love and harmony of God came down to earth.

In a parallel reality or universe of a higher dimension, Jerusalem already exists as this wondrous, crystalline holy city healed of all its conflicts, but will remain beyond our awareness until we raise our vibrations enough so that the three religions and their followers who claim it as their own can embrace their common purpose, to know God, and adhere to the intended attitudes and qualities they were based on. We will only reach that awareness when hatred, divisiveness, and conflict are replaced with love, unity, and harmony—despite our differences.

The cities of light not yet visible to most of us are already being used by the higher-dimensional beings for our benefit. Quan Yin states that Mt. Shasta now acts as a retreat for "the Great White Brotherhood: a mystical order of Light-Beings, both human and higher-dimensional, who are working on behalf of Earth's spiritual awakening and ascension."[13] As we release the constraints of our limited awareness and vision, we may have occasional glimpses of these highly spiritual manifestations of love and harmony and be invited to visit them for spiritual enhancement and physical healing.

Gentle, Enlightened People to Lead Us Into the Future

Every generation has come forth more enlightened that the last. Every time-frame of our history has produced light holders to guide us out of our dualistic thinking, but we usually ignored, belittled, or even killed them. However, we are now better prepared to support those who come to lead us into a more harmonious world, and most of the youth of today are rejecting the corrupt politics and selfish business tactics that further inequality and injustice. They have come into the world enlightened enough to demand the empowerment they know is their right and that of all people. They will not adhere to societal norms based on prejudice or inequality nor buy into the fear those in power positions attempt to wield.

Many of us now understand or have even tasted empowerment as the lack, fear, and greed paradigms we have lived under have been exposed and have started to crumble. We are no longer interested in relinquishing our individual sense of hope and power this has left us with. New, bright, shining lights and leaders are now among us to continue the work of those who, in our most recent history, paved the way for us to see more clearly into a bright and better future.

In the past few years, Malala Yousafzai's example of courage and fearlessness against insurmountable odds exemplifies how we can move gracefully beyond our hurts, rise above injustices put upon us, and despite these still work toward a more egalitarian society. I also believe that the influence of this Shift brought with it many people in high standings who will use their great power for the good of all.

World and Government Leaders Coming
Forth to Answer the Shift's Call

The recent appointment of Pope Francis is another manifestation of the Shift toward a more honest, fair, and gentle society. While promoting changes from within the Church, as he walks among the people, he encourages believers and impresses those with no religious affiliations. He is starting to challenge outdated principles the Church held to that do not align with the attitudes of the Shift, is addressing past behaviors perpetrated by the Church that hurt others, and has reached out to the leaders of the Christian Orthodox Church and some within the Muslim and Jewish faiths.

In the fall of 2015 Pope Francis wrote a paper on climate change that he delivered to the world, which was widely praised by environmentalists. I even heard David Suzuki say in an interview that it was so insightful and knowledgeable that he wished he could take credit for it. This new Pope has reminded us that we no longer have authority over our lives because money rules all aspects of it, and has asked the political and financial leaders of the world to adopt financial practices taking into account and based on moral principles.

On numerous occasions Pope Francis has publicly apologized for priests who molested children (boys & girls) and has put in place internal measures to remove future offenders. He has also publically apologized for the mistreatments of Indigenous peoples by those representing the Church as they created settlements in new countries and attempted to control and convert the native people with cruel and abusive methods. He has communed and prayed with leaders of the Muslim and Jewish faiths, and met with the leader of one of the largest Russian Orthodox churches—the first meeting of these two sects within the last 1000 years—all with the aim to break down the barriers that divide them so that they can work together to help those who are suffering in the world. He has even now told Christians to stop trying to convert Jewish people.

Pope Francis has clearly come through at this time of the Shift to help us reconcile what has gone on in the past at the hands of those who claimed to represent the Catholic Church, as well as guide us towards a safer, kinder, gentler, more compassionate and egalitarian world.

Infused with the energy this Shift has ushered in within the last few decades, young royals throughout much of the world are now attuned to the plight of their subjects and to people around the world—much more than their predecessors were. I believe their futures will be characterized by a more judicious use of their energy, wealth, and power to help bring about a safer, fairer, and more equitable world.

This Shift is also bringing forth government leaders who align with the attitudes it is asking of us. In the fall of 2015 Canada elected the candidate to lead our country whose aim is to foster a co-operative, transparent, government promoting inclusiveness, with its focus on unity and hope rather than exercise a dictatorial approach perpetuating divisiveness and fear. Marrying both gender and cultural equality, Mr. Trudeau appointed a 50/50 female/male cabinet which included individuals from nearly every ethnic and religious background of our citizens. He has not only made addressing the many First Nations issues a priority, but encourages us to look to them for guidance regarding the environment. This government recognizes the necessity to factor ecology into their decision making, and vowed to partner and consult with the First Nations communities when making decisions that could impact their land.

Trudeau also gave Parliament the mandate to accept 25, 000 Syrian refugees as soon as possible (with more to follow) at a time when it was not very popular to do so. With the necessary due diligence to immigration processes, this forward-thinking attitude based in positivity and hope instead of negativity and fear demonstrates how we *can* reconcile present realities while creating a better future for the world. Never having been especially patriotic, I now feel *very* proud to be a Canadian. I believe this new government answered the call of the people and this Shift with its positive attitude and co-operative, inclusive, consultative approach.

May of 2016 saw more proof of the focus on our differences fall away, as London voted in Sadiq Khan, a human rights activist, and the first Muslim mayor in the Western world.

As this book is in its final proofreading stage in June of 2016, the Unites States is in the midst of a contentious election whose main contenders hold a variety of attitudes and approaches—from calm, composed, and respectful focusing on the issues, to aggressive, bullying, tactics that promote divisiveness and aim to undermine their opponents. The immense and unexpected support for the two anti-establishment candidates shows that people are now more motivated than ever to take back their sense of empowerment, which is a clear indication of the Shift at work.

The surprising support for Bernie Sanders, who ran his campaign free from the tutelage of establishment government, shows that the people in the U.S. are no longer interested in being at the beck and call of the machine that disenfranchises them. And although Donald Trump's platform has a negative spin, which preys on fear and harbors prejudices and aggressive tactics, he has still garnered much support. However, in the face of what is going on in the world today, it is hard not to get lured into fear scenarios, so some of us will continue to be drawn to support that which is not 100% ideal as we attempt to reach for our empowerment in a world that does not yet totally support all the qualities of the Shift. Clearly though, much inner-juggling is going on and people want to feel empowered and be free of corrupt establishment government and their mignons.

One generation, one bright-light, or a single leader can drastically shift the trajectory of where we are going as they answer the call of what people are ready to hear and embrace. Change has always come about because people cry out for it and the Universe answers.

However, change often requires letting go of what we know, are used to, and are comfortable with. Some are willing to embrace the required changes to create a better, fairer, and more egalitarian world where we all live in relative comfort on a healthy Planet. Some refuse to relinquish their power positions, while others afraid of change want to keep the status-quo. Still others are unbelievers or simply pessimistic pronouncing that the hopes and dreams for a fairer, egalitarian world are lofty, unattainable, and pie-in-the-sky aspirations to be scoffed at.

Thankfully, the energy of the Shift is evoking powerful forces to bring about what is required at this time in our evolution, including bringing moral principles into our financial practices like Pope Francis asked of our political leaders. Working towards fairness and equality for all is spirituality/Godliness made manifest. More and more people are starting to do so and inspiring others to join them or continue their work.

In Mark Schmanko's recent insightful article "Bernie Sanders: A Deeply Spiritual Politician" he tells us that "Bernie Sanders manifests the potential … to ignite a movement of 'civic spirituality,' something we desperately need in these times [and is] … a voice not just of hope and idealistic change, but a deeply motivating and highly practical force in the world, committed to transformation, social justice—and showing, not telling, leadership and goodness in action."[14]

Sanders is clearly answering this call to change the Shift brings with it, and is a good example of how a proclaimed non-religious person can promote highly spiritual ideals with such honesty, clarity, and conviction so as to create a movement. His unexpected rise in popularity shows that he has voiced what many want to hear and that he has gained their trust. He is the inspiration inducing the next generation to come forth and participate in the political process. They will be the vanguards to usher in the world their beautiful souls came here to bring about.

I will end this chapter with a quote from a letter by the late Jack Layton, former Leader of our National Democratic Party (NDP), who throughout his political career consistently stood for fairness and equality for all. Shortly before his death in August 2011, he addressed Canadians in writing, encouraging us toward the ideals he stood for. These principles outline the future we were all promised eons ago and are now ready to work toward and embrace.

> *We can build a better one—a [world] of greater equality,*
> *justice, and opportunity. We can build a prosperous economy*
> *and a society that shares its benefits more fairly.*
> *We can look after our seniors. We can offer better futures for our children.*
> *We can do our part to save the world's environment.*
> *My friends, love is better than anger.*
> *Hope is better than fear. Optimism is better than despair.*
> *So let us be loving, hopeful and optimistic. And we'll change the world.*
> —Jack Layton[15]

Conclusion

It is both our commission and our destiny
to fully awaken … and eventually return home.
—Drs. Ronald and Mary Hulnick[1]

It Doesn't Matter …

To be happy and contented, feel empowered, and to ascend with Gaia it doesn't matter whether you believe in, understand, or practice any of the spiritual concepts within this book, or elsewhere. Nor do you have to believe in the Shift or Ascension. It doesn't matter whether you believe in or care about our connection to ETs, the existence of Atlantis and Lemuria, who the masters were or the details of their births, deaths, or time on earth. You just have to embrace love and its qualities and find your empowerment. What matters is what is in your heart.

By embracing life and your passions, finding joy, and making choices that do not harm others or instil shame or guilt within your being, you are riding the wave of the Shift on your way to eventual reemergence with the Source we all came from. You just need to align with your God-self and uncover the place within you where peace and joy abide.

Feeling love, peace, joy, happiness, and empowerment is our birthright!

Embracing Our Birthright: Who We Are Meant to Be

You have to claim your birthright. You have to have the courage and audacity to reach for and then embrace it! You have to listen to what your heart whispers to you. It is guiding you towards your Best Self, so you have to believe what it is telling you and mobilize your being into the positive and/or empowering direction it is guiding you towards. You *can* create the life you really want—the one that whispers to you within the depths of your heart but that you have often silenced—the one most of us have not dared believe we can achieve. And if you hear any murmurs of fear, limitation, or thoughts of not being good or deserving enough, remove what is in the way of reaching your most fulfilled and empowered Best Self.

Truly Loving Ourselves / Getting Addicted to Love

The Shift brings with it an impetus to release propensities to hold on to the emotional weight and burdens of buried pains and misperceptions. It encourages us to replace these with the peace and harmony that truly loving ourselves can bring. We can then live embracing our full potential as limitless beings becoming the empowered *unique* expressions of the Oneness we were meant to be. In his article "Addicted to Love and the Middle Way," Steve Beckow shares insights that came to him as he was releasing deep-set vasanas that helped him embrace being "addicted to love" rather than holding on to the pain of the past. We can use these as guidelines to live by and as affirmations to help us do so.[2]

- I love myself. I take care of myself. I'm responsible for my own well-being;
- My life is a workshop. My life is an experiment. My life is a meditation;
- My life is a walk of faith. There's no other way I could do it;
- I get to craft my life in any way I want. But I remain responsible for what I do with every minute of every hour of every day;
- I almost-completely walk forward in my life and use reverse gear sparingly and in emergencies;
- I keep my engagements but make them seldom, to avoid stress, and only after having estimated the cost.

Answering Our Calls to Passion

We all came here with a higher purpose: to learn, to experience, and to help others through their life lessons. These show up as the passions within us, and they play out in many ways. Our passions always bring us joy, make us feel alive, and keep us feeling empowered. (The article "How Embracing our Passions Helps the World" found on the book's website expands on these suggestions below).

- If your passion calls you to work for the betterment of people, animals, the Planet, or the world in general—*do it!*
- If your passion calls you to teach—*become an educator!*
- If passion calls you to create a loving family—*do it!*
- If you feel passionate about cooking, farming, or the food industry in general—*embrace it!*
- If passion calls you to the business community, technical industry, or any other seemingly everyday job or career path—*answer the call!*
- If you feel passionate about art, music, dance, writing, and so on—*embrace it!*

It doesn't matter what we do in life. What is important is that we answer the call of our hearts, make conscious decisions, and have passion for and bring integrity into what we do.

Help and Compassion for Others, While Still Empowering Them

Ultimately we are only responsible for our own lives and spiritual growth. We all have our own life plan and lessons to learn, or not learn, and can actually curtail others' growth by stepping in too much, as we disempower them from finding authority over their own lives. Not only are we not privy to others' soul life plans, they also have to do their own work to grow spiritually and become their Best Selves. Those around us are not meant to evolve in the same way we do nor on the same timeline.

In *Loyalty to Your Soul*, Drs. Ronald and Mary Hulnick explain that one of their principles in living with loyalty to our souls is to understand that the "physical-world reality exists for the purpose of spiritual evolution … [through our] different spiritual curriculums." When we understand this, we can stop projecting our ideas of happiness or life purpose onto others. They recount an incident when they witnessed a young man in a wheelchair who clearly had physical disabilities and seemed to be mentally distant. The attending physician noticed their discomfort at the man's situation and explained that if they could see past his disabilities, they would perceive that this was all part of his spiritual curriculum in this lifetime. The Hulnicks realized that in their judgment of the young man's situation, their sympathy was "self-referenced."[3] We tend to put ourselves into other people's situations and decide we do not like or could not handle that and then project this onto them. We must remember the well known axiom that God doesn't give us more in life than we can handle. So even if we think we could not handle a certain situation.

> *We all have individual life curriculums: it is our life purpose to discover and respond to them!*

Sometimes it is in our souls' life plan to simply bear what life has given us and find peace with our circumstances, while for others it may be to overcome life's conditions. It is a fine line to walk to be nonresistant and not push *against* life, create a better life situation, while still being grateful for what we now have. We all have to find the balance between working within the realities of our lives and our world while aiming to create new and better realities wherever possible.

> *When creating new realities we have to acknowledge the current ones.*

Steps to Overcoming Unhappiness, Frustration, Inertia, Limitation, or Addiction

Even if we are simply plagued with inertia or have been in a holding pattern not knowing what to do in life, we can rise above feeling unsettled. We *can* overcome unhappiness, frustration, limitation, bad lifestyle choices or addictions that keep us from being the best we can be. To do so however, requires being proactive and taking the necessary steps—even if it is just making life lists or lists to help us find or reconnect to our passions. And it is important to match the type of problem with the correct approach. Lofty spiritual concepts cannot address deeply entrenched issues or addictions. We must use the appropriate tool geared towards the specific problem. Below is a recap of some of the suggestions I have discussed. (The article "Aids to Overcoming Our Issues" found on the book's website expands on these suggestions).

- Acknowledge and deal with what is making you feel bad;
- Make life lists;
- Do or redo any of my worksheets;
- Use affirmations daily;
- Get help with any issues in your life—NOW;
- Buy/rent/borrow material you are drawn to;
- Cultivate joy;
- Take up a centering practice;
- Make necessary life changes;
- Yell at God or the Universe—if you must.

We all have what we need inside us to become the most empowered versions of our self. So remove what is in the way of doing so, and grab onto it!

Don't let the sun go down on your Best Self.
Decide now! Take action!

Self-Forgiveness Is Paramount in Making the Required Shifts

Forgiving ourselves for all that we have done and not done, the time we have wasted in life, money we have squandered, addictions we have succumbed to, or the hurt we have caused others is vital to becoming our Best Self. (The article "Self-Forgiveness Is Paramount" found on the book's website explains the importance of these two concepts listed below).

- <u>We forgive ourselves for undermining becoming our Best Selves</u>: for any attitudes or behaviors that have kept *us* from living empowered or life to the fullest; and/or
- <u>We forgive ourselves for hurting others</u>: if our attitudes, actions, or non actions adversely affected others, or even our loved ones.

Overcoming the effects of our dysfunctional attitudes and behaviors helps others as well. When those around us see that we can move from acknowledgment to remorse, and then to healing and wholeness, they may realize that they can as well. Metaphorically jumping off a bridge because we have done bad things doesn't show others how to move on from their mistakes. Most of us have something to forgive ourselves for, make peace with, or overcome. And sometimes it is simple inertia and not being able to move forward in life.

Do Not Lose Hope if You Feel Stuck

For a few years before this book started coming together, and after I had finished with my university classes, I spent three or so years feeling as if I was flailing around in life. I knew I had something to say, and I spent every day writing something, reading associated material, and browsing related websites. However, the writing had no form or goal. I felt like a loser when I whittled the day away reading or perusing websites that engrossed me, which I now know were part of the learning groundwork I needed to do for this book. However, it did not feel like that at the time. Nor did I understand that I was in a holding pattern preparing and waiting for clearer instructions from the Universe— as have many of us in recent years.

The energy of this Shift may have kept us from going in the wrong direction, but we may not always have been able to connect to what to do next.

Those three years when I was plagued with inertia and felt inadequate and lazy were actually like a classroom for me, and I came out the other end clear, fresh, and ready for the next stage in life. Here I am now four years later having finished a book of this scope. So you need not despair if things do not appear to be coming together for you right now as it is often in times of great inertia that there is much inner juggling going on, but because it is difficult to recognize as such, it may make us feel inadequate.

Society has dictated that we should always be doing something concrete to move ourselves forward, but we are now learning the importance of being present and taking time to rejuvenate ourselves and to listen to what our souls are trying to tell us. This Shift is encouraging us to move away from the rat race type of existence that has plagued us for more than half a century. I believe the generation just entering the work force innately knows this. So as long as we are not hurting others, jeopardizing our job (unless it is time for a change), or shirking the responsibilities we have to others, it is best to just go with the flow. We will be given what we need. I had the good fortune to be set up in life to take those years to do what I now realize was research (not wasted time as it then felt) and did not have anyone to answer to nor responsibilities to take me off task.

There is a cosmic purpose to all our circumstances, as well as to our relationships: the good parts and the seemingly bad parts. And often when we find our way out of our misery, we share that journey with others, along with our new understanding of the pitfalls, tools, and practices that helped us—just as I am with this book. This usually just happens naturally.

When our way forward is not clearly defined, going with the flow
of where we are now keeps pathways open to the wisdom
within us needed for the next step.
Fighting where we are now closes those pathways.

When Our Life, or the World, Is Not How We Want

Most of us are just doing our best to get along in the world. We are either acting in ways we think we need to be happy, feel empowered, or to be a good person, or we are under the influence of unconscious influences. We have all been heavily influenced by the conditioning that Humanity has encouraged, and we were never taught other than to allow our feelings and their reactions to have their way. This has often created conflicts in our lives and derailed our efforts toward happiness.

Our Feelings Are Often Untrustworthy

It is important to acknowledge our feelings, as they are how our inner beings let us know where we are aligned or misaligned with Source, and when acted upon can guide us toward change and betterment. However, we cannot trust and act upon *all* our feelings, as they may be based in neediness or the result of being stuck in a spiral of negativity. Our feelings do not always show us a true picture. To examine what our feelings are urging us to say or do, we can ask ourselves questions like the following:

- Will giving in to this urge *ultimately* make me feel better?
- Will it solve the problem?
- Will I be filled with guilt and remorse later?
- Will it guide me toward changes I know I need to make for a better life?

- Will it serve the ideals I want to hold?
- Will it harm others?

When we act on an urge it is often our way of dealing with a feeling we cannot face, such as frustration, loneliness, sadness, anger, disempowerment, feeling inadequate, etc. This may cause us to overeat, overdrink, overspend, do drugs, hang out with people who derail us from attaining our goals, take a job only for the prestige and/or money, or hook up with someone because they are sexy, rich, or powerful. However, these attempts to overcome our feelings will not satisfy us in the end.

We need to start directing our energies toward things that will bring us, and the world, peace and happiness—the things that matter. In *The Only Thing That Matters: Conversations With Humanity*, Neale Donald Walsch tells us that 98% of the world is spending 98% of their time doing things that don't matter. He explains that the soul knows what it is supposed to be doing, what will bring us joy, and be in our best interests. He says that we uncover this not by finding what we are supposed to be doing, but by remembering: this is not a discovery process that needs to be researched but a *recovery* process whereby something is retrieved. Walsch tells us that when both our minds and souls have the same understanding, we are then living consciously.[4] When we live consciously and in touch with our True Self, we can hear our soul's reminders of what we came here to do. However, we still have to stay mindful of where our feelings are coming from.

Trust your feelings, your gut-instincts.
At the same time, be wary of neediness masquerading as true feelings:
these phony urgings may lead you to unhealthy attitudes or choices.

Maintaining Mindfulness and Conscious Awareness

To become conscious of the effects we are or will have on our own and others' lives, be that a decision we have to make or continuing to hold to old or outdated attitudes or beliefs, questioning ourselves helps determine whether our attitudes reflect the ideals we strive for and gives us insight into our real intentions. We can ask ourselves:

- What is the purpose for my words or actions regarding this issue?
- What will the ultimate consequences be to me and those involved?
- Do my thoughts, attitudes, words, and actions uphold the idea of God's love and the Oneness we all emanated from, or do they uphold ideas of our separateness?
- Do my thoughts and attitudes create harmony within my being?

- Do they create a cavern between me and my True Self, and thereby with others?
- Do these thoughts and attitudes promote harmony with all others?
- Do they align me fully with my God-self?

We have to be honest when we ask our self these questions. Our unconscious influences can encourage us to act impulsively or make forceful suggestions we think will help another. Clinging to any outdated or misguided beliefs or ideals may be based in fear of change and can influence us to criticize others' choices, lifestyles, or ways of being in the world.

When we promote beliefs, ideals, or how we think people should be in the world by pointing out how others are wrong—even if we are sincere—doing so only endorses divisiveness: it does not promote unity or God's love. Our beliefs may offer us a very valuable support system and by promoting them we are doing what we think is helpful or right but we can be erroneous in our interpretation of them or misguided in our approach. This Shift's energy is flushing out all divisive attitudes or actions, and they will be exposed for what they are. If in our approach we judge others and focus on peoples' differences, we create conflict. If we do not change our methods there will be fallout. When we create conflict it always reverberates back to us, sooner or later. When we push too hard to make our point, or push against something, at this point in our evolution the Universe will push back: we will experience the repercussions of our endorsement of divisive attitudes.

Unconditional love accepts:
it does not blame, shame, criticize, belittle, or push against.

Are Our Attitudes and Behaviors Bringing into
Our Sphere Who and What We Want?

When things around us are not as we would like them to be, it may simply be because timing and circumstances are out of our control. Things rarely change immediately, so be patient, keep positive, and take care to ensure that your attitudes and behaviors do not undermine what you want. It does not compute to:

- Demean family members and generate conflict in our household and then expect a loving, peaceful family life;
- Criticize the wealthy and then complain that we are not experiencing abundance;
- Marry or partner-up *only* for security and then wonder why we have no passion and intimacy in our lives;

- Marry *only* for passion and intimacy without considering practical matters and wonder why we have no security in our lives;
- Promote our ways as loving, right, and godly while at the same time criticize other people, their beliefs, or how they express themselves in the world;
- Choose to have a quiet, stress-free, peaceful life and then be envious of what high achievers are manifesting and experiencing.

If we are lonely, have trouble connecting with people, or are not invited along with others, examining how our attitudes, reactions, and actions may be perceived by people may offer important insights as to why they may not want to socialize with us.

- Are we loud, pushy, or constantly interrupt others thereby dominating conversations?
- Are we negative, a complainer, critical, argumentative, or judgmental?
- Are we needy—always expecting others to do everything, entertain us, or answer our every whim?
- Do we draw others in, like answering the phone with "nice to hear from you," or push them away with a dismissive response like "what's up?"

In the Universe there is no right or wrong, only the understanding that everything is just the playing out of duality and our perceived separation from Source. We can hold on to any attitude and behave in any way we want, but if we want things to change we have to ensure that what is held in our Life Matrix supports what we want in life.

If life is not going your way;
first look to your own attitudes, responses, and behaviors.

Giving up All Ideas of Separation is a Required Course

We all have to overcome concepts based in duality and its temptation to focus on our differences. A Course in Miracles tells us that it is a "required course." This does not mean that we all have to study its big blue book or use its terminology. It means that at some point in our soul's journey we have to stop focusing on our separateness. The *me-and-you* and *me-versus-you*, and the *me-and them* and *us-versus-them* attitudes uphold ideas of separateness. They only promote divisiveness. Where divisiveness treads love cannot flourish. Where there is no love, peace, joy, and happiness cannot survive. *Getting this* is what will change us and the world!

Taking issue with or being upset by others' attitudes, cultural, religious, or sexual differences, or allowing certain situations to bug us only serves to reinforce the illusion of our separateness from God, from each other, and distances us from the only thing that is real: Love. While practicing and living in accord with the concepts of this Oneness paradigm, we create the peaceful feelings we all crave as well as the positive life experiences we all want, because what we extend to others gets infused into our vibratory mix and becomes part of our Life Matrix.

Love and its qualities changes the world for the better.
Not rules; not religions; not government!
However, these may facilitate change.

Creating the World We Want

It is essential to focus on what we want the world to be, not on what it has been. If we focus on all the negativity that has gone on or is still going on, we reinforce those low vibrations within our being and they become part of our Life Matrix and thereby attract more negativity to us, as well as into the world. We also need to feel grateful for all the recent positive efforts and progress concerning the treatment of people, animals, and Gaia. However, to create the world we want we have to acknowledge past actions that benefited us at the expense of others and address the fallout.

We may proudly pronounce that we want to continue to uphold the values and ideals of our countries' forefathers, but are we aware enough to recognize that we have not, in essence, held onto many of those high ideals, such as equality for all?

We certainly did not! The truth is that we continuously laid claim to land to build our wonderful nations through cheating, lying, and broken treaties with the Indigenous people whose lives, livelihood, and culture we changed forever. Nor were they upheld as we used or abused immigrants that came to our lands looking for a better life, or allowed segregation and thereby marginalization of African Americans to flourish. Once we acknowledge and understand these facts and then support efforts for reconciliation, we can then move forward proudly with a positive attitude based in truth not denial.

Because the mass media tends to focus on the negativity that is going on in the world, it can be difficult to recognize the significant advances Humanity has made in the past few years leading up to and within the recent timeframe of the Shift. In all walks of life people are standing up for the rights of those who are abused or marginalized because of race, sex, religion, social status, and sexual orientation, as well as for the plight of animals and the betterment of our Planet. We are starting to reject the rat race which has made us stressed, mentally and physically tired, and even sick. It has also stunted our spiritual growth.

Ten years ago "living in the moment" and "being present" were relatively unknown concepts. These terms are now part of our vernacular and are regularly used by individuals, teachers, and ministers. Even media personalities and celebrities increasingly use and endorse these notions. Our world *is* changing! But we must remember to continue to be grateful for all that we have and are becoming, as gratitude attracts back to us more of the same and thereby moves our world in a positive direction. Focusing on the negative aspects of what is still going on in the world or what has gone on in our past does not move us forward.

Within the course of Humanity's history and our various lifetimes we have all been perpetrators and victims. This fact, coupled with the understanding of the dualistic system of the lack and fear paradigm we have been under, allows us to forgive what has and is still taking place in the world. It is only when we do understand and forgive our collective past that we erase the impact of its negative attitudes and actions still held in our cellular memories. This opens up the space for forward movement to create a better world. Forgiving attitudes about what happened in the past anchors in the possibility for a future full of good stuff for all of us.

To help achieve this, it can help to reflect on the examples of those of the recent past, notably Gandhi, Mother Teresa, Martin Luther King Jr., and Nelson Mandela who offered us glimpses of how to truly exemplify love, compassion, cooperation, and forgiveness. We can take action if we feel inclined to do so—sign petitions, send money, or do whatever is appropriate for our life circumstances to help—while keeping alive the spirit of the peacemakers who came before us. It may be difficult at times to avoid negative attitudes seeping through regarding a distressing situation, but we must challenge ourselves to do so. Mother Teresa once said that she would march *for* peace, but *not against* war. She did not give war any mental energy. This is the type of focus we need to help bring about a peaceful life for ourselves, our communities, and the world.

> *We must acknowledge Humanity's past—without blame;*
> *We must forgive it all—we were all only living in darkness;*
> *When we aim to fix, we must do so without blame, judgment, or vengeance.*

Most of us will not be directly involved in helping to bring about major changes in the world, but we can all do our little parts as well as ensure that our attitudes and actions are attuned with concepts of unity, compassion, and Oneness. Even small shifts in attitudes affect those around us, and this then influences those around them. This will trickle down to all the generations afterward. On an individual level, we must ensure that our attitudes and actions are consistent with what we want to see in the world. It does not compute to:

- Complain about what is happening in our communities, cities, and countries yet not vote for or support efforts for improvement;
- Continuously shop at the dollar store or buy imported goods and then complain about the lack of jobs at home;
- Drive gas-guzzling cars and then complain about pollution;
- Be prejudiced against other cultures and then complain about the lack of world peace;
- Cheat on our taxes or fudge our expense accounts while complaining about corruption in government and big business.

This is not a judgment on how we behave, but a reminder to connect the dots between our attitudes and actions and what we wish to see in the world. As we adjust our attitudes and do our little parts, we align ourselves with the benevolent creative force that is overseeing the big picture. And even though there is still much negativity in the world, it is also vital to keep hope alive.

The Audacity of Hope5

- Hope is the fiber that holds our fears at bay and the thread that keeps our dreams alive;
- Hope allows us to dream of better lives for ourselves and our families and for a safe, fair, and equitable world—even if we cannot see evidence of it now;
- Hope gives us courage to go on when we are in pain, our families are in pain, or pain is splashed all over our newscasts;
- Just as with love, hope has no form. However, after love and gratitude, it is the most powerful attribute we can hold;
- Hope is the reason we dare to dream. For without the hope of the dream coming true, why bother to dream. Hope allows us to believe our desires and dreams are possible;
- At its highest level, hope brings with it the belief that there is a benevolent force that oversees everything and that all will eventually be ok.

It is the name of Barack Obama's book *The Audacity of Hope* that inspired me to write this section. As with any request or prayer, if we waver in the belief that a better world is attainable, we create static in the request. This lower vibration reduces the possibility of our creating a better world! So we *must* keep this hope alive—even in the face of all that is still going on.

We Must Do Our Part So Our Hopes Manifest

We are being hopeful when we believe that God/the Universe will take care of everything. Many believe that God will look after healing the Planet and help end the wars. This belief is somewhat valid, but we have gone against the laws of nature. We have not used the "free will" given us to maintain loving, reciprocal relationships with the Planet or with each other. So *we* must address and attempt to correct the effects of our misuse of her and make smart choices to help our Planet recover; it is also on us to attempt to mend the rifts within our families and those around us. Only then can God/the Universe step in to help further our cause. And when aiming to help the people in dictatorial or war-torn countries we must make wise choices taking into account the ripple effects of our efforts. We must also keep to attitudes that create positive vibrations regarding these worldly concerns so the collective vibration of Humanity encourages only constructive changes for the future. However, help may not come about as we may think.

Will governments finally take initiatives to enforce smart environmental practices? Will we support these, or complain about the costs? Will we encourage supporting inventors of technologies that could clean up the Planet, or denounce them as quacks? Will the technologies come from the extraterrestrials currently surrounding the Planet? We can pray for and encourage our governments to make the best choices regarding their defense strategies, but are we encouraging harmony within our families and communities? Are we being completely fair, loving, and accepting of those around us? Are we aware of the ripple effects our actions have on others? As well as doing our part, hope must be accompanied by an openness as to how changes will come about and the vibration of our attitudes must match what we are hoping our world will become.

We Can at Least Aim to Be Neutral, Not Adding Negativity to the World

Even if we have not overcome all of our unconscious influences or if our life circumstances do not allow us to actively participate in societal concerns, we can at least aim to be neutral, thereby not adding any negativity to the world. In *Power vs. Force* Dr. David R. Hawkins explains that neutral vibrations do not negatively influence the world. On his scale of vibrational Energy Levels (see chapter 7) he equates feelings and attitudes of neutrality with an energy level of 250, which is above the 200 minimum vibrational level to not negatively influence the world.[6] To become neutral we must work toward being accepting of those who are different from us, and avoid negatively pushing against situations that upset us. We can aim to:

- Practice nonresistance instead of total judgment and opposition towards others who are different than us. Finding some common ground helps, like recognizing that he, she, or they are only concerned about their family's welfare;
- Aspire to do no harm. Avoid creating disharmony around us, or adding fuel to volatile world situations with negative attitudes or discordant behaviors.

We cannot all positively affect world issues in concrete ways, but we can aspire to "do no harm." In an *Astronaut's Guide to Life on Earth*, Chris Hadfield suggests that until the time we *can* add value to the world we can at least "aim to be a zero." He says that by doing no harm and not creating disharmony around us our "impact is neutral and doesn't tip the balance one way or the other." Until that time when we can become "a plus one ... who actively adds value" to the world, we at least are not someone who is "a minus one: actively harmful."[7]

However, even when our actions are not negative, we are often unaware that we are creating negative vibrations, as our attitudes can hold mild disapprovals and biases that we may not consciously recognize, but which come through subtly, nonetheless. These can put us slightly on the minus side of zero, but we can avoid being there by ensuring our thoughts, words, and attitudes do not hold *any* negative or judgmental slants. While aiming for this zero effect may appear to be an ineffective way to deal with life and the world as we know it, we will all benefit if more of us shift from being minus one to zero, as we will not be negating those who are living as a plus one.

If all people who held any negativity in their Life Matrixes aimed for the zero effect, Humanity would quickly make a huge upward spiral.

Our Different Contributions Back to Oneness

We are all making different contributions to bring about the world we want on our way back to Oneness. However, we cannot all focus on everything, nor can we help everyone. There is *much* need in the world. We have all come out of the same history of duality playing itself out.

On an individual level most of us are (or have been) living in the grip of unconscious influences or neediness, and therefore many of our decisions had repercussions that left us further disconnected from our True Selves, feeling discouraged, and even needier. So many of us are needy in some way! It is impossible to answer the needs of everyone within our sphere or who fall across our path all the time. If we were to try to do so, our life-energy would be drained and there would be no room left for joy, a much needed quality which helps raise the Planet's vibration to the level that will bring about the world we want. We can at the very least be careful not to judge what others are or are not doing, as our souls' journeys and various contributions to this end are all different.

There is a lot of need in the world—individually and collectively: we cannot answer it all.

Some contributions are overt for all to see, like those who work on the world stage and rally others to help people or the Planet. They make things happen. Others' offerings are more covert, such as monks, yogis and people who spend hours a day in prayer or meditation, or even quiet, gentle people who live simple, uncomplicated existences savoring life's little pleasures. They help to stabilize and raise the vibrations of the Planet to the benefit of all. Both overt and covert offerings are needed, but these people often frustrate each other and do not get along because their different focuses require differing and contrasting energetic make-ups. Illustration 22 shows how our contributions all work together:

#22: Different Contributions Back to Oneness

No matter what your personality type, or what you feel guided to do in life, both overt and covert efforts are crucial in helping to raise the vibration of the Planet!

Relinquishing Our Ideals of Might-and-Fight

Our world is based on the *might-and-fight* paradigm. Humanity has been stuck in the fear and lack paradigm for so long that pitting ourselves against one another for power and control is our baseline. We have warred over land, goods, and anything else that has given us a real or false sense of security. We have trained our men and women to fight for and defend what is ours and to conquer what lies beyond. Indeed, all our borders have been erected in blood—all in the name of power, control, and money. Many of us are proud to say that *my country's army is the strongest in the world*. Protecting our citizens is important, however, the psyches of those trained to defend us are forever altered, as are those of the societies that have lived through the brutalities of war.

Even in our most recent history, as men and women took up positions in the various bodies to uphold justice, a controlling mind-set often took root, and superiority and brutality all too often became ingrained in the consciousness of these defenders. We have as a whole had to deal with the fallout from training people to kill, and have also had to contend with the fact that for the most part we are still upholding this might-and-fight ideal in many areas of society other than combat, like with our police forces. It is time for us to overcome this might-and-fight attitude. And the effects of doing so will not only help earth's inhabitants but will also reverberate throughout the whole Universe.

It is now clear that many of the gods of old were extraterrestrials. The ancient myths from the different cultures as well as our scriptures tell of some angry, warring, controlling, or power hungry gods. It is now pretty evident that most, if not all of us, originated from other planets. If these supposed gods were our guides, we may have adopted their warring mentalities. Part of this Shift and Humanity's challenge is to overcome this might-and-fight attitude—for us—but maybe also so that others in the Universe who still may be holding onto controlling, warring attitudes can pattern themselves after us for overcoming it. Fully embracing the Shift so that we can one day live in a peaceful world requires relinquishing the *might-and-fight attitude*. We can help bring about a more peaceful world if we replace notions such as *my country's army is stronger than yours* with those similar to *my country's people are contented*. This can come about, but we must ensure our attitudes match peaceful concepts and address past and current injustices that are affecting the contentment of some.

Making Right Our Past Injustices

Even though we have to forgive what Humanity has done in its past, we also have to make right the injustices we created that do not uphold the concepts of Oneness. We do this by creating new and supporting current programs that work toward:

- Lifting all our citizens out of poverty, as well as people around the world;
- Ensuring equality within the sexes and re-empowering women;
- Making right past injustices and eliminating all discrimination toward Indigenous people;
- Making right past injustices and eliminating all discrimination regarding those of a different color, race, culture, creed, or sexual orientation, etc.;
- Helping the men and women and their families who chose to serve to protect us by providing them with all necessary support after their return from duty, including healing from any fallout of the might-and-fight attitude that were instilled in them.

As outlined in his book, *The Last Hours of the Ancient Sunlight*, Thom Hartmann suggests it is to our benefit that we continue to re-empower women. He tells us that "in virtually all Older Cultures the women were of equal status with the men, and in a few they were even in charge ... They ran the show because they controlled life itself" by giving birth to the future generations. His research documented that in the Iroquois society, the women who were in places of power made assessments and choices based on the flourishing of the people rather than from arrogance or based on power struggles.[8]

Our Countries' Harmony Is Linked to Helping Indigenous People Heal

Many of us have not been aware of the extent and repercussions of the abuses of the Indigenous peoples when settlers came from Europe to the West in search of a better life and took over their land. This conquest paved the way for their comfortable lives, and now ours. To ensure we create a good and safe future for all of us it is important to acknowledge and address what our ancestors did.

Indigenous peoples tap into and retain their empowerment through their connection to the land and by adhering to their cultural traditions. By appropriating their lands and imposing our ways upon them we disempowered them, to say the least. As this Shift is guiding us towards fairness and equality, it is imperative that we now partner with the descendents of the Indigenous people to assist in their healing from the accumulative effects of past abuses, and to acknowledge and stop what we continue to do today to undermine their health, general welfare, and connection to the land which is *essential* to them being able to thrive. We need to create a partnership and work together to create a harmonious future that will benefit us all, and our future generations, on the lands we now share.

It is arrogant, even ignorant of us to complain about immigration and how those seeking a better life are changing the cultural landscape while we have not righted the wrongs made when our ancestors not only changed the Indigenous peoples' cultural landscape, but in many cases eradicated some tribes completely. If we want a harmonious future with those who are now immigrating into our countries as well as ensuring that our laws and the spirit of them are upheld, we must connect the dots between how we acted in the past towards the Indigenous people we usurped, the karma that was created, and what we want for our future. Past karma *can* be overcome when we choose to hold to positive attitudes around similar concepts and if we address the repercussions of past negative attitudes and their actions.

A New Normal: A New You

As you embrace what brings you joy and make any necessary attitude shifts, you are beginning to create a new normal. Whereas before you may have allowed yourself to live in a lackluster state in which life was only okay, you now make choices and embrace the things that bring you joy. If you were once inclined to automatically react with anger or blame, as you work to dismantle your false perceptions, you may begin to adopt neutral qualities that may appear dispassionate, and then slowly and surely move toward compassionate responses, acceptance of others, and a desire for fairness for all. These qualities will then become your new normal: the New You will emerge. Your new normal:

- Can connect more easily to light-heartedness and pure joy;
- Finds its sense of empowerment from within;
- Embodies self-confidence;
- Finds conviction in any newfound purposes;
- Personifies integrity and humility.

As the blocks and static to your True Self are removed you will be more attuned to natural gifts and abilities that have remained latent in you and can now be rekindled.

- You will have greater clarity of mind;
- You will be able to feel, hear, and sense things more easily;

- Your ability for discernment will be enhanced;
- Your intuition will increase;
- You will be able to create your own realities.

As your True Self is free to step forward and reveal itself, the New You that emerges is connected to the truth of who you are and your power base. You feel empowered, but from within, not through others or weak substitutes. There is no longer a need to *feel* powerful and significant—you embody power and significance. Past tendencies toward arrogance, greediness, or manipulative approaches disappear. A new way of being emerges.

As your new normal unfolds, your male and female energies will become more balanced. You will be able to embrace the positive aspects of your male and female energies while overcoming tendencies to bring forward the negative ones.

- Aggressive inclinations are tamed and redirected toward firm action;
- Passive tendencies are replaced by quiet, confident assuredness.

In *The New You*, Mother Mary, speaking through Linda Dillon, tells us that "balancing our masculine and feminine energies within ourselves is the key to understanding and expanding our beingness, of stepping into and anchoring the New You." She goes on to explain that neither energy is superior to the other but society has focused more on the alpha, male, doer, protection-oriented energy and has forgotten to "feed the goddess" parts of ourselves. Attention to the subtler parts within us is being revived and the remnants of old ways of perceiving ourselves are disappearing.[9]

The balancing of our male and female energies will make us feel energized, as the imbalance of these seemingly opposing forces encourages us to deny the important more subtle aspects of ourselves.

Taking Responsibility for Our Lives Empowers Us

Once you have cleansed yourself of the attitudes that detract you from being your Best Self, the New You that emerges encourages you to:

- Take responsibility for your happiness and life so you no longer blame others or circumstances;
- Take responsibility for your attitudes and actions toward others;
- Become conscious of the effects your decisions have on others and the world around you;
- Rise up and find your empowerment;

- Step into the full potential of why you came here at this important time in our history.

To take responsibility for our lives and be aware of how our attitudes and behaviors affect others means we must live consciously. Jean-Paul Sartre, one of the leading philosophers of the 20th century, tells us that "to be conscious is to be faced with choices about what to believe and what to do. To be conscious is to be free."[10] Once we are free of our unconscious influences, we can more easily discern attitudes and actions that empower us without negatively impacting others, which would create conflict or incur karmic debt. We are also better equipped to question any misguided or outdated beliefs that do not ultimately serve us or promote harmony around us. We are then ready to fully embrace our empowerment and allow our life-path to reveal itself to us.

Our Cleansing Done; Our Path Unfolds

Once we start to release the blocks to our God-selves, we will have glimpses of what our new paths will look like. In *Positioned to Bless*, Faisal Malick tells us that we have been in a "season of preparation ... of alignment ... The Lord is causing his people to change, to look deep into their hearts." Malick reminds us what we are told in Joshua 3:5: "Consecrate yourselves, for tomorrow the Lord will do amazing things among you." We must cleanse ourselves of influences that detract us from stepping into the highest expressions of ourselves so we can embrace why we came here at this important time in our history.[11]

It is time for us all to step into our God-given power. For some this may just be to speak up for them self so that they can have authority over their lives. Their example will also serve to teach others in their sphere about empowerment. For others it may mean finally taking action regarding how to proceed on a certain issue that has stumped or intimidated them. Still others may now feel inspired to speak up, support, or rally others to correct some kind of unfairness or abuse of people, animals, or the Planet.

Knowledge, Belief Systems, the Gods, Universal Help

Our Religions Hold Much Healing Power, but also Many Conflicts

It is understandably difficult for one who strongly adheres to a religious belief to question which parts of its practice or scriptures speak the truth and which do not. This is especially true for those whose lives have been completely turned around by embracing a certain faith or belief system to better cope with grief, severe depression, addiction, etc., because in order to heal they had to give themselves to it 100% and embrace it fully.

The best way to deal with perceived conflicts within our scriptures or with what clashes with them today is to hold fast to the concepts that uphold notions of unconditional love, and to ask for insight or clarification of those that do not. Despite all their discrepancies our scriptures still hold great power. We can find comfort and connect to Spirit and our God-self through any of the spiritual paths or different religions. We may even be guided to draw on different aspects of more than one of them, as I do.

It was intended that we could all find our own ways, through whichever path or paths we choose. I once heard Rabbi Susan Silverman explain in an interview that we are all prophets and that when the Torah was given, there was an understanding that it was to speak to us directly and be interpreted through our hearts. We are only now finally beginning to do this, as the knowledge of our ability to allow the texts to speak directly to us was kept hidden from us. This was done to control us, but also for our own good.

Knowledge Was Hidden from Us Until We Were Ready to Use It Wisely

Knowledge of the powers we hold to direct our lives is only now being unearthed within mainstream society. This is being done within the individual religions, as well as by laying them alongside one another. Dr. Jim Richards, a theologian working under the Christian umbrella, also uses ideas from Eastern philosophies so we may benefit from *all* the knowledge given to us throughout the ages.

Although many within the Christian community denounce Eastern beliefs, there are few correlations within them that we may have overlooked. For instance, the Bible states that it was three *wise men* from the East who brought Jesus gifts, and there are also many themes within Proverbs that are based in wisdom congruent with the Tao and other Eastern religions and philosophies. Completely rejecting the wisdom found in these or other religions seems counterproductive, especially at this time of the Shift when we are being urged towards reconciliation in all areas.

Within the hierarchical systems of the original Christian church as it was being formed almost two thousand years ago, many of the truths about our inner power were hidden. The political systems of the day were based on power and control, so rather than encouraging the growing Christ followers to create their own power structures, the government stepped in and created the Church under its own political system. However, this may have been agreed upon by the true followers for our individual protection, as many at that time were not enlightened enough to make judicious use of the powers within the practices and heightened spiritual connections.

Don Miguel Ruiz concurs that we were not ready to use our power wisely before this new millennium. In *The Four Agreements* he explains how one thousand years ago, his ancestors, the Toltecs of Mexico, were forced to "conceal the ancestral wisdom and maintain its existence in obscurity." Because of a few apprentices' abuses of the power, it was feared that common knowledge of our inner power be misused for personal gain. This esoteric knowledge was then passed on through generations of the different lineages until the time when Humanity was evolved enough to handle the responsibility of the full impact of these esoteric understandings.[12] The time is now!

Messages of Love, Forgiveness, Compassion, and Acceptance: the Most Important Elements

Our connection to Spirit and our God-selves does not depend on the form it takes or on our belief in the various rituals and symbols within our belief systems. There has been so much confusion and contention regarding the symbols and who and what they represent within the different belief systems, so that instead of their uniting us in God's love, we allowed them to separate us. It is the messages and intentions within our belief systems as well as our ability to revel in the energy our scriptures impart into our being that are important.

In Ken Wapnick's article, "The Treachery of Images," he compares our ability to understand the real meaning between the words from the messages of written or oral teachings to understanding the intention behind the notes in a great piece of music or an opera.[13] The premise is that it is not the form or the perfection in the notes that moves us, but the spirit and intention with which they were written and performed. And so it is with the stories, symbols, and explanations in our scriptures. It is not the form they have taken but the intended teachings and the experiences they direct us to that is important.

Likewise, we do not have to believe the full story of the Buddha's or Krishna's journey and lives to allow the wisdom of their teachings to guide us. Embracing Jesus' messages of unconditional love and forgiveness is more important than concerning ourselves with particulars such as the Virgin Mary's immaculate conception.

Respect for All Belief Systems

We often think we are observing the basic messages of our belief systems because we extend them to the people we love and to those who look and act in ways consistent with our beliefs. Embracing the masters' concepts of compassion and unconditional love means we should extend them to *all* people—even when their beliefs or ways of being in the world are different than ours. We have to be especially careful when promoting spiritual or religious beliefs—especially if they promote judgment of others and/or foster divisive attitudes.

Because of the energy, light, and love this Shift brings with it, the darkness of non-acceptance will stand out and we will have to address it. If we continue to harbor divisive attitudes we will be reproached, and create disharmony around us. At this time in our evolution, when we push against or criticize anything or anybody for their beliefs or ways of being in the world, Universal Laws will prevail and we will get a push-back. And the stronger we push the stronger the push-back. No matter how our belief system may help and nourish us spiritually or how strongly we adhere to their doctrines, it is vital that we be non-judgmental of others' beliefs and what *their* belief systems bring to them.

During a public lecture in Montreal in the fall of 2011, the Dalai Lama said that it is good to embrace and believe in the power of our belief systems—110%. He also stated that it is crucial to recognize that this is *our* chosen path, that all other paths are equally good, and that we *must* respect others and their beliefs. However, we can all learn from and even adopt practices from each other. It would be beneficial to work together to try to help each other discover all the truths within our belief systems.

The Master's Messages Come Through in Many Ways

The messages inherent in our belief systems come through to us in many forms—and not just through formal religion. Throughout history people have been inspired to teach, write, and sing about the basic principles the masters taught.

Many are still comforted and inspired by the writings of Ste. Teresa of Avila and St. John of the Cross from the 15th century, Shakespeare from the 16th century, the poets Rumi from the 13th century and Walt Whitman from the 19th century, and yogi Sri Ramana Maharshi in the 20th century. Songwriters like Bob Dylan, John Lennon, Neil Young, and Bono encourage us to call for a more loving, fairer, and peaceful world, while most of the messages of the younger musicians of today embrace concepts of love, acceptance, fairness, freedom, and empowerment, like Katy Perry telling us in "Firework" to get out from under and let our light shine. Whether through books or for the screen, writers have also been inspired to help us see our erroneous ways.

In one of the original Star Trek episodes the Enterprise lands on a less evolved planet because of malfunctions and it needing repairs. Although the ship was hidden in a large cave and the crew thought they would be undetected, some of the planet's inhabitants stumbled upon them. As the people came to know the visitors they became enthralled with all they could do and started to perceive these more evolved beings as gods. They eventually started fighting among themselves over how much adulation and power they should give them. This episode helped sensitize viewers to what we are now discovering about those we once called gods.

In an episode of one of the earlier seasons of the television series, Game of Thrones, Catelyn Stark speaks of how she now understands that the hate she always held for her husband's illegitimate child brought about the tragedies which befell her family. She connected the dots between what she put out into the world and what came back to her. Although now a commonly understood tenet among spiritual seekers, seeing her make this connection may have inspired those not aware of it to further explore this concept, or even examine their own attitudes.

I believe there is more than a superficial reason for cult followings of musicians, writers, and shows such as these. While entertaining they address, explain, and even guide us to a new perception of many of the issues we have had, or now face—from both an individual and societal perspective. Those of us not involved with any formal spiritual or religious group have gotten their intended messages indirectly through people who are inspired in many different ways to move and enlighten us. Coming from within that surge of peace and love energy of the '60s, how can one listen to John Lennon's "Imagine" and not see how he was encouraging us to bring about a world of love and peace most of us hoped for then and are now making concrete efforts to bring about? It may have taken another half century, but the spark that was lit back then is now a blazing fire.

The ET Connection Is Not the Be-All-End-All of Our Existence

Even if we could prove that those who were considered to be gods were extraterrestrials, establish that we did come from the stars, and that we can and will discover our planetary origins—then what? This would still not answer the question of "Why are we here?" or, "What is our ultimate purpose?" Finding our planetary origins is but one step in discovering the truth—that we (and everything within the Universe including the stars, planets, solar systems, the archangels, masters, the ETs) emerged from the Oneness and are part of the playing out of the concepts of duality we originally chose, and that our ultimate purpose is to transcend *all* ideas of duality and separateness (of me-and-it, me-and-you, and us-and-them) within the Universe so we can *all* merge back with the Oneness. The ET connection is but one aspect of our journey.

In the past the extraterrestrials may have shared their technologies, other devices, or highly energetic stones or jewels and when discovered these artifacts may still retain the power to help us access other realities or higher dimensions, enabling us to create and manipulate energy and matter. However, this would only take us so far. Accessing power through technologies is not our ultimate purpose just as joining with our space brothers and sisters is not our final frontier. In our ultimate journey back to the Oneness source we emanated from, we will all at one point or another have to *energetically align* with all its qualities. The last remnants of dualistic thought systems and attitudes can only be completely replaced through the vibrations of our attitudes and choices based solely in concepts of love, harmony, unity of purpose, and Oneness.

I have attempted to tie the different areas of study in this book together and focus on what is similar so that we all have a better understanding of the mysteries of our existence, why we are the way we are, how to overcome our individual tendencies of negativity, blame, judgment, and biases, why hate and cruelty still exist in the world, and how to effectively deal with the negativity and chaos still going on without *us* falling into negative attitudes. However as I am not an academic I have approached subjects at a basic level aimed at the general public, and hopefully pointed those of you who wish to further investigate these subjects in the right direction.

In addition to the insights and knowledge I have garnered over the years, this book also draws extensively from many people I have met, heard speak, or read about. I may not agree with or embrace *all* their philosophies or their lifestyles, and do not suggest that you should, either. Nor do I expect you to agree with all that I have said. Most of us doing this kind of work are sincerely seeking to uncover many truths, but none of us have *all* the answers or can put all the pieces of the puzzle together.

So if something someone says here resonates with you in some area but not another, I suggest that you accept the insight as a gift, and practice some type of forgiveness to deal with what does not ring true within you. The love and light this Shift brings with it allows us to make peace with all our differences and interpretations, more than ever before.

The Shift and Our Near Future

This Shift brings with it light, love, and beautiful energy that opens up our hearts. It has the power to shift our attitudes and perceptions by giving us many aha moments, allowing us to make peace with others and/or difficult situations. It has inspired people like Malala Yousafzai (as well as her parents who believed she, not just her brothers, should be educated) Pope Francis, and Bernie Sanders, as well as many others all over the world, to speak to our innermost desire to create a fair and egalitarian world, articulate in very practical ways how to bring the necessary changes about, and mobilize people to action. Without bringing religion or dogma into the mix, these way-showers demonstrate how our spirituality and Godliness is made manifest by promoting and working towards fairness, equality, social justice for all, and for the health of our Planet.

This light, love, and energy of this Shift works to inspire us to relinquish the darkness within and that which supports darkness and separation in the world. The love and compassionate actions for and towards others are the result of this light, love, and energy becoming manifest. They will work in concert until all the darkness has been removed from each of us. I believe this last point I leave you with in this section, inspired by Ellen DeGeneres's final words on her daily show, "be kind to one another," will go a long way to shape our individual and collective near and distant futures.

Be authentic! Be kind to one another! Be good to Gaia!

Effects of Influx of Light and Love to Be Felt for Years

This Shift will continue to bring with it much light and love for many years until the light is fully reanchored in every cell of our beings. This light is crucial as it dispels the darkness within us. Its love reminds us of the truth of who we are. We need both of these. The light cuts through the darkness to dislodge it, and the love shines through the subsequent cracks and rekindles itself within us. These influxes of light and love often come in waves, bringing with them different sensations.

An influx in the spring of 2014 that some call the Tsunami of Love brought with it huge bursts of energy that penetrated to the core of our beings. These influxes of energy often just come upon us and we may feel like we have been hit by a wave or are overcome by a welling up of love or well-being. If we have the spiritual opening and have been taught how to deal with this, we simply embrace and revel in the experience. Should this happen to you and you feel like it is too much to take, ask Spirit (your inner self) to lessen it or to send it away. This may also be experienced as anxiety.

In his May 2014 article "Just Allow It," Steve Beckow tells us that during the middle of the night he awoke with an incredible sense of anxiety, which he interpreted as the Tsunami of Love that was currently in effect. Had he not recognized it as "a sense of alarm or panic in the face of an upwelling of energy," he might have thought he was "losing it." To overcome any sense of panic of this nature, we must tell ourselves that everything is okay and use one of the spiritual tools to send the energy of panic away. Beckow visualized the connection to the upsetting feelings being snipped away with a "pair of garden shears ... [and was left] feeling expanded, more stable, more loving, etc."[14] Abnormal physical sensations like light-headedness, headaches, or stomach upsets can also be attributed to these unaccustomed bursts of energy. If they persist seek medical council.

These bursts of light and energy may also stimulate issues to bubble up in us or dislodge remnants of buried past hurts, angers, or unmet expectations. These can lead to brief periods of sadness or mild depression. They are coming to the surface for release and our eventual liberation from the emotional component. When the light aiming to penetrate us meets any darkness still lurking within (conscious or unconscious) it stresses our beings and can manifest as either emotional or physical upsets. Collective pains of the past or present may also be stirred up and cause emotions to well up, even though we may not be aware of the collective connection.

The collective history of Humanity is still etched in our cellular memories, making it almost impossible to ignore what is still going on in the world that is not of love. With growing evidence that we have been controlled for years by the cabal and illuminati who infiltrate our governments, businesses, the Vatican, control the world monetary systems, and promote wars, our beings have to deal with the associated conscious or unconscious anger that comes with all this. So from now on, should you feel any physical or emotional sensations arise with no apparent cause, do the following:

- Check to ensure that any physical pain or symptom does not have a natural cause, or that it is not your inner being warning of danger nearby or reminding you that you are way off track on your soul's life plan;
- If none of the above, release your feelings of fear, anger, or panic and open yourself up to allow the love and light to penetrate you. It if becomes too much, ask for it to be removed;
- Momentarily acknowledge any bad feeling or fatigue, which may be the result of these infusions of light waves dislodging buried negative emotions, and then dispel the bad feelings or fatigue by using a releasing tool, such as Beckow's example to visualize the link being cut. If major feelings or issues arise, take the appropriate extra quiet time until you find your emotional equilibrium and/or joy surfaces;
- If you feel the need to cry or metaphorically pull the covers over your head, do so. These confusing feelings are the result of inner juggling from the pull-and-push of the light energy trying to penetrate your being through your created barriers.

These negative feelings should quickly abate as the light and love are powerful and will quickly do their job unless we fight it, and we are usually left with a beautiful, peaceful feeling. This influx of light and love has been necessary because Humanity became mired in living so far below the vibrational level we need to be at now. There is a link in my List of Recommendations to a meditation by Linda Dillon to engage this Tsunami of Love.

The Specialness of Humanity Now Understood

These influxes of light and love are part of the love and support we are given because of our importance in the Universe. Even our scriptures suggest that Humanity is special. One theory is that we were placed on earth to reclaim lost DNA as other beings in the Universe had lost some of theirs and could no longer recover it. We now understand that as we raise our consciousness out of third-dimensional attitudes and embrace the qualities inherent in the higher dimensions we are reclaiming our original 12-strand DNA. We also now know that this Shift and our and Gaia's Ascensions are raising the whole Universe into a higher dimension.

Humans were and still are well-respected within the higher realms for agreeing to manifest on earth to learn some of our lessons in the denseness of the third dimension with its duality and polarity: this is part of our specialness. It was also understood that we could become entangled in the darkness. Throughout history many of us have, as evidenced by all the brutality we inflicted on one another. But we have also received much help and support from those in the higher realms, like the masters and ETs who came to guide us.

We have been given all this attention because classroom earth held great potential. Crawling out of the denseness of the third dimension with duality and polarity firmly entrenched in it, free-will in place, the temptation of power, and the enticement of making solid form the most important aspect of our existence (most notably our bodies and their survival) would be a momentous feat with the benefits reverberating throughout the entire Universe. However, just as space is not our final frontier, earth is not our real home, and our bodies are but a tool with their principal function being to serve our ultimate purpose.

Earth—Our Temporary Home; Body and Mind—Our Vehicles

While we live in this world of form on Gaia, it is important to do all we can to make it a fairer, more loving and egalitarian place. However, earth is not our final home! The entire Universe was created to play out the duality we chose before any form existed, and the Universe and Gaia's purpose is to serve as a classroom to learn to reconnect to the Oneness we emerged from. Once we understand this, we can find comfort in creating a loving and compassionate world, as this is a step on the ladder of our returning to the Oneness. This understanding also helps us to more easily forgive any manifestations of duality still apparent in our world. However, embracing the qualities of Oneness while we are here helps us to climb out of the dualistic systems we have been stuck in. Our world is not our raison d'être, and neither are our bodies!

When we shift from being mind-centered to heart-centered and embrace the qualities of Oneness, we release our identification with the ego and its prize possession—the body. Our bodies act as masquerades of the separated Self and are a visible proof we buy into our differences and that we are separate from one another. We overcome our propensity to see our differences by relinquishing our identification with our minds and bodies. In *Power vs Force*, Dr. David R. Hawkins writes there is "great freedom in the realization that I 'have' a body and a mind, rather than I 'am' my mind or body."[15] Once we make this shift, we can use the mind and body as vehicles for endeavors guided by Spirit that will bring us joy individually and aim to unite rather than separate us. For the first time in our history, we now know how to temper the body and mind so that we can bring about inner shifts that will create new attitudes and actions which foster the qualities of love and Oneness, rather than those of fear and divisiveness.

Even though we came close many times in the past, the continued flourishing of highly spiritual ancient civilizations on earth like Lemuria, Atlantis, and ancient Egypt was never part of our cosmic plan. Their journeys were cycles Humanity had to undergo, and our cellular memories hold the lessons learned through their failures. Our cellular memories also retain all that was good. The lost civilizations were a vital part of the grand scheme of our unfolding, as the inner knowledge of their experiences continues to guide us. We are at the pinnacle of our evolution. Now is our time to complete Gaia's and Humanity's cycle mapped out in the cosmos at its very beginning.

> *Every choice of who and how to be is a choice of great consequence,*
> *as all of our choices reverberate through the ages ...*
> *The universe holds its breath as we choose, instant by instant,*
> *which pathway to follow;*
> *for the universe, the essence of life itself, is highly conscious.*
> *Every act, thought, and choice adds to a permanent mosaic;*
> *our decisions ripple through the universe of consciousness*
> *to affect the lives of all ...*
> *Everything in the universe is connected with everything else.*
> —Dr. David R. Hawkins[16]

Definitions
(see back page for code to download from the book's website)

Abundance Paradigm: An awareness of enough—without any awareness of limitation or lack. (chapter 1)

A Binding Universal Truth: We *all* came forth as loving expressions of the creative force of the Universe. Thus there is a pervasive Oneness that binds us together. (Introduction)

Best Self: We are our Best Self when we are aligned with our True Self. This manifests as happiness, acceptance of life and our circumstances, and connection to that part of our self that feels empowered, confident, assured, loving, giving, and emotionally healthy. (chapter 1)

Conscious Awareness: When living consciously we are aware of, have made peace with, or are simply not under any negative influence from our personal, cultural, or generational conditioning. (chapter 1)

Default Position: The reactionary, nonreactionary, or responsive way of dealing with others or situations. We respond with aggression, passivity, or neutrality. (chapter 1)

ego: On an *individual* level, ego is the manifestation of the separated Self. It is engrossed in itself, in the "I" of it all. It gives a running commentary of everything that is going on, could go on, or has gone on with us, with others, and in all situations. It upholds all ideas of separation, luring us away from being present in the moment, thereby separating us from the truth of who we are. It constantly compares, judges, and blames, thereby further separating us from others. It can be relentless, needs to protect itself, and is thereby defensive of upholding all its ideas of separateness. On a *cosmic* level, the ego, or Satan, is the negative energy that arose from the original judgment of the *false* notion that we separated from our Source, and thereby relinquished all the qualities it embodies. Ego was perpetuated by shame and guilt of what we thought we had done, as well as the fear of retribution. All our issues and everything that is *not of love and unity* is a manifestation of ego (or Satan). (chapter 1)

forgiveness: The forgiveness suggested by *The Course* is congruent with "making peace with." *The Course* suggests that we forgive ourselves and all others for all our *perceived* errors because we never did anything wrong: we only ever act from misperceiving who we really are, because we believe we are separated from our Source and behave from within the illusion of fear and lack. We forgive all situations because everything that appears to happen is perceived from within the illusionary world we believe we exist in, based on our perceived separation and the associated ideas of pain, fear, and lack. By using this type of forgiveness (not the usual type of forgiving in which somebody did something wrong), we aim to see beyond the illusion. *The Course*'s forgiveness is a tool that aims to dismantle the illusions of the ego by overriding its ideas of separation. (chapter 1)

Emotional Body: The storage house of all the impressions and interpretations that we have gathered from our life experiences. Our innate characters influence to what degree these affect us. (chapter 1)

Illusionary Constructs: Thoughts, attitudes, beliefs, and ideas based on past emotional impressions that we unconsciously constructed or appropriated from others, or from past situations. These are held within our Emotional Bodies and create misperceptions about current situations. (chapter 1)

Hidden Agendas: Ulterior motives or unconscious driving forces created by our Perceived Needs that we constructed for our emotional survival. (chapter 1)

Life Matrix: Is the lens through which we see and navigate the world. It holds *all* our underlying perceptions or misperceptions and all our unconscious influences. It supports what we think we need to be, as well as what we think we need to do to uphold our perceptions, whether real or false. (chapter 1)

Oneness: The pervasive universal creative force that everything and everybody emanated from, are still connected to, and will eventually return to: we still hold a memory of that Oneness within us. (chapter 1)

Our Truth: Our True Reality. We are love; we came from love; we are all *unconditionally* loved by our Creator; and we hold all the power of that creator energy. Even though we have forgotten this, we are still connected to that reality. (Introduction)

Peaceful Honesty: The feeling that is created within the depths of our being when we no longer have buried hurts or pain, inner conflicts, or their attached emotions. As we have acknowledged the illusions that we created, there is no longer a barrier between our consciousness and our True Self. (chapter 4)

Perceived Needs: What we think we need to do and who we think we need to be, to appease any disempowering, negative inner beliefs we have amassed in our Emotional Bodies. (chapter 1)

Protective Mechanisms: The methods we use to uphold, protect, and defend false, limiting inner beliefs, biases, and insecurities. (chapter 1)

The Standard: What we must align ourselves to so we are working at our highest potentials: happy, peaceful, and in harmony with all in the Universe, embracing the qualities of its creative force, or God. (chapter 2)

True Self: The truth or memory of who you really are—free of any Illusionary Constructs. (chapter 1)

Unconscious Awareness: The effect of our created perceptions that were birthed from the attitudes and inner beliefs we amassed within our Emotional Bodies and that we appropriate to the world. If our Unconscious Awarenesses hold biases, negativity, or misappropriated perceptions, we will develop *needs* to try to uphold them and *strategies* to keep them buried. (chapter 1)

Meditations, Visualizations, and Other Practices
(see back page for code to download these to your device from the book's website)

Meditations and Conscious Breathing Exercises – are available to download from the book's website, using the appropriate code located on the last page of the book.

Energetic Attunements

1: Healing Torn Energy Fields That Deplete You (From chapter 4)
- First thing in the morning as soon as you awake (or anytime something depletes you), take a few deep breaths, and put your awareness into your heart center.
- Then gently make the request that any torn energetic fields be healed.
- Take a few more gentle breaths, until you feel a bit lighter or in a better mood.

You can do this exercise whenever you feel depleted energetically in any way, and whether you feel a huge difference immediately or not, this exercise works through your heart center and subtly affects your whole energetic being. If you do it regularly, it will eventually shift your whole energetic field. You also don't have to know or pinpoint what exactly is affecting you for this to work. By requesting your heart center's energetic system to be healed, Spirit, who understands this process, steps in and reconnects you. Your life force is then reattuned to the higher vibrations inherent within you as you are now connected to the healed places within your heart center (where all emotional lows gather). Your energy is then rejuvenated, just as being connected to broken places within the heart center depletes your energy.

Visualizations

1: Bodily Upsets Leaving (From chapter 4)

This technique is simply a matter of visualizing bodily upsets oozing out from you and drifting away so that a cognizant intelligence can dissipate them.
- Take a few deep breaths.
- Connect with the anxiety, ache, pain, fatigue, or state of discomfort.
- Create an image in your mind of the upset leaving: a hand signal to offer them up to the Universe, a visualization of them floating away in a balloon, or any other symbol that works for you.
- Then visualize a cord being cut from the events.

This exercise dissipates the emotional component of the event, but the event will not be erased from your memory. However, when you think of it again, you will not be emotionally affected anymore. This works quickly for minor upsets, but for major hurts or abuses it usually takes multiple visualizations for the emotional effects to dissipate. For prolonged or life-threatening events, I recommend professional help.

2: To Release Any Negative Attitude, Stress, or Fatigue (From chapter 4)

You can use this exercise if you find yourself unable to let go of any negative or disempowering attitude or if you feel bad, tired, angry, or simply stressed. Use this visualization for a momentary boost, as it resets your vibrations. Do not try this when your full attention is needed elsewhere.

- Close your eyes, and take a few slow, deep breaths.
- See yourself at the top of a mountain with the vast expanse of a lush green valley ahead of you.
- Breathe it in, and claim it within your whole being.

This embodiment of expansiveness overrides whatever is holding you in limiting or unhealthy attitudes or emotions. The exercise can be done once slowly, repeated again, or done a few times in a row until the desired shift within your being is attained.

3: Set or Reset Your Path or Mind-Set (From chapter 4.)

Do this visualization to set or reset your path or mind-set if you are unable to release old attitudes or habits or are having trouble getting out from under the muck of your old story.

- Sit in your quiet place, close your eyes, and take a few deep breaths.
- Visualize a road or a pathway.
- See a fork in the road.
- One path is laid with gold, the other with muck.
- See yourself at the fork in the road choosing to walk on the path laden with gold.
- Step onto it and walk forward while embracing its brilliance, breathing it into your being.
- If you feel resistance to follow that path, turn away from it for a moment.
- Then do a 180-degree turn toward it, jump on it, and run as fast as you can until you are halfway down the path.
- Slow down, and embrace the path's brilliance, breathing it deeply into your whole being.
- Walk slowly to the end of the path reveling in its beauty and embracing how you now feel free of any old, negative, or limiting attitudes. Notice and welcome the clarity of mind you have now obtained.

Come back to this visualization as often as needed, until you experience a shift away from being stuck in stuck in any negativity or atmosphere of the past.

4: Recap of Inelia Benz's "Meet Yourself in the Future; Successful and Healed" (From chapter 7,8,9)

- Sit in a quiet, comfortable place.
- Make a mental image of yourself in the future: the way you want to see yourself.
- Envision sitting across from that future Self.
- Ask your future Self questions of how you got there. Listen attentively to the answers.
- Envision yourself stepping into that future Self.
- Revel in and feel what it is like to be the new you for a while.
- Bring back the vibrational signature of your future Self.
- Revel in it within you now.

Reconnect back to that feeling whenever you feel yourself slipping into negative or disempowering thoughts or attitudes regarding what you want to have or be in the future.

Affirmations and Self-Talks

Self-Talk to Help Us Forgive (Louise L. Hay, from chapter 8)

- It is easier for me to forgive than I thought.
- Forgiving makes me feel free and light.
- The more resentment I release, the more love I have to express.
- I am learning to choose to make today a pleasure to experience.[1]

Self-Talk to Anchor in Health (Dr. Christiane Northrup, chapter 8)

Repeat before you go to sleep for thirty days: "I am intending vibrant health."[2]

Self Talk / Affirmation from Arten to Use When Judgmental of Another. (Arten, Gary Renard's teacher from *The Disappearance of the Universe*, chapter 4).

"You are Spirit. Whole and innocent. All is forgiven and released."[3]

Self Talk / Affirmation - To Dispel Resistance (Louise L. Hay, from chapter 4).

"I see any resistance patterns within me only as something else to release. They have no power over me. I am the power in my world. I flow with changes taking place in my life as best I can. I approve myself and the way I am changing."[4]

Exercises

Inelia Benz's Fear-Processing Exercise (From chapter 4):

http://goldenageofgaia.com/2011/08/11/inelia-benz-fear-processing-exercise/

Inelia Benz's Reconnect with the Spirit of Money (From chapter 9): http://www.youtube.com/watch?v=V78VtQXKfV8.

Recaps

The Two Elements To Making this Shift: (From chapter 3)

A) Connect to and Anchor in Our Truth: Seven Steps to Help Us Connect to, Anchor in, and Align with *Our Truth*

> 1) Aligning to Material that Supports Ideas of Unconditional Love and Joy, Opens Us Up to that Love, and Reawakens Our Being.
> 2) Reaffirming through repetition.
> 3) Directing Our Thoughts and Words With Concepts of Empowerment and Self-Love.
> 4) Lightening Up, Embracing Laughter, and Infusing Our Lives with Joy.
> 5) Calming Our Minds; Centering Our Beings.
> 6) Aligning With the Oneness Paradigm.
> 7) Taking Control of Our Lives; Aiming to Live Consciously.

B) Dismantle What Is in the Way of Accessing *Our Truth:* Six Steps to Unravel What Is in the Way of Accessing Our Truth

> 1) Recognizing.
> 2) Acknowledging.
> 3) Understanding: Getting in Touch with Our Feelings and Connecting the Dots.
> 4) Forgiveness: Making Peace with Self, Others, Situations, the World.
> 5) Letting go: Releasing Emotions / Shifting Attitudes / Improving Reactions.
> 6) Uncluttering the Inner and the Outer.

List of Recommendations

(Cover all aspects at this time of the Shift, including our personal journeys, Gaia's journey, health, current events, religion, science, spirituality, extraterrestrials).

General Websites
- articles, workshops, spirituality/self-development, sacred site tours: http://www.grailproductions.com/
- articles, exercises, workshops: https://ascension101.com/
- articles, meditations, workshops: http://counciloflove.com/
- articles, practices, workshops: http://onenessofbeing.org/center-for-planetary-awakening.html
- articles, insights, meditations/prayers, workshops: http://www.celestinevision.com/
- health, science: http://www.forbiddenknowledgetv.com/
- self-development: men, women, soul mates: http://www.evolvingwisdom.com.
- spirituality, current events, Ascension, ETs: http://goldenageofgaia.com/
- spirituality, self-development, relationships, workshops: http:// http://davericho.com/.

Radio Talk Shows
- spirituality, ET's, Ascension: http://www.blogtalkradio.com/inlight_radio.
- health, science, arts, paranormal, world events, etc., http://www.coasttocoastam.com/.
- science, world issues, business, religion, philosophy, etc., http://www.ted.com/.

Meditations
- Against the Stream Buddhist Meditation Society. http://www.againstthestream.org/audio.
- Dillon, Linda. *Tsunami of Love.* Spring 2014. http://counciloflove.com/category/tsunami-of-love/.
- Redfield, James. "Biweekly Group Prayer/Meditation for the World." http://www.celestinevision.com/.
- Renard, Gary, and Cindy Renard. *Meditations for Couples.* Berkeley, CA: Fearless Books, 2012. CD-ROM. 74 minutes. http://www.fearlessbooks.com/Meditations.html.
- Salzberg, Sharon. *Real Happiness: The Power of* Meditation: *A 28-Day Course.* New York: Workman, 2010. http://www.sharonsalzberg.com/.

On ETs
- Blog-Talk Radio. "Cosmic Vision News." http://www.blogtalkradio.com/search?q=cosmic+vision+news/.
- Dolan, Richard. "The Future Is Now." UFOTV Studios. June 30, 2012. http://www.youtube.com/watch?v=AsspNhvKZJU.

- Eisenhower, Laura. "Laura Eisenhower Interview: Who Are We?" By Roxy Lopez. February 17, 2012. Golden Age of Gaia. http://goldenageofgaia.com/2012/02/20/laura-eisenhower-interview-who-are-we/.
- History Channel. "Ancient Aliens." Prometheus Entertainment. http://www.history.ca/ancient-aliens/.

Uplifting, Vibration-Raising, Energizing Music
- Ripa, André. "Children of the Sun Song." http://childrenofthesun.org/children-sun-song/.
- Torgeson, Mark. "Rapture." http://www.marktorgeson.com/Videos/RaptureMovie.mov.

Abundance and Prosperity
- Beckow, Steve. "Prosperity! Remembering Divine Principle." Golden Age of Gaia. April 24, 2014. http://goldenageofgaia.com/2014/04/24/prosperity-remembering-divine-principle-12/.
- Benz, Inelia. "Reconnecting to the Spirit of Money." http://www.youtube.com/watch?v=V78VtQXKfV8.

Couple Relationships
- Carter, Christian. *Communication Secrets*. http://www.catchhimandkeephim.com. Targeted towards women.
- Forest, Jenna. "The Stages of Twin Flame Relationships." June 30, 2011. https://www.youtube.com/watch?v=3aIV5okbDZQ.
- Grey, John. http://www.marsvenus.com/john-gray-mars-venus-daily-advice.htm.
- Hendricks, Gay, and Katie Hendricks. http://www.hendricks.com.
- The Meisners. http://www.mynewday.tv/. Christian based.
- Richo, David. http:/ http://davericho.com/. Books, articles, video presentations, etc.

Health
- Brill, Stephen. "Bitter Pill: Why Healthcare Costs Are Killing Us." *Time*. March 2013. http://livingwithmcl.com/BitterPill.pdf.
- http://www.chakrahealing.com. Audio explanation of chakras and little chakra tests.

Planetary, Global Concerns
- Nocera, Dan. "A Solution to the Global Energy Challenge." http://www.ForbiddenKnowledgeTV.com/page/724.html.

Tools, Practices, Teachers: Personal Growth, Spirituality, Ascension.
- *A Course in Miracles*: teachers, programs, books, and YouTube videos
    Hoffmeister, David. http://www.livingmiraclestv.org/.
    McSween, Jennifer. http://www.pathwaysoflight.org/facilitators/ministers_profiles/details/188/.
    (Montreal area).

Renard, Gary. *The Disappearance of the Universe.* http://www.garyrenard.com/. (Like an ACIM 101).

Wapnick, Ken. Q&A archive, http://www.facimoutreach.org/.

- Benz, Inelia. "Ascension 101 Program." https://ascension101.com/.
- Dwoskin, Hale. "The Sedona Method." http://www.sedona.com/.
- Fitzpatrick, Carol. http://www.carolynnfitzpatrick.com. (Virginia area).
- Ford, Debbie. http://www.thefordinstitute.com/SearchResults.asp?Cat=348.
- Katie, Byron. "The Work." http://www.thework.com/index.php.
- Meyer, Joyce. http://www.joycemeyer.org/.
- Mirdad, Michael. http://www.grailproductions.com/.
- Richards, Jim. "Heart Physics Program." http://impactministries.com/.
- The Meisners. http://www.mynewday.tv/. Christian-based family life, and couples.
- Wallace, David Foster. "This Is Water." http://www.youtube.com/watch?v=8CrOL-ydFMI. On our propensity to judge.

Books

I recommend all books mentioned in the text. Complete information on those books can be found in the endnotes. The following list details other books that have either inspired me or helped me over the years.

<u>Uplifting Fictional Stories with Helpful and Insightful Messages</u>

Brooks, David. *The Social Animal: The Hidden Sources of Love, Character, and Achievement.* 2012.*

Coelho, Paulo. *The Alchemist.* 1998.

Dekker, Ted. *Black, Red, White,* and *Green.* The Circle Series. 2011.

Laurie, Jamie B. *The Big Summer.* 2014. A coming-of-age tale of first love and the struggles of coming out and self-acceptance; inspired by the author's experience.

Redfield, James. *The Celestine Prophesy.* 1993.

<u>Accounts of Spiritual Healing Through Forgiveness</u>

Lewis, Scarlett. *Nurturing Healing Love: A Mother's Journey of Hope and Forgiveness.* 2013.

Wolfe, Joe. With Gary Renard. *Letter to a Prisoner: From a Career Criminal to Seeker of the Truth,* 2011.

Young, William P. *The Shack.* 2007.

<u>For Personal and Spiritual Growth</u>

Brooks, David. *The Social Animal: The Hidden Sources of Love, Character, and Achievement.* 2012.*

Chopra, Deepak, & Nacson, Leon. *A Deepak Chopra Companion, Illuminations on Health and Human Consciousness.* 1998, 1999.

Dyer, Wayne. *Being in Balance.* 2006.

Canfield, Jack. The Success Principles. 2005, 2015.

Hollis, Marica. *God Meets Us Where We Are*. 1989.

Moore, Thomas. *A Religion of One's Own: A Guide to Creating a Personal Spirituality in a Secular World*. 2015.

Richo, David. *The Power of Grace, Recognizing Unexpected Gifts on the Path*. 2013.

Richo, David. *When Catholic Means Cosmic, Opening to a Big-Hearted Faith*. 2015.

Ruiz, Don Miguel. *The Voice of Knowledge*. 2004.

Ruiz, Don Miguel. *The Mastery of Love*. 1999.

Shambhala Publications. http://www.shambhala.com/.

Szaccero, Peter. *Emotionally Healthy Spirituality: It's Impossible to Be Spiritually Mature, While Remaining Emotionally Immature*. 2014.

Twyman, James W. *The Moses Code*. 2008.

Vaughan-Lee, Llewellyn. *Sufism, The Transformation of the Heart*. 1995, 2012.

Walsch, Neale Donald. *Conversation with God: An Uncommon Dialogue*. Books 1, 2, and 3. 1997, 1997, 1998.

Walsch, Neale Donald. *The New Revelation*. 2002.

Ward, Matthew. Channeled through Suzanne Ward. *Tell Me about Heaven*. 2002.

Practical Solutions

Beattie, Melody. *The New Codependency*. 2009.

Canfield, Jack. *The Success Principles*, 2005,2015.

Dwoskin, Hale. *The Sedona Method*. 2007.

Dyer, Wayne. *Excuses Begone!* 2009.

Meyer, Joyce. *Conflict Free Living*. 1985.

Wooding, Scott. *Rage, Rebellion, & Rudeness*. 2003.

Couples / Relationships / Sexuality

Grey, John. *Men Are from Mars, Women Are from Venus*. 1992.

Grey, John. *How to Get What You Want and Want What You Have*. 1999.

Love, Patricia, and Steven Stosny. *How to Improve Your Marriage without Talking about It*. 2007.

Richo, David. *How to Be an Adult in Love; Letting love in Safely and Showing it Recklessly*. 2013.

For Women

Breathnach, Sarah Ban. *Simple Abundance: A Daybook of Comfort and Joy*. 1995.

Deida, David. *Dear Lover: A Woman's Guide to Men, Sex, and Love's Deepest Bliss*. 2002.

Eldredge, John, and Staci Eldredge. *Captivating: Unveiling the Mystery of a Woman's Soul*. 2005.

Meyer, Joyce. *The Confident Woman, Devotional*. 2011.

Williamson, Marianne. *Tears to Triumph*. 2016.

For Men

Deida, David. *The Way of the Superior Man: A Spiritual Guide to Mastering the Challenges of Women, Work, and Sexual Desire.* 2004.

Eldredge, John. *Wild at Heart, Discovering the Secret of a Man's Soul.* 2001.

For Families

Tsabary, Shefali. *The Awakened Family; A Revolution in Parenting.* 2016.

Spiritual, Cosmic, and Scientific Connections

Campbell, Joseph. *The Hero With a Thousand Faces.* 1949 (revised 2008).

Robinson, Jason C & Peck, David A (editors). *Irreconcilable Differences.* 2015.

Wilber, Ken. *A Brief History of Time.* 2007.

Wilber, Ken. *The Integral Vision.* 2007.

Worksheets

Always start with a small, two-minute meditation, or prayer, or energetic attunement:
(Invite in your Best Self, True Self, higher Self, Spirit, Holy Spirit, Buddha, Jesus, or any other deity to join with you as you aim to clear the pathway to peace).

Worksheet 1: Illusionary Constructs, Misperceptions, and Projections

You can use my examples as guidance or inspiration for your own self-reflection.

My Illusionary Constructs:
- Ex: I believed my thoughts, feelings, emotions, and reactions were founded and based in reality and that everyone around me should yield to what they dictated.
-
-

My Misperceptions:
- Ex: I believed being quiet and unassuming was unempowering and always led to victimization and that being in control led to empowerment.
- Ex: I believed that creating an organized household would bring about a sense of love and security.
-
-

My Projections:
- Ex: I projected onto those around me my unconscious angers at my upbringing, my fears of becoming unempowered like my mother, and my frustrations about not creating the life I felt I needed to avoid becoming unempowered.
-
-

Understanding My Misperceptions and Projections:
- Ex: I expected others to fulfill the Perceived Needs I had erected and answer to the neediness within me rather than allowing life to unfold and allowing for my own happiness.
- Ex: I blamed others for the conflict and discord I had created in my family with my attitudes, demands, and projections.
- Ex: I often felt hurt and frustrated when people did not answer my calls of neediness or comply to my every whim.
-
-

Re-empowering New Awareness:
- Ex: Discovering how my unconscious awareness and how my perceptions and projections were misappropriated helped me understand that much of my frustration in life was of my own creation, and this helped alleviate any leftover frustration and anger at others or life.
- Ex: I now understand that I can shift my thoughts and attitudes from disempowering ones to those that will help me feel peaceful and bring harmony into my life.
-
-
-

Worksheet 2a: Desires/Needs: Real or Perceived

Start with a small, two-minute meditation/prayer/attunement. Invite in your Best Self, True Self, higher Self, Spirit, Holy Spirit, Buddha, Jesus, or any other deity to join with you as you aim to clear the pathway to peace.

Real Desires/Needs:
- Ex: I desire a good job and career so that I can provide my family with security, a good education, and lots of fun experiences.
-
-
-
-
-
-
-

Perceived Needs:
- Ex: I need to have a successful job that brings with it good social standing so that my family will look good in the community and not be unempowered in life.
-
-
-
-
-
-
-

Examine Where the Perceived Needs Come From:
- Ex: Was poor in childhood and our family was shunned and my parents had no power to change their circumstances. They could never afford to join me in activities or sports.
-
-
-
-
-
-

Worksheet 2b: Neediness: How It Plays Out in My Life

Neediness Playing Out in My Life:

- Ex: I draw others into my sphere to fulfill my selfish need for love, companionship, acceptance, or security without a conscious awareness of what they have to offer or the repercussions I am amassing.
- Ex: If they get too close and start to make demands of me, I pull away and feel angry and put-upon.
- Ex: If they do not fulfill what I expect of them, I pull away and feel angry, cheated, frustrated, or confused.
-
-
-
-
-
-
-

Possible Solutions:

- Ex: Rather than always looking for a companion, I will acknowledge the loneliness or insecure feelings I have because of my life situation. To move past these feelings, I will work on my self-esteem by reading books that build confidence, take a class, or find activities I like that give me some social outlet. These will boost my self-confidence and help me feel secure in myself so that I can develop the strength of character to choose only healthy relationships based on commonalities and likes and dislikes rather than on my neediness.
- Ex: I will acknowledge that I want friends or a girlfriend or boyfriend. However, if I feel myself considering that the person(s) I am out with will solve all of my problems, make me feel secure, and fulfill all my dreams, I will consciously choose to keep it casual. Until then I will find activities I like and go out casually with groups of people.
-
-
-
-
-
-
-

<u>Worksheet 3: My Boundaries</u>

Healthy Boundaries:
- Ex: I have healthy boundaries with my friend. We love each other but respect each other's opinions and space. While giving advice or a shoulder to cry on if asked, we allow each other to make our own decisions and find our own empowerment and path in life.
- Ex: We lean on each other in times of need or comfort, but as soon as emotional healing has taken place and the situation dictates, we release each other emotionally so that we can draw on our own inner strength to make necessary decisions or changes and move forward in life.
-

Unhealthy Boundaries:
- Ex: I have unhealthy boundaries with my brother. Because I love him deeply, I try to accommodate his harmful lifestyle and choices. He has not held a steady job in years, and when he needs money or a place to stay, he calls me and plays on my guilt about how I can afford to help him, and I always fall for it.
- Ex: He never pays me back when he says he will, and as soon as I realize I've been taken advantage of again, I feel bad, angry, and embarrassed. When he leaves after overstaying his welcome and eating me out of house and home without any offer to help with chores or chip in with expenses, I feel used.
-

Diagnosis:
- Ex: My brother is playing on my emotions and using me. I allow this to happen because I understand life is hard for him because our father left when he was so young.
- Ex: By continuously bailing him out, he feels no impetus to make a good life for himself. I am enabling him to continue with his life of drugs, drinking, and irresponsibility.
-

Solutions:
- Ex: I can tell him I love him when he calls and asks for help but refuse to give him money or a place to stay. When he balks, I must be strong and know it is the only way he will find his own empowerment.
- Ex: So he doesn't starve, I can give him a gift card from a grocery store for a small amount to get him through the day or a few days. I can offer to organize a professional help meeting or drive him to a recovery group.
-
-

Worksheet 4: Conflicting Messages and Their Pulls and Pushes

Conflicting Messages within Me: Undermining myself
- Ex: I want to have enough money to eat out, travel, and do fun things, but my parents frowned on being successful, doing fun things, and having nice things. We had to be very frugal.
- Ex: When I see/hear someone who has the things I want, I think/say things that are negative and judgmental.
-
-
-
-
-
-
-
-
-
-
-
-
-

Solutions:
- Ex: When I catch myself making either mental or verbal judgments regarding someone who is successful or has what I want, I will shift my focus to how nice it would be and feel to have those things.
- Ex: When I turn to limiting attitudes like thinking, *I could never afford that*, I will instead think, *Wouldn't it be nice ...?* and revel in how delicious it would feel.
-
-
-
-
-
-
-
-
-
-
-
-

<u>Worksheet 5: Hidden Agendas</u>

Attitudes That Bring Conflict into My Life:
- Ex: I try to control and organize everyone and everything in my life.
- Ex: I place work, money, and financial security above all else.
-
-
-
-
-

Possible Hidden Agenda and Causes:
- Ex: I am looking for security and empowerment. My childhood was chaotic with an alcoholic or abusive parent.
- Ex: I felt marginalized, was hushed, or had no discipline or affection in childhood.
- Ex: I want to create a perfect home. I believe this will bring me a sense of balance and security I was missing as a child.
- Ex: I want to become wealthy to overcome feeling less than or disempowered from a poor childhood.
-
-
-
-
-

Solutions:
- Ex: I will ask others for their opinions and bring them into the decision-making process. My way is not the only way, and I understand others will do things differently (or not to my high standards).
- Ex: I will relax a little with creating a perfect outward appearance and try to foster a calm, relaxed home atmosphere
- Ex: I can find peace and happiness when I create a more harmonious household. This can also make me feel empowered.
-
-
-
-
-
-

Worksheet 6: Being at the Effect or the Cause of My Life Experiences

Situations I Find Difficult:
-
-
-
-
-
-
-

My Perceptions about the Situations:
-
-
-
-
-
-
-

Where I May Be at the Effect of My Thoughts and Attitudes:
-
-
-
-
-
-
-

Where I Am / Could Be at the Cause of Good or Better Life Experiences:
-
-
-
-
-
-
-

<u>Worksheet 7a: My Default Position</u>

My Usual Reactions:
- Ex: Anger, impatience, blaming or judging others, avoiding confrontation, burying hurts and feelings, staying neutral, dealing with the situation at hand calmly, etc.
-
-
-
-
-
-

Reactionary Default Position—Projecting Hurts/Feelings Outward:
- Ex: Anger, impatience, blaming or judging others, manipulation, revenge, etc.
-
-
-
-
-
-

Passive Default Position—Burying Hurts/Feeling:
- Ex: Avoiding confrontation, never speaking up, always giving in to others, never standing up for myself, etc.
-
-
-
-
-

Neutral Default Position—Staying Neutral or Dealing with the Situation at Hand Calmly
-
-
-
-
-
-

Worksheet 7b: Protective Mechanisms: My Masks of Fear

Pinpoint the Underlying Issues: (anger, judgment, criticism, blame, control, manipulation, revenge, passivity, etc.)

- Ex: I like to control or organize everything and everybody because nobody can do it better.
- Ex: I blame others because I think somebody else must be controlling my circumstances.
-
-

Problems with These Attitudes:

- Ex. Controlling everything and everybody creates conflict in my life and wears me out. I have decided the people around me cannot look after their own lives. This discourages and disempowers them.
- Ex: Blaming others does not solve the problems in my life. It does not allow me to face the fact that my attitudes, actions, or nonactions may have caused this issue.
-
-
-

Real Issue with These Attitudes:

- Ex: I think I am better than other people. *I need* the validation or security of controlling and organizing everything and everybody around me. I am not in touch with my own true value.
- Ex: I blame others because *I am* unempowered regarding my own life.
-
-
-

Solutions and Benefits:

- Ex: I allow others to look after and organize things, although they may not be done my way or to my standards. I will be less busy and stressed and will have less conflict with those in my life. I will work to develop an accepting attitude for how others approach life,
- Ex: I will organize myself to do what I need to do to attain what I want. I will make lists, make the phone call, or send the email - and follow up. I will become conscious of my commitments, like bills to pay. I will make a budget and put the necessary money aside. I will feel more empowered.
-
-

<u>Worksheet 8: Compulsions, Dysfunctions, or Addictions</u>

Compulsions:
- I always …
- I need to …
-
-
-

Dysfunctions:
- I am/do …
-
-
-

Addictions:
- I am …
-
-
-
-
-

My Feelings When I Fall into These (Angry, Sad, Lonely, Frustrated, Invalidated, Etc.):
- I feel …
- I am trying to overcome …
-
-
-
-

My Hurt or Fear Is Being Unloved, Alone, No Good, Good for Nothing, Etc.:
- I am …
- I am trying to overcome feeling …
-
-
-
-

<u>Worksheet 9: Unconscious Limiting Beliefs / Outdated Principles and Ideals</u>

Life Issues (Money, Weight, Self-Worth, Work, Spouse/Partner, Etc.):
- I … because I feel …
-
-
-
-
-
-

Limiting Beliefs (Shoulds—It/I/He/She Should Do or Be …):
- I believe …
-
-
-
-
-
-

Outdated Principles or Ideals:
- I hold to …
- I want to keep …
-
-
-
-
-
-

Attitude Shifts I Could Make:
-
-
-
-
-
-
-

<u>Worksheet 10: Moving Toward or Away from Something</u>

Where I Have Moved Away from Something:
- I am running or have run away from …
-
-
-
-
-
-
-
-
-

Where I Have Moved toward Something:
- I am moving or have moved toward …
-
-
-
-
-
-
-
-

Differences in My Attitudes:
- Ex: When I run away from something, I feel an urgency and feel glad to be away from certain people.
- Ex: When I am moving toward something, I feel excited for this next step in life.
-
-
-
-
-
-
-
-
-

<u>Worksheet 11: Aggressive and Passive Behaviors</u>

Aggressive Behaviors:

- Ex: I lash out and want to manipulate and control.
- I am trying to avoid feeling ...
-
-
-
-
-
-

- I feel ...
-
-
-
-
-
-
-

- I am trying to overcome ...
-
-
-
-
-
-

Passive Behaviors:

- Ex: I internalize my feelings.
- I am afraid to ... because ...
-
-
-
-
-

<u>Worksheet 12: Other Limiting Attitudes or Behaviors</u>

Other Possible Limiting Attitudes (Defensiveness, Envy, Jealousy, Victim Mentality, Etc.):
*   I often become …
*   I am trying to overcome …
*
*
*
*
*
*
*
*
*

*   I sometimes become …
*   I am trying to feel (or avoid feeling) …
*
*
*
*
*
*
*
*

*   I can't help becoming …
*   ….. is my natural reaction, and I don't know how to overcome it.
*
*
*
*
*
*
*
*

<u>Worksheet 13: Mindfulness and Mindlessness</u>

Where I Am Mindful:
- I am mindful when/with …
- This creates … in my life.
-
-
-
-
-
-
-
-
-
-
-
-
-
-

Where I Am Mindless:
- I am mindless when/with …
- This creates … in my life.
-
-
-
-
-
-
-
-
-
-
-
-
-

<u>Worksheet 14: Life Lists and Goals</u>

Where do I want to be in life <u>one year from now</u>?
- In my personal life (e.g., relationships, health, finances, etc.):
-
-
-
-

- In my professional life (e.g., start or go back to school, find a better job, change careers, etc.):
-
-
-
-

Where do I want to be in life <u>two years from now</u>?
- In my personal life:
-
-
-
-

- In my professional life:
-
-
-
-

Where do I want to be in <u>life five years from now</u>?
- In my personal life:
-
-
-

- In my professional life:
-
-
-
-

What steps can I take to make that happen (for one year from now)?

-
-
-
-
-
-
-
-
-
-
-

What steps can I take to make that happen (for two years from now)?

-
-
-
-
-
-
-
-
-
-
-

What steps can I take to make that happen (for five years from now)?

-
-
-
-
-
-
-
-
-

/2

<u>Worksheet 15: Lens through Which I View the World</u>

How I See the World with a Clear Lens:
- Ex: I see the best/good in people, the beauty in things, and have hope for the future.
- Specifically …
-
-
-
-
-
-

How This Has Affected My Life:
-
-
-
-
-
-
-

How I See the World with a Cloudy Lens:
- Ex: I see the worst in people, the ugly in things, and feel the future is hopeless.
- Specifically …
-
-
-
-
-
-

How This Has Affected My Life:
-
-
-
-
-
-
-

Worksheet 16: My Thought Processes: What They Invite into My Life

How do my thought processes affect what I am trying to create in my life?

Do my thought processes support what I am trying to create in my life?
-
-
-
-
-
-
-

Do my thought processes regarding myself promote love and harmony within my being?
-
-
-
-
-
-
-

Do my thought processes promote harmony and unity with others?)
-
-
-
-
-
-
-

What thought processes, if any, do I need to change to help create the life I want?
-
-
-
-
-
-
-

<u>Worksheet 17: False Perceptions, Their Beliefs, and How It Should Bes</u>

False Perceptions I Hold:

-
-
-
-
-
-

False Beliefs I Hold:

-
-
-
-
-
-

Should Bes I Maintain:

-
-
-
-
-
-

Solutions:

- Ex: I will replace any false or outdated perceptions, beliefs, or how it should bes that create conflict or undermine those in my life with new, realistic ones based in love and support of who they are; I will work to change my attitude and how I speak to and what I expect of the people around me; I will aim to do my part to create a more relaxed atmosphere at home, with family, or at work, etc. leading to more harmonious relationships.
-
-
-
-

<u>Worksheet 18: Forgiveness</u>

A) Self-Forgiveness:
- I need to forgive myself for ...
-
-
-
-
-
-
-

B) Forgiving Others:
- I need to forgive others for ...
-
-
-
-
-
-
-

C) Forgiving Situations:
- I need to forgive the situation ...
-
-
-
-
-
-

D) Forgiving the World: Humanity and Its History
- I need to forgive the world regarding ...
-
-
-
-
-
-

Worksheet 19: Small/Large Shifts I Can Start With

Small Shifts

Replacing Judgment with Acceptance:
- I can replace judgment with acceptance regarding ...
-
-
-

Replacing Blame with Understanding:
- I can replace blame with understanding regarding ...
-
-
-

Replacing Anger with Self-Control:
- I can replace anger with self-control regarding ...
-
-
-

Replacing Indifference with Empathy:
- I can replace indifference with empathy toward ...
-
-
-

Replacing That Which Causes Discord with That Which Embraces Harmony:
- I can replace my words, attitudes, or actions toward ...
-
-
-

Large Shifts in Attitudes or Behaviors I can Make
-
-
-
-

Worksheet 20: Judgments of Self, Others, Groups, or Situations

Where I Judge Myself:
-
-
-
-
-
-
-

Where I Judge Others:
-
-
-
-
-
-
-
-

Where I Judge Groups of People:
-
-
-
-
-
-
-
-

Where I Judge Situations:
-
-
-
-
-
-

<u>Worksheet 21: Opened or Closed to Universal Powers regarding Different Attitudes</u>

Where I Am Open with No Blocks (Worry, Money, Health, Job, Life Partner, Etc.):

-
-
-
-
-
-
-
-
-
-
-
-
-
-
-
-
-

Where I Am Closed with Unconscious Blocks (Worry, Money, Health, Job, Life Partner, Etc.):

-
-
-
-
-
-
-
-
-
-
-
-
-
-
-
-

<u>Worksheet 22: Lurking Negative or Limiting Thoughts or Attitudes</u>

In which areas of my life, if any, are my feelings, which influence my thoughts, words, and attitudes not in alignment with what I want or want to become?

-
-
-
-
-
-
-
-
-
-

Which of my feelings, if any, undermine me with limiting thoughts?

-
-
-
-
-
-
-
-
-

Do I harbor feelings of negativity or jealousy regarding someone else's success?

-
-
-
-
-
-
-
-

Do I *really* feel deserving?

-
-
-
-
-
-
-
-
-
-
-
-
-
-
-

To what extent do I feel that there is enough love, success, and goods to go around? To what extent do I believe in scarcity and limitation?

-
-
-
-
-
-
-
-
-
-
-
-
-

/2

Endnotes

Preface

1   *A Course in Miracles* is a profound philosophical and self-study program with 365 daily lessons that guide us toward undoing the ego and its false illusions of separateness. While its philosophy resembles Buddhist concepts of multiplicity and of the world being an illusion, it uses Christian terminology. It also proposes that our world, the Universe, as well as all our illusions of separateness are actually projections of our mind and are therefore *all* unreal.

Introduction

1   The third dimension is the realm of form and solid density that Humanity has inhabited for eons (from within the twelve cosmic dimensions). It is characterized by duality and embodies qualities of lack, fear, limitation, greed, judgment, blame, and cruelty. It fosters conflict and separation.

2   The fifth dimension is the realm of a higher consciousness with a lighter density that Gaia and her inhabitants are moving into with the current Shift. It is characterized by Oneness and its qualities of love, joy, compassion, fairness, equality, abundance, acceptance, and empowerment. It fosters unity and harmony.

3   Shelley Yates, "Fire the Grid—Vancouver Speech," YouTube video, 1:25:03, posted by "bigal888888," June 6, 2012, http://www.youtube.com/watch?v=KHGyu AXNWg.

4   Dan Harris, *10% Happier* (New York: It Books, 2014), 56.

5   Ibid., 58, 59.

6   Ibid., 56–8.

Chapter 1

1   Aldous Huxley, "Aldous Huxley Quotes," http://www.goodreads.com/author/quotes/3487. Aldous Huxley.

2   Inelia Benz, "Unit 13: The Emotional Body," Ascension 101, eCourse.

3   Angela Peregoff, "5D-Spring Nesting-Instincts," Golden Age of Gaia, April 9, 2012, http://goldenageofgaia.com/2012/04/angela-peregoff-5-d-spring-nesting-instincts/.

4   Leslie Stevenson and David L. Haberman, *Ten Theories of Human Nature*, 3rd ed. (New York: Oxford University Press, 1998), 54–5.

5   Ellen J. Langer, *Mindfulness* (Reading, MA: Addison-Wesley, 1989), 26.

6   Amy Casement, "Encountering the Shadow in Rites of Passage: a Study in Activations," Journal of Analytical Psychology 48, no. 1 (2003): 29–46.

7   Anne Katherine, *Boundaries: Where You End and I Begin* (New York: Fireside/Parkside, 1991), 75.

8   Arten, quoted in Gary Renard, *The Disappearance of the Universe*, 2002, http://www.garyrenard.com/Preview.htm#law.

9   Debbie Shapiro, *Your Body Speaks Your Mind: Decoding the Emotional, Psychological, and Spiritual Messages that Underlie Illness* (Boulder, CO: Sounds True, 2006), 3.

10 Gloria Wapnick and Kenneth Wapnick, *Awaken from the Dream: A Presentation of A Course in Miracles* (Temecula, CA: Foundation for a Course in Miracles, 2006), 3.

11 Ibid., 3.

12 John English (lecture, SSF-IIIHS Conference, Montreal, Quebec, June 2009).

13   Stevenson and Haberman, *Ten Theories of Human Nature*, 46.

14   G.W. Hesketh, *The Soul of the Messenger* (Nine Hawks Books; 2015). 15.

15   The forgiveness suggested by *The Course* is congruent with "making peace with." *The Course* suggests that we forgive ourselves and all others for all our *perceived* errors because we never did anything wrong: we all only ever act from misperceiving who we really are, because we believe we are separated from our Source and behave from within the illusion of fear and lack. We forgive all situations because everything that appears to happen is perceived from within the illusionary world we believe we exist in, based on our perceived separation and the associated ideas of pain, fear, and lack. By using this type of forgiveness (not the usual type of forgiving in which somebody did something wrong), we aim to see beyond the illusion. *The Course's* forgiveness is a tool that aims to dismantle the illusions of the ego, by overriding its ideas of separation. (This is also found in "Definitions" at the back of the book).

16   Jim Richards, "Miraculous Probabilities: The Science of Faith," *New Day*, Vision TV, August 2012, http://www.mynewday.tv/shows/miraculous-probabilities-the-science-of-faith.

17   Ibid.

18   Mary Addenbrooke, *Survivors of Addiction: Narratives of Recovery* (New York: Routledge, 2011), 1.

19   Brad Blanton, *Radical Honesty: How to Transform Your Life by Telling the Truth* (Stanley, VA: Sparrowhawk, 2005), 25.

20   John D. Knight, *Change Your Conversations … Change Your Life* (Atlanta, GA: Life is for Living, 2001), 29.

21   Gerry Clow, "Biodynamic Craniosacral Therapy," accessed January 15, 2014, http://www.wiseawakening.com/home.php?var=gerrybio.html.

22   21 Dennis de Young, singer from the band Styx, performed at Bourbon Street, Ste. Adele, Quebec, June 23, 2007.

23   Langer, *Mindfulness*, 78.

24   "An Old Cherokee Tale of Two Wolves," *Wizdompath* (blog), March 5, 2008, http://wizdompath.wordpress.com/2008/03/05/an-old-cherokee-tale-of-two-wolves/.

25   Harris, *10% Happier*, 218.

26   Timothy Freke and Peter Gandy, *The Hermetica: The Lost Wisdom of the Pharaohs* (New York: Tarcher, 1977), 126.

Chapter 2

1   Joyce Meyer, Christian preacher with daily broadcasts, Vision TV, https://www.joycemeyer.org/broadcasthome.aspx.

2   Almine, *The Lemurian Science of Immortality* (Newport, OR: Spiritual Journeys, 2013), 8.

3   JRobert/Oasis was a spiritual group with JRobert as the channel for four light-beings who called themselves Oasis. They held meetings and workshops, and many books have been written from the messages that came though over the years. They are no longer active but were for over thirty years. All their work was in French, as are the books (for now), as this was based in Montreal.

4   Hadi Subiyanto, *Eat, Pray, Love*, directed by Ryan Murphy (Los Angeles, CA: Plan B Entertainment, 2010).

5   Louis Pauwels, Jacques Bergier, *The Morning of the Magicians* (Rochester, NY: Destiny Books, 2009), 229.

Chapter 3

1   Louise L. Hay, *You Can Heal Your Life* (Carlsbad, CA: Hay House, 2004), 1.

2   Harris, *10% Happier*, 87.

3   Carol Fitzpatrick, "Open Your Heart, and Allow Joy to be Your Guide" (workshop, VA, 2013), https://www.carolynnfitzpatrick.com/.

4   Gay Hendricks, Conscious Breathing: Breathwork for Health, Stress Release, and Personal Mastery (New York: Bantam Books, 1995), 7–8.

5   Hermann Hesse, *Siddhartha*, trans. Hilda Rosner (New York: New Directions, 1951), 118.

6   Neale D. Walsch, *Conversations with God for Teens* (Charlottesville, VA: Scholastic / Hampton Roads, 2001), 56–7.

7   Parmenides, *Poem of Parmenides: On Nature*, trans. John Burnet (1892), 8.19–21, http://philoctetes.free.fr/parmenidesunicode.htm.

8   Christiane Northrup, Women's Bodies, Women's Wisdom: Creating Physical and Emotional Health and Healing (New York: Bantam Books, 1998), 639.

9   Greg Mackie, *How Can We Forgive Murderers?* (West Sedona, AZ: The Circle of Atonement: Teaching and Healing Center, 2003), 173.

10   Ibid.

11   David Foster Wallace, commencement speech, Kenyon College, 2005, http://www.youtube.com/watch?v=8CrOL-ydFMI.

12   Langer, *Mindfulness*, 68.

13   Hulnick and Hulnick, *Loyalty to Your Soul: The Heart of Spiritual Psychology*, 160–1.

14   Almine, The Lemurian Science of Immortality, 330.

15   Ibid., 241.

16   Phil McGraw, *Self Matters: Creating Your Life from the Inside Out* (New York: Simon & Schuster, 2001), 30.

17   Sakyong Mipahm, *Turning the Mind into an Ally*, accessed May 25, 2014, http://www.goodreads.com/author/quotes/28647.

Chapter 4

1   Khalil Gibran, *The Prophet* (New York: Alfred A. Knopf, 2008), 55.

2   Esther Hicks and Jerry Hicks, *Ask and It Is Given: Learning to Manifest Your Desires* (Carlsbad, CA: Hay House, 2004), 110-1.

3   Ibid., 114-7.

4   Ibid., 115.

5   Michael Mirdad, *You're Not Going Crazy … You're Just Waking Up* (Bellingham, WA: Grail Press, 2009), 11–13.

6   Iyanla Vanzant, *In the Meantime: Finding Yourself and the Love You Want* (New York: Fireside, 1998), 88–9.

7   Joyce Meyer, daily broadcasts, https://www.joycemeyer.org/broadcasthome.aspx.

8   Vanzant, *In the Meantime*, 180.

9   Byron Katie, *A Thousand Names for Joy: Living in Harmony with the Way Things Are*, with Stephen Mitchell (New York: Three Rivers Press, 2007), 247.

10   Vanzant, *In the Meantime*, 296–97.

11   Robin McGraw, *Inside My Heart: Choosing to Live with Passion and Purpose* (Nashville, TN: Thomas Nelson, 2006), 92.

12 Ronald L. Holt, "The Christ Grid," interview by Julia Griffin, *Spirit of Ma'at: "Earth Energies"* 3, no. 12 (July 2003), http://www.spiritofmaat.com/archive/jul3/prns/ holt.htm.

13 Rick Warren, "A Journey with Purpose," introduction to *The Purpose Driven Life: What on Earth Am I Here For?* (Grand Rapids, MI: Zondervan, 2002).

14 Arten, quoted in Gary Renard, *Your Immortal Reality: How to Break the Cycle of Birth and Death* (Carlsbad, CA: Hay House, 2002), 80.

15 Nicky Gumbel, Alpha Course, UK DVD series. A series of DVDs that explains Christianity, basically a Christianity 101. Attended course at Lakeshore Evangelical Church, Dorval, QC, 2010.

16 Kurt Bruner and Jim Ware, *Finding God in* The Lord of the Rings (Wheaton, IL: Tyndale, 2001), 41.

17 Hicks and Hicks, *Ask and It Is Given*, 118.

18 Bernie Glassman and Jeff Bridges, *The Dude and the Zen Master* (New York: Plume, 2012), 75.

Chapter 5

1 Vanzant, *In the Meantime*, 167.

2 Knight, Change Your Conversations, 47–8.

3 Don Miguel Ruiz, *The Four Agreements* (San Raphael, CA: Amber-Allen, 1997), 6–7.

4 Jean Liedloff, "Who's in Control? The Unhappy Consequences of Being Child-Centered," *Mothering* (Winter 1994), http://www.continuum-concept.org/reading/whosInControl.html.

5 Gary Chapman, *The Five Love Languages: How to Express Heartfelt Commitment to Your Mate* (Chicago: Northfield Publishing, 1992), 107.

6 Ibid., 165–6.

7 M. Scott Peck, *The Road Less Traveled: A New Psychology of Love, Traditional Values, and Spiritual Growth* (New York: Touchstone, 1997), 152.

8 Shefali Tsabary, *The Conscious Parent*, (Vancouver, BC: Namaste Publishing, 2010), 5, 10-1, 111-16.

9 Ibid., 10-1, 5, 116.

10 James W. Goll, "A Radical Faith," three-part series, *New Day*, Vision TV, November 2011.

11 *Conversations with God for Teens*, 228–9. 231.

12 Scott Wooding, *Hear Me, Hug Me, Trust Me* (Markham, ON: Fitzhenry & Whiteside, 2003), 40–5.

13 Tsabary, *The Conscious Parent*, 11-2.

14 Harville Hendrix, *Getting the Love You Want: A Guide for Couples* (New York: Owl Books, 2001), 105.

15 Katherine, *Boundaries*, 161.

16 Hendrix, *Getting the Love You Want*, 141–2.

17 Lerner, *Marriage Rules*, 181-2.

18 Oprah, "Night with Oprah Tour" (Place Des Arts, Montreal, April 12, 2013).

19 John Gray, *How to Get What You Want and Want What You Have* (New York: HarperCollins, 1999), 169.

20 Chapman, *The Five Love Languages*, 37–121

21 Gumbel, Alpha Course.

22   Tolle, *A New Earth*, 88.

23   Peck, *The Road Less Traveled*, 91–92.

24   Ibid., 117.

25   Ibid., 119

26   Chapman, *The Five Love Languages*, 149–50.

27   Steven Stosny, *Love without Hurt* (Philadelphia, PA: Da Capo Press, 2008), 39–40.

28   Ibid., 259.

29   Ibid., 260–7.

30   Leo Godzich, "Men Are from Dirt, Women Are from Men," *New Day*, Vision TV, April 2012.

31   Matthew Ward, April 11, 2013, message, *The Matthew Books*, channeled through Suzanne Ward, http://www.matthewbooks.com/mm/anmviewer.asp?a=162&.

32   Ibid.

33   Ibid.

34   Shmuley Boteach, "Bringing Up Spiritual Children," podcast, www.shmuley.com

35   John English, The Little Book on Relationship: How to Guide Your Life with Meaning, *Purpose and Power* (Phoenix, AZ: Dreamtime, 2009), 87.

Chapter 6

1   Ben Kingsley, *Gandhi,* directed by Richard Attenborough, (UK/India: 1992).

2   *A Course in Miracles,* M-21, 9–10.

3   Dave Schmidt, "Repentance; Oh That Nasty Word … Or Is It?" Golden Age of Gaia, July 25, 2012, http://goldenageofgaia.com/2012/07/repentance-oh-that-nasty-word-or-is-it/.

4   Sadhguru J. Vasudev, "Delinking Religion and Politics," *Isha eNews,* April 2009, http://www.ishafoundation.org/component/option,com newscomponent/Itemid,/act,view/id,2305/.

5   Kirpal Singh, *The Wheel of Life*: *The Law of Action and Reaction* (Blaine, WA: Ruhani Satsang, 2007), xii, http://ruhanisatsangusa.org/pdf/WHEELOFLIFE.pdf.

6   Maurice Turmel, "The Process of Self-Awareness," Golden Age of Gaia, October 19, 2011, http://the2012scenario.com/2011/10/dr-maurice-turmel-the-process-of-self-awareness/.

7   Steve Beckow, "Vasanas vs. Fears and Beliefs," Golden Age of Gaia, January 15, 2012, http://goldenageofgaia.com/2012/01/15/vasanas-vs-fears-and-beliefs/.

8   C. J. Chaput, "Yeshiva Lessons," *First Things*, no. 225 (August/September 2012): 19–21.

9   Shelley Yates, "Fire the Grid," talk/workshop/video presentation, http://www.firethegrid.com/eng11/index-2011.htm.

10   Gary Renard, *The Disappearance of the Universe: Straight Talk about Illusions, Past Lives, Religion, Sex, Politics, and the Miracles of Forgiveness* (Carlsbad, CA: Hay House, 2004), xiii–xiv.

11   Stephen Mitchell, *Meetings with the Archangel: A Comedy of the Spirit,* advanced uncorrected proof (HarperCollins, n.d.), 1, 2, 5–9.

12   Carolyn Sayre, "Confusing Signs," *Time,* February 19, 2007, 19.

13   Manfred Lurker, *An Illustrated Dictionary of the Gods and Symbols of Ancient Egypt* (New York: Thamas & Hudson, 1974), 27.

14   Richards, "Miraculous Probabilities."

15   Todd Burpo and Lynn Vincent, *Heaven Is for Real* (Nashville, TN: Thomas Nelson, 2010), 60–76.

16 Ibid., 65–67.

17 Gibran, *The Prophet*, 78.

18 Vasudev, "Delinking Religion and Politics."

19 Marc-Joseph Chalfoun, "Our True Nature," *New Times Ahead*, July 2013, https://sites. google.com/site/mjchalfoun/yoga/subscribe/archives.

20 Lori Smith, "Chanting," Christians Practicing Yoga, accessed February 2014, http:// www.christianspracticingyoga.com/chanting.htm#.

21 Carl W. Ernst, *The Shambhala Guide to Sufism* (Boston: Shambhala Publication, 1997), 2–5.

22 *Columbia Electronic Encyclopedia*, s.v. "Glossolalia," accessed November 2013, http:// www.infoplease.com/encyclopedia/society/glossolalia.html.

23 "Speaking in Tongues," Time, August 15, 1960, http://content.time.com/time/ subscriber/article/0,33009,939776-2,00.html.

24 Jeffrey Weiss, "A River Runs through Them: World Religions: How Water Shaped Our Beliefs and Rituals," *Science & Spirit* 18, no. 3 (July 2007).

25 Patricia Diane Cota-Robles, "11-11-11 The Cosmic Moment Is Now," Golden Age of Gaia, October 21, 2011, http://goldenageofgaia.com/2011/10/21/ pat-robles-11-11-11-the-cosmic-moment-is-now/.

26 David B. Dillard-Wright and Ravinder Jerath, *The Everything Guide to Meditation for Healthy Living* (Avon, MA: Adams Media, 2011), 24, 96.

27 Audrey Meisner, "I Am a Child of God," *Audrey's Blog*, November 26, 2012, http://www. mynewday.tv/ blog/audreys blog/post/I Am a Child of God/.

28 Leonard Cohen, *Ladies and Gentlemen … Mr. Leonard Cohen*, directed by Donald Brittain and Don Owen, originally filmed in 1965, rebroadcast on Sundance Channel, January 20, 2013.

29 Richards, "Miraculous Probabilities."

30 Zhi Gang Sha, *Divine Transformation: The Divine Way to Self-Clear Karma to Transform Your Health, Relationships, Finances, and More* (Toronto, ON: Atria Books, 2010), 5.

31 Mitchell, Meetings with the Archangel, 165–66.

32 Steve Beckow, "When Time Stood Still," epilogue to *Eight Seconds Out of Time*, revised 2010, http://www.angelfire.com/space2/light11/epilog.html.

33 Steve Beckow, "Everywhere Are Clues about Life," *The Divine Plan For Life*, Golden Age of Gaia, http://goldenageofgaia.com/spiritual-essays/the-divine-plan-for-life/ everywhere-are-clues-about-life/.

34 Linda Dillon, *The Great Awakening: A Spiritual Primer* (n.p.: CreateSpace, 2012), 46–47.

35 Stanislav Grof, *The Holotropic Mind: The Three Levels of Human Consciousness and How They Shape Our Lives* (New York: HarperCollins, 1993), 164.

36 Barbara Hand Clow, *Awakening the Planetary Mind* (Rochester, VT: Bear & Company, 2011), 240–3.

37 Inelia Benz, "The 5th Dimension Is Not a Location It's a Creation," November, 2012, http://ascension101.com/en/home/free-articles/68-november-2012/286-the-5thdimension-is-not-a-location-its-a-creation.html.

38 Yvonne Kason, *Farther Shores: Exploring How Near-Death, Kundalini, and Mystical Experiences Can Transform Your Life* (Toronto, ON: HarperCollins, 2000), 133–37.

39 Paul Wallace, *The Iroquois Book of Life: White Roots of Peace* (Santa Fe, NM: Clear Light Publishers, 1994), 25.

40 Steve Beckow, "Christianity and Hinduism Are One," updated January 2, 2010, http://www.angelfire.com/space2/light11/hinduism1.html.
41 Stevenson and Haberman, *Ten Theories of Human Nature*, 46–49.
42 Ibid., 47–48.
43 Ibid., 47.
44 Mitchell, *Tao Te Ching*, 6.
45 Ibid., 25.
46 Joyce Meyer, Joyce Meyer Ministries, various broadcasts, https://www.joycemeyer.org/broadcasthome.aspx.
47 Stevenson and Haberman, *Ten Theories of Human Nature*, 49.
48 Vanamali Mataji, *The Complete Life of Krishna, Based on the Earliest Oral Traditions and the Sacred Scriptures* (Rochester, VT: Inner Traditions, 2012), xiv–xv.
49 Ibid.
50 Gibran, *The Prophet*, 67.
51 Richards, "Miraculous Probabilities."
52 Ken Wapnick, "How Can I Explain to My Church That the Course Is Christian Based?" question 1218, September 26, 2007, *A Course in Miracles* Outreach, http://www.facimoutreach.org/qa/questions/questions259.htm#Q1218.

Chapter 7
1   David R. Hawkins, *Power vs. Force* (Carlsbad, CA: Hay House, 2002), 234.
2   Matthew Ward, November 1, 2012 / October 21, 2012, message, *The Matthew Books*, channeled through Suzanne Ward, http://www.matthewbooks.com/mm/anmviewer.asp?a=154.
3   Hawkins, *Power vs. Force*, 79–98.
4   Ibid., 79.
5   Ibid., 88.
6   Richards, "Miraculous Probabilities."
7   Northrup, Women's Bodies, Women's Wisdom, 630.
8   Grof, *The Holotropic Mind*, 6.
9   Ibid.
10 Kryon, "The Quantum Factor," channeled through Lee Carroll, Edmonton, Canada, April 10, 2011, https://www.kryon.com/k channel11 edmonton.html.
11 Inelia Benz, "Units 2, 3, 4: Setting Goals," Ascension 101, eCourse.
12 Ronald L. Holt, "The Spiral and the Holographic Matrix," Seed of Life Institute, 2012, http://www.solischool.org/uploads/1/5/7/1/15716170/art-holomatrixspiral.pdf.
13 Ibid.
14 Ibid.
15 Ibid.
16 Matthew Ward, September 9, 2011, message, *The Matthew Books*, channeled through Suzanne Ward, http://www.matthewbooks.com/mm/anmviewer.asp?a=139&.
17 Fred A. Wolf, *Quantum's Little Book of Big Ideas: Where Science Meets Spirit* (Needham, MA: Moment Point Press, 2005), 25.
18 Northrup, *Women's Bodies, Women's Wisdom*, 759.
19 Abraham-Hicks (workshop, Asheville, NC, September 1998).

20   Amanda Gefter, "Bang Goes the Theory," New Scientist 214, no. 2871 (June 30, 2012): 32–37.

21   Robert J. Sawyer, "Big Ideas," TVO, November 2011, rebroadcast May 10, 2013.

22   Masaru Emoto, "Hado Crystal Water Experiment," YouTube video, July 2012, http://www.youtube.com/watch?v=PDW9Lqj8hmc.

23   Ramana Maharshi, *The Collected Works of Ramana Maharshi*, authorized 10th ed. (San Rafael, CA: Sophia Perennis, 2001), 139.

24   Parmenides, *Poem of Parmenides*, 8.35.

25   Wolf, Quantum's Little Book of Big Ideas, 108.

26   Workbook lesson 169, *A Course in Miracles*, combined volume, 3rd ed. (Mill Valley, CA: Foundation for Inner Peace, 2007), 323:4, 4.

27   Julianne Everett, "Reclaiming Your 12-Strand DNA," Golden Age of Gaia, October 17, 2011, http://goldenageofgaia.com/2011/10/julianne-everett-reclaiming-your-12-strand-dna/.

28   Almine, The Lemurian Science of Immortality, 214.

29   Hand Clow, *Awakening the Planetary Mind*, 11.

30   Ibid., 16.

31   Dillon, *The Great Awakening*, 17.

32   Ibid., 15.

33   Gary Renard, *Fearless Love: The Answer to the Problem of Human Existence* (Louisville, CO, Sounds True, 2008), CD-ROM.

34   Sananda, "Activating the Andromedan StarGate at Lake Louise, BC," channeled through Elizabeth Trutwin, May 1, 2015. http://cosmicascension.com/the-messages/.

35   Ronna Herman, "The Mystery of the Vesica Piscis," October 2010, http://www.ronnastar.com/messages-aam/messages-aam/607-aam-10-2012.html.

36   Everett, "Reclaiming Your 12-Strand DNA."

37   Ibid.

38   Dave Schmidt, "What's All This Talk about Life Being an Illusion," The 2012 Scenario, June 12, 2012, http://the2012scenario.com/2012/06/whats-all-this-talk-about-life-being-an-illusion/.

39   Kryon, "The Quantum Factor."

40   Ibid.

41   Hand Clow, *Awakening the Planetary Mind*, 11.

42   Helyn Hitchcock, *Helping Yourself With Numerology* (New York: Parker, 1972), 5.

43   Stephen Knapp, "Lord Vishnu," accessed June 10, 2014, http://www.stephen-knapp.com/lord vishnu.htm.

44   Sananda, "Activating the Andromedan StarGate at Lake Louise, BC."

45   Lynne D. Kitei and S. Lantz, *The Phoenix Lights: We Are Not Alone* (A Kitei & Lantz Production, 2008), DVD.

46   Kryon, "The Quantum Factor."

47   Kevin Engstrom, "Manitoba UFO Sightings Up in 2012," *Winnipeg Sun*, May 13, 2013, http://www.winnipegsun.com/2013/05/13/manitoba-ufo-sightings-up-last-year.

48   Germane, "ET Civilizations," channeled through Lyssa Royal, accessed May 15, 2014, http://www.lemuria.net/article-et-civilizations.html.

49   Inelia Benz, "The 5th Dimension Is Not a Location, It's a Creation," November 2012, http://ascension101.com/en/home/free-articles/68-november-2012/286-the-5thdimension-is-not-a-location-its-a-creation.html.

50   Stephen Hawking and Leonard Mlodinow, *The Grand Design* (New York: Bantam Books, 2010), 155.

Chapter 8

1   David Ehrenfeld, *The Arrogance of Humanism*, quoted in Northrup, *Women's Bodies, Women's Wisdom*, 638.

2   Northrup, *Women's Bodies, Women's Wisdom*, 578.

3   Joan Hunter, *It's a New Day*, Vision TV, October 12 and 31, 2011.

4   Kat Duff, *The Alchemy of Illness* (New York: Bell Tower, 1993), 23.

5   P. Kendall-Reed and S. Reed, *The Complete Doctor's Stress Solution: Understanding, Treating, and Preventing Stress and Stress-Related Illnesses* (Toronto, ON: Robert Rose, 2004), 8–11.

6   Hendricks, *Conscious Breathing*, 7–8.

7   Tolle, *A New Earth*, 246.

8   Everett, "Reclaiming Your 12-Strand DNA."

9   Kelly McGonigal, "How To Make Stress Your Friend," TED Video, 14:28, filmed June 2013, http://www.ted.com/talks/kelly mcgonigal how to make stress your friend.html.

10   Debbie Shapiro, *Your Body Speaks Your Mind: Decoding the Emotional, Psychological, and Spiritual Messages That Underlie Illness* (Boulder, CO: Sounds True, 2006), 3–6, 35–6.

11   Beverly A. Musgrave and Neil J. McGettigan, *Spiritual and Psychological Aspects of Illness: Dealing with Sickness, Loss, Dying, and Death* (Mahwah, NJ: Paulist Press, 2010), 4, 5, 121.

12   Ken Wilber, *Grace and Grit* (Boston: Shambhala Publications, 2000), 258–9.

13   Northrup, *Women's Bodies, Women's Wisdom*, 52.

14   Hay, *You Can Heal Your Life*, 1.

15   Daniel J. Siegel, *The Developing Mind: How Relationships and the Brain Interact to Shape Who We Are* (New York: Guilford Press, 2012), 44.

16   Ridha Arem, *The Thyroid Solution* (New York: Rodale, 2008), 295.

17   Northrup, Women's Bodies, Women's Wisdom, 578.

18   Hay, You Can Heal Your Life, 74.

19   Northrup, *Women's Bodies, Women's Wisdom*, 638–39.

20   Ibid.

21   David Lykken, *Happiness, the Nature and Nurture of Joy and Contentment* (New York: St. Martin's Press, 1999), 211–12; Northrup, *Women's Bodies, Women's Wisdom*, 577.

22   Margaret Trudeau, *Changing my Mind* (Toronto: Harper-Collins Publishers, 2010), 3.

23   Ibid., 97.

24   Colin Cameron in Margaret Trudeau, *Changing my Mind* (New York: HarperCollins, 2010), 351.

25   Northrup, *Women's Bodies, Women's Wisdom*, 577.

26   Arem, *The Thyroid Solution*, 294–95.

27   Wilber, Grace and Grit, 42–43.

28   Musgrave and McGettigan, *Spiritual and Psychological Aspects of Illness: Dealing with Sickness, Loss, Dying, and Death*, 4-5, 121.

29   Joel Fuhrman, "3 Steps To Incredible Health!," PBS, originally aired 2012, rebroadcast September 2013.

30 Christina Scott-Moncrieff, *Detox: Cleanse and Recharge Your Mind, Body and Soul* (London: Collins & Brown, 2001), 18–20.

31 *The Sugar Solution, by the editors of Prevention* magazine, ed. Anne Fittante (New York: Rodale, 2007), 35–6.

32 Ibid.

33 Cristin Couzens, report by Kelly Crowe, "Sugar Industry's Secret Documents Echo Tobacco Tactics," by Kelly Crowe, posted March 8, 2013. http://www.cbc.ca/news/health/sugar-industry-s-secret-documents-echo-tobacco-tactics-1.1369231.

34 Joseph Mercola, "Why Is Wheat Gluten Disorder on the Rise?," July 23, 2009, http://articles.mercola.com/sites/articles/archive/2009/07/23/Why-is-Wheat-Gluten-Disorderon-the-Rise.aspx.

35 Vandana Shiva, "The Problem with Genetically Modified Seeds," Moyers & Company, PBS, July 13, 2012, http://billmoyers.com/segment/vandana-shiva-on-the-problem-with-genetically-modified-seeds/.

36 National Research Council, Global Sources of Local Pollution: An Assessment of Long-Range Transport of Key Air Pollutants to and from the United States (Washington, DC: National Academies Press, 2010), 97–101.

37 Paul Connett, "Warning: This Daily Habit is Damaging Your Bones, Brain, Kidneys, and Thyroid," interview by Joseph Mercola, July 1, 2010, http://articles.mercola.com/sites/articles/archive/2010/07/01/paul-connett-interview.aspx.

38 Inelia Benz, "Raising Our Vibration with Food," YouTube video, http://www.youtube.com/watch?v=zTK2GRvr8NA.

39 Nancy Hearn, "Health Benefits of Drinking Water: The Healthy Cell Concept," http://www.waterbenefitshealth.com/health benefits of drinking water.html.

40 Everett, "Reclaiming Your 12-Strand DNA."

41 Lawrence Peltz, *The Mindful Path to Addiction Recovery* (Boston: Shambhala Publications, 2013), 17.

42 Jeff VanVonderen, "Trying to Measure Up," three-part series, *New Day*, Vision TV, April 2012.

43 Addenbrooke, *Survivors of Addiction*, 1, 7, 21.

44 Peltz, *The Mindful Path to Addiction Recovery*, 85–88.

45 VanVonderen, "Trying to Measure Up."

46 Neale D. Walsch, Evolving Wisdom, promotional e-mail for "Conversations with God: The Essential 7-Week Online Course," http://evolvingwisdom.com/nealedonaldwalsch.

47 Douglas J. Davies, *A Brief History of Death* (Oxford: Blackwell, 2005), 133–34.

48 Ibid., 135.

49 Stephen Levine and Ondrea Levine, *Who Dies? An Investigation of Conscious Living and Conscious Dying* (New York: Anchor Books, 1982), 220–22.

50 Taryn Crimi, "Death Is Not the End but the Start of Something New," June 5, 2013, http://angelicguides.wordpress.com/2013/06/05/death-is-not-the-end-but-the-start-of-something-new.

51 Stephen Levine, "Conscious Living, Conscious Dying," posted by "ThinkingAllowedTV," hosted by Jeffrey Mishlove, August 23, 2010, http://www.youtube.com/watch?v=pxY0RXq04E.

52 Ram Dass, preface to *Who Dies?*, by Levine and Levine, vii–ix.

53   R. Zalenski and R. Raspa, "Maslow's Hierarchy of Needs: A Framework for Achieving Human Potential in Hospice," *Journal of Palliative Medicine* 9, no. 5 (October 2006): 1120–27, http://www.ncbi.nlm.nih.gov/pubmed/17040150.

54   John Wren-Lewis, review of *Grace and Grit*, by Wilber, 2007, http://www.kenwilber.com/Writings/PDF/GG--Wren2-p.pdf.

55   David Hoffmeister, "*A Course In Miracles*: Forgiving Relationships," YouTube video, 2009, http://awakening-mind.org/about-us/.

56   Almine, *The Lemurian Science of Immortality*, 151.

Chapter 9

1   Thom Hartmann, *The Last Hours of Ancient Sunlight: Waking Up to Personal and Global Transformation* (Northfield, VT: Mythical Books, 1998), 191.

2   Gore Vidal, quoted in Hartmann, *The Last Hours of Ancient Sunlight*, 110.

3   Fernando Vossa, "The Engines of Mass Creation. Part 1 and 2," YouTube video, http://www.youtube.com/watch?v=9v-Z FfBD5E&feature=player embedded.

4   Hartmann, *The Last Hours of Ancient Sunlight*, 110.

5   Severn Cullis-Suzuki, "The Girl Who Silenced the World for 5 Minutes," YouTube video, http://www.youtube.com/watch?v=TQmz6Rbpnu0.

6   Sandra Steingraber, "Raising Elijah & Living Downstream," Moyers & Company, PBS, April 21, 2013.

7   John Stanley and David Loy, "At the Edge of the Roof: The Evolutionary Crisis of the Human Spirit" essay in *Spiritual Ecology, The Cry of the Earth*, edited by Llewellyn Vaughn-Lee (Point Reyes, CA: The Golden Sufi Center, 2013), 41.

8   Ibid., 43.

9   Ibid., 43-4.

10   Hartmann, The Last Hours of Ancient Sunlight, 235.

11   Thomas Berry, "The World of Wonder" in *Spiritual Ecology, The Cry of the Earth*, a collection of essays edited by Llewellyn Vaughan-Lee, (Pointe Reyes, CA: The Golden Sufi Center), 15-17.

12   Ibid.

13   Barbara Hand Clow, *Awakening the Planetary Mind* (Rochester, VT: Bear & Company, 2011), 240–3.

14   Hartmann, *The Last Hours of Ancient Sunlight*, 245.

15   Ibid.

16   Mitchell, *Tao Te Ching*, 25.

17   Charles Eisenstein, "The Three Seeds," Golden Age of Gaia, June 9, 2012, www.the2012scenario.com/2012/06/charles-eisenstein-the-three-seeds.

18   Ibid.

19   Ibid.

20   *Mine, Story of a Sacred Mountain*, narrated by Joanna Lumley, (Survival International) http://www.survivalinternational.org/films/mine.

21   Susan Murphy, "The Koan of the Earth," Essay in *Spiritual Ecology, The Cry of the Earth*, edited by Llewellyn Vaughan-Lee, (Pointe Reyes, CA: The Golden Sufi Center), 113.

22   James Lovelock, *The Revenge of Gaia: Why the Earth Is Fighting Back—and How We Can Still Save Humanity* (London: Penguin, 2006), 2–4.

23   Charles Eisenstein, *The More Beautiful World our Hearts Know Is Possible* (Berkeley, CA: North Atlantic Books, 2013), 9-14.

24   Ruiz, *The Four Agreements*, 2.

25   Charles Eisenstein, *Sacred Economics, Money, Gift & Society in the Age of Transition*, (Berkeley, CA: Evolver Editions, North Atlantic Books, 2011), xviii-xix.

26   Hicks and Hicks, *Ask and It Is Given*, 121.

27   Stanley and Loy, "At the Edge of the Roof: The Evolutionary Crisis of the Human Spirit," 43.

28   Eisenstein, *Sacred Economics*, xii. xv.

29   Gibran, *The Prophet*, 19–20.

30   Eisenstein, *Sacred Economics*, 367.

31   Ibid., 365.

32   Inelia Benz, "Clearing Your Wealth Lines," Ascension 101, http://ascension101.com/en/store/product/13-clearing-your-wealth-lines.html.

33   Inelia Benz, "Reconnecting with the Spirit of Money," YouTube video, 2012, http://www.youtube.com/watch?v=V78VtQXKfV8.

34   Eisenstein, *Sacred Economics*, xviii-xix, xi.

35   Ibid., 353, 350.

36   Ibid., 349-50.

37   Richards, "Miraculous Probabilities."

38   Inelia Benz, *Meet Yourself in the Future*, Units 2, 3, 4: Setting Goals, Ascension 101, eCourse.

39   Mark Boyle, *The Moneyless Manifesto*, (Hamshire, UK: Permanent Publication, 2012), xxvii, 298-9, xxvii-iii.

40   Stanley and Loy, "At the Edge of the Roof: The Evolutionary Crisis of the Human Spirit," 42-3.

41   Kurt Bruner and Jim Ware, *Finding God in the Lord of the Rings* (Wheaton, IL: Tyndale, 2001), 10.

Chapter 10

1   Sananda, *The Crystal Stair: A Guide to the Ascension*, channeled though Eric Klein, 3rd ed. (Livermore, CA: Oughten House, 1994), 16–17.

2   Dillon, The Great Awakening, 31.

3   Steve Beckow, "Ascension: The Larger Picture," Golden Age of Gaia, accessed January 15, 2014, http://goldenageofgaia.com/ascension/what-is-ascension/ascension-the-larger-picture.

4   Inelia Benz, "The 5th Dimension Is Not a Location, It's a Creation," November 2012, http://ascension101.com/en/home/free-articles/68-november-2012/286-the-5thdimension-is-not-a-location-its-a-creation.html.

5   Ibid.

6   Everett, "Reclaiming Your 12-Strand DNA."

7   Mark Torgeson, "DNA Activation and Music," video 20 of 29, accessed March 15, 2014, http://www.onenessofbeing.org/mark-torgeson 1.html.

8   Mark Torgeson, "Nature, Consciousness and Ascension," video 21 of 29, accessed March 15, 2014, http://www.onenessofbeing.org/mark-torgeson 1.html.

9   Steve Beckow, "What Is the Golden Age of Gaia?," Golden Age of Gaia, April 15, 2014, http://goldenageofgaia.com/2014/04/15/what-is-the-golden-age-of-gaia/.

10   Kryon, "The Quantum Factor," channeled through Lee Carroll, Edmonton, Canada, April 10, 2011, https://www.kryon.com/k channel11 edmonton.html.

11   Sandra Walter, "November Waves and Responsible Creation," Golden Age of Gaia, November 17, 2013, http://goldenageofgaia.com/2013/11/17/sandra-walter-november-waves-and-responsible-creation/.

12   Dillon, *The Great Awakening*, 183–84.

13   Mark Torgeson, "On Ascension," video 22 of 29, accessed March 15, 2014, http://www.onenessofbeing.org/mark-torgeson 1.html.

14   Steve Beckow, "Ascension Has Been in the Works for a Very Long Time," Golden Age of Gaia, September 18, 2012, http://goldenageofgaia.com/ascension/what-is-ascension/ascension-has-been-in-the-works-for-a-very-long-time/.

15   Dillon, *The Great Awakening*, 31.

Chapter 11

1   George Eliot, quoted by Dr. Tony, Awakening Potentials Inc., http://awakeningpotentialsblog.com/ultimate-wakeup/it-is-never-too-late-to-be-what-we-might-have-been.

2   Walter, "November Waves and Responsible Creation."

3   Tolle, *A New Earth*, 25–26.

4   Steve Beckow, "Lifting the Veil—Part 7," Golden Age of Gaia, December 5, 2013, http://goldenageofgaia.com/2013/12/lifting-the-veil-part-7/.

5   Ibid.

6   Maria Forleo, "Why Women in Their 20s Are Yearning for Fulfillment," Oprah's Super Soul Sunday: Own Network, accessed July 30, 2014, http://www.oprah.com/own-super-soul-sunday/Why-Women-in-Their-20s-Are-Yearning-for-Fulfillment-Video.

7   Gumbel, Alpha Course.

8   Matthew Ward, June 2, 2014, message, *The Matthew Books*, channeled through Suzanne Ward, http://www.matthewbooks.com/mm/anmviewer.asp?a=185.

9   Ilie Pandia, "Free Energy," May 2013, http://ascension101.com/en/home/free-articles/77-may-2013/346-free-energy.html.

10   Bernie Sanders, "Letter #30, 2016: Bernie's Remarks in Rome," Inside the Vatican, April 15, 2016, http://insidethevatican.com/news/newsflash/letter-30-2016-bernies-remarks-rome?gclid=CjwKEAjwmdu5BRCg1O3a-tDY0AQSJACKPgRKpiBrEhfNYkXwO1EJNRkC8GtCTiFRw_CMZrAJydoAvxoCumDw_wcB.

11   Shelley Yates, "Becoming High Frequency" (talk, Montreal, 2011), http://lightworkers.org/node/191727.

12   Amorah Quan Yin, "Crystalline Cities of Light," Pleiadian Lightwork, accessed August 16, 2014, http://www.amorahquanyin.com/articles/a cities.html.

13   Ibid.

14   Mark Schmanko, "Bernie Sanders: A Deeply Spiritual Politician," *The Huffington Post, March 3, 2016,* http://www.huffingtonpost.com/mark-schmanko/bernie-sanders-a-deeply-spiritual-politician_b_9368406.html.

15   Jack Layton, "Letter To Canadians: NDP Leader's Last Words For The Public," *Huffington Post Canada*, August 22, 2011, updated October 22, 2011, http://www.huffingtonpost.ca/2011/08/22/jack-layton-dead-letter-to-canadians n 933012.html.

Conclusion

1   Hulnick and Hulnick, *Loyalty to Your Soul*, 165.
2   Steve Beckow, "Addicted to Love and the Middle Way," Golden Age of Gaia, August 26, 2014, http://goldenageofgaia.com/2014/08/26/addicted-to-love-and-the-middle-way/.
3   Hulnick and Hulnick, *Loyalty to Your Soul* 45–46.
4   Neale Donald Walsch, *The Only Thing That Matters: Conversations with Humanity* (Ashland, OR: Emnin Books, 2012), 1–7.
5   Barack Obama, *The Audacity of Hope* (New York: Three Rivers Press, 2006).
6   Hawkins, *Power vs. Force*, 88–89.
7   Chris Hadfield, *An Astronaut's Guide to Life on Earth* (Toronto: Random House Canada, 2013), 181–82.
8   Hartmann, The Last Hours of Ancient Sunlight, 233.
9   Dillon, *The New You*, 205.
10 Jean-Paul Sartre, quoted in Stevenson and Haberman, *Ten Theories of Human Nature*, 176.
11 Faisal Malick, *Positioned to Bless: Secrets to Fulfilling Your Divine Assignment* (Shippensburg, PA: Destiny Image, 2008), 22–23.
12 Ruiz, *The Four Agreements*, xiii.
13 Ken Wapnick, "The Treachery of Images—Part II," *The Lighthouse* 24, no. 7 (December 2013).
14 Steve Beckow, "Just Allow It," Golden Age of Gaia, May 1, 2014, http://goldenageofgaia.com/2014/05/01/just-allow-it/?utm source=rss.
15 Hawkins, *Power vs. Force*, 128.
16 Ibid., 152.

Meditations, Visualizations, and Other Practices

1   Hay, *You Can Heal Your Life*, 74.
2   Northrup, *Women's Bodies, Women's Wisdom*, 638–39.
3   Arten, quoted in Gary Renard, *Your Immortal Reality: How to Break the Cycle of Birth and Death* (Carlsbad, CA: Hay House, 2002), 80.
4   Hay, You Can Heal Your Life, 62.

Download Page
(codes for those who bought the book and want
to download some or all of the aids
located at the back of the book)

To download the information from the back of the book, go to
the book's website www.yourjourneytopeace.com and click on the
Download Link. You will be able to choose one, or more, of the elements
available for downloading and you will be asked for the associated
code. You can download for printing, or to your electronic device.

Download Codes

Affirmations and Self-Talks: AST0616

Definitions: D0616

Energetic Attunements: EA0616

Exercises / Releasing Techniques: ERT0616

Meditations: M0616

Recaps: R0616

Visualizations: V0616

Worksheets: W0616

Printed in the United States
By Bookmasters